Romantic Voices

Romantic Voices

Listening to Nineteenth-Century Music

DOUGLASS SEATON

SUNY PRESS

Cover image: Pierre-Auguste Renoir, *Woman at the Piano*, 1875–76, oil on canvas. Mr. and Mrs. Martin A. Ryerson Collection.

This publication has been made possible, in part, by funding provided by the John Daverio Fund and General Fund of the American Musicological Society (AMS).

Published by State University of New York Press, Albany

EU GPSR Authorised Representative:
Logos Europe, 9 rue Nicolas Poussin, 17000, La Rochelle, France
contact@logoseurope.eu

For information, contact State University of New York Press, Albany, NY
www.sunypress.edu

Library of Congress Cataloging-in-Publication Data

Name: Seaton, Douglass, author.
Title: Romantic voices : listening to nineteenth-century music / Douglass Seaton.
Description: Albany : State University of New York Press, [2025]. | Includes
    bibliographical references and index.
Identifiers: LCCN 2025014803 | ISBN 9798855804331 (hardcover : alk. paper) |
    ISBN 9798855804355 (ebook) | ISBN 9798855804348 (pbk. : alk. paper)
Subjects: LCSH: Music—19th century—History and criticism. | Music—19th
    century—Analysis, appreciation. | Music—19th century—Philosophy and
    aesthetics. | Romanticism in music. | Narrative in music.
Classification: LCC ML196 .S43 2025 | DDC 780.9/034—dc23/eng/20250331
LC record available at https://lccn.loc.gov/2025014803

Contents

List of Figures

List of Tables

List of Music Examples

Acknowledgments

Two invitations broke the ground in which I was able to plant the seeds of the first two chapters of this book, from which the entire volume grew. The first, in 2003, came from Jan Christoph Meister, who proposed that I should speak on narrativity in music to an interdisciplinary gathering of scholars at the Second International Colloquium of the Narratology Research Group at the University of Hamburg. That opportunity led me to start formulating my ideas about applying narratological theory in a paper on Beethoven's "Tempest" Sonata, now considerably refined and amplified in chapter 2. In 2015 Arianne Johnson Quinn, at the time still a doctoral student at Princeton University, invited me to speak at a musicology colloquium there, which prompted me to develop my thoughts about definitions and approaches to identifying persona in Romantic works, represented in this book by chapter 1.

Four decades of teaching graduate students in my courses in nineteenth-century music and various seminars at Florida State University nurtured this project. Those students prepared, thoroughly and often even eagerly, the assigned music analyses and readings for our discussions of most of the works explored here. I am grateful for their interest, their challenging questions (including those that sometimes came from left field), and occasionally just their raised eyebrows when confronted with ideas that were still evolving, all of which spurred me to range more broadly over the intellectual landscape and delve more deeply into the music and the historical evidence.

Several colleagues have particularly encouraged my research and writing in this area. Márta Grabócz of the University of Strasbourg has been constantly warm and encouraging. Robert S. Hatten and Ralph Locke gave support to this book along its slow path toward publication. The kind collegiality and friendship of my faculty colleagues in musicology at Florida

State University has meant the world; I feel especially indebted to Jeffery Kite-Powell, Dale Olsen, Charles Brewer, Denise Von Glahn, Michael Bakan, Frank Gunderson, Sarah Eyerly, Michael Broyles, Panayotis League, and Eduardo López-Dabdoub for together cultivating a scholarly community more supportive and congenial than any other faculty I have heard of anywhere.

I must express my enormous appreciation for the support of the libraries on which I have depended. For this project the most important was naturally the Warren D. Allen Music Library at Florida State University. The New York Public Library, both at Fifth Avenue and Forty-Second Street and the Library for the Performing Arts at Lincoln Center, and the Gabe M. Wiener Music & Arts Library at Columbia University provided outstanding assistance, especially following my move to New York and through the latter part of the COVID-19 pandemic.

SUNY Press has assisted and accommodated my work in this project attentively and cordially. Thanks to my acquisitions editor, Richard Carlin (book shepherd extraordinaire); to the book's diligent and thoughtful reviewers; to Jenn Bennett-Genthner for patient, practical advice; to the copyeditor, Megan Zid; to Diane Ganeles and Ryan Morris for their help with production matters; to the cover designer, Kirk Warren; and to Michael Campochiaro for handling marketing.

No one who knows me will be surprised that my greatest thanks must be reserved for my wife, Gayle. She tolerates with infinite grace the inconveniences of going through life married to a scholar, her musicality and intellect make her an indispensable sounding board for ideas and style in my writing, and—not least—her good sense curbs my curmudgeonliness ("no, you can't really say *that*"), when it needs reminders from a kindlier spirit. She deserves my professional gratitude along with my love.

Preface

Historical Framework

Several years ago, after teaching music history courses at all levels for about fifteen years, I began to realize that the usual ways of explaining "style" periods in the history of Western music did not seem convincing. What justified the identification of historical phases in music did not fundamentally come down to a particular constellation of musical style elements. The contours of musical change through the centuries depended rather on the models according to which musicians believed musical expression did or should operate.

This way of putting the issue takes a middle ground between trying to conceive musical developments as really nothing more than periods to which students might apply particular style-based names (the period of the basso continuo, the era of sonata form) or even checklists of style traits and, on the other extreme, the artificial borrowing of terms from other disciplines (Baroque, Impressionism), or even a mere reduction of history to the counting of centuries. Yet we cannot evade the observation that developments in music history proceed in phases, just as cultures form and fade. The expressive models for music necessarily arise from the cultural epistemes in which they emerge, and they naturally produce music that employs the elements of style in distinctive ways.

Thus, to begin, from the twelfth to the fifteenth century the cultural epistemes were rooted in ecclesiastical or classical authority and in hierarchy. These produced Gothic cathedral architecture and the scholastic approach to thought. From the point of view of musical expression, music was conceptualized as expressing order. Following Pythagoras and Boethius, musical thinkers envisioned this order as inherently mathematical. In music such order found its embodiment in the authority-based and hierarchical structure of cantus firmus polyphony and in the governing force of the perfect intervals and mathematical proportion, manifested in its most sophisticated form in the ars nova motet.

The end of the Middle Ages brought a radical shift in the models according to which music was thought to work. From the fifteenth century to the nineteenth, the old mathematical model yielded to new ones, thought of in the same ways as literature. Music in the period of Renaissance Humanism conceptually shared its expressive model with poetry—musical structure corresponding to poetic lines, phrase designs mirroring poetic declamation, and musical ideas resembling poetic imagery. During the Rationalist movement, a new model—still literary—took over: rhetoric. Solo melodic inflection and harmonic intensity in a basso continuo texture combined with the use of figures and the essay-like forms of da capo aria and fugue to produce music that intended to convey an affect or passion. In the Enlightenment, empiricism led to a musical model based on literary plot, achieved by character contrast and the rise of tension and its resolution across the course of a piece or movement and best represented by the sonata form. At the arrival of the twentieth century, then, these literary models gave way, first in Impressionism to a model of sensualism, then in Stravinsky, Varèse, and serialism to a new objectivity suggesting the model of mathematics and engineering, and in aleatory music perhaps to models as varied as Zen or chaos theory.

Because my teaching had to deal most often and most in depth with the music of the periods reaching roughly from the 1720s to 1900, it became obvious that the overarching "plot model" required refinement in order to explain the relationship between the so-called Classic and Romantic movements. The foundation of nineteenth-century musical culture came from the increased importance of subjectivity, an idea that grew out of Enlightenment empiricism and dominated the art that called itself Romantic. The crucial element here, it appeared, was the rise of the "aesthetic subject," the personality of the individual understood as the source of the artistic expression. When we listen to the music, we attend to the personality speaking in the work's *Romantic voice*.

The personality of that aesthetic subjectivity is not to be confused with the actual composer of a musical work. Musical works are not accounts of their composers' lives. If they were, hearing them would resemble reading someone's diary, an enterprise mostly dull and sometimes voyeuristic. The Romantic voice of a work is a specific personality whom we understand to be expressed in our hearing. That voice or personality emerges from all the factors that inform our listening, but only from those that belong to each particular piece. Speaking casually, we might of course refer to the Romantic voice by a composer's name, but that can mislead us into what is sometimes called the biographical fallacy (perhaps more appropriately thought of as the autobiographical fallacy). The composer of the *Missa solemnis* was deaf, but the personality we encounter in that work is not a deaf person, nor is it the same personality as the lover's lyric voice of *An die ferne Geliebte*. To say that we hear the voice of Beethoven in any of his works merely invites the question of whom we are calling "Beethoven" in that work. In the end, attaching Beethoven's name to the aesthetic subject simply creates a misleading distraction.

In the sense that aesthetic subjectivity begins around 1800 to become equally important as a work's plot (if not even more so), we can say that the model for an eighteenth-century sonata movement resembles that of a stage drama, where interest resides in the actors and actions presented directly to the audience, while a Romantic work is more akin to a novel, in which the narrator's voice intrudes into the plot, so that the reader's perspectives, understandings, and sympathies arise from interaction with that narrator. As I will point out in some of the studies that follow, Romantic voice can also become the key to nonplotted, lyric compositions.

In nineteenth-century music, then, what has come to interest me most is the voice of a musical work. The importance of voice to the Romantics was embodied in a variety of quite different phenomena, including the vital public interest in composers' lives and the ways in which musicians created images of themselves to shape the understanding of their music as well as the appearance of the conductor on the podium and the solo performer in a highlighted position. And of course, as we shall see, the voice can emerge from the musical tones themselves. The desire or need of the Romantic imagination to establish an identity for—or at least a representation of—each work's voice seems undeniable.

This book therefore explores how the voice of the musical work, whether a narrative voice in a plotted movement or the lyric voice of a brief character piece, might emerge in the music or in the listener's understanding. Most of the pieces dealt with are instrumental works, partly out of a perhaps perverse idea that it makes best sense to challenge one's thinking with the topics that provide the least explicit help, but some of the discussions also demonstrate how the idea of the subject voice can apply in song and opera. The task consists principally of identifying the voice for each work. No formula will enable this project: The Romantic voice might emerge from close analytical hearing of the music, from surrounding literary material stemming from the composer, from considerations of performance situations and practices, from contemporary commentary, from reception history. Once we can identify the voice of the work, we can then engage with that voice as a means of understanding the work hermeneutically, of the musical aesthetic on which it depends, or of the cultural context from which it arises.

Romantic Voices opens with a consideration of how I approach this task, with chapter 1 distinguishing my perspectives from the work of other scholars who have dealt with related issues and pointing to some of the general kinds of evidence I shall adduce. The remaining chapters, organized loosely by chronology, show how the experience of voice manifests itself in what might seem to be dizzyingly, but are certainly dazzlingly, different ways—an inherent consequence of Romantic individuality itself. Chapter 2 takes up what seems to me to be an enlightening early Romantic work, Beethoven's "Tempest" Sonata, where the voice is extremely clear and the clues to its acquaintance are a remarkable demonstration of just how unexpected and idiosyncratic evidence can be. In chapters 3 and 7 I study song cycles, revealing in these cases how individual lyric voices hold the songs together as well as noticing the important difference between the speakers here and those of the more conventional, folk-song-based Lied. Chapter 4 turns to the issue of personality in virtuosic variations in and of opera arias, situating the idea of virtuosity in relation to gender. Chapters 5 and 13 deal with instances of composers experimenting self-consciously and explicitly with narrative positions, Berlioz in *Harold en Italie* and MacDowell in his "Keltic" Sonata. Chapter 6 tackles an aesthetic claim by Mendelssohn based on statements by the composer and by Schumann, applied to *Songs Without Words*, whereby the identity of the voice is shifted onto the performer and hearer. In chapter 8 I take up two contrasting types of plot, each revealing a kind of feminist perspective, as well as clues to the fictive narrative voices for Hensel's Piano Trio and Chopin's B-Minor Sonata. Schumann's Symphony No. 2 in C Major occupies chapter 9, which shows how a combination of plot and intertextual reference reveals the voice of a composer claiming a position in history. The focus in chapter 10 is on Liszt's "Vallée d'Obermann," which provides versions of the same piece voiced by a traveler (in the early version) or a pilgrim (in the second) and furnishes an unusual wealth of paratextual information. A completely different kind of voice emerges in Verdi's *Otello*, the topic of chapter 11, where both the character of Jago and devices in the music of Jago's so-called "Credo" enact a deconstructive personality. Chapter 12 probes a brief and ostensibly simple song by Wolf, bringing together a Mörike poem, a painting, and musical style to propose two possible alternative types of lyric speaker for that piece.

The discussions here provide neither a comprehensive history of the voices in Romantic musical works nor a surefire methodology for studying the topic. As the brief outline above will have made clear, they instead demonstrate the range of possibilities, both of the voices of a variety of works and of ways by which we can discover, know, and appreciate those voices. Because the nature of the endeavor requires bringing together the widest spread of relevant information for any piece of music, I look forward to new studies that will amplify, refine, or even supersede the arguments presented in this book. Ideally, readers will take the studies here as motivation to pursue the Romantic voices of many more works.

With that last wish in mind, I acknowledge that, although along with many of my colleagues in the discipline of musicology I am deeply committed to including and valuing the work of composers of color, minority figures do not appear within the frame of this book. The problems of voice in the works of those composers, especially Black composers in the Western so-called "art" music of the nineteenth century, raise issues that differ inherently from those that apply to the European (and European American) composers discussed here. The Romantic voices for particular pieces of music by composers in minority groups would always have to be subsumed within the context of another layer of discourse, which renders making their acquaintance different in an essential way from doing so for those in the studies in this monograph. In a sense that does not apply to the music of white composers, an inescapable challenge in any Romantic work by a Black composer was inevitably to embody a persona negotiated between two predetermined types of voice: on one hand, speaking a stylistic idiom that communicated with the expectations of audiences and critics for classical music and, on the other, articulating the diverse impulses that individual composers felt to maintain an authentic Black identity both personally and for other Black people. To make sense of these issues would demand multiple case studies and require unsnarling strands of constructed identities more tangled with the multiplicity of their specific social histories than we can sort out within the necessarily limited page count of a monograph such as this one. Although I believe that the insights and methodologies I offer here can contribute profoundly to such a project, to do justice to enough variety of Black composers (not to mention composers of other minority groups) to deal fairly with these issues clearly merits another book.

Chapter 1

Hearing Voices

A Termino-Methodological Prolegomenon

Romanticism in Music Historiography

This book must begin with definitions, specifically to establish clearly at the outset what the terms *Romantic* and *voice* will mean throughout this discussion. This would apply to the topics of books (or any other writing) generally, but especially in this case, because each term carries a variety of meanings as well as complex and subtle connotations. In fact, both terms are used inconsistently and uncritically not only in daily conversation but equally so in academic discourse about music in the nineteenth century. For that reason we need to make sure that the intended meanings start and stay clear; nothing frustrates as much as trying to explain one's thinking to readers who have not understood the meanings of the core terms one uses, unless it is trying to understand an author who uses core terms in inconsistent ways. The first parts of this chapter will therefore position my usages in relation, or in contradistinction, to the usages of other writers, ranging from historical authorities to recent critics.

The concept *Romantic* here refers, probably not unexpectedly, to the qualities that mark the literature, art, and music that we associate with the dominant works of the nineteenth century in Western Europe. I accept, for reasons that I shall hasten to explicate, the conventional historiographic distinction between the music in a period that occupies roughly the latter half of the eighteenth century, which music history textbooks often call *Classic*[1]—though they would perhaps better designate it *Enlightenment*—and that of a new movement arising roughly at the beginning of the nineteenth

1

century, identified already in its own time as *Romantic*. We need to keep in mind that these two ideas and styles depend closely on each other; in fact, central ideas in the Enlightenment provided the seed from which the basic assumptions of Romanticism grew, and Romantic musical style importantly relies on established Classic models, specifically to disrupt them. For this reason, we must also emphasize a distinction between the two centuries as chronological periods and the epistemological, aesthetic, and stylistic values, respectively, of both Enlightenment and Romantic thinking and music. Especially, not all the music of the nineteenth century is automatically Romantic.

To set this historiographical perspective into context in its essentials, the Enlightenment, which defined itself by turning away from the idealized and abstract model of thinking that governed Rationalism (corresponding to or, perhaps better, generating the music that later acquired the regrettable moniker *Baroque*), relied to a new degree on empiricism (not that Galileo and Newton had not made their own observations of the world; they obviously had). Enlightenment artistic expression, like contemporary thinking in general, came to depend not on abstract reason but on experiential development of ideas. This manifests itself, in writing of all kinds, in an unprecedented dependence on *plot*. As Peter Brooks has observed, for the Enlightenment, when faith in a sacred master plot gave way, things had to be explained by stories of causation: "From sometime in the mid-eighteenth century through to the mid-twentieth century, Western societies appear to have felt an extraordinary need or desire for plots, whether in fiction, history, philosophy, or any of the social sciences, which in fact largely came into being with the Enlightenment and Romanticism."[2]

Plot and Musical Form

From the point of view of music, the Enlightenment's most significant contribution for our present purpose was the sonata form. The effect of a fully developed system of tonal contour, integrated with thematic activity and events, responded to the empiricist imagination in that the meaningful content of the musical movement fundamentally resided not in its melodic material or its rhythmic or harmonic affect, as had been primarily the case in the Rationalist Baroque, but in the course of the entire experience. In that sense, as Charles Rosen expressed it, "Dramatic sentiment was replaced by dramatic action."[3] As Schiller wrote about tragedy, it must constitute a complete action made up of events to be followed:

In order that a tragic picture may be complete, a whole series is required of particular actions, rendered sensuous and connected with the tragic situation as a whole . . . tragedy might be defined as the poetic imitation of a coherent series of particular events (forming a complete action): an imitation which shows us man in a state of suffering, and which has for its end to excite our pity. . . . It is, therefore, important that we should be able to follow in all its concatenations the action that is represented to us, that we should see it issue from the mind of the agent by a natural gradation, under the influence and with the concurrence of external circumstances.[4]

And this is likewise true of late-eighteenth-century music.

The underlying principle of the sonata form—and of its various affiliated forms—is dramatic action. In order to forestall any misunderstanding here, I must emphasize that I do not mean that the music is somehow a stepchild of theatrical drama. Rather, both theatrical works and sonata forms depend on a common way of achieving expression, which we can name the *dramatic mode*.[5] Literary drama and dramatic musical form stand side by side as sister arts. Their relationship is not filial; the latter is not the child of the former. Returning to Brooks's point, we can say that the central principle of both a stage play and a sonata-form movement is the idea of plot. All considerations of the idea of a plot begin with Aristotle, who in the *Poetics* established the fundamental concept, defining creativity (*poiesis*) as the making of plot (*mythos*), which is an imitation (*mimesis*) of action. In the nineteenth century, Schopenhauer described well what this means when he wrote that

the common end of the drama and the epic, to exhibit, in significant characters placed in significant situations, the extraordinary actions brought about by both, will be most completely attained by the poet if he first introduces the characters to us in a state of peace, in which merely their general colour becomes visible, and allows a motive to enter which produces an action, out of which a new and stronger motive arises, which again calls forth a more significant action, which, in its turn, begets new and even stronger motives, whereby, then, in the time suitable to the form of the poem, the most passionate excitement takes the place of the original peace, and in this now the important

> actions occur in which the qualities of the characters which have hitherto slumbered are brought clearly to light, together with the course of the world.[6]

To turn to one of the leading recent scholars of cultural and literary theory, Tsvetan Todorov describes a plot as consisting of propositions that are grouped into higher units in sequences, of which he says there are always and only five: a stable situation, disturbance by a new force, disequilibrium, a new force in the opposite direction, and reestablishment of stability.[7] These descriptions of plot apply precisely to the processes of sonata form. Indeed, the philosopher Stanley Cavell has noted that in the eighteenth century music became

> dramatic in a more fundamental sense . . . when it . . . achieved its own dramatic autonomy, worked out its progress in its own terms. . . . [The dramatic nature of music in this period] is secured only with the establishment of tonality and has its climax in the development of sonata form . . . I will say that the quality we are to perceive is one of *directed motion*, controlled by relationships of keys, by rate of alternation, and by length and articulation of phrases. We do not know where this motion can stop and we do not understand why it has begun here, so we do not know where we stand nor why we are there. The drama consists in following this out and in finding out what it takes to follow this out.[8]

We can see what Rosen and Cavell have in mind when we consider that the two necessary (and sufficient, one presumes) elements of a plot are characters whose roles are to be agents and a contour that begins at some point of stasis, proceeds through a middle in which that condition is disturbed, and ends by establishing a new point of stasis.

The leading approach to the analysis of sonata forms presently is Sonata Theory, laid out in a definitive study by James Hepokoski and Warren Darcy, copiously describing and classifying the norms typical of substantial instrumental movements of the late eighteenth and nineteenth centuries, and opening up the range of "sonata deformations" in actual practice.[9] Oddly, Hepokoski and Darcy at first describe the form in architectonic terms not at all consistent with the Enlightenment thinking on which the music was based, reflecting an anachronistic conception that scholars abandoned decades ago:

> A sonata-form project was a feat of engineering, like the construction of a bridge "thrown out" into space. In the eighteenth-century style this temporal span was to be built from rather simple materials: trim, elementary musical modules whose brevity and small-scale balances seemed best suited to short-winded compositions. In the hands of most composers, constructing a sonata-form movement was a task of *modular assembly*: the forging of a succession of short, section-specific musical units (spaces of action) linked together into an ongoing linear chain—pressing down and connecting one appropriately stylized musical tile after another.[10]

Later in the book, however, they reformulate their view in terms of dramatic action and plot, much more in keeping with the epistemology underlying the musical thinking and practice of the time. For reasons that will become clear shortly, in the following passage I replace their word "narrative" with "plotted" and "plot," which represents their point more accurately.

> A sonata is a linear journey of tonal realization, onto which might be mapped any number of concrete metaphors of human experience. Since a central component of the sonata genre is its built-in teleological drive—pushing forward to accomplish a generically predetermined goal—the sonata invites an interpretation as a musically [plotted] genre. A sonata dramatizes a purely musical plot that has a beginning (P, the place from where it sets out with a specific tonal-rhetorical aim in mind), a middle (including a set of diverse musical adventures), and a generic conclusion of resolution and confirmation (the ESC and subsequent music). It is in the nature of the sonata to set up a quest [plot]. . . .
>
> A sonata is a metaphorical representation of a perfect human action.[11]

Which is in fact the conception that the writers and composers of the time had in mind.

Character in Musical Expression

In eighteenth-century music-aesthetic thinking, a musical theme possesses character—unlike the earlier, Rationalist conception in which a musical theme served as the topic of a piece, more or less like the topic of an essay. In fact, the use of the term *topic* to identify expressive types in music of the late eighteenth and nineteenth centuries is an anachronism. The concept of musical expression based on topoi belongs to an earlier epistemological framework, in which musical forms were likened to rhetorical ones and musical ideas sometimes referred to as *loci topici* or conventional motives for development—in short, the Rationalist (so-called Baroque) way of treating music.[12]

The failure to observe this distinction has led to some misrepresentation of the epistemological differences that underlie the history of musical ideas and styles. In recent decades theorists have adopted the term *topic*, appropriate for the rhetorically conceived music of the Rationalist aesthetic, to identify the nature of a musical idea in Enlightenment and Romantic works of the late eighteenth and nineteenth centuries. Leonard Ratner initiated this usage in his book *Classic Music: Expression, Form, and Style*, and it has unfortunately been widely adopted.[13] Among Ratner's most influential successors were his students Wye J. Allanbrook, who applied the idea to the expressive use of dance rhythms in Mozart's operas, and Kofi Agawu, who developed the concept of topics into a theory of semiotics for Classic music.[14] Raymond Monelle elaborated at length on three so-called topics: the hunt, military music, and the pastoral.[15] Monelle admits that "the idea of the topic was discussed by contemporaries, *though they used different language* . . . and by modern writers not actually topic theorists."[16] Kofi Agawu compiles lists of "topics" identified by himself and other topic theorists, encompassing dances, moods, repertoires, textures, figurations, tempo markings, social positions, ethnicities, genres, idiomatic styles of instruments and singers, nature sounds, and so on.[17]

The fact that the writers contemporary with the music discussed in this book did not employ the word *topic* should be a clue that they did not have that rhetorical concept in mind. The identification of types of passages under the term *topic* has both become ubiquitous and extended to all sorts of musical features, and indeed writers who use it often offer perceptive and useful categorizations for discussions of thematic ideas and their references.[18] Nevertheless, the usage itself remains unfortunate. For one thing, it obscures the real intention of the historical concept of a topic within the rhetoric-based style to which it is relevant. For another, it misrepresents the nature and functions of themes in the late eighteenth and nineteenth centuries. The fact that late-eighteenth- and nineteenth-century writers do not identify musical ideas as "topics" in the language of an earlier time and episteme indicates that they thought of music in an importantly different way from their predecessors. The language that writers use does matter, and what drives and develops in a plot, whether literary or musical, is not a topic. Here I deliberately steer away from the concept and therefore from the use of the term *topic* to describe a theme.[19]

Consistent with the Enlightenment aesthetic model of plot, contemporary thinkers described the expressive aspect of a theme, passage, or even a whole movement heard as manifesting expressive unity by the word *character*. For example, in his guidance for piano players in 1789, Daniel Gottlob Türk identifies the expressive quality in music by the word *character*: "Every good piece of music possesses some specific (governing) character, which is to say, the composer has expressed in it a certain degree of joy or sorrow, humor or seriousness, rage or calmness, etc."[20] He then lists performance indications that help the performer to realize that character. Some of these characters are exactly congruent with the categories that, as just noted, recent writers misleadingly include among the so-called topics, such as lament, pastoral, siciliana, and so on. Likewise, in 1792 Johann Georg Sulzer wrote in his article on "expression in music,"

> Every piece of music, whether it is a melody actually accompanied by words or only composed for instruments, must have a distinct character and arouse a specific kind of mood in the listener's mind. It would be foolish if the composer wanted to begin his work before he had settled on the character of his piece. He must know whether the language that he wants to use should be the diction of a proud or a humble person, a brave or a fearful one, one who pleads or one who gives orders, a gentle or an angry one. And if he has discovered his theme by chance, or if it came to him by accident, he should analyze its character so that he can also sustain it in the working out.
>
> Having established the piece's character, he must then place himself in the mood that he wishes to evoke in others. The best approach is to imagine a plot, an occasion, or a situation, in which this would naturally reveal itself.[21]

The concept of character and its relationship to plot are already suggested here. Anton Reicha similarly illustrates the usage of *character* where earlier writers might have employed *affect* or, more rarely, *topic*: "Melody expresses different characters. . . . Two tunes composed in the same key and with the same meter, modulated in the same way, and having the same rhythm and the same structure, can nevertheless be completely opposite in character."[22]

Themes have not only recognizable character but also effective functions within a movement and in that sense serve as agents. Contemporary writers never used the term *agent* or *actant* in discussing musical form. Nevertheless, the concept is suggestive in relation to the use of the term *motive* in identifying a theme. While our usage of *motive* in discourse about music has come to suggest an inanimate object—a rhythmic/melodic configuration of a few notes to be manipulated in the course of a composition—the word should imply more than that. The Italian term *motivo* in fact seems to carry more connotation than does our English counterpart of the sense of being responsible for the course of action or conduct, that is, an active or animating force. The characters represented by the themes/motives of a sonata form establish keys, lead the music from place to place, interact, heighten or relax activity, and so on. They genuinely function in the sonata plot as agents.[23]

Because thinkers and writers about literary or musical plots in the nineteenth century did not employ either the term *topic* or *agent*, I employ their preferred term, *character*, throughout this book. In making this decision, I intentionally maintain the conviction, adopted directly from nineteenth-century musical thinkers, that character in a plot signifies two inseparable concepts, which the ideas of topic and agent artificially separate. First, in Romantic works a musical element *possesses* character in the sense of an identity determined by recognizable features. Second, that element *functions as* a character in that it takes an active part in the events of a piece, or it can passively experience—or, to put it less anthropomorphically, at least undergo—the action. These two senses of the word are inseparable because, as the music makes abundantly clear, the characteristic features of musical elements determine how they can work as characters within a plot.

The assumption that a character is implicitly human—that is, that themes have a sort of anthropomorphic identity—seems natural. We can easily find examples of this sort of thinking in recent scholarship. The statement quoted earlier from Hepokoski and Darcy's *Elements of Sonata Theory*, "A sonata is a metaphorical representation of a perfect human action," which is shortly followed by the assertion "It is 'human' primarily within eighteenth-century European conceptions of humanness,"[24] provides one such instance. Hepokoski and Darcy use "human" as an adjective and so do not explicitly claim that a theme represents a real or imagined person. On the other hand, Seth Monahan, writing about Mahler's Sixth Symphony, does adopt from Adorno the idea of "themes as anthropomorphic 'characters'" and says, "The more thoroughly we examine how these oppositions play out over time, the sharper a sense we get of the work's materials as dramatic characters, integral entities distinct from one another in terms of their goals, their anthropomorphic 'personalities,' and even their planes of origin."[25] We need to tread cautiously the boundary between taking up the eighteenth- and nineteenth-century commitment to the idea that themes or passages have character and the mistaken inference that music represents people. That is, we should never assume that, just because themes have characters and pieces of music are plotted, they programmatically recount actions or experiences of specific human beings, actual or fictional. As I will emphasize in what follows, this kind of programmatic explication is not what we should mean by saying that a work is narrative.

Finally, to make clear how explicitly and intentionally the nineteenth century regarded sonata form as consisting of characters and plot, we need only read Carl Czerny's synopsis of the form, dating from the late 1840s:

> Just as in a romance, a novel, or a dramatic poem, if the entire work shall be successful and preserve its unity, the necessary component parts are: first, an exposition of the principal idea and of the different characters, then the protracted complication of events, and lastly the surprising catastrophe and the satisfactory conclusion:—even so, the first part of the sonata movement forms the exposition, the second part the complication, and the return of the first part into the original key produces, lastly that perfect satisfaction which is justly expected from every work of art.[26]

Narrative and Voice

The eighteenth century offered musical forms as plots with somewhat conventional characters and conventional contours of stability, increasing tension, conflict, climax, and resolution and dénouement. The nineteenth century, by contrast, employed these resources in more idiosyncratic ways. The themes partake less of conventional types, and the courses of the action become less predictable. Moreover, nineteenth-century music does not merely present dramatic plots but represents these as narratives, making the subjective individuality expressing the action as interesting as the thematic characters and action themselves.[27] And this marks the defining difference between Enlightenment (or Classic) music and Romantic.

Crucial to the point here, Rousseau introduces his *Confessions* with the observation that "I am not made like anyone I have seen; I dare to believe that I am not made like anyone who exists. If I am not worth more, at least I am different. Whether nature has acted rightly or wrongly in breaking the mold in which she cast me, one can only judge after having read me."[28] Crucial, because it establishes the premise that humans derive their worth not from their positions within the large framework of society but from the effective expression of their individuality. Thus, not only does Rousseau set up a basis for fostering personal development beyond artificial social constraints, he implies that each person merits our interest uniquely, based on our experience of what each has to say. This understanding served as philosophical justification for a new conception of human rights and for the revolutions of the last quarter of the eighteenth century, and it set up for the coming century a new way of thinking about an individual's personality and self-expression.

The position that Rousseau articulated led to new interest in the emotional life of the individual. A person is intrinsically different from all others on the basis not of objective reason but of subjective experience. Thus objective Enlightenment empiricism projected itself into the exploration of subjectivity that defines Romanticism. This philosophical trajectory manifests itself in the move toward an aesthetic that expects a work of art to express an individual subjectivity. This justifies the premise of the studies that follow: that the Romanticism of a work consists in the sense that it gives of a personality expressing itself—in other words, a voice. We can turn to the flowering of lyric poetry of the nineteenth century for one instance of this. For another, we may take the explosion of the novel, which, during the nineteenth century, adds to the actions of the plot the point of view, the personal position, the values, and even the feelings of the narrator.

For this reason, I again stress the importance of distinguishing between the terms *plot* (and *drama*) and *narrative*, terms unfortunately often treated as synonymous.[29] Narrative incorporates plot, but it differs from drama by the presence or perception of a narrative voice. One of the clearest statements of this comes from Robert Scholes and Robert Kellogg in *The Nature of Narrative*: "By narrative we mean all those literary works which are distinguished by two characteristics: the presence of a story and a story-teller. A drama is a story without a story-teller. . . . For writing to be narrative no more and no less than a teller and a tale are required."[30] Seymour Chatman reminds us that the history of this point extends back to Antiquity: "Direct presentation presumes a kind of overhearing by the audience. Mediated narration, on the other hand, presumes a more or less express communication from narrator to audience. This is essentially Plato's distinction between *mimesis* and *diegesis*, in modern terms between showing and telling. Insofar as there is telling, there must be a teller, a narrating voice."[31] For the Greek philosophers, drama is mimetic; *epos* or narrative, diegetic.[32] Only one of the two images in figure 1.1 depicts a narration.

Figure 1.1a. Moritz von Schwind, *Der Erlkönig*. *Source:* Heritage Image Partnership Ltd. / Alamy Stock Photo. Used with permission.

Figure 1.1b. Albert Anker, *Der Grossvater erzählt eine Geschichte*. *Source:* Artmedia / Alamy Stock Photo. Used with permission.

In the period on which this book focuses, that distinction continued to be articulated in the same way. As Schiller put it, "In tragedy particular events are presented to our imagination or to our senses at the very time of their accomplishment; they are present, we see them immediately, without the intervention of a third person. The epos, the romance, simple narrative, even in their form, withdraw action to a distance, causing the narrator to come between the acting person and the reader."[33] Genette, as we have already noted, differentiates these as the two modes of representation in fiction.[34]

This differentiation is not always observed in discussions of either literature or music; writers frequently use the word *narrative* where they clearly just mean *plot*. Michael J. Toolan poses what he calls a "minimalist definition of narrative": "a perceived sequence of non-randomly connected events."[35] Tzvetan Todorov gives a somewhat more elaborate description: "The minimal complete plot consists in the passage from one equilibrium to another. An 'ideal' narrative [*sic*] begins with a stable situation which is disturbed by some power or force. There results a state of disequilibrium; by the action of a force directed in the opposite direction, the equilibrium is re-established; the second equilibrium is similar to the first, but the two are never identical."[36] In both cases, these writers describe what I, for reasons that will be obvious, shall rigorously call not "narrative" but "plot"; in fact, Todorov here neatly demonstrates the all-too-common casual slippage between the two words.[37]

I have already noted Hepokoski and Darcy's use of "narrative" for what is more properly regarded as plot.[38] A prominent recent example of this use of the term *narrative* to mean plot in music (only one of many) is Byron Almén's impressively sophisticated *A Theory of Musical Narrative*.[39] Almén explores his topic in admirable detail, but that topic is not really "narrative" at all but rather plot and plot archetype. The demonstrations that form the second part of his book illustrate the application of the four *mythoi* framed by Northrop Frye,[40] and, as we have seen, the authoritative meaning of *mythos* (and I think that we can comfortably take Aristotle as authoritative here) is plot, not diegesis.

Other recent discussions of the activity within musical pieces have developed theories of agency in and around musical plots. Seth Monahan's 2013 article "Action and Agency Revisited" lays out a framework of nested layers of agency as it is used or implied in analytical writing about music. He distinguishes assertions that treat as agents individuated elements that writers describe as performing particular roles within compositions, the putative work-persona that seems to direct those elements (i.e., a narrator), a fictional composer taken as expressing ideas by creating the work-persona or the musical elements (i.e., an implied author), and finally the analyst whose writing might set up any or all of the lower-level agents. Monahan undertakes to explain the relationships in this hierarchy, illustrating them with quotations from analytical writing, and he observes the considerable complexity and open-endedness of the possibilities.[41] Robert S. Hatten builds on Monahan's propositions in his book *A Theory of Virtual Agency for Western Music*. He describes a number of ways in which agency unfolds or is perceived in musical works. He outlines how the inference of agency in the listening or analytical process extends from basic understanding of the identities of events, through the interactions and relationships in the music, to perception of volition and subjectivity, and culminates in the development of communication among hearers and the codification of cultural meaning.[42] My thinking has profited from the ideas of both Monahan and Hatten, but my approach is not primarily concerned with agency in the action of musical plots nor with issues of the metaphors by which we write about music. The body of this book also does not undertake a systematic layout of approaches, since each of the works discussed here (like Romantic works generally) brings up its own, idiosyncratic conditions and requires a specific kind of synthetic interpretation.

Karol Berger, pursuing an alternative line of thinking, follows Ricoeur in adopting a definition of *narrative* that is "thematic" rather than "modal." Distinguishing between types of work that deal with enacting rather than directly with feeling, he lumps together the dramatic and the genuinely narrative, in order to separate them from the expression of emotion that we encounter in lyric poetry. Thus epic and drama, because they both have plot, are both called "narrative," while lyric constitutes the alternative element in a dyad. Thus, in disregard of Plato and Aristotle, the distinction between mimetic and diegetic modes becomes irrelevant to Berger's definition of narrative.[43] It is not that Berger's point here is invalid in its own right within the framework of his thinking. His thematic grouping is, however, not useful to the issue of Romantic voice that will interest us here. To put this in perspective, the point of view I shall take in this book draws the dividing line in a modal rather than thematic way. Where Berger distinguishes plotted from lyric works in an unbalanced division thematically (see table 1.1), I shall distinguish them modally (see table 1.2).

Table 1.1. Berger's thematic categories and genres they include

So-called "narrative"—i.e., plot-based	Drama Narrative
Lyric	Lyric poetry

Table 1.2. Modal categories and genres they include

Represented	Drama
Voiced	Lyric poetry Narrative

Unlike Almén, Berger does not fail to recognize the modal classification; nevertheless, by conflating drama and narrative, the use of the latter term confuses the reading of the broader literature generally.

Michael Klein offers a definition of narrativity that abandons the Aristotelian distinction between the mode of the drama and that of epic to the point of meaninglessness: "The whole question of *mimesis* (showing) and *diegesis* (telling), of whether the action is mediated by a surviving narrator or whether it unfolds before us, has no bearing on the question of whether music, drama, poetry, or painting can be narrative. The requirement for a narrative is that we apprehend that the story might have been arranged in another way. Narrative is any showing or telling of events."[44] This essentially denies the existence of mimesis—quite apart from the problem that a story arranged another way is another story. Moreover, a narrator apparently need not be a survivor in the implicit sense of having been present in the action narrated. Ultimately, Klein confesses, "We tell stories about music,"[45] and that seems to be the most honest usage of the idea of narrative he offers—narrative analysis means that the analyst creates a narrative—in other words, the fourth level in Monahan's hierarchy. In that case, one has to agree that the mode of presentation of the work itself might have no bearing.

My point in this critique of the usages of the term *narrative* is not to disregard and certainly not to disparage the interesting work of Almén, Berger, or Klein. Rather, by identifying what I believe is a problematic conflation of the principle of plot, or plot archetype or drama, with the idea of narrative, I mean to indicate the more specific definition that I shall employ throughout my own argument.

Now it will also be useful to examine some of the ideas of writers who resolutely reject the possibility of narrative in music. We can start with Jean-Jacques Nattiez, who in 1990 published the article "Can One Speak of Narrativity in Music?," in which he decisively rejects musical narrativity as a possibility.[46] The core of his argument is that, unlike literature, which employs words and hence enables denotative references, musical tones do not name persons and actions and thus cannot represent stories of events in a nonmusical world. Famously, he ran an experiment in which he played *The Sorcerer's Apprentice* for schoolchildren without telling them the title, and he asked them to write the story that they heard in the music. As we might expect, the children did not "get it right." It is helpful here to remind ourselves that a rigorous structuralist would quickly point out that plots expressed verbally in literature also do not reconstruct real-world happenings but construct verbal objects. Given that principle, it absolutely does not make sense to expect listeners to hear a musical plot as an enactment of an extramusical story. We should, moreover, turn Nattiez's argument back on itself by remembering that plottedness (or drama) and narrativity do not come to music by borrowing from literature but exemplify a conception of artistic expression that can be instantiated in either literature or music. For the same reason that Dukas could compose a piece that presents the dramatic contour of the regrettable adventures of the sorcerer's apprentice, the children could also compose adventure stories that traced the contour of Dukas's music. Neither literature nor music depend on the other in order to create a plot; each depends on a larger idea about understanding sequences of actions and events, an idea that supersedes both art forms. Such a plot can equally well be expressed in a good description or diagram of a piece's form.[47] Nattiez also claims that "it is not within the semiological possibilities of music to link a subject to a predicate."[48] That grammatical construction, however, turns out to be specious, again in the sense that it blames music for not being verbal language. Identifiable themes do accomplish actions within a piece—they establish tonal areas, carry the listener from one key to another, spread themselves across the orchestra, fall apart into fragments and reassemble, and so on. To say this straightforwardly in terms of a subject and predicate, in music, "stuff happens."

Read in another way, Nattiez might seem to adopt the peculiar idea that narrativity in music means that music should recount (in contradistinction to enacting) the events of some particular story—in other words, that "Music" assumes the position of narrat*or* in relation to a literary or, one presumes, historical tale. But this pushes the issue down to a level that simply doesn't make sense. No one should seriously expect music to become the narrator of the misadventures of a sorcerer's apprentice or the career of Napoleon. The events of a piece of music actually are the music. The concept of narrativity does not apply to music in the way that Nattiez suggests.

One of the ways of understanding narrative that has occupied some music scholars in the past couple of decades depends on making literary narrative the model for narrativity in music. The argument is that in literature (including drama as well as the novel) a work presumes a series of actual—even if fictive—events that the work enacts or recounts. The difference between the events and their representation in the work is the shift from reality (or some implied reality) in the past to narrative in the present. Narrative in this case means only the emplotment of events, descriptions, and so on. But unless the music intends a naive kind of programmaticism, this does not apply convincingly in music, where the only events are the events in the music itself, and they are all present in the hearing.

To get around this, some theorists mine for discontinuities in a work as evidence that different musical events might be parts of two different chronologies. That is, some of what we hear appears to comprise actions or moments narrated, and some comprises or at least invokes an act of narration. For example, Raymond Monelle gets at this issue in making a distinction between "genre" and "structure." For Monelle, the musical mark of genre is the evocative passage or fragment occurring within a work, while the structure asserts a unifying principle to bind the fragments in ways that arise from a specific concept or ideology.[49] Michael Klein offers a distinction between types of time in Chopin's music, asserting that passages in salon styles (like those of the nocturne, mazurka, and waltz) can be associated with "lyric time" and those in bravura style (like the etudes and virtuosic passages in concertos and polonaises) with "narrative time." The shifts between styles suggest shifts between past and present.[50] Andrew Davis, who also takes Chopin as a prime example, finds that some passages within a movement seem to constitute a predictably directed succession of events, while at other moments the music does not belong to that predictable vector—he calls these passages "temporal" and "atemporal," respectively, and for him this appearance of atemporality suggests narrativity.[51] Of course, we might object that both Klein's lyric and narrative time and Davis's "atemporal" passages take place in and occupy stretches of present time—and these fall within the same listening time as the rest of the music, and the events generally do seem to relate to each other coherently as the music unfolds. I shall examine some specific issues in their arguments when I discuss Chopin in a later chapter.

Narrators' Voices

In literary fictions and histories, narrators recount events, and we read the events through the voices of their literary narrators and historians. In hearing a tone poem or a symphony movement, we hear actions and plots in the music, but in addition, as Robert Hatten rightly observes, "we as listeners are predisposed to engage with a kind of subjective identification whenever we listen to music."[52] I would argue that this engagement amounts to getting to know the subjective identity from whom we instinctively imagine the music to come, and I would assign this kind of engagement particularly to Romantic music, where it is most intrinsically part of the aesthetic presupposition of a work. (And when we have that experience with other music, I believe that we are bringing to it an approach that belongs to that Romantic aesthetic—in effect, romanticizing it.) What I hope to do, then, is explore how we locate and identify the voices of the narrators or lyric egos that we hear behind those plots.

An issue that troubles skeptics about the possibility of narrativity in music is the observation that for music, unlike literary narrative, they cannot find a way to separate in a musical work what narrative theory in literary criticism calls *story* from *discourse*—in Russian, *fabula* and *sjužet*; in French, *histoire* versus *discours* (Todorov) or *histoire* versus *récit* and *narration* (Genette)—or sometimes *plot* and *story*, which is a bit confusing because "story" comes to be employed for both of the two ideas.[53] Typically, in fiction the two differ in terms of chronology; that is, we easily notice that the time taken by the action is different from the time taken to recount it. Sometimes events might have occupied a very much longer time than we need to read the narrator's report in a paragraph that summarizes them, and in other situations time stands still while we read the narrator's description or learn what happens or what characters perceive in an instant. In fact, as Genette points out with examples from Proust,[54] we might even read in a single sentence about a large number of events recounted in imperfect tense—the sort of thing that reports, "On Sunday afternoons, we used to walk . . ." For Paul Ricoeur, a (the?) distinctive feature of narrative is that the time of telling is assumed to be later than the time of the events narrated.[55] Carolyn

Abbate articulates the point by observing that music has no past tense.[56] True enough. But it takes a sort of naive listening to miss, or prejudgment to lead one to ignore, the fact that time in music does have layers. Let us grant that we listen continuously through a musical work or movement, so that the tones are always present to us. Even so, musical time does not flow along at a constant, clocklike pace but slows down and speeds up. Too, we remember even as we listen, so that past and present both become part of the listening, when we notice repetition and variation. Furthermore, there are other treatments of time that break out of musical continuity. As we shall see, the forward flow of a coherent musical action can be broken by an interruption so independent of the plot that we are following (as in the first movement of Beethoven's Piano Sonata in D Minor, op. 31, no. 2) that it undeniably pauses the action and takes place in a separate time frame of its own. Or a cyclic work may represent experiences by recounting them to us in an unplotted sequence that need not represent chronological order, so that the individual pieces clearly do not belong to the same time as the telling (as in Schumann's Eichendorff *Liederkreis*), and in this case one can hardly think of the separate pieces as anything other than past in relation to the work as a whole. So when Seymour Chatman says that narrative must always structure the time of telling in relation to the time of the action, this can apply to musical narrative as well as to literary fiction.[57]

Some musicologists have espoused the concept of narrativity that I am using here. In a 1998 conference paper summarizing musical applications of narratology, Thomas Christensen points out that "if we pause to reflect upon the basic meaning of narration, we recognize at once a missing element in the structural descriptions noted above: narration demands some agent telling a story. Narrative is fundamentally a process of 'recounting,' not 'representing' (the distinction between *diegesis* and *mimesis*)."[58] Hatten writes, "Generally speaking, Classical musical discourse is an enacted discourse, more akin to drama than narrative. Only when a narrative agency is explicitly staged in the music do I consider a Classical work to constitute a narrative. My position thus differs from those for whom the mere ordering of events by a composer can reflect what I would call a narrative agency."[59]

In his 1990 dissertation, David Loberg Code takes note of some of the issues involved in the distinction between action and narration in a musical work. He observes that we might initially be inclined to doubt the possibility of separating the two: "How can a performance medium which is non-linguistic project a temporality other than that which exists in real-time performance? We must either postulate that the narration is completely synchronic in relation to the story (that the story and narrational sequences are identical), or that the narration is completely achronic (that the differences between the story and narrational sequences are indeterminable)."[60] But he then suggests that we might hear "cracks or seams within the musical text" that indicate a difference between the events in the main course of the plot and another temporal level or perspective. Among the ways in which this might happen, he suggests quotations, of other musical works or even from within the piece itself. In an analysis of Brahms's Intermezzo in B-flat, op. 76, no. 4, Code demonstrates that

> it is possible to discern a difference between an underlying story and its narration through musical (i.e., non-verbal) means. Temporally, a narrational sequence can differ from the story's sequence of events with regard to order, frequency, and . . . duration. By treating repetitions of similar thematic material as narrations of the same event, it is possible to construct alternative ordering from the one we hear in real-time performance. . . . Additionally, by comparatively inspecting the differences between these multiple narrations, we can isolate some of the elements which belong separately to both the story and narration.[61]

Further,

> Narration is perhaps most evident in tonal compositions . . . by the events which it omits. It is through implication, harmonic or otherwise, that we are aware that what we hear (i.e., what we are told) is not the whole story. These narrational ellipses may involve the implication of single pitch, a chord, a small phrase, or entire section of music. . . . Anywhere that the music appears to lead us to an awareness of events which are not aurally present, a distinction is made between story and narration.[62]

Carolyn Abbate does emphasize the instantiation of narrative in music at moments of disruption:

> The *narrating voice* . . . is not merely an instrumental *imitation of singing*, but rather is marked by multiple disjunctions with the music surrounding it. These disjunctions, their forms and signs, . . . change from work to work; they are fugitive. They

exist on many levels. I propose that we understand musical narration not as an omnipresent phenomenon, not as sonorous encoding of human events or psychological states, but rather as a rare and peculiar act, a unique moment of performing narration within a surrounding music.[63]

In her path-breaking study, Abbate works primarily with opera, and she focuses methodologically on analysis of the notes and the performative act of singing. (Her treatments of instrumental music, Dukas's *The Sorcerer's Apprentice* and the third movement of Mahler's Second Symphony, have drawn more skeptical responses.)[64]

Listening for Romantic Voices

Whether we think of narrative (where it seems to have caused so much confusion) or lyric, the most important factor in Romanticism is the presence of *voice*. The epoch-making study of this, and one that has been enormously influential on my interest in the topic, is Edward T. Cone's *The Composer's Voice*. In turn, Cone derived central elements of his thinking from Wayne C. Booth's *The Rhetoric of Fiction*.[65] For Booth and for Cone, a central point was to differentiate the figure of the actual author or composer of a work from the voice that both presents and is embodied in the content of the work. Scholars miss the central issue when they ask, as Abbate does, "How does music narrate?" or, as Klein puts it, "Music, what is your story?"[66] The question I pursue in this book is rather, "Music, whose story are you?" The fundamental assumption in this book is not at all that a work of Romantic music is like a narrative because it tries to tell a story. A work is narrative because it is told. What will concern us is *who narrates music*. This is the voice, whether lyric or narrative—the so-called lyric ego or the narrator—whose presence, I argue, determines Romanticism.[67]

The voice in this sense is sometimes referred to by the term *persona*, which I shall also use throughout this book to identify the speaker of a lyric piece or the guiding narrator of a plotted one. The idea of the persona gained currency in musical studies from its application by Cone. Writers have also employed it in ways unlike our interest here, and sometimes skeptically. The aesthetician Peter Kivy, for example, resists an application that he and others have adopted, a hypothesis that the emotions that music expresses must be the emotions of some so-called "persona" behind it.[68] This seems to me a misuse of the concept of persona in the first place, not least because the narrative subject in a work might assume quite an impersonal stance in regard to the emotions that the work expresses—or even reveal entirely contrary emotions.

My intention in the following chapters is not to explicate a philosophy of emotion in music generally but to become acquainted with each work's Romantic voice, the mind or the guiding imagination (not, however, identical with the biographical composer) responsible for the musical ideas—that is, to get to know whose kinds of thinking we encounter in specific pieces of music. Precisely this goal distinguishes this book from most recent work in narrative theory. I do not propose an analytical method for locating narrativity, because the idiosyncrasies of Romanticism eventually, inevitably, confound method. Nor am I satisfied to have located the narrative moment or the traces of narrativity in a narrative work, although that forms a crucial step in many cases. Essentially, I want to get to know the personalities of the voices—the lyric egos or the narrators—behind each of the pieces that I study. This book shares the experience of acquaintance with those personalities.

The aspiration to get to know the voices (or personas, or speakers, or minds) of particular works makes sense when we remember that what we call the Classic-Romantic period, or, as we have seen above, the Enlightenment moving into Romanticism, is the age of the novel. For one thing, the modern novel, as opposed to its predecessors the epic and the romance, emerged at about this time. Characteristically, the eighteenth-century novel adopts a first-person voice and is presented as if it consisted of the eponymous author's documents such as a journal (*Robinson Crusoe*) or letters (*Pamela*). Increasingly in the nineteenth century the plot is recounted in the third person, where the narrative voice stands outside the action; in other words, the novel becomes more obviously voiced.

Evidence of the Romantic interest in—we might even say obsession with—the voice emerges in music, too. The first modern composer biographies date from the turn of the century, starting with Johann Nikolaus Forkel's *Über Johann Sebastian Bach's Leben, Kunst, und Kunstwerk* in 1802. Forkel takes pains to give Bach's music a voice for nineteenth-century listeners, German listeners in particular, representing Bach as the genius-hero who speaks in his music for German posterity. The eighteenth century had not felt it necessary to depend on personalities as voices for its music. Enlightenment listeners knew composers' names and admired their music and its compositional craft, but only later did writers invent the Haydn whose troubled marital stresses he expressed in the so-called Sturm und Drang symphonies of the 1770s. Beethoven, the socially prickly but artistically commanding figure, partisan of the Revolution, suffering with a shattering disability, naturally played into the Romantic impulse to create a voice for his challenging musical expressions. Within the first quarter of the nineteenth century, the fictional (in the sense of created, even if out of actually—or supposedly—factual information) biographical constructions of composers to invoke as voices in their music could be taken for granted.[69] Nevertheless, the voice so constructed remains a fiction. We must avoid the error, often referred to as the biographical fallacy, of thinking of the composer as the narrator of a plotted musical work or the speaker in a lyric one. Artists reveal attitudes and ways of thinking in their work, but they do not air their personal laundry. What musical works tell us biographically about composers is just that they composed them, not about their individual activities, ailments, and emotional experiences.

In *The Beethoven Syndrome: Hearing Music as Autobiography*, Mark Evan Bonds notes the distinction between the interpretation of composers' works through their lives, which he identifies as the meaning of the term "biographical fallacy," and "perceptions of compositional subjectivity."[70] Bonds points out that the latter is not a fallacy at all. In fact, it is a historical fact of nineteenth-century reception history. Bonds does not sufficiently recognize that the actual fallacy is the assumption that the perception of subjectivity in a piece implies that the narrative or lyric voice of a work is identical to the person of the composer. That is what leads the uncritical to carry information about a composer's life into (mis)interpretation of the music. Likewise, the reverse: a work's perceived subjectivity does not reveal the subjective experience of its composer; it can do no more than represent some fictive subjectivity that the composer's imagination adopts for that work. In this sense, the biographical fallacy becomes the autobiographical fallacy. Any autobiography read from a musical work is merely a fictive construction by a naive listener, not by the composer.

In manners of performance, too, the assumption that an identifiable figure represented the voice of a work made itself evident. The early nineteenth century first saw the regular appearance of a conductor standing on a podium with a baton (scepter or weapon?), controlling the music of a symphony. Audiences could read the conductor in that performance practice as a visual representation of or as a surrogate for the narrator's voice in the work, especially when composers led their own works. Romanticism idealized composer-conductors, notable among them Mendelssohn, Berlioz, Wagner,

Mahler. Audiences also conceived the conductor as the Romantic voice for a marked performance when specialist virtuoso conductors came on the scene with their distinctive public personalities, so auditors wanted to know Hans von Bülow's Beethoven's Ninth Symphony. Likewise, concerts in the eighteenth century had featured diverse performers in potpourri programs, but the nineteenth century invented the solo recital, in which the master (as in Liszt's case) or mistress (in Clara Schumann's) of the music voiced his or her husband's music. Performers also cultivated personas that guided the hearing of their work by their audiences, as we shall discuss in the cases of Paganini and Liszt.

Evidence

To locate and identify the Romantic voices in musical works of the nineteenth century requires that the critic exercise alertness both to analytical features of the music as it is heard and to external evidence. In every instance the specific elements belong only to the single work, so we can never rely on a methodological formula to reveal the voice; Romanticism, after all, glories in the idiosyncratic. As I have said, this book offers no theoretical method for discovering voices in works, for an adequate method is impossible. Nevertheless, an overview of some possibilities can help to open up our critical insight. Since the remainder of this book demonstrates a variety of ways to approach specific works, the discussion that follows will merely offer some general observations and mention a few instances, several of which I shall develop later.

To begin with the internal, textual, what Genette calls the immanent aspects of the work, we can think of several ways in which the music indicates a voice behind the action. A particular idiom governing the work immediately provides clues about the voice.[71] The texture of a lyric piano piece represents a different speaker from that of a dense, symphonic texture. The songlike melody and rocking, compound-meter accompaniment of a barcarolle specifies the voice of a gondolier. Certain kinds of virtuosity, as we shall see, carry implications about voice. A listener will undoubtedly hear a work for one instrument that mimics another—we might think of Gottschalk's *The Banjo*, for instance—as displaying a voice. Likewise, the evocation of the orchestra in a piano piece introduces us to a narrative voice not of the salon soloist but of a more ambitious, public figure. A fugal passage not only represents a thematic character but suggests for the work a voice knowledgeable in a learned style or historically conscious.

Beyond the use of an idiomatic style or technique, even more specificity can arise from the use of actual quotation or allusion. When one musical work quotes another, we are obviously compelled to hear the voice of the work as that of someone who knows the music quoted. Even more, we will understand from the position and nature of the quotation how the voice regards the composer or work to which the music refers. The *1812 Overture* does not simply recount an event; it reveals where its narrator's sympathies lie. A symphony that incorporates the Lutheran hymn "Ein' feste Burg ist unser Gott" or one that grossly parodies the melody of the "Dies irae" definitely reveals something of the voices from which it comes. These examples might seem so obvious as to be almost trivial; they demonstrate, however, that what we are thinking about here is not foreign to our hearing of Romantic music—even if we overlook it by taking it for granted.

Cyclical recurrences of thematic ideas among movements in cases where we would not normally expect them also suggest narrativity. Naturally, they affect the understanding of the form of a work, but in doing so they imply the imposition of the storyteller on the action. Thus even a piece that has no program tends to move from dramatic action toward narrative recounting of action when cyclic recurrences connect separate movements. Schumann's D-Minor Symphony, like Liszt's *Faust Symphony*, presents a final movement essentially reinterpreting the first, and although the former has no program, unlike the latter, the implication of an external, controlling presence is equally strong.

Yet another possibility for immanent evidence of the voice in the musical text of a piece is the inclusion or intrusion of music that evidently does not belong to the body of the work's form and style. In such cases, as Robert Hatten convincingly argued in 1991, the music appears to present multiple levels of discourse, perhaps suggesting that the main activity takes place in one plane but that some occurs in another.[72] This sometimes relates to the idea of idiom, except that instead of governing the music as a whole it applies to limited segments of a form. Such a passage might occur as a framing section, especially at the close of a piece. (Introductions in a formulaic "introduction" style, inherited from the earlier French *ouverture*, are so well established in the eighteenth century that we would not necessarily respond to such passages as suggesting voice rather than as conventional structural frame.) If in Mendelssohn's A-Minor Symphony we hear the body of the work as "Ossianic" and the finale's coda as German,[73] then it hardly seems likely that the ending logically belongs to the same action as the fourth movement "Allegro guerriero," programmatically representing—well, what? After the Scottish battle, the arrival of a chorus of German university students on tour? Too farfetched. But it certainly suggests that outside the

Scottish landscape and stormy weather of the first movement, the folklike gapped scales and "snap" rhythms of the scherzo, and the warlike action of the finale there stands a German presence. Commenting interruptions also form an indication of such a voice for a piece. The paradigmatic example, as we shall see, is the opening movement of Beethoven's Piano Sonata in D Minor, op. 31, no. 2, where a recitative intrudes directly to tell the listener how, or perhaps how not, to follow the musical plot.

In addition to the notes of the score we also encounter paratextual elements that guide our attention to the voice of a piece. The components of paratexts have received their most extensive coverage from Genette.[74] He separates these into two categories: peritext, which for our purposes here includes the visual and verbal materials that accompany a score itself; and epitext, written or oral statements that the composer understands will be known by readers. For music, the peritext often includes much the same material as for works of literature, including titles, epigrams, prefaces, dedications, explanatory notes, and intertitles for separate movements, but it would especially include the programs of program music.

The composer's name on a title page (or, presumably, a concert program) can also reveal an identity of voice. On the famously torn and discarded manuscript title page of the "Bonaparte" Symphony the composer's name was given as Louis van Beethoven, clearly marking a national affinity, even if not actual identity, for the voice of the work. The published title page of the "Eroica" Symphony gives the Italian, and therefore cosmopolitan, name of Luigi van Beethoven. Anonymity or the use of a pseudonym is less common in music than in literature, but at least one exemplary case of what Genette calls an apocryphal attribution—the use of a borrowed name in place of a real composer's—comes to mind. The songs of Mendelssohn's first two published collections, opp. 8 and 9, are mostly by the composer Felix Mendelssohn Bartholdy, which makes our approach to them the same as for any Romantic song. Three songs in each set, however, fall into a completely different category, since they were composed by Fanny Mendelssohn Bartholdy (later Hensel) and thus introduce a different and very interesting relationship between composer and voice.[75]

Titles contribute to our understanding of the voices of works, whether those titles are *rhematic*, such as *Sonata* or *Symphony*, which identify pieces by their genres, or *thematic*, as in programmatic works.[76] The music that we typically think of as "absolute" generally offers only rhematic titles. Listening to a piece titled only String Quartet, we naturally attend primarily to theme and motive, interplay between instrumental lines, and form. A symphony headed "From the New World" obviously places the narrator geographically, and we listen for marks of exoticism in themes and styles. A symphony titled *Harold en Italie*, as I shall discuss later, sets up several layers of voices by its reference to those within Byron's *Childe Harold's Pilgrimage*, as well as the symphony's commentary on that work.

In dealing with program music, we must remember that events and actions named in a program do not themselves constitute evidence of narrative. Programs do, however, represent a layer of discourse that stands beside the musical tones themselves and in that sense can imply narrative (or possibly, in some instances, lyric) voices. In some cases, works that are not explicitly programmatic in the sense of representing an identified plot come with epigrams that contribute to our understanding of the voice.

We should also observe cover design and typography or engraving style, illustrations, and the like. Two examples of title pages for works of Chopin will illustrate this point. The first (figure 1.2) is for his first published work. The title, "RONDEAU," appears in a Gothic font, decorated by a banded treatment of the broader strokes in each letter. The whole is embellished by curlicues. Thus we meet the music as expressive of both historic tradition

Figure 1.2. Title page of Chopin's Rondo, op. 1 (1825). RONDEAU | composé pour le | PIANOFORTE | et dedié | à Mme de Linde | PAR | FREDERIC CHOPIN | Propriete de l'editeur | à Varsovie chez A. Brzezina. *Source:* Public domain.

and rococo ornamentation. The largest and most elegant letters express the name of the dedicatee, Luiza Linde, in the center of the page. The small italics for "composé pour le [PIANOFORTE]" and "et dedié" belong to the same basic style as the identification of the publisher at the bottom of the page. The explosive lines radiating from "PAR" suggest the composer's bursting onto the scene or a flash of inspiration, yet Chopin's name is in a relatively plain and modern typeface. The use of French in a publication in Warsaw reminds us of the cultural affinities of Poland at the time.

By contrast, the title page of the Impromptu, op. 51 (see figure 1.3), leaves a completely different impression. The lettering is far more uniform

Figure 1.3. Title page of Chopin, Impromptu in G-flat, op. 51 (1843). ALLEGRO VIVACE | POUR LE | PIANOFORTE | DEDIÉ | À MADAME | LA COMTESSE ESTERHÁZY | NÉE COMTESSE BATHYANY [sic] | PAR | FRÉDERIC CHOPIN. | OP. 51. PR. 20 NGR. | Propriété des Editeurs. | Enregistré aux Archives de l'Union. | LEIPZIG, CHEZ FRÉDERIC HOFMEISTER. | LONDON, CHEZ WESSEL & Cie. PARIS, CHEZ M. SCHLESINGER. | St. PETERSBOURG, CHEZ C. F. HOLTZ. | VARSOVIE, CHEZ G. SENNEWALD. | 2900. *Source:* Public domain.

and modern; indeed, it seems relatively matter-of-fact. The decoration is a repeating frame comprising what might seem to be small flames, although it is difficult to identify them for certain, with corner and center medallions, and the text itself is printed on a field of diagonal hatchwork. The decoration, like the typeface, is more functional than expressive. The dedicatee, Countess Jeanne Esterhazy, née Batthyany, again represents Polish heritage but is far higher in rank than Madame Linde and with grand international prestige. Nevertheless, the composer's name now appears more prominently than that of the dedicatee. The cosmopolitan reach of the music is also indicated by the inclusion of a list of the publishers who will distribute the score in different countries, extending from England to Russia.

These title pages tell us much about styles and tastes in different times and places in the nineteenth century, and about the composer's career. But they also influence how the reader of the score will understand the voice of the music. How such information is interpreted depends on the reader we have in mind. As historians, we will try to reconstruct imaginatively the reader of the time at which the print appeared. As critics, we also have the opportunity to read with our own insights.

Epitext could, as for literary works, include a composer's diaries or memoirs, interviews, and compositional drafts. Additionally, musical epitexts might extend to explicit guidance for or even presumed conventions of performance. To cite an example in which the epitexts can contribute to the listener's sense of the voice, we have for Berlioz's works generally the *Treatise on Instrumentation*, standing as an external source that offers a guide to indicate expressive effects of the various instruments. At the same time, his *Mémoires* suggest specific experiences in Italy that can come into play by leading a public familiar with the *Mémoires* to a way of understanding the kinds of perceptions and attitudes in the voice behind *Harold en Italie*. For the same work, the composer's instructions about the placement of the instruments in performance reinforces the explicitly multilayered nature of its discourse.

Important cues to the awareness of identifiable voices in nineteenth-century listening come from reception history. I have already noted the interest in composer biographies as evidence of the eagerness to establish a voice for a composer generally. Critical writing and popular journalism offer us additional insights. Even if we regard specific cases as completely wrongheaded, these documents demonstrate the importance that voice had in listeners' approaches to the understanding of music. Beethoven's case constitutes a model for the construction of voice by listeners and critics. As Tia DeNora and Scott Burnham have shown in two quite different studies, Beethoven (or rather "Beethoven") was largely a creature of patrons, audiences, theorists, and critics.[77]

The Project

In summary, in this book I explore some approaches to identifying aesthetic subjects, that is, the Romantic voices—whether narrative personas or lyric egos—in a variety of nineteenth-century works. As the preceding discussion will have suggested, I shall stick rigorously and consistently to "strong" definitions of terms, most particularly of *narrative*. The project does not amount to bringing musical works together under some consistent model. That would be a fool's errand for nineteenth-century Romanticism. Instead, my intention is to show the expansiveness and diversity that the idea of voice, the idea that makes a work Romantic, can encompass. This exploration cannot blaze a well-marked trail to be pursued by other scholars for other works, but it should encourage others to strike out and explore more paths through the landscape of Romantic musical voices.

Music analysis will form a significant part of the method, but I will do my best to avoid dragging the reader through tedious, technical explications of music-theoretical analyses. Rather, I shall focus on features that establish musical character and the plot lines of narrative works. The explication of the details of plot in plotted musical works deserves thorough discussion, but that is not the material of this book.[78] I deliberately look beyond action to isolate the evidence of narration and the identities of narrative voices; for that reason I resist the impulse myself to "narrate" the detailed events and dramatic contours of pieces. Nevertheless, we must certainly look in musical forms for evidence of narrativity such as disruptions in the continuity of a plot, interruptions by extrageneric music, or quotations and allusions.

We shall also need to go beyond the notes themselves. This book will stay resolutely historical, so that different sorts of information surrounding our works will always come into play. Peritextual evidence will include, among other things, composers' names, titles of works, dedications, epigraphs, verbal texts of vocal music, programs, instructions for performance, and the physical aspects of musical sources themselves. Among epitexts that we might consider are composers' writings such as memoirs, statements by composers recorded by biographers, and compositional notations.

Broader contextual information will also come into play. The social contexts for which composers intended their works (or in which listeners heard works, whether consciously intended by the composers or not) must affect the sense of voice on any occasion. Conventions of performance practice bear particular implications for the voice of a work. A work's relations to other works, including works of music or literature or art, necessarily form a backdrop for listeners. Assumptions about class and gender are implicated in music.

The treatment of other writers' thoughts here—broadly speaking, the reception history of the works to be discussed—deserves brief explanation. This has two distinct purposes. First, I take into careful consideration the kinds of responses that earlier listeners have had to the music, partly in close proximity to the creation of the compositions themselves and partly over time since then. While these reactions rarely speak intentionally of the task at hand here, identifying the personality of a work's fictive voice, they sometimes observe aspects of it or sense its presence. Such experiences of the music deserve attention as evidence of the way in which listeners actually have heard it speak.

Second, most of the pieces I shall examine have seemed problematic to other critics. Their analyses and interpretations have variously prompted my curiosity, aroused my skepticism, and inspired me to think harder. Although they have sometimes seemed to me to veer off course and sometimes to be completely misguided, they constantly help me to steer my thinking to just the point that turns out to be enlightening. For that reason I cannot ignore them, and I acknowledge them gratefully, even when my discussions will disagree with them.

The methodology here will not resolve itself into a formulaic procedure. We cannot discover the voice by running the music through an analytical process, tabulating data about its peritexts and epitexts, or viewing it through a series of historically colored lenses. In fact, we should not even expect the kinds of results that emerge to be of the same type for every piece. The following chapters will intentionally—even necessarily—be empirical and adaptive.

Chapter 2

The Voice of the Genius

Interruption in Beethoven's "Tempest" Sonata

Keys to Understanding Beethoven's Music—An Anecdote

Anton Schindler tells a story about Beethoven's Piano Sonata in D Minor, op. 31, no. 2, that raises intriguing questions. He leads up to his anecdote by discussing the nature of expressive content in Beethoven's music:[1]

> By far the most important and most unusual characteristic of our composer was his practice of drawing an idea for a composition from nature or from a poem that had made an impression upon his imagination. He would allow himself to be completely sub-jugated by this idea, at the same time moulding it into a form that was precise and definite, but having little in common with traditional forms, and this formal structure even differed from composition to composition. . . . Each one different, and yet the master leads us by way of his form along such a sure, clear path that requires little imagination, provided the performance is adapted to the content, to retain the thread of the poetry without losing it for even an instant. Anyone capable of following the form in Beethoven's sonatas, of penetrating it to its foundations, must come to the conclusion that in this respect no other sona-tas can compare with Beethoven's. His form is exceptional, and expresses an exceptional musical poetry.

> . . . In the piano sonatas . . . we find the musical Shake-
> speare . . .—the poet who tells us in music all that can be expressed:
> the struggles hidden deep within the heart, the sweet magic of love
> in the most innocent soul, the bitterest, most poignant sorrow,
> the delights that rejoice to the skies, the depths of sincerity, the
> fires of ecstasy, the greatest nobility, the utmost grace. It is not
> overbold to say that a performance of these sonatas, or at least
> of certain movements, presents problems comparable to those of
> portraying certain Shakespearian characters if we aim, as we should,
> at exploring the inner being and at presenting it logically and
> forthrightly. Just as with Shakespeare most actors grasp only the
> word and not the spirit behind the word, so also the musicians
> who play Beethoven sonatas study only the technical aspects of
> the music, having neither the head nor the heart to penetrate its
> depths. Ferdinand Ries . . . says . . . , "When composing, Bee-
> thoven often bore a specific object in mind." These words must
> be interpreted in the light of what we have just said.
>
> Carl Czerny expresses himself more cogently . . . when
> he speaks of the character and the correct performance of the
> sonata in F minor opus 57. He says . . . ,
>
> Beethoven, who was so fond of portraying scenes from
> nature, was perhaps thinking of ocean waves on a stormy night
> when from the distance a cry for help is heard, then such a
> picture will give the pianist a guide to the correct playing of
> this great tonal painting. There is no doubt that in many of his
> most beautiful works Beethoven was inspired by similar visions
> or pictures from his reading or from his own lively imagination.
> It is equally certain that if it were always possible to know the
> idea behind the composition, we would have the key to the
> music and its performance.[2]

Then Schindler continues with his anecdote:

> One day when I was telling the master of the great impression
> that Carl Czerny's playing of the D minor and F minor sonatas
> opp. 31 and 57 had made upon the audience, and he was in a
> cheerful mood, I asked him to give me the key to these sonatas.
> He replied, "Just read Shakespeare's Tempest." It is, therefore,
> to be found in that play. But where? Questioner, it is for you
> to read, to ponder, and to guess.[3]

We learn here that Beethoven's friends and contemporaries—not only Schindler but also Ries and Czerny—understood him to have employed a poetic approach to composition, in which he created under the inspiration of literary works or nature. Further, if performers could know the sources of inspiration, they could render the works rightly. This places on the player the burden of discovering the images behind the music, and to find these images or ideas becomes vitally important.

For this reason, after a very successful performance of both the D-Minor Sonata and the F-Minor Sonata, op. 57, Schindler asked Beethoven to give him the key to the music. Beethoven's reply was "Just read Shakespeare's *Tempest.*" Schindler obviously did not feel confident that he understood what Beethoven was saying, but he urged his readers to probe the subject: "Questioner, it is for you to read, to ponder, and to guess."

Now I should say here that Schindler has long been known as a highly unreliable witness.[4] He maintained a close relationship with the composer for some time in the early 1820s, but Beethoven later accused Schindler of cheating him, and for a while they were estranged. Schindler did return to assist Beethoven at the end of the composer's life and thus gained possession of musical manuscripts, conversation books, and other items, which he sold, to his own profit. Schindler's Beethoven biography distorts facts in order to place its author in a favorable light, and he even mutilated and forged documents. We cannot simply disregard his reports, however, because he certainly does count as an eyewitness, even if of a dubious sort. This particular anecdote, while scholars have often assumed that it should be consigned to the apocrypha among Schindler's writings,[5] does, I think, probably deserve some credibility. The most striking feature in Schindler's reminiscence is that he reveals his own failure to understand Beethoven's admonition to read *The Tempest.* It seems highly unlikely that a biographer would invent a story about his subject that he evidently did not understand, and given Schindler's persistent determination to represent himself as a confidant of the master, the improbability that this anecdote is pure invention or deliberate misrepresentation becomes very high indeed.

In any case, Beethoven's remark has led commentators to speculate about how the music of op. 31, no. 2, reflects Shakespeare's *The Tempest.* One could certainly argue that the minor key and animated motion of the first movement make it sound stormy. Donald Francis Tovey, presumably tongue in cheek, suggested that "it will do you no harm to think of Miranda at bars 31–38 of the slow movement."[6] Arnold Schering offered one of the more imaginative treatments of the Sonata. He interpreted the first movement as representing act 1, scene 2 of *The Tempest,* in which "Fernando [*sic*] hears the calling song of the invisible Ariel and listens in enchantment to the ballad of the drowned father." He goes so far as to underlay some melodic passages with text taken from Schlegel's translation of Shakespeare's play. The second movement, corresponding to act 3, scene 1, depicts a "love duet between Fernando and Miranda." The third movement renders a "character portrait of the airy spirit Ariel, modeled on his song in act 5 scene 1."[7] Schering later even demonstrates his willingness to invent programmatic readings by creating an image for music that Beethoven never composed: "If Beethoven had wanted to construct the sonata in a four-movement design, he would apparently not have hesitated to set the misshapen Caliban as a musical monument in a grotesque Scherzo."[8] Josef Pembaur likewise contrived similar detailed programs for both op. 31, no. 2, and op. 57. Pace Shakespeare, in Pembaur's version the first movement is entirely about Prospero and the conjuring of the storm, the second represents Ferdinand's unfulfilled love for Miranda, and the third reveals how the waves of time carry away all human experience.[9]

Several problems must make us resist this approach to relating Beethoven's statement to the music. For one thing, in no sense does the structure of op. 31, no. 2, suggest the action of *The Tempest*. At best, one can claim only that a character of tempestuousness or of feminine grace emerges from various passages in the sonata. This would be equally true of any number of sonatas by Beethoven and by other composers of the early nineteenth century. Further, as Schindler's story makes clear, the composer's reference to Shakespeare's play must apply as much to the F-Minor Sonata op. 57 as to op. 31, no. 2, and one might argue that op. 57 is even more tempestuous. The name of the play became attached to op. 31, no. 2, only because op. 57 already had its own name, "Appassionata."

All of which probably suggests that Schindler's anecdote offers nothing of use in understanding Beethoven's op. 31, no. 2. But in the end I am going to argue that we might yet find it helpful. Nevertheless, we shall have to hold it in abeyance for a while and look closely at the music.

Opus 31 in Historical Context

Beethoven composed the three sonatas that form his op. 31 in 1802, at a turning point in his career—and consequently also one in our conception of music history. The composer spent much of the year in Heiligenstadt, where he hoped to find some remission of his hearing loss, a sojourn that culminated in the Heiligenstadt Testament, in which he came to grips with the inevitability of his deafness and resolved to persevere in spite of that terrible condition. Scholars generally regard the three sonatas as having been composed in the spring and summer of 1802, shortly preceding the Testament, which is dated in October.

At about this time, according to Carl Czerny, Beethoven told his friend Wenzel Krumpholtz, a mentor to Czerny, "I am not satisfied with the works I have written so far. From now on I am taking a new direction [*neuen Weg*]." Czerny continues, "Not long afterward the three Sonatas Op. 29 [*recte* 31] were published."[10] Not only does the music come from a time that we recognize as pivotal in Beethoven's life, therefore, but he explicitly aspired to a new approach to his music, and his close friends associated this change with the op. 31 sonatas.

Since the middle of the nineteenth century, Beethoven's biographers and writers about his music have regarded this time as marking the division between the first and second of three periods in his creative life. The D-Minor Sonata, with its two companions in op. 31, stands at the threshold between the first period (traditionally, "period of imitation") and second ("period of extroversion" or "heroic period"). Beyond the specific life and works of Beethoven, though, this moment offers a compelling marker for the first blossoming of the bud of nineteenth-century Romanticism in music. As the following discussion of the "Tempest" Sonata will suggest, this work presents a groundbreaking instance of narrativity in instrumental music and, in that sense, can lay claim to launching an era.

Sonata and Plot

We must first return, however, to the issue of plot expressed in music, so neatly summarized by Rosen's aphorism that in the course of the eighteenth century "dramatic sentiment was replaced by dramatic action."[11] In simple terms, we can take as a definition that we have a plot in any action in which characters become involved in a sequence of events in which tension arises and is resolved. The idea of the sonata form as a dramatic plot is treated as an important metaphor in Sonata Theory, as Hepokoski and Darcy describe the form, including their assertion that "a sonata is a metaphorical representation of a perfect human action."[12] I would quibble with this formulation only in the sense that a sonata-form movement is a plotted action in its own right and not a metaphor for something else at all.

We have already observed that in the eighteenth century musicians began to employ a new way of describing musical themes—rhythmic/melodic units—no longer according to their "affect," as in the past, but according to "character." Furthermore, the main melodic units of a piece were no longer referred to as "subjects" but as "motives," suggesting that they represented not material to be dealt with in the work but rather a sort of agency that motivated the music. Thus, a musical passage might be identified as "military" or "amorous," "aristocratic" or "rustic," and even "masculine" or "feminine."[13] Such characterizations are not all mutually exclusive, and so a theme might be both aristocratic and amorous, or it might first appear as lyrical and return as heroic.

At the same time, Enlightenment composers began to adopt a powerful and flexible approach to long-range harmonic contour in substantial movements of musical works, which produced the principle that became known (after the fact) as "sonata form" (see table 2.1).[14] Fundamentally, the principle is fairly straightforward. At the outset a movement establishes a stable home key or tonic. The music then modulates, rising into another key (usually the dominant, or in minor keys the relative major), which creates a heightening of tension. (This setting up of the movement's fundamental opposition is often referred to as "exposition," not a term used for this in the Enlightenment.) A more or less extended period of harmonic instability, sometimes called "development" (misleadingly, because development of musical characters and action may take place anywhere in the movement), ultimately leads to a moment of climactic anticipation. The return of the tonic provides harmonic resolution, restoring stability.

Also crucial to this musical plan is the coordination of the different musical themes or passages, recognizable by their respective characters, with the harmonic events. Because of this concinnity, the themes motivate, accomplish, or experience the harmonic progress of the music; in other words, we can legitimately consider them "agents" or "patients" in the work, exactly as we would understand the roles of the dramatis personae in a play. Standard functions, each with its conventional (although far from universal) character, include the following:

- *Opening themes,* the point of which is to create anticipation at the beginning of the action. These tend to be fragmentary and open-ended, perhaps even unsettled in character. They are frequently external to the harmonic plan and thus not involved in the plot.

- *Principal themes,* which establish the tonic key of the movement both at the beginning and at the moment of resolution.

Table 2.1. Sonata form as plot

Introduction		**Plot contour:** Prologue • **Harmonic level:** Leading to tonic • **Musical material:** Opening (O) • **Typical thematic character:** Anticipatory
Part I (conventional designation: beginning of "Exposition")	**Section 1**	**Plot contour:** Stable situation, followed by increasing tension • **Harmonic level:** Tonic, followed by modulation • **Musical material:** Theme(s) associated with principal key (P) and with harmonic transition (T) • **Typical thematic character:** Affirmative, forceful for P; active and lively for T
Part I continued (conventional designation: continuation of "Exposition")	**Section 2**	**Plot contour:** Contrasting situation, followed by closing • **Harmonic level:** Dominant (or relative major) • **Musical material:** Themes associated with secondary key (S) and closure (K) • **Typical thematic character:** Contrasting to P, often lyrical for S; affirmative, often "stock" character for K
Part II	**Section 3** (conventional designation: "Development")	**Plot contour:** Rising action to climax • **Harmonic level:** Unstable • **Musical material:** Development of previous material; new material (N) may be introduced • **Typical thematic character:** Unpredictable
Part II continued	**Section 4** (conventional designation: "Recapitulation")	**Plot contour:** Resolution, followed by dénouement • **Harmonic level:** Arrival of tonic, with stabilization and closure in that key • **Musical material:** P, T, S, K • **Typical thematic character:** As in sections 1 and 2

Abbreviations:

O — opening
P — material associated with the principal key
T — material associated with harmonic transition
S — material associated with the secondary key
K — material associated with closure
N — new material introduced in part II

Themes in this position are likely to be strongly rhythmic and bold in character.

- *Transition themes,* which destabilize the key and move toward the contrast key. We expect such themes or passages to be lively and active.

- *Secondary themes,* which is to say, themes associated with the secondary key, which serve to stabilize the secondary key and to contrast with the character of the principal theme. Often, secondary themes are lyrical and long-breathed.

- *Closing themes,* which confirm the secondary key. Closing themes tend to be formulaic and predictable in character.

What focuses our interest in listening to any given piece is the interplay among the characters of the themes and their roles within the movement. Generally, the style tends to assign a controlling, active role to the principal theme or character, because it establishes the main key at the beginning and marks the return of that key at the resolution. The other themes (or characters) are eventually brought from their original harmonic levels into the main key, so that especially the character associated with the secondary key seems to assume a more passive role. The way in which all of this plays out in any given work will be specific to the piece, just as any plot in any artistic medium is specific, and that is what holds our interest.

It is not at all necessary, I hasten to emphasize, to translate pieces of music into verbal or pictorial stories. This has been done many times, sometimes more and sometimes less amusingly. The point here is that the musical characters and musical shaping of tension in a work are at the same time entirely specific and refer to nothing else. Naturally, we communicate about musical works in words (or, in more technical explications, in symbols). We can do this in great detail by using the technical terms of music analysis, but that approach inevitably sacrifices the immediacy of the character and the experiential contour of tensions and resolutions that we perceive directly in hearing the music. We can also describe music in metaphors or assign names to the characters (identifying a heroic theme as Promethean, for example), but that either brings too much external baggage to the character or fails because the metaphor or name means something different to anyone with whom we share such caprices.[15] The fundamental principle in the discussion that follows here (and in other chapters), then, is that, although entirely without reference to extramusical imagery or stories, the music of a movement in sonata form presents characters and enacts a plot of its own. The following discussion does not intend to invent a story based on a Beethoven sonata but much more simply to let the music express its own character and enact its own plot, avoiding both highly technical analysis and programmatic fairy tales.

The Sonata Begins—but Where?

Beyond Schindler's perplexed anecdote and the position of op. 31, no. 2, at a crucial moment in Beethoven's life, the music itself has entertained critics and analysts for more than two centuries now.[16] What has provoked most discussion about the sonata is its first movement's failure to produce a proper thematic statement in the principal key. Specifically, theorists have argued about whether the first twenty measures constitute an introduction or really amount to the beginning of the movement's sonata structure proper and, consequently, whether to hear (or play) the passage that occupies the next twenty measures as principal theme or as transition. Given Schindler's setup for his report of his fruitless conversation with Beethoven, he certainly did not have in mind this conundrum when he asked for the key to the music, but in fact analysts since his time have always sought the key to solve this particular problem.

The movement does not start out like a sonata (for an overview of the trajectory of the whole movement, see table 2.2). Its perennially puzzling beginning merits some specific description, so I must request the reader's patience for a few paragraphs of detail. We first hear (m. 1) only an arpeggiated A-major chord in first inversion, largo and pianissimo, rising out of a low register in an unmeasured strum, arriving on A3. This then extends through semi-staccato C♯4 and E4 quarter notes, marking some sort of regularization of rhythm, which, however, pauses for an indeterminate moment on A4 (m. 2). The whole is sustained by the pedal (example 2.1). The effect is of the keyboard player starting in a sort of reverie, just listening to the intonation of the A-major chord, testing the touch of the instrument. The pensive fermata seems to give the player time to consider what to do next. Robert Hatten identifies this rolled sixth chord as a "recitative chord," and he regards such chords as a topic within the extensive repertoire of conventions that make up topic theory for Classic music.[17] At this stage it does not lead to recitative but instead to something for contrast—a quick,

Table 2.2. Form of the first movement of Beethoven's Piano Sonata in D Minor, op. 31, no. 2, "The Tempest"

Introduction?/ Exposition? (mm. 1–20)		**Plot contour:** Unstable • **Harmonic level:** Leading to D minor • **Musical material:** *O?/P?* • **Thematic character:** Anticipatory
Part I— Exposition? (or Exposition continued?)	**Section 1** (mm. 21–41)	**Plot contour:** Immediately increasing tension • **Harmonic level:** Only momentarily in D minor, then modulatory • **Musical material:** *P?/T?* • **Thematic character:** Bold
(Part I continued)	**Section 2** (mm. 42–92)	**Plot contour:** Contrasting situation • **Harmonic level:** A minor • **Musical material:** S (mm. 42–55); K (mm. 55–92) • **Thematic character:** Mercurial S and stern K
Part II	**Section 3—** Development (mm. 93–142)	**Plot contour:** Rising action to climax • **Harmonic level:** Unstable • **Musical material:** Development of O?/P? (mm. 93–98), T?/P? (mm. 99–121), K (mm. 122–42) • **Thematic character:** As in part I
(Part II continued)	**Section 4—** Reprise (mm. 143–228)	**Plot contour:** Resolution(?) unfulfilled • **Harmonic level:** Arrival of D minor, immediately destabilized • **Musical material:** *O?/P?* (mm. 143 and 149–54); ***Recitative*** (mm. 144–48 and 155–71) • **Thematic character:** Anticipatory O?/P?; declamatory recitative **Plot contour:** Dénouement • **Harmonic level:** D minor • **Musical material:** S (mm. 172–85); K (mm. 185–228) • **Thematic character:** As in section 2

Abbreviations:

O — opening

P — material associated with the principal key

T — material associated with harmonic transition

S — material associated with the secondary key

K — material associated with closure

N — new material introduced in part II

Example 2.1. Beethoven, Sonata in D Minor, op. 31, no. 2, "Tempest," mvt. 1, mm. 1–6.

descending gesture in eighth notes in the right hand, rushing down from scale degree 5 to 1 in D minor, articulated in gasping slurs, accompanied by contrary motion in the bass (m. 3). Repeat. Repeat again a fourth higher, on G minor, with a crescendo, and pause on the dominant of D, embellished, now Adagio, by suspensions and an ornamental turn around A4 (m. 6). None of this produces any sense of theme, but at least the key of D minor is established. Fermata again to think of a new move.

The new move is the largo arpeggio once more, but this time on C major (mm. 7–8), which is not a chord in D minor at all. This sounds like mere whim, an entirely arbitrary shift, suggesting that we are not listening to a composed piece at all, merely eavesdropping on a pianist feeling out the instrument. The reverie this time leads to a variant of the rushing gesture beginning on F major, jerking upward melodically over rising and partly syncopated chromatic harmonies, crescendoing its way to a high $^6_4$ in D minor (mm. 9–13).

The left hand drops out as the right picks out the D-minor triad descending precipitously through nearly three octaves, each pitch embellished by a lower chromatic neighbor (mm. 13–16), until it arrives on the fourth D4/A3, disturbed by neighbors C♯4 and B♭3, and the right hand is joined by the left to make a sort of roar (mm. 17–18). The full chromatic scale from A3 to A4, harmonized by the $^6_4$ and V7 in D minor (mm. 19–20), completes this brief cadenza. The music now turns out to be a lead-in to the arrival of D minor.

Altogether, the music of measures 1–20 belongs not to the genre of the sonata but to the fantasia. The abrupt, unmotivated shifts of material, the indeterminate pauses, the juxtapositions of tempo, the arbitrary change of key—all suggest improvisation rather than composition. Some listeners have clearly recognized this. Arnold Schmitz in 1923 described the passage as "merely an attempt at a theme, an improvisation."[18] More recently, Kenneth Hamilton has also heard the opening as akin to an improvised prelude to a composed piece.[19] The listener who knows that the music is a sonata must surely hear this passage as an introduction and expect next a principal theme, melodically coherent, metrically stable, and harmonically grounded in D minor.

The resolution of the V7 in measure 20 leads directly to a new idiom (example 2.2). The downbeat of measure 21, clearly in the tonic key, introduces a triadic motive rising in the bass under a vibrating right-hand accompaniment. The rhythm echoes that of the first measure, now in the Allegro tempo, and the arpeggiated pattern starts on the triadic root, D2, rather than the third, but the listener will undoubtedly recognize measures 21–22 as a logical adaptation of an idea promised at the opening. To this, a turn figure in the treble responds in measures 23–24, recalling measure 6. The next four measures reproduce this pattern on a dominant seventh chord, inverted to place E2 in the bass (mm. 25–28). This four-measure unit compresses to two, climbing sequentially over a rising bass line through F2, G♯2, A2, B2, C3 (mm. 29–30, 31–32, 33–34, 35–36, 37–38). A further compression, made by repeating the last measure of the sequence, stands on the diminished seventh of E (mm. 39–40), and this finally resolves to the V of A minor (m. 41). This twenty-measure passage, taken as a whole,

Example 2.2. Beethoven, Sonata in D Minor, op. 31, no. 2, "Tempest," mvt. 1, mm. 21–32.

sounds as though it started with a typical sonata-form "retake" of a principal theme and launched the transition, driving forward by means of sequence and fragmentation, from D minor to the dominant of A. In the terms of Sonata Theory, this works like a transition starting with a "dissolving restatement,"[20] except that its beginning is not actually a restatement at all.

These forty measures have challenged commentators for two centuries. Apparently, this sonata form has no proper beginning. An evidently introductory passage leads immediately to an evidently transitional one. What the listener most naturally expects—a defining feature of any sonata movement—a stable thematic-sounding statement in the principal key, simply does not appear at all.[21] Because this problem has occupied scholars so continuously for so long, it is worth pursuing how they have variously dealt with it. The difficulties that have troubled analysts reveal the issues that constitute the movement's musical plot itself, so they will reward a detailed review. We can group the analyses into a few categories.

The first category includes writers who regard the movement's first twenty measures as introduction and the principal theme as starting at the confirmation of D minor in measure 21. One of these, closest historically to Beethoven, is Adolf Bernhard Marx, who wrote in 1863,

> Everything previously discussed up to measure 21 is *introduction*, preamble to the movement that begins in bar 21; in itself it is unfulfilling, it is incomplete, it still is and remains in process, juxtaposes two entirely different motives. This struggling, this indecisiveness must be expressed, and as a result no fixed tempo is possible, but also no abrupt entrance of the Allegro. Because nothing exists yet, certainly nothing determinate and decisive, all uncertain, vague, questionable. Consequently, however, grasped in the correct sense, everything is suggestive, anticipating what is to come, agitated.
>
> The *main theme* enters in bar 21, immediately full of decisiveness, and at once in a fixed and lively tempo and with full strength. Here, therefore, the first statement of the Allegro begins.[22]

This tradition in the Sonata's analysis is represented by Hugo Leichtentritt in 1955 and Steven Vande Moortele in 2009, who asserts that "any experienced listener . . . who first encounters the opening movement of the *Tempest* Sonata will be tempted to hear bars 1–21 as an introduction."[23]

A second group of analysts take the position that the improvisatory or fantasia-like music of the beginning of the movement forms a true principal thematic area. Among the first important theorists to hear the passage this way was Hugo Riemann, who in 1919, despite recognizing its inherent fantasia-like qualities, found a way to analyze the first six measures as a perfectly balanced period made up of two phrases and eventually proposed that the entire passage occupying the first forty-one measures constitutes the principal area, without distinguishing introduction from thematic statement or transition.[24]

Ludwig Misch rules out the idea that the material beginning at measure 21 can be understood as the statement of the principal theme, largely because it does not return in the recapitulation.[25] Further, because measures 21–41 modulate to the dominant key, the passage "lacks one decisive characteristic of a principal theme. The principal theme of a Beethoven sonata movement regularly represents and circumscribes the principal key."[26] Ultimately, Misch determines that only the first six measures of the movement can be regarded as the principal theme.

To this category of analysis, we must add the detailed and much-cited study of the D-Minor Sonata's first movement by Janet Schmalfeldt from 1995. Schmalfeldt also presents a case for hearing the first twenty-one measures as the principal theme, closed with a perfect authentic tonic cadence. Rather than treating the first six measures as a period, as Riemann had done, however, she regards those six measures as an antecedent phrase, closing on the dominant, answered by an expanded (and admittedly "fantasialike") consequent of fifteen measures.[27] The passage thus meets the requirements of a principal theme for a sonata-form movement.

James Hepokoski offers a related analysis in a 2009 essay. According to his hearing of the first part of the movement, "bars 1–21 are devoted to laying out a D-minor 'primary thematic zone' (P)—the '*Hauptgedanke*' and initiator of the sonata process—which drives toward and elides with the *forte* onset of the transition (TR), bar 21." He does not find the style of this passage a deterrent to interpreting it solely in terms of it structure and function, concluding that "The anacrusis ('not yet') quality of the compound-modular bars 1–21 does not call into question the generically unambiguous P-function of that passage."[28]

Yet a third way of dealing with the first section of the movement (mm. 1–41) is to accept these ambiguities as the musical idea per se. Commentators have handled this in various ways. Most notable in this is Carl Dahlhaus, who straightforwardly accepts the idea that the first twenty measures are "not yet" and the next twenty are "no longer" a principal theme.[29] For him, this in itself constitutes the essence of the movement. Dahlhaus argues,

> Nothing could be more abstract than the arpeggiated triad in the first movement of the D minor Piano Sonata, Op. 31 No. 2, which serves, without rhythmic specificity, to link the preliminary form of the theme (bar 1) with its more substantial manifestation (bar 21): the latter modulates, however, so that the preliminary form is endowed retrospectively with the function of an exposition in the tonic. . . .
>
> The beginning of the movement is not yet a subject, the evolutionary episode is one no longer.[30]

Schmalfeldt, positioning the work as a representation of the dialectical thinking of the early nineteenth century, acknowledges Dahlhaus's treatment of the movement. The title of her article is "Form as the Process of Becoming."[31] Despite her argument that the first twenty-one measures constitute the statement of a principal theme, as discussed earlier, she emphasizes that this does not become clear until after the listener discovers that the next twenty measures effect the transition to the new key and therefore cannot qualify as presentation of the principal theme. In that sense, she says, in this movement "introduction becomes main theme" and "main theme becomes transition." Eventually, too, "codetta becomes presentation." The wording here, and in fact the concept as well, might seem a little problematic, however, because what is really meant is not exactly that the passages in question "become" something new as the music continues but that after they have passed by they *turn out to have been* different in function from what they appeared to be in the moment. That is, the "becoming" takes place not in the music but in the analysis. Whether this qualifies as an instance of Hegelian dialectic is arguable.

Erwin Ratz had already anticipated this kind of understanding twenty years earlier, explaining it as a matter of *Phasenverschiebung* (phase displacement). The characters and positions of the musical materials and their functions are misaligned, in his hearing, such that the first twenty measures, which have the character and position of an introduction, function as principal theme; the next twenty, which have the character and position of a main theme, function as transition; and so on.[32]

But Dahlhaus also makes the point that the listener need not—even should not—feel it necessary to sort out the materials and their functions decisively. The listener, he argues, will come to "the recognition that the unpretentious broken triad, which he first misconstrued as introduction, was actually already the theme but traverses a process of transformation in which the designations 'prelude,' 'anticipation,' and 'exposition' are layered on top of each other, so that the one would not be suppressed by the others,"[33] and "anyone who feels confused by the sonata should not try to impose on it an unambiguous solution, which would be incorrect by virtue of being imposed; rather, the ambiguity should be perceived as an artistic factor—an attribute of the thing itself, not a failure of analysis. The very contradictions of the form constitute its artistic character."[34] I want to focus on this ambiguity in regard to the appearance (or nonappearance) of a putative principal thematic statement, but before continuing to consider this issue, it is worth observing that analysts find problems, as well, in identifying secondary-area and closing thematic and structural units in the remainder of the first part of the movement's form. While there are distinct passages of contrasting thematic and figurational content, their functions as secondary or closing themes come into question because of the absence of clear periods in the secondary key and the misalignment of thematic and harmonic units.

The second part of the form opens with a development based on the material of the first forty measures. Three iterations of the Largo arpeggio of measures 1–2 sound in measures 93–94, 95–96, and 97–98, in the course of which the mode shifts to F♯ minor, and the Allegro material of measures 21ff. returns, effecting a modulation that brings the music to settle on the dominant of D minor (mm. 121–38), preparing the reprise.

Now what the listener surely hopes for is a clarification of the roles of the ideas in the first forty measures. As Schmalfeldt observes, "Decisions about the large-scale formal divisions of sonata-form movements often depend on the uncomplicated task of comparing the exposition with the recapitulation . . . recapitulations in late eighteenth-century sonata forms tend to be marked by a return of main-theme materials in the home key."[35] Thus, if what at first appeared as introductory gestures really constituted the principal-key thematic material, then it ought to reemerge as the defining material of the return of the tonic. On the other hand, if the material that led so quickly into harmonic instability now comes to be understood as the beginning of the sonata form proper, then it ought to reappear in a tonally stable form here, where no modulation is necessary. And so we may expect the return of D minor to resolve questions about the roles of the thematic characters that the movement presented at its outset.

No chance. Schmalfeldt says, "Suffice it to say that in this case the beginning of the recapitulation has the effect of obfuscating rather than clarifying the design at the beginning of the exposition."[36] The opening rolled chord—again in inversion—does sound (mm. 143–44), and now it leads directly into a passage that comes from another world entirely, a recitative (example 2.3). The right hand declaims the recitative within the haze of the A-major harmony sustained by leaving the dampers up. This melody, marked "con espressione e semplice," leads from A4 to F4 and is left to linger under a fermata rest. The pianist releases the damper pedal and plays measures 3–6 from the opening, as if the recitative were merely a parenthesis and the movement would continue conventionally to the hoped-for answer to the initial question. The C-major chord from measures 7–8 ensues, but this again leads to recitative, now shifted to F minor and ending on A♭4, the local third scale degree, still against the lingering C-major harmony. Any hope of a clarification of the thematic and structural questions raised at the beginning is now lost.

Apparently, no smooth continuation makes sense after this disruption. A neat chromatic progression leads to the dominant of D, where the material of measures 41ff. appears "out of the woods," after which the movement continues simply with transposition of the end of its first half. Once D minor is finally established, the music rumbles into silence.

In short, then, the question that has perpetually puzzled analysis, left hanging throughout the course of the movement—whether to consider

Example 2.3. Beethoven, Sonata in D Minor, op. 31, no. 2, "Tempest," mvt. 1, mm. 143–58.

measures 1–21 or 21–41 the actual principal thematic area—remains open, even when we might have thought it must be answered. At the reprise, the opening fantasia-like passage, so far as it recurs, has become even less clearly expository; the passage that followed, which began so assertively but continued as modulation, has not returned at all. Instead, the moment of reprise is interrupted and frustrated by interloping recitatives.

Talk and No Action

Thus, since the first part of the opening movement of Sonata op. 31, no. 2, opens questions regarding characters and plot, analysts naturally look to the reprise to sort these out. Yet the passage from the reestablishment of D minor at measure 143 to the arrival of the material from measures 42ff. in measures 173ff. simply refuses any sort of solution. As we have noticed, what does reappear of the first twenty measures is truncated and interrupted, and the material of the next twenty has disappeared completely. But whereas anything remotely like normative thematic clarity fails to materialize, two passages of recitative emerge entirely unexpectedly. The recitative must certainly engage with the musical substance of the rest of the sonata, however—unless we toss up our hands and regard it as merely arbitrary. If it has any intention, and we must accept that it does, then as such a singular component of the work it should, in fact, convey some sort of insight into this puzzling movement.

It is possible, apparently, to concoct ways to treat the recitative statements as participating in the action of the rest of the movement's plot. Walter Riezler, who was concerned to resist the imposition of verbal texting of the purely instrumental music, argued, "Here the creative power of absolute music stands the test with particular success. A form [i.e., the recitative] that originally only had significance when allied with a text is gradually so permeated with music that it no longer requires the support of words. The notes now speak for themselves."[37] In some cases commentators acknowledge the interruptive and foreign quality of the recitatives in relation to the design of the movement. For Salinas the recitative passages "create the illusion that time itself stands still right before the drama is about to reach its zenith."[38] Salinas thus places all his emphasis on what is *absent* here, however, and does not take into account the addition of the recitative as a vocal *presence* interrupting the instrumental plot. In another philosophical/critical treatment, Eduardo Marx offers a detailed discussion of the movement as a representation of Heidegger's thinking about the arts. He identifies the recitatives as the "voice of Be-ing" itself (*die Stimme des Seyns*).[39] Scott Burnham draws an interesting spatial image when he describes the recitatives as realizing "one of the realms suggested by the *largo* arpeggios, a realm that is oblique to the reality of the *allegro* music."[40]

Less abstractly, writers have incorporated the recitative statements into the understanding of the movement as a whole by the expedient (which, however, we rejected earlier) of creating a verbal program, within which some character in the story actually speaks. Riezler, although he does not believe that such programmaticizing is justified, nevertheless acknowledged the impulse, writing, "The entry of the recapitulation provides a much-discussed 'surprise': the broken chord with which the movement opens is expanded into a recitative passage—a welcome occasion for programmatic commentary."[41] He resisted, but not everyone has done so. Notorious is the handling of the movement by the Beethoven biographer Paul Bekker, who contrived a program entirely unrelated to Shakespeare's play, so vivid that it rewards quotation in full:

> A simple dominant triad resounds, whose tensely questioning expression is uncannily intensified by the third used as the bass note. And out of this mystical depth arises a ghostly apparition, groping upward with soft steps. Furiously resisting, energetic eighth-note rhythms, steady bass quarter notes hurry away from the menacing specter, first coming to rest on an adagio measure that broadly dies away. Yet the phantom returns, warning even more seriously by means of the startling choice of C major. More furiously than before the resisting figures answer, in frightful agitation traveling up to F6 and then plunging into the depths, where a chromatic scale releases the storm. Amid rolling eighth-note triplets the theme appears: it is the Largo apparition. With demonic strength it rises up. A painfully pleading phrase, winding chromatically around one pitch, answers twice. Then it is overwhelmed by the theme, which, ascending level by level in lapidary chordal steps, makes its way with annihilating force. The fluctuating eighth-note rhythms storm on, until an apparently new motive bids them halt. Apparently new. It is the chromatic answering phrase, read backwards, which in this form takes on rhythms of menacingly stubborn force: by its reversal the lament forms itself into resolute resistance. Slowly the

agitation gives way. The gloomy peace of the beginning returns, yet with it also the Largo apparition. Out of the lowest registers upward-seething arpeggios raise again the expression of the hideous phantasm. A development follows, which, as the second theme ceases, resembles the antecedent statement throughout. The main idea alone dominates. Then—at the second return of the beginning, the curse appears to be broken. The theme begins to speak. A recitative struggles, painfully pleading, out of the chord motive. In vain. In muffled, thumping chords and uprearing chordal passagework a merely suppressed, not calmed, agitation proclaims itself. Powerfully it strives for liberation, the second theme struggles out yet again, nevertheless, as the first time, to die away in dark bass passagework. A grandly simple cadence closes the fading piece in dark minor harmonies.[42]

Here the recitatives are the sound of an actual voice of a character who resists the threatening specter introduced in the first two measures. August Halm, in particular, lambasts Bekker's "analysis" as idle nonsense.[43] But more recent critics also hear a quality of spookiness in this place. Hepokoski, for example, who analyzes the movement rigorously in terms of Sonata Theory and accounts specifically for each moment in conformity with that theory, at the same time turns the music into a series of illustrative metaphors in a "predator-prey drama" where the opening major chords constitute "grinning Tragedy."[44] In this programmatic context "the individual voice raised twice in poignant recitative . . . may be heard as a double-plea of weary supplication—'Must we continue?'—as sonata-time proper is put on hold."[45] Hatten finds the uncanny presence not in the arpeggiated first-inversion chords but in the "spooky recitatives."[46] This perception has historical precedents going back to Czerny's reports of conversations with Beethoven. In one case, the composer, explaining the indication that the dampers are to be released throughout the recitative passages, is said to have told Czerny that he "wanted the effect to suggest someone speaking from a cavernous vault, where the sounds, reverberations, and tones would blur confusingly."[47] In his guide to performing Beethoven's works, Czerny wrote that "the pedal is held down during the recitative, which must sound like one complaining at a distance."[48]

Karol Berger takes the alternation of tempo and style in the movement's opening as representing a shift from the "real" world of plotted action to an "imaginary" world of aesthetic contemplation. In his discussion the recitatives come "from beyond" as "a human voice," and "the other world, the world beyond, turns out to be the world within."[49] Without falling back on the invention of a parallel verbal story to explain the dramatic action of the music, Berger recognizes the two aspects of the recitative that should surely come into play in interpreting their place in the work: their representation of a human voice, and their location in a plane outside the world of the rest of the movement.

What the Composer Said

Now we can return to Schindler's exchange with Beethoven and consider again what the composer said. As Schindler reports it, he asked Beethoven for the "key" to understanding his sonatas (two of them, we should remember). Beethoven told him just to go read *The Tempest*. Schindler passes along to his reader this "key," which he himself evidently did not know how to use to unlock the meaning of the music. Interpreters have made various choices in dealing with this information—for example, to try to locate the action or characters of the play in the music (of just the one sonata, which seems impossible to justify in the first place), to set bits of the play's text to phrases of the music (à la Schering), to make vague comparisons between ideas about Shakespeare and about Beethoven as creative geniuses, or to ignore the issue altogether.[50]

We might, however, interpret Beethoven's comment in an entirely different way, a way that Schindler seems not to have understood—or perhaps chose not to understand. Beethoven's reply, a direct enough response to Schindler's question, need not have answered that question in its own terms. Let us reconsider the exchange: Schindler asked Beethoven for the key to the sonatas, and Beethoven responded, but did not actually "answer," that he should go read *The Tempest*. What might Beethoven have meant, since it seems self-evident that he did not simply mean that the D-Minor Sonata told the story of or was inspired by Shakespeare's play?

We might read the anecdote as suggesting that Beethoven simply wanted Schindler to go away and leave him alone, and so he gave his annoying disciple something edifying to do, and that was the end of it. There might have been more deliberate intent in the assignment, however. Central to *The Tempest* is Prospero's relationship (or, better, lack of relationship) with the other characters. The former duke of Milan, Prospero, lives on a desert shore in isolation from the world. He came there as a consequence of his

earlier withdrawal from everyday affairs into his own realm of magical studies, having first entrusted his dukedom to his brother, who then usurped
Prospero's position; treacherously conspired with Prospero's rival, the king
of Naples; and cast Prospero asea in a leaky boat with only his books and
his infant daughter. In act 1, scene 2, Prospero explains his history:

> . . . being so reputed
> In dignity, and for the liberal arts
> Without a parallel; those being all my study,
> The government I cast upon my brother
> And to my state grew stranger, being transported
> And rapt in secret studies . . . (lines 72–77)

> I thus neglecting worldly ends, all dedicated
> To closeness, and the bettering of my mind
> With that which, but by being so retired,
> O'er-prized all popular rate, in my false brother
> Awaked an evil nature, and my trust,
> Like a good parent, did beget of him
> A falsehood in its contrary as great
> As my trust was, which had indeed no limit,
> A confidence sans bound . . . (lines 89–97)

What can this have to do with Schindler's request? Beethoven's response
to the naive question might have intended to draw a parallel between the
composer and Prospero. Not unlike Prospero, Beethoven had withdrawn
into his own art, leaving the common world behind.[51] Also like Prospero,
the composer had little patience for the petty questions of small minds. To
tell Schindler to read *The Tempest* was not an attempt to provide a key to
the sonatas but rather a way to indicate the futility of—and probably the
composer's frustration with—such a conversation. In other words, Beethoven's
reference to *The Tempest* relates not to the action or any specific passages in
the music of the two sonatas—still less specifically to the D-Minor Sonata in
particular—but to the place of the music in the experience of the composer
on the one hand and his interlocutor on the other.

   We can therefore reasonably think of the character of the magician in
The Tempest as a model for the character of Beethoven in Schindler's anecdote. Clearly, Beethoven's response to Schindler's request does not appear
to have been intended as a direct answer to the question as it was asked.

Instead of giving Schindler an explanation of the sonatas' contents (always keeping in mind that the conversation applied to the "Appassionata" as well as the "Tempest"), Beethoven's retort simply indicates that Beethoven, like Prospero, saw himself as different from others, a figure isolated by his own unwillingness to trouble himself with the petty interests and naive questions of duller intellects.

But What About the Music?

At this point we might abandon the discussion of the D-Minor Sonata itself in terms of *The Tempest* or Prospero—but to do so would overlook a chance to understand something about the music. To avoid, if possible, being misinterpreted here, I must reemphasize that Beethoven said *nothing at all* about the music of the first movement of op. 31, no. 2. Nevertheless, understanding what he apparently did say does—purely fortuitously—provide a model for understanding how the movement actually goes.

Let us consider the music of the opening movement of op. 31, no. 2, in the light of the history of musical analyses. The piece presents a puzzle recognized by every critic, that of identifying the functions of measures 1–21 and 21–41, respectively, or, to put it another way, of finding the principal theme. As we have seen, some analysts have claimed that these two twenty-measure passages are introduction and principal theme, respectively; others, that they are principal theme and transition; others, that each passage has dual or shifting functions; and still others, that each in turn is not yet or no longer a principal theme. One can certainly sympathize with Schindler's plea for a key to the sonata.

And what about that recitative? Here we encounter one of those remarkable moments where the discourse shifts audibly in the midst of the music. Recitative does not belong to the world of the action of an instrumental sonata. It is a specifically vocal style, which comes from the world of opera; "extra-generic" to the piano sonata, it interrupts the action of an instrumental sonata as an alien voice.[52] As such, it should not sound as though it constituted a part of the sonata plot at all. It comes as a surprise and even as an intrusion. Rather than participating in the substance of the musical action, it takes the part of an outside voice, commenting on the action taking place (or not taking place) in the rest of the music. Halm found one way to frame this: "as if the author suddenly started to lecture, as if the artist spoke instead of creating."[53] Halm takes this as an indication that the recitative points to the rest of the music that it interrupts; by appearing precisely where it does, it certainly must do that. Riezler also hears the wordless recitative as referring to the composer's experience, though internally, saying that it comes appropriately "here, where the opening improvisation returns and the composer slips back into his dreams again for a few moments after the strenuous exertion he has been through."[54] Some commentators have pursued the question of what type of expression the recitative constitutes and what it actually means to say, not as part of some invented program but actually about the music itself. Ratz hears that "the recitative enters in place of the transition motive that has stepped forward with elemental force in the development, which no longer appears in the reprise, whereby Beethoven must have been pointing out something significant."[55] Martin Geck, who rejects sonata-form analysis as a red herring in the attempt to understand this movement ("It is the plot that it is") and instead frames it as an instance of the mythic archetype of binary opposition, nevertheless observes that the recitative appears at a crucial moment in the piece, where the main theme is expected but dispensed with: "The recitative, it appears, has shoved aside this stable, almost conventional element [a main theme] in order to open up new spaces for the movement—not thematic but nevertheless free spaces." He hears the recitative as clearly embodying an evident kind of meaning: "this time an expressive cry breaks away from the binary opposition of the beginning, which can hardly be explained as anything but a pronounced utterance or even as an objection by a subject."[56]

As we have already established, sonata form presents a plot or enacts a drama. But the recitative here is not part of the dramatic plot of the movement. Whether we perceive it, like Burnham, as oblique to the piece's trajectory; like Berger, as part of an "imaginary world" separate from the movement's "real" one; like Halm and Riezler, as somehow revealing the composer himself, it always seems like "something else."

Here the recitative functions to draw the listener's attention to the fact that, though we have carried a certain kind of question about the music through our listening to the movement so far, we will not receive an answer (or a "key") in the form in which we expect it. Whereas we presumed that we knew what the movement was about, we must now understand that the meaning of this work goes beyond resolving a structural, analytical problem the music poses. Instead, we learn that at times we encounter a mind that does not intend to give us answers to the questions with which it confronts us.

Entering at the very moment when tension might be resolved and uncertainties clarified, the intruding voice of the recitative comments on the plot, constituting an instance of discourse that stands outside the movement's action. It functions as a narrative voice, in this case interrupting the action explicitly in order to rebuff the listener's desire for clarification. To recognize this moment as a narrative interjection becomes the means to elucidate the real nature of the movement.

Which returns us to Beethoven and Prospero. For if this (admittedly hypothetical) interpretation of Beethoven's retort to Schindler seems probable, then it does, however unintendedly on the composer's part, indeed share a viewpoint with the first movement of op. 31, no. 2. In both cases the issue turns out to lie beyond the immediate question that Beethoven's listener asks. In both cases the response, refusing to be drawn into the realm of thinking in which the question is posed, speaks from an outside position that at worst we do not comprehend at all and at best takes us by revelatory surprise.

The first movement of the "Tempest" Sonata demonstrates clearly how we can hear different levels of discourse in a piece. The movement's peculiar plot takes place on one level, that of Classic sonata form. The interrupting recitative comes as a voice from another world, a voice that speaks in a different idiom, a voice that draws attention to and at the same time denies us a solution to the questions that trouble conventional expectation.

Whose voice? This is not Beethoven's voice in an externally biographical sense. Beethoven did not compose the movement to represent his life, as if it were an autobiography or a memoir. Rather, we hear the voice of a fictional persona, created for this movement and this meaning. To characterize it, however, we can turn to the parallel moment in the anecdote from Schindler's dubious recollection. Taking into account its separateness from the world around it and its focus at the point where the commonplace question fails, we must regard it as the persona of isolated genius. To characterize it we can hardly do better than to call it "Prospero-like," wizard-like, or, more generally, the voice of "alienated genius."

A Brief Methodological *Peroratio*

The "Tempest" Sonata's first movement illustrates how internal and external levels of discourse (plot and voice) can operate within a piece of music. A story about the composer—one often regarded as apocryphal (though perhaps not, and in the end it would not matter)—demonstrates how mythology can come into play to characterize the narrative voice in a work. In this case, admittedly a somewhat remarkable one, the return from the story to the music connects Schindler's "biographical" paratext to the immanent content of the music.

The "Tempest" Sonata, both in its tones themselves and in its history (or fictional afterlife, if we prefer), thus offers a lesson in musical narrativity. The lesson is this: To the extent that this or any instance can serve as a paradigm, it can do so only in a very general way. No other work will present this plot and its intractable problems, and no other work will bring the same kind of striking—and fortuitous—analogy to an anecdote about its composer. Each musical work will have its own plot and reveal its own narrative persona in its own way. The process of narrative analysis will differ from work to work, as will the insights offered by music-historical or other extramusical evidence. Nevertheless, this sonata demonstrates that narratology, which we still struggle to apply in musicology, has much to offer specifically to the study of the music of nineteenth-century Romanticism.

Chapter 3

Nonchronological Narrative in the Song Cycle

Schubert's Heine Songs

Cycle and Voice

Defining what makes a song cycle presents multiple problems. We expect a cycle to have a degree of intentional unity that we would not necessarily find in every assemblage of songs into a single volume. That coherence might come from the representation of a linear plot, from the presence of a central theme, or from some structural resemblance among the songs.

Most compellingly, we understand a group of songs as a cycle because we attribute a single governing persona to them—that is, we recognize an integral voice for all the songs. In some cases we allow for more than one fictive speaker/singer, however. The overall persona might, for example, quote another speaker, or more than one. A cycle might even include multiple personalities, possibly reflected in multiple singers in performance, in which case the cycle likely forms a dialogue or drama. An extreme case is Schubert's settings of Walter Scott texts from *The Lady of the Lake*, published as the composer's op. 52, which consists of three songs for a woman's voice (Ellens Gesänge I–III), two for men's voices (Normans Gesang and Lied des gefangenen Jägers), one for men's chorus (Bootgesang), and one for women's chorus (Coronach).[1]

For the solo song with piano, we must not overlook the integral place of the piano part in determining the lyric persona. It is true that in some cases the piano enacts the function of an instrument accompanying a singer and might in that sense take the role of an instrument played by a singer.

An example of this might be the "Ständchen" from Schubert's Rellstab songs in the *Schwanengesang* set, in which the instrument evokes the serenader's guitar. Very often—and surely more often than not—the vocal part and the "accompaniment" form a united persona.[2] The piano does not merely represent music accompanying a singer but constitutes an intrinsic part of the lyric persona. In the piano we come to know the inner experience of the persona who expresses ideas in the words sung. That might take the form of an audible experience—"Ich hör' ein Bächlein rauschen"—or a visual one such as the circling crow in "Die Krähe" in *Winterreise*, or the feeling of a cold gust of wind as in "Die Wetterfahne" or the third stanza of "Der Lindenbaum" in that cycle. In those cases, as in others not so explicitly pictorial, however, the piano unmistakably conveys the speaker's inner feeling. With the piano we learn what the singer experiences, both physically and emotionally, and thus we come to know the song's persona.

This chapter and chapter 7 consider two song cycles, both fraught with questions: Schubert's six Heine settings in the *Schwanengesang* and Schumann's *Liederkreis*, op. 39, on poems of Eichendorff. Each raises questions about whether and/or how it forms a cycle. These questions inevitably direct our attention to the character of the lyric persona, which is to say, the identity of the Romantic voice for the experiences expressed in the songs.

Nonchronological Narration Versus Absence of Plot

The most obvious problem with considering Schubert's Heine songs as a cycle is the absence of a direct, linear plot. Schubert derived his songs from the *Heimkehr* section of Heine's *Buch der Lieder*, where there is a storyline, but he chose poems too few and too widely spaced to convey Heine's event sequence, and then he scrambled their order.

The case of Schubert's Heine songs is complicated by the historical fact that the composer did not live to arrange their publication. They appear in a collection of manuscript pages in the order in which he wrote them out. No documentary evidence survives to indicate that they had been drafted previously in another order (such as the order in which they appear in Heine's book of poetry) or whether the composer ever considered changing their order (for instance, to correspond with Heine's). Their evident disordering has led to two different ways of treating them. On one hand, it is not unreasonable to regard them as merely a group of text settings that Schubert made while occupied with a particular source, in no sense conceived as a cycle at all.[3] This is certainly the way most scholars have treated the seven songs on poems by Rellstab that occupy the beginning of the same manuscript as the Heine songs. On the other hand, some scholars have proposed to justify a Schubert Heine cycle by seizing upon the composer's not having brought the songs to publication, which they take as an opportunity to suggest the possibility that the manuscript merely reflects a haphazard order of the songs' notation on those folios. They then presume that the composer should have wanted the songs ordered into a plot-based sequence as in Heine's *Die Heimkehr*, following the approach he adopted in his two Wilhelm Müller cycles.[4]

To be sure, the need for a linear course of action in order to establish a song cycle is not to be taken for granted. The earliest definition of *Liederkreis* appeared in 1865:

> A coherent complex of different lyric poems. Each of the latter is self-contained; [it] can also be distinguished from the others externally in its meter and stanza structure; but they all maintain an inner relationship to each other, because through them all runs one and the same fundamental idea. The individual poems always give it only different turns of expression, represent it in multiple and often also contrasting images and from different sides, so that the basic feeling can be drawn out in rather comprehensive completeness. . . . Compared to the dramatic solo cantata, the Liederkreis actually lacks no more than the recitative and the aria-like form of the song instead of the Lied-like; beyond that one will find it closely connected to the cantata, or will regard it as an intermediate genre between the through-composed song and the cantata.[5]

This gives us a somewhat self-contradictory description, however, because the first part of the discussion allows for an assemblage of loosely related songs around a central idea, but the closing statement suggests something quasi-dramatic and in that sense plot-like. Schubert's Heine songs (and Schumann's Eichendorff songs, as we shall see) seem better described by the beginning rather than the end of the lexicon entry.

Constructing Schubert's Cycle of Heine Songs

I am going to assume that the six Heine songs in Schubert's manuscript and in the original edition, as well as publications since then, constitute a cycle, and one that reflects Schubert's intentions. If we were to dismiss them as a cycle, there would be, of course, no compelling reason to seek a voice common to them all. As will become clear, accepting Schubert's order leads to insight into the lyric persona, a personality so closely bound to the sequence of pieces that it in turn reinforces the composer's plan.

To start with, we must recognize that the six songs reflect events and experiences that hold easily understood places in a storyline, which would be, in fact, the order in which they had appeared in *Die Heimkehr*. At the same time, the musical sources present the moments in that story nonchronologically. That does not, however, make it impossible—or even especially difficult—to regard the songs in Schubert's order as a cycle.

My fundamental claim in this chapter will be that the integrity of a song cycle depends on the recognition of persona and not on analytical arguments based on locating recurring details or the discovery (or creation) of an architectonic structure for a sequence of songs. Nevertheless, close listening to musical features in the work is essential. Before dealing with the ordering of Schubert's six songs—and subsequently the persona—we can profitably pay attention to a number of musical details among the six songs that have been adduced by some sharply perceptive commentators to help justify the claim for a degree of unity among them, supporting the assumption that they form a cycle.[6] Harry Goldschmidt noted the "unmistakably unified 'tone' of the Heine songs, their tragic accentuation, and not least of all the elevated stylistic unity, connected to the new declamatory-melodic rhetorical style" in these songs.[7] Numerous analyses have pursued in detail a variety of more specific melodic, harmonic, textural, and registral relationships.

Edward T. Cone points out the unifying effect of the appearances of the melodic motive consisting of a skip, usually from the tonic pitch, to the third of the scale, followed by a drop to the leading tone, sometimes resolved to the first scale degree (e.g., "Der Atlas" in the bass, mm. 1–2 and passim, as well as mm. 22–23ff.; "Ihr Bild," mm. 3–4; "Das Fischermädchen," mm. 7–9; somewhat obscured in "Die Stadt," mm. 11–14; "Am Meer," mm. 3–4; and in retrograde with an added passing tone in "Der Doppelgänger," mm. 1–5).[8] There are also recurring instances of a melodic pitch surrounded by its chromatic neighbors in the vocal lines of "Der Atlas" (mm. 50–51, G, A♭, G, F♯, G) and "Die Stadt" (mm. 32–33, C, D♭, C, B♮, C), as well as the piano postlude of "Der Doppelgänger" (mm. 56–63, B, A♯, [D], C♮, B). Michael Hall tracks an emphasis on the pitch class F♯/G♭ and its chromatic neighbor tones through the six songs.[9]

Analysts have often pointed out the importance within and among these songs of harmonic moves based on semitones in the voice leading.[10]

Among the most striking instances of this is the harmony A♭, B♭, D, and
F♯ at the cadence of the voice part in "Der Atlas" (mm. 50–51), a dominant
substitute made by chromatic alteration of the root of the G-minor tonic
triad in both directions to create an augmented sixth. Other augmented sixths
include the mysterious German augmented sixth coming into focus on C
major that opens and closes "Am Meer" (mm. 1–2, 44–45), and in "Der
Doppelgänger" both the French (mm. 32–33) and German (mm. 41–42)
forms of the augmented sixth. The Neapolitan in root position appears just
at the end of "Der Doppelgänger" (m. 59), sliding down in parallel octaves
and fifth to the V/iv and the plagal conclusion, which also moves from the
minor iv $^6_4$ to the tonic major by chromatic semitones in the inner voices.

Suggestive key relationships also mark the Heine settings. A noteworthy
feature is the use within four of the six individual songs ("Der Atlas," "Ihr
Bild," "Das Fischermädchen," "Der Doppelgänger") of third relations to
set off the inner stanzas of three-strophe songs from their framing stanzas.
It is also worth noting that two songs share the key of C, minor in "Die
Stadt" and major in "Das Meer," and that the key of B (or its enharmonic
respelling) turns up three times: B major in the middle of "Der Atlas,"
C♭ major in the middle of "Das Fischermädchen," and B minor in "Der
Doppelgänger" (which ends on B major).

Writers who have argued for the coherence of the six songs as a
cycle based on reordering them to follow their storyline sequence in *Die
Heimkehr* have argued on the basis of key relationships between what then
become adjacent songs and across the group as a whole. Goldschmidt, first
of all, begins by arguing that "Das Fischermädchen" leads in the course of
the action to "Am Meer" and pointing out how the A♭ tonic that ends
the former is subtly altered to form the augmented sixth that opens the
latter in C major. Likewise, the reappearing augmented sixth at the end of
"Am Meer" changes to the diminished seventh that permeates the C-minor
"Die Stadt," by the chromatic alteration of A♭ to A♮. The C at the end
of "Die Stadt" links to the B minor at the beginning of "Der Doppelgänger" as its Neapolitan, a harmonic move reiterated at the end of that
song, as we have already noticed. The downward semitone shift to the B♭
minor of "Ihr Bild" seems to Goldschmidt to reveal an overall tonal plan
for descending keys. The key of "Der Atlas," G minor, represents another
descent, this time by a minor third—although Goldschmidt hypothesizes
that this song might originally have been conceived in A minor, continuing
the semitone plan, but that it had to be transposed downward a whole
tone, on the assumption that the vocal range became impracticably high
at the end of the song.[11]

Richard Kramer likewise assumes that Schubert originally conceived the Heine songs as a cycle following the succession of events according to the order in which they appeared in *Die Heimkehr*. He points out the same kinds of relationships between what would then become consecutive songs that Goldschmidt had created. Kramer is not convinced by Goldschmidt's suggestion that "Der Atlas" would originally have been conceived in A minor, however. To explain the tonal plan of the whole set, he arrives at a quasi-Schenkerian diagram that makes C the tonic key for the complete cycle, which composes out a long-range move from ♭VI (A♭) in "Das Fischermädchen" to V (G, although expressed in minor) in "Der Atlas."[12] Thus Goldschmidt and Kramer adopt the same organization of the material, and they adduce the same features, but they arrive at different ways of explaining the same conclusion.

So there is sufficient analytical evidence to show that the songs share considerable common material and to suggest that there is value in exploring harmonic relationships within and among them. Of course, in an absolute sense this need not make them a cycle, for on the basis of shared style features alone we might construct all sorts of cycles out of cleverly chosen groups of pieces, if we picked out ones that had a few details in common and organized them according to their keys in a sequence of our choosing (even without going to the lengths of transposing a song that did not fit the analyst's predetermined plan, as in Goldschmidt's case, or imposing a linear analysis that neither establishes nor concludes in the presumptive tonic, as in Kramer's). Moreover, Schubert's two major song cycles, *Die schöne Müllerin* and *Winterreise*, do not manifest thoroughgoing motivic unity or long-range tonal plans, so we cannot make that a requirement for cyclicity in the Heine songs. If we do find those features, it must indicate something new and special in the composer's approach to the genre.

As I indicated earlier, I assume that Schubert, if he did intend a cycle, intended the songs to proceed in the order in which he deliberately placed them—the order in which they are preserved in his manuscript. But let me make a few observations about the presumable Heine-based order of the poems that Schubert chose. To begin with, the six songs that Schubert selected from among the eighty-eight poems in *Die Heimkehr* should not suggest any attempt to convey Heine's work itself or even a synopsis of it. After all, Heine's poems do not form a continuous, uninterrupted story in the first place. Some of them report events; sometimes the events are substantially separated in time; and some poems suspend time to take the form of reflection or confession. In addition, omitting Heine's first seven poems and starting with number 8, skipping ahead by six to number 14 and again slightly to 16, then ahead four to number 20, and ending with the only two consecutive texts, 23 and 24, and stopping at that point does not remotely suggest an attempt to represent Heine. This sequence would in any case have to be understood as a construction out of nuggets extracted from Heine's lode. But then we have no rationale for placing them in the order in which any prospector would initially have found them. In fact, the only justifiable order for the six songs is the order in which the composer arranged them. As I have argued in an earlier study, one can create a work according to one's own plan, but then it is neither the composer's work nor any form of critical interpretation; it is merely evidence of one's failure to "get it."[13]

Schubert's Heine Cycle—How It Really Goes

This naturally leads to the obligation to discover and elucidate Schubert's cycle. To do so, we can begin with the poems as we encounter them in the music, then follow up some musical details—many of the same important ones that earlier critics have noted, although now treating them in a manner better integrated with the texts and the speaker(s) they disclose—to confirm Schubert's approach to the texts and become closely acquainted with the character of the lyric persona.

Schubert's first song, "Der Atlas," introduces a speaker who immediately states his view of himself:

> Ich unglücksel'ger Atlas, eine Welt,
> Die ganze Welt der schmerzen muss ich tragen.
> Ich trage Unerträgliches, und brechen
> Will mir das Herz im Leibe.

"I, wretched Atlas! A world, the whole world of pain must I bear. I bear the unbearable, and my heart wants to break in my body." The song and the cycle open with agitated tremolos and the pounding, jerky, stubborn bass figure in the piano that immediately introduces the key of G minor and a recurring motive for the six songs—tonic note, third scale degree, and leading tone. The third immediately expresses the minor key, while the fall of a diminished fourth to the leading tone, which has to slide up to return to the tonic, indicates frustration and struggle. The vocal line in the first section of the song roughly doubles the bass, which is already doubled in octaves, so that the melody sounds very unlike a typical Lied melody and carries enormous intensity (example 3.1). As the Atlas reaches the final clause and speaks of his breaking heart, the key shifts quickly by way of a diminished seventh (first spelled on G♯, then E♯) to B major.

The mention of his heart brings the Atlas to realize that the cause of his misery was his heart's ambition:

> Du stolzes Herz, du hast es ja gewollt,
> Du wolltest glücklich sein, unendlich glücklich,
> Oder unendlich elend, stolzes Herz,
> Und jetzo bist du elend.

"You proud heart, you wished for it. You wanted to be infinitely happy, or else infinitely miserable. And now you are miserable." This second part of the song begins softly with a reinterpretation of the bass motive in B major, in regular rather than dotted rhythm, the tremolo replaced by cantering triplets. Against that accompaniment, the vocal part starts with fanfare-like, triadic figures in dotted rhythms. The overall effect is that the heart goes adventuring. To the listener who knows Schubert's songs well enough,

Example 3.1. Schubert, "Der Atlas," mm. 1–8.

the move from minor to major might represent a contrast between harsh reality and deceptive optimism.[14] This gives way, when the text refers to unhappiness, to more even note values and a move, by turns, to E minor and then back to G minor.

The speaker then returns (in Schubert's setting, not in Heine's poem) to his own crushing wretchedness. Only the first two lines of text come back, as the point here is that the Atlas must simply go on forever bearing the world of sorrow. The pain of this weight emerges at the final cadence, when the melodic line (paralleled, as before, by the bass) overreaches G to its upper chromatic neighbor, A♭, placing the ♭2–1 motion and the turning figure A♭/G/F♯/G at the climax of the song, as the singer conveys something like a cry of hurt and a groan of effort (example 3.2).

The overall harmonic plan of "Der Atlas" will become essential to understanding the cyclicity of Schubert's Heine songs and the issue of lyric persona for them. To lay the groundwork, we must consider the problem of the contrast between G minor and B major. The relationship—really, the lack of relationship—of these keys is crucial. The modulation from a minor key to the major key based on its raised third, here the change from G minor to B major, means changing all seven available pitch classes. For that reason, Schubert presumably turned to it as the most remote relationship possible. In this song it expresses unmistakably the self-alienation that the Atlas experiences with his own heart; the Atlas is embodied in G minor, and the heart, in B. (This is a relatively rare move, but it later occurs for a similar reason in Liszt's *Faust Symphony*, where the respective keys are C minor and E major.)

In addition, we must take note here of the connection between the key of B major and the heart, whom the Atlas addresses in (therefore as a) second person. Although several scholars have proposed special meanings

Example 3.2. Schubert, "Der Atlas," mm. 49–52.

for Schubert's use of the key of B, none has yet taken sufficient account of the significance of the striking contrast of keys in "Der Atlas." In her very detailed discussion of the Heine songs, Susan Youens remarks on the effect of B major for this song, but she hears the key as a reflection of something both isolated and abstract: "B major, we soon realize, is the key of the past, the Titan remembering an earlier time when he thought that the greatest happiness was within his grasp" or "the key of 'glücklich' possibility."[15] Michael Hall identifies B major as "the key that [Schubert] almost invariably used for the transcendence of suffering," but he mentions it only in the context of "Der Doppelgänger" and not the middle of "Der Atlas."[16] Litterick says, "B major and its enharmonic equivalent seem to be associated with fantasy and wish fulfillment in this group of songs, as elsewhere in Schubert."[17] These interpretations appear to be valid here, but they do not get to, well, the heart of the matter. Indeed, the speaker's heart, as a specific and personal subject, has experienced past happiness, transcendent suffering, and (unfulfilled) fantasy, but there is more to the story of the Atlas and his heart than that.

As an opening for the cycle, this poem made an excellent choice, and the music that Schubert contrived for it reinforces its purpose. First, we meet the "lyrisches Ich" explicitly.[18] He introduces himself as Atlas and describes his experience of bearing the weight of the whole world's anguish. This self-introduction comes not in simply-metered rhyme but in prose-like blank verse, so that it stands apart from the songs that will follow, as a prologue.[19] The speaker then addresses his own breaking heart, accusing that part of himself, compelled in the past to seek bliss or accept condemnation to misery, which in the end has brought on him his cruel situation. And he returns to lamenting his present unhappiness. Based on such a prologue, we will hear the rest of the songs surely not as marking succeeding experiences for this character but rather as expressing moments of past experience that have brought him to this present state. Already, we are cued in to understand the cycle as nonchronological. We must also understand from the juxtaposition of G minor and B major that the speaker experiences self-alienation. Further, the key of B identifies the first speaker's heart, suffering from the disappointment of its earlier fantasies of happiness, and we should remember that when we encounter it again.

The second song, "Ihr Bild," again begins with "Ich" and describes a moment in the past, and it brings into the story an encounter with a woman, or at least the portrait of a woman:

Ich stand in dunkeln Träumen
Und starrt' ihr Bildnis an,
Und das geliebte Antlitz
Heimlich zu leben begann.

"I stood in dark dreams and stared at her likeness, and the beloved countenance secretly came to life." Two tolling B♭ octaves provide all the introduction for this song. The piano continues in bare octaves to double the first vocal phrase (the first two lines, the grammatical clause), of which the structural core is the play between B♭ and its upper neighbor C♮, from which the line drops abruptly by a tritone to G♭, sixth scale degree in the key of B♭ minor (example 3.3). The brief interlude that echoes the phrase's last two measures features C♮ and G♭, as well, in its outer voices. The remainder of the stanza turns to a more hymnlike texture and B♭ major, an expressive warming appropriate to the text's second clause. Again the motion of C♮ to B♭ dominates, developed from above first by D (now natural) and then E♭.

After an interlude still in B♭ major and ending on an imperfect cadence, the speaker continues,

Um ihre Lippen zog sich
Ein Lächeln, wunderbar,
Und wie von Wehmutstränen
Erglänzte ihr Augenpaar.

"Around her lips a smile played wondrously, and her eyes shone as if from tears of sorrow." Beginning again from unison B♭s, sustained as a top-voice pedal,

Example 3.3. Schubert, "Ihr Bild," mm. 1–6.

the melody walks down through A♭ to G♭, which then turns the music to G♭ major. Notably, as in "Der Atlas"—and as in two of the remaining four songs—the structural tonal contrast is between keys a third apart. The upper neighbor to B♭ is now C♭ (fourth scale degree in G♭) on *Lächeln* ("smile") and *erglänzte* ("shone"), which the listener hears in contrast to the earlier C♮. Schubert's handling of key and melodic design captures the strange enlivening of the image in the picture. The major key hints at the possible happiness suggested by the smile, but the fact that the key is G♭—so darkly minor at its earlier occurrence—forces us to remember the minor mode of the song's beginning, and the tension in the downward pull of C♭ captures the pang of sorrow in the tears.

The final two notes of the stanza's melody, D♭ (as escape tone from C♭) and B♭, at this point recur three times in the piano part, harmonized respectively as G♭ major, by B♭s filled out by the augmented sixth G♭/E♮, and by a mode-less B♭/F harmony. Then the speaker responded, too, as he tells us, with tears:

> Auch meine Tränen flossen
> Mir von den Wangen herab—

"My tears, too, flowed down from my cheeks." The music is identical to the first two lines of the song: "I stared. . . . My tears flowed"—seeing and weeping seem inseparable for the speaker. But then he says something quite remarkable,

> Und ach, ich kann es nicht glauben,
> Dass ich dich verloren hab.

"and ah, I cannot believe that I have lost you." Why remarkable? First, because it moves from reporting an action in the past to expressing his (i.e., the speaker's) situation (having lost) and experience (inability to believe) in the present. The speaker can clearly look backward, reliving the past events that have caused his present condition. Forgoing chronology is no impediment to understanding events and their significance—it wraps them in context.

Even more remarkably, perhaps, the final couplet uses the second person singular, and in the intimate form, "dich." The dear one whom the speaker (the Atlas) has lost can hardly be the woman in the picture, because he refers to her in third person. In fact, there is a compelling identity for the lost one, which comes by reference to the preceding text (as is true also in *Die Heimkehr*); it is the "du" of the first poem, the too-proud heart. In this second song we still hear the divided self from the first, the man and his estranged heart.

The fact that this third stanza uses the music of the first, so that the loss of the most beloved is set to the same music—that is, in the major key—used for the picture's coming to life, gives the closing line of text an oxymoronic effect. One might imagine that the tone expresses an effort at consolation, if not of the lost one addressed then of the speaker himself. In any event, the postlude returns brutally (forte) to B♭ minor.

The third song shifts to another time and place, as well as to a somewhat distant key, A♭ major, and it must appear to mark the beginning of a love story—or what its speaker had hoped would become one. Although the speaker uses the present tense, the previous songs have prepared us to understand this as flashback and as the speaker's self-quotation. In its musical style this song differs sharply from its predecessors. The style of a barcarolle in conventional ⁶⁄₈ meter and simple chordal texture, with a lilting melody, marks it strongly as a "song" in contradistinction to the more declamatory pieces that make up the remainder of Schubert's Heine settings (example 3.4).

The speaker stands on the shore and calls to a young fisherwoman to come sit and flirt with him:

> Du schönes Fischermädchen,
> Treibe den Kahn ans Land—
> Komm zu mir und setze dich nieder,
> Wir kosen Hand in Hand.
>
> Leg an mein Herz dein Köpfchen
> Und fürchte dich nicht zu sehr,
> Vertraust du dich doch sorglos
> Täglich dem wilden Meer.

Example 3.4. Schubert, "Das Fischermädchen," mm. 8–11.

> Mein Herz gleicht ganz dem Meere,
> Hat Sturm und Ebb' und Flut,
> Und manche schöne Perle
> In seine Tiefe ruht.

> "You pretty fisher-maiden, drive your boat up onto the land—
> come to me and sit down, and we will dally hand in hand.
> Lay your little head on my heart and do not be too afraid;
> you trust yourself every day to the wild sea. My heart is just like
> the sea; it has storm and ebb and flow, and many a beautiful
> pearl rests in its depths."

The fact that the speaker addresses only the girl, not his heart or us as his auditors, separates this song from its predecessors in place and time, so that its setting in his past cannot be missed. The poem's introduction of a location and characters leaves no doubt that, whatever its position in the cycle, it belongs at the beginning of the speaker's story. As we have observed, however, we are by now fully prepared to accept a nonchronological presentation of events.[20]

A second notable element of this song is that the man makes much of his heart, now in third person. Here, unlike in the preceding songs, he and his heart have not yet become alienated from each other. Rather, he seeks the girl's closeness for his heart, or, to put it another way, the man's heart serves him as the locus of an intimate relationship with the girl. He actually argues in its defense—he assures the fisher-maiden that although his heart might seem dangerous in the disturbances on its surface, it hides beauty in the calm of its depths.

Again, the middle stanza is set off by a move to a third-related key, here from the tonic A♭ to C♭. If we can hear across the breaks between songs, we recognize the pitch class as having been set up in the middle verse of "Ihr Bild." We might also recognize the tonality as the enharmonic equivalent of B major in the middle of "Der Atlas."[21] The key reflects that first song, for here the speaker mentions his heart, on which the song invites the fisher-maiden to lay her head. Our understanding of the heart from the accusation in "Der Atlas" is consistent with the allusion here to the young woman's qualms—the heart is characterized by extremes: in the first song, the desire for endless happiness or misery; in this one, its storms and floods, and the pearls in the depths.[22]

Another vignette from the past follows—again in present tense, at least until the final line. The speaker is in a rowboat.

Am fernen Horizonte
Erscheint, wie ein Nebelbild,
Die Stadt mit ihrem Türmen,
In Abenddämmrung gehüllt.

Ein feuchter Windzug kräuselt
Die graue Wasserbahn;
Mit traurigem Takte rudert
Der Schiffer in meinem Kahn.

Die Sonne hebt sich noch einmal
Leuchtend vom Boden empor
Und zeigt mir jene Stelle,
Wo ich das Liebste verlor.

"On the far horizon appears, like a cloud of mist, the city with its towers, enveloped in evening twilight. A moist gust of wind ruffles the gray water-track; with sorrowful strokes the boatman rows in my boat. The sun lifts itself once more, shining from the surface, and shows me the place where I lost the dearest one."

Because we the audience are not yet present, nor does the speaker address anyone else, the poem seems to articulate an interior monologue. In the evening twilight he sees a city. The light is muted, the water troubled by a breeze, the motion of the rower slow. When a ray of sunshine does break out, the speaker sees the place where he lost the most precious object.

The text here leaves us with several curious questions, since some facts that we might assume are not actually stated. For one thing, we might not be sure of the speaker. We probably take for granted that it is the man who introduced himself as Atlas and that he is also the one who addressed the fisher-maiden in the previous song, but the poem does not say this explicitly.[23] (For all we really know, it might even be the girl; after all, we do know that she possesses a boat.) We don't know for sure, although we probably assume, that the city shrouded in mist in the first stanza is the sad location that the sunlight reveals in the third. It is not clear what time frame the poem encompasses, with the evening twilight followed by the rising sun—does an entire night pass after the first stanza? Crucially, we might not immediately understand the direct object of the last clause, especially since the speaker has lost "das Liebste," rather than "den" or "die." In fact, the article calls into question whether the lost one is a woman here, who (despite the German use of the neuter for "das Fischermädchen") would far more likely be identified as "die Liebste" in this context. Yet we might realize (perhaps with some astonishment) that we—we the listeners to Schubert's cycle in contradistinction to the readers of Heine's book of poems—do know a lost beloved that would have to take the neuter article: "das Herz," that proud heart of the first song, the lost one of the second.

The music first establishes the rowing motion and the lassitude of the weary oarsman, in a prelude made up of arpeggiated diminished seventh chords over a pedal tone C. In addition to the impressionistic mistiness of the harmony, the rhythm provides an example of Schubert's gift for deriving from a poem a rhythmic motion that also expresses emotion. Here the slow triple meter (the "trauriger Takt" of line 7) mimics in each measure the drag of the oars through the water, followed by the dull clunks of the oarlocks as the rower lifts the oars and resets them for the next stroke (example 3.5). (Fast rowing, by contrast, uses duple rhythm.) This music occupies the introduction, the speaker's explicit description in the second stanza of what it feels like to be in the boat, and the postlude. The vocal part in the second stanza places the singer on the water by merely outlining the diminished seventh chord, descending from E♭ to C a tenth lower.

Example 3.5. Schubert, "Die Stadt," piano, mm. 1–6.

The first and third stanzas, where the speaker looks away toward the horizon and sees the distant city and the place where he lost the beloved one, contrast markedly with the middle stanza. In these two stanzas the piano plays in block chords, using a shuddering, dotted rhythmic ostinato, expressing both somber grandeur and sorrow.[24] The key is C minor, and the harmony moves in conventional style from tonic through subdominant and dominant to a firm cadence on the tonic. The third stanza features a strongly marked chromatic upper neighbor, the D♭ that produces a straining Neapolitan sixth as the singer mentions that place there ("*jene* Stelle"), where he lost his beloved. The vocal line is in declamatory style. In the first stanza the speaker describes the appearance of the distant city in the twilight mist. The line is somewhat constrained, mostly reciting each phrase on a single pitch in gradually rising steps. The third stanza alternates those static lines with new variants containing bold leaps when the singer sees the sun burst upward and when he mentions his loss.

The moment represented by this song evidently follows the flirtation of "Das Fischermädchen," with its more naive (even if disingenuously so) tone of voice. It might either appear as a second flashback, in which the present tense reenacts an experience at some point between "Das Fischer-mädchen" and "Der Atlas," or else more or less the same present as the opening song. The loss mentioned here in the past tense will certainly be understood as the same as the loss in "Ihr Bild," also in past tense and in that song's last line, although it is now referred to not in second person but third—addressed not to the lost one but to the song's listener. We probably place "Die Stadt" before "Ihr Bild" in our understanding of the chronology because of the musical treatments of these two corresponding references to the same loss. In "Die Stadt," the minor key, the effect of the accompaniment, and the outcry on the leap to the high G in the last line suggest a still fresh and painful anguish, whereas in "Ihr Bild," the major key, the more regular rhythm, and the hymnlike texture, setting a much more constrained vocal phrase, carry a sense of resignation.

The fifth song actually narrates a past event, describing the fatal moment in the speaker's history in three of its four stanzas:

Das Meer erglänzte weit hinaus
Im letzten Abendscheine,
Wir sassen am einsamen Fischerhaus,
Wir sassen stumm und alleine.

Der Nebel stieg, das Wasser schwoll,
Die Möve flog hin und wieder;
Aus deinen Augen, liebevoll,
Fielen die Tränen nieder.

Ich sah sie fallen auf deine Hand
Und bin aufs Knie gesunken,
Ich hab von deiner weissen Hand
Die Tränen fortgetrunken.

"The sea shone in the distance in the evening's last radiance. We sat at the lonely fisher's house; we sat mute and alone. The mist rose, the water swelled, the seagull flew back and forth; from your eyes, full of love, the tears fell down. I saw them fall on your hand and I sank to my knee; I drank up the tears from your white hand."

The speaker here recalls to his companion that they sat on a lonely shore, alone and silent, and she wept. The reason for this remains unknown; her emotion appears to have been love, so perhaps the two found themselves forced to part. Interestingly, the verb tenses slip from the preterite for the depiction of the setting (in the sense of "the sea was shining," etc.) for the first nine lines to the perfect for the speaker's particular actions ("I knelt" and "I drank the tears"). The speaker recounts the scene and the woman's weeping as simply having taken place in the past. The kneeling and drinking of the tears are viewed, in contrast, as actions that, from a present point of view, he reports having done—in fact, actions performed, almost as a sort of devotional ritual that he has accomplished.

In the final stanza he describes his present condition:

Seit jener Stunde verzehrt sich mein Leib,
Die Seele stirbt vor Sehnen;—
Mich hat das unglücksel'ge Weib
Vergiftet mit ihren Tränen.

"Since that hour my body is wasting away, my soul is dying of longing. The wretched woman has poisoned me with her tears."

He confesses—no longer addressing the woman, to whom he refers here in the third person—that his demonstration of love or devotion led to a deadly longing.[25] Despite its position among its neighbors, we understand this event to have taken place between "Das Fischermädchen" and "Die Stadt," which is indeed the position of the poem in Heine's order. Although the presentation in the cycle is nonchronological, we interpret this as the turning point in the story between hopeful attraction and bitter disappointment, the experience that brought the Atlas to his world of pain.

The song opens with a curious version of an augmented sixth chord, played twice. Rather than functioning as a predominant harmony, the augmented sixth here is framed by three octaves of Cs, so that it merely strains into the C-major chord by approaching the third and fifth by semitones; it conveys a feeling of yearning toward the tonic. With no more context, the gesture opens a question: What accounts for this longing?

The first stanza is set as a doubled duet above a simple bass of tonic and dominant, the vocal line doubled in the piano and paralleled in thirds above and sixths below. Although in some sense this appears chordal, it does not really resemble the texture of a hymn setting. Such paralleling of a vocal melody can evoke friendship and even, in an opera duet, handholding or an embrace of lovers. Here the speaker is accompanied by a present but vocally silent partner. The simple melody, outlining an eight-measure period in the key of C, sets up the situation as entirely innocent—so innocent, indeed, that the attentive listener probably anticipates a twist of fate. The cadence is reiterated in the piano alone, reflecting the mute isolation of the pair of lovers ("stumm und alleine").

Immediately the texture changes, tremolo chords expressing both the increasing motion in the scene of the mist, the sea, and the gull and the speaker's emotional agitation; the chord of C minor launches a drive to a cadence in D minor; a crescendo brings a climax at the second line. The singer's agitation also becomes clear in the shorter, declamatory phrases. A quick move to a D half-diminished seventh with C in the bass allows a move back to the original key, but only as far as a half cadence.

The third stanza uses the music of the first, restoring the naive sense of intimacy, so that the drinking of tears seems as innocent as the scene described at the song's beginning. The twist comes at the lead-in to the final stanza, which returns to the agitated music of the second, and the gull's flying back and forth now seems to have been an anticipation or even an omen of the soul's dying of longing. The melody changes for the close of the fourth stanza, incorporating a dominant minor ninth chord for the "wretched woman," produced by A♭ in the doubling part above the singer in measures 40–41, and adjusting to produce a perfect authentic cadence. The final word, "Tränen," receives a curious embellishment. Perhaps the idea is to ameliorate the bitterness of the speaker's experience by the elegant turn on the C-major close, and yet he can only convey this by an artificial figure that has nothing to do with the rest of the song, or even of the entire cycle. The potential for ironic interpretation is obvious; at the very least, one suspects that the suffering lover only hopes to comfort himself.[26]

The song closes with a return of the opening chords of yearning. They provide a frame, by which we know that the song's entire plot closes in on itself around this governing feeling. Unlike the beginning, however, as an ending they draw back from the finality of the preceding authentic cadence and now serve as a meditative, quasi-plagal extension of the sustained tonic Cs.

The speaker of the final song has returned to his sweetheart's home:

Still ist die Nacht, es ruhen die Gassen,
In diesem Hause wohnte mein Schatz,
Sie hat schon längst die Stadt verlassen,
Doch steht das Haus auf demselben Platz.

"The night is silent; the alleys rest; in this house my sweetheart lived; she left the city long ago, but the house still stands in the same square."

The first stanza situates the speaker in the city in the present, the silence and darkness of his location rendered emptier by the memory that his sweetheart departed long ago. Notably, the house on the city square suggests that the beloved of this song was not the fisher-maiden of the third song, whom we would hardly expect to find living in such a place. In this case, we learn that the speaker's story is not one of a single love and loss but of a life of multiple desires and disappointments.

Da steht auch ein Mensch und starrt in die Höhe
Und ringt die Hände vor Schmerzensgewalt;
Mir graust es, wenn ich sein Antlitz sehe,
Der Mond zeigt mir meine eigne Gestalt.

"A man also stands there and stares upward and wrings his hands
from the force of pain; I shudder when I see his countenance;
the moon shows me my own form."

The speaker sees a man standing there, as well, and realizes that this man reflects his own face; with trembling he recognizes his alter ego, from whom he stands apart and to whom he refers in third person. But he then addresses this figure:

Du Doppelgänger, du bleicher Geselle,
Was äffst du nach mein Liebeslied,
Das mich gequält auf dieser Stelle
So manche Nacht, in alter Zeit?

"You double, you pale companion, why do you mimic my
love's sorrow, that tormented me in this place so many a night
in time long past?"

Here the speaker accuses his double of taking him back through the story of his painful love, putting him through the bitter experience all over again.[27] As a reflection on the cycle to this point, this forces us to consider the identity of both the pale double and the present speaker. The one who has been repeating the failed love story and its pain is, of course, the speaker of the preceding songs. In other words, the original lyric persona, the Atlas, appears here as the Doppelgänger. In fact, the songs themselves have been reenactments of his past.[28] Consequently, the speaker of this poem, whose face is mirrored by that of the Atlas, who addresses the "Mensch" as "du," surely must be the heart of the first song.[29] Accused in the first text of bringing the man to his miserable state, the heart asks in reply why the man continues to wallow in his past and its pain. In terms of chronology, the "now" of "Der Doppelgänger" follows the "now" of "Der Atlas" (reversing the order of these poems in Heine's book) as a response to the Atlas's reliving of his unhappy history through the intervening songs.

The identification of the speaker in "Der Doppelgänger" emerges immediately from the return to the tonality of B for this song—referencing the B that formed the tonal centers of the middle sections of "Der Atlas" and "Das Fischermädchen," where it referred explicitly to the heart. Rather than B major, the key here is B minor—although the first harmony has no third, so that the mode is ambiguous until measure 3. The harmonic structure that governs the song, which is mostly a repeating eight-measure progression creating a sort of passacaglia, employs a succession of harmonies that all contain a double internal pedal tone F♯. The outer parts in the harmony at the start outline an approximate retrograde form of the motive that opened "Der Atlas," as we noted at the beginning of our discussion (example 3.6). Each repetition closes with an unresolved chord, either the dominant seventh (in second inversion in mm. 12–14, 22–24) or augmented sixths (mm. 32–33, 41–42), so that there is no strong cadence until the perfect authentic cadence at the last word of the song (mm. 55–56). The insistent F♯ and the open ending of each repetition might be taken as an enactment of the Doppelgänger's compulsion through the first two stanzas; it certainly creates the experience of constant failure to achieve closure.

Like the piano part, the vocal line holds insistently on F♯ in a strikingly declamatory style—even more so than the hardly lyrical preceding songs. In the second stanza it works its way up to the higher octave F♯ (*fff*) and collapses back at "Schmerzensgewalt," repeating that process and extending to high G at the horrifying realization that the speaker sees his own face in his pale companion. That G breaks the lock of F♯ on every harmony.

Example 3.6. Schubert, "Der Doppelgänger," mm. 1–8.

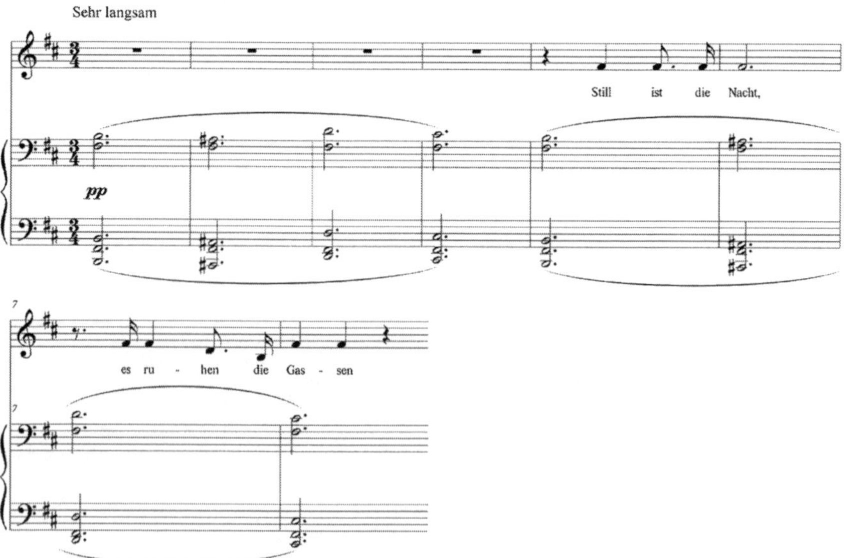

It also leads to a new progression that modulates to the key of D♯ minor, the same move from the minor key to the key of the raised third scale degree that marked "Der Atlas," at the text "Why do you mimic my love's suffering." The singer's part rises again from F♯ to its upper octave, fortissississimo, falling back in a surprisingly lyrical descent, including an elegant little melisma, to B for the close, pianissimo, of the stanza.

The piano postlude begins as another statement of the opening progression, but these eight measures move to a new kind of closure, with the Neapolitan in the fourth measure (in root position, m. 59), then the secondary dominant seventh of the subdominant (now *ppp*), the subdominant, and the major tonic to end the cycle. The relaxing parallel semitone descent from C major to the B seventh chord, the sustained Bs in the outer parts, and the inner parts' falling chromatic voice leading from G to F♯ and E to D♯ (mm. 61–62), together with the Picardy third, create the feeling of resignation and peace at the close (example 3.7).

The song does not reveal what brings about this ending or what it means. By tradition, an encounter with one's double leads to death, and the postlude here might represent gentle death, as in "Der Tod und das Mädchen." Alternatively, once the Doppelgänger is recognized and challenged, it fades away or actually merges back into the reunified person of the speaker. Whatever the listener's understanding, the essential aspect of the outcome of the song brings resolution and closure beyond itself to the cycle as a whole—and it does so more effectively than any other one of these songs would, if they followed an alternative order.

As a cycle, these songs (in Schubert's order) follow a tight and rigorously logical plan. The composer selected and organized the texts to cycle between the present and the beginning of the story, as well as intervening times, but the lack of chronology in the order of the songs in no way interferes with the understanding of the chronology of events.[30] Schubert chose as a frame two texts complementary in that in each the speaker and his alter ego

Example 3.7. Schubert, "Der Doppelgänger," piano, mm. 56–63.

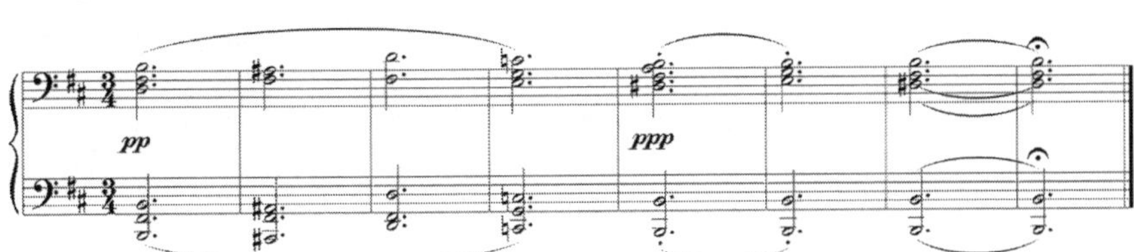

explicitly accuse one another. The interior songs recount specific past events as causes of specific present emotional experience. For the Atlas, the actions of the past develop his case against his own heart. From the point of view of his heart—to whom the Atlas finally appears as Doppelgänger—it is the obsessive revisiting of those moments that loads the Atlas with the whole world of pain. Out of just a few of Heine's poems, Schubert constructed a work that exposes the back-and-forth movement between present and past, dealt with in terms of two ways of approaching the divided subject's life history and memories.

Clearly this divided subject is a more sophisticated persona than the public would have expected from songs before this time. As Siegbert Salomon Prawer wrote in his study of Heine's *Buch der Lieder,*

> Der Doppelgänger [but, as the song incorporates its predecessors, one could include here Schubert's complete six-song cycle] presents, with entire seriousness, the dilemma of a post-Romantic poet who has lost even the naïveté of suffering; who is forced to watch his own gestures of sorrow with an all-too-conscious eye. So watched, these gestures become ridiculous, a mockery of grief that may once have been spontaneously real but has now become self-conscious and hollow. The ultimate subject of this magnificent poem is not so much grief over lost love as grief over the lost simplicity of grief.[31]

Song Style and Cultural Status of the Speaker in Eighteenth- and Nineteenth-Century Germany

The model of the songs in Schubert's two great cycles on poems of Wilhelm Müller, as for the Lied generally, had been the *volkstümliche* (folklike) style, but nothing of that remains in the Heine songs, except for the deliberate appropriation of the folk idiom in the seduction scene of "Das Fischermädchen." Heine's texts still adopted, for the most part, the structure and metrical style of folk-song-modeled poems, despite their quite unfolklike content. In 1826 Heine wrote to Müller, "In my poems, by contrast [i.e., to Müller's], only the form is somewhat folklike, the content belongs to conventional society."[32] By "conventional society," presumably, he had in mind the sophisticated world of post-Napoleonic city life. In Gernot Gruber's view, "It is also conceivable that Schubert's settings of his poems do not express Heine's representations of musical Volkstümlichkeit."[33] What Heine's poems set up, Schubert's music captures unmistakably. Prawer's disillusioned post-Romantic poet, Schubert's Atlas and his heart, speaks from this "conventional society" as a bourgeois, urban voice.

The unmistakable difference between the style of Schubert's Heine songs and the tradition of the Lied makes it worthwhile to reflect on the musical features and meanings of German songs from the middle of the eighteenth century to the middle of the nineteenth. In the fourth decade of the eighteenth century the Lied began a long period of growth in terms of social use, cultural significance, and economic success. The first phase brought songs with keyboard accompaniment to a market eager for such a commodity. In the burgeoning bourgeois economy, when a sudden expansion of wealth to the mercantile and commercial class allowed families to purchase both keyboard instruments and sheet music or periodicals that included music for the home, composers and poets raced to fill the demand. Poetry espoused an ideal of clear, directly expressed sentiment and sometimes didactic intent, turning away from the rhetorical and courtly literary complexities of the Italian-dominated Baroque. Music adopted simple forms and transparent textures. In some cases, poets or musicians generated songs quickly by adding texts to create contrafacts of existing instrumental dances.

By the end of the eighteenth century, an interest in songs in a folklike style had emerged. The collection of folk poetry by writers and philologists led to publication of actual songs with folk tunes, the setting of traditional texts (or invented texts purporting to represent actual folk songs), and songs with both words and music newly created in what the writers and the public understood to be a style representing *Volkstümlichkeit*. Part of the interest in folk songs stemmed from the Enlightenment's drive to seek encyclopedically for new knowledge, especially in culture that seemed close to nature. Equally, however, as the German population in particular moved rapidly in the late eighteenth and early nineteenth centuries from rural settings to urban, cosmopolitan centers, evocations of folk culture helped people to maintain a connection—even if a fictitious or imaginary one—to a German identity rooted in the land.

The assumptions of a *volkstümlich* style for Schubert's Lieder, then, include a transparent and figurational keyboard part, a symmetrical tune, and strophic form. This type largely governs the two great cycles, *Die schöne Müllerin* (identified on its title page as "Cyclus von Liedern / gedichtet von / WILHELM MÜLLER") and *Winterreise* (which bears no specific genre designation). Schubert took advantage of the style to establish the persona of each cycle as a young wanderer—in *Die schöne Müllerin* explicitly of the working class, and in both cases in a rural setting. The artistic brilliance of his songs comes from the adaptation of idiomatic keyboard (or guitar-like) accompaniment patterns to capture both imagery and feeling and the freedom to treat poems in modified strophic forms as a means of adapting to changing ideas within a song. The protagonist's voice emerges as both German and inextricably connected to the sylvan landscape.

Starting in the 1830s, then, the old-fashioned *Volksstil* becomes retrospective. In some cases it might seem exotic in the manner of a fairy tale. In others it serves an escapist function, as an imaginative flight from the city to the culturally remembered forest and village. The general abandonment of those quasi-*Volkslied* conventions marks the Heine songs as an entirely different type. They mostly avoid the kinds of figurations and the tuneful melodic style that the earlier cycles exploit, and the strophic form is highly attenuated. They instead present an urban and sophisticated Romantic voice, in comparison with which the *Volkstümlichkeit* of earlier songs seems naive, exactly the voice that Heine mentioned to Müller.

Chapter 4

Prima Donna or Composer

Opera Variations and Chopin's Op. 2

Anti-Romantic Virtuosity?

Virtuosity has a vexed standing in Romanticism. Friedrich Blume went so far as to call it "anti-Romantic."[1] Virtuosity certainly held a large place in Romantic musical life and experience, however, and it hardly deserves a summary dismissal. Virtuoso performers remained as important in the public musical culture as ever, and in some repertoires the adaptation of musical designs to the demands of virtuosity provides the justification for musical structures. This chapter proposes a hypothetical generalization about virtuosity and gender in one part of the nineteenth-century repertoire. It also considers some exceptions to the general conception, actually suggesting that they confirm rather than contradict it. Centrally, the chapter takes as its topic Chopin's variations on a Mozart opera theme, focusing specifically on the way in which Schumann, as Romantic critic, used his review of Chopin's music to enforce a particular hearing of the music's voice.

The opera stage provided one obvious venue for virtuosic performance. Among the most prominent performers were the great divas of nineteenth-century bel canto opera, and their elaboration of their arias constituted a considerable part of their stock in trade. The design of the opera aria consequently adapted itself to virtuosic embellishment (even rewriting). Just as in the Baroque the da capo aria form had provided the framework for such a play of skill, in the nineteenth century arias tended to strophic forms, which the prima donna would turn into variations, or rondos, in which each return of the rondo theme would become a venue for decoration.

As Carl Dahlhaus has pointed out, these forms do not develop but rather allow for elaboration.[2] Unlike the sonata form or its deformations, the rondo and variation do not unfold as plots. Nor do they suggest the subjective voice of the narrator within the notated tonal object. Thus, unlike the listener to a Romantic symphony, the listener to a virtuoso opera aria performance (especially on the concert stage) does not primarily attend to the experience of a character nor hear what, in a fictive sense, we sometimes refer to as "the composer's voice."[3] Instead, the listener hears the musical imagination of the singer qua singer. And thus the persona projected in performing these arias is that of the diva, not the dramatic protagonist and not the storyteller.

Nineteenth-century Italian opera audiences, in particular, listened to opera singers in this way. At an opera's first performance they generally paid attention throughout, became acquainted with the characters, and followed the plot. But audiences often returned for later performances, when those in the private boxes could alternate between listening to the arias of the star singers and playing cards, discussing politics, or enjoying snacks. Sections of recitative or the arias for *comprimario* singers (so-called *arie di sorbetto*, by convention treated as opportunities to indulge in flavored ices) might find the front curtains of the boxes closed. In that context the public clearly did not attend to plot or character, rather selecting out the "hit" arias and their favorite *prime donne*, opening their curtains only for these and then closing them again.[4]

Singers also cultivated this kind of listening. Manifesting the usual display of skill that attends any competitive sport, the operatic divas found chances to embellish the notated vocal line at any fermata, major cadence, or repetition. Sometimes they departed from the score in ways more imaginative than musical.[5] It was common practice for leading singers to substitute their favorite arias for those that the composer had written—so-called *arie di baule*, or "trunk arias"—and that made it hardly reasonable to expect them to portray the personalities of specific characters in any given opera.

The behaviors of twenty-first-century opera audiences and singers make it less obvious that we attend to the voices of the performers and not of the characters. Audiences no longer return to the theater night after night for the same staging of an opera, and few theaters feature boxes easily closed off from the house for snacks and card games. Singers no longer feel free to replace the music written by the composer with arias taken from some other opera, even by another composer. Yet it is still true that we hear the opera arias of the Italian bel canto as manifestations of the voice not of the character but of the performer.

For an example of how the form of an early-nineteenth-century Italian aria explicitly foregrounds the virtuosity of the performer, we can take the closing section of the final scene of Rossini's *La Cenerentola*, the title character's "Non più mesta." The passage consists of increasingly virtuosic variations on a simple tune, followed by a coda. The form invites the display of flexibility and articulation across the mezzo soprano range, as well as creativity in personalizing the notated passagework with figuration and interpolated extremes of pitch, according to the individual singer's abilities and imagination. It has become conventional to start the section at a fairly moderate tempo and then to double the speed at the third variant of the theme in continuous sixteenth notes—but this is not marked in the original score, and not all singers follow this practice. For this piece, the musical experience should be in the performance, not the score.

In Cecilia Bartoli's performances of "Non più mesta," we listen to Bartoli, the prima donna or even the diva, as the audience at the 1817 premiere would have listened to Geltrude Giorgi-Righetti (1793–1862)—not to Cinderella and not to an imagined fairy-tale teller, "Rossini." It is hard to imagine that the audience member at this point in the opera hears shades of Cinderella's happiness at the outcome of the plot in Bartoli's machine-gun articulation of the passagework in the variations or the choice of B5 for the penultimate note. The listener who hears Bartoli's various performances might notice the relatively direct rendition of the readings in the score in one and the much more individual, creative treatment of the notes in another.[6] Every interesting performance, by any singer, must accomplish this. A mere execution of the score will mean nothing at all. In any case, in the opera we should not expect to experience the voice of Cinderella, nor the voice of any fictive teller of a folk tale, but the prima donna's voice.

This does not make the repertoire "anti-Romantic," however, for the key to Romanticism lies in the listener's acquaintance with the personality of the musical voice, not in any foreordained type of persona per se. Indeed, in the sense that the *virtuose* of the nineteenth-century opera stage cultivated distinctive personae, such virtuosity constitutes a manifestation, not a contradiction, of Romanticism.

Here is a hypothesis: Virtuosity in the performance of the opera aria (especially on the concert stage) tends to invoke a specifically female persona. Even a male performer who enacts the behavior of a "star" performer might be referred to as a "prima donna" or "diva." As an example of how the term might be applied to a nonfemale singer, Luigi Marchesi (1755–1829) not only excelled in embellishment but insisted on special treatment. Francis Toye reports that, as an unusually short man, he insisted on making his entrances from a height or on horseback, with a costume crowned by a high plume.[7] In gender-biased everyday parlance, there has been a convention of describing such an attitude as reflecting the personality of a diva or prima donna, not a primo uomo.

The Pianist as Diva

Instrumental virtuoso-composers mined the operatic aria repertoire for their themes. We might take, for example, Henri Herz's treatment of "Non più mesta," a flashy set of six variations, loaded with the pianistic tricks of the day. The piece is transposed from E to C major. The general design is as follows:

> Introduction—Fantasy-like: fast passages in broken thirds, a brief cantabile moment, scales, rapid repeated notes, and suggestions of the theme followed by a lead-in

> Theme—The aria's sixteen-measure rounded-binary-form tune, presented simply and clearly

> Variation 1—A variant of the theme in triplets, increasing the motion, with parallel thirds and sixths at the end of each segment

> Variation 2—Increasing the speed to sixteenth notes, a galloping variation, with the beginning of the second segment (mm. 8–12 of the variation) featuring an inner voice trill effect

> Variation 3—The melody played straightforwardly in the right hand over rushing scales in the left running up and down two and a half octaves, the second segment starting in broken chords

> Variation 4—The melody varied in quick, densely voiced, staccato eighth-note chords, with measures 8–12 showing off "pearly" trills and sixteenth-note slurred passagework

> Variation 5—The fastest passagework yet, featuring sextuplets and very fast descending scale in parallel thirds (which might be handled as a double glissando)

Variation 6—A romance or nocturne variation in A minor and
$\frac{12}{8}$ meter that ends by accelerating into a transition back to
C major[8]

Finale—A string of Rossinian comic finale moments in a variety
of pianistic styles

In short, Herz extends the operatic convention into the idiom of the piano in the salon or concert hall. This was a common genre in the period, and it had at least two functions. First, it provided skilled pianists, starting with the composer himself, repertoire that would be easy for the listeners to follow and make a stunning impression. Second, before the availability of recordings, it gave opera audiences opportunities to hear favorite tunes more frequently than if they had to wait for them to turn up in the opera house.

What my hypothesis suggests is that in such cases, although the composer was male, and even when he played the variations on "Non più mesta" himself, in a conceptual sense the voice in the music and performance is that of a prima donna. At any rate, just as the public listened to the opera aria to hear the singer, in the virtuoso concert they attended to the pianist qua pianist. In the sense that the opera diva stood as the conceptual model for this sort of thing, then, the musical role of virtuosity in general takes on a feminine position. Moreover, the musical style itself plays into nineteenth-century gender codes. The virtuosic variation as a genre does not feature constructive but rather ornamental or decorative talent—it is a matter of embellishment or embroidery applied to the original music. A favorable review by G. W. Fink in the *Allgemeine musikalische Zeitung* of January 1831 describes some of Herz's sets of opera variations with such terms as "charming," "dainty," "gracious," "glittering," "alluring," "prettiness," "fashionable," "flirtatious," and says that they are "art not for art's sake, but rather motivated by the desire to please."[9] In other words, Fink regarded even a set of variations (or a variation rondo) composed and performed by a man not as a masculinization of the music but as a feminization of the persona.

Overriding the Diva Persona—Paganini

In the remainder of this chapter, however, we shall consider what appear to be some very deliberate and self-conscious exceptions. Some virtuoso performers clearly sought to create new kinds of personas for themselves, overriding the convention of the diva voice. As he was the most notorious virtuoso of the period, we inevitably have to bring Paganini into the picture. Paganini also composed variations on "Non più mesta," and we hear there some of his familiar virtuosic tricks, including difficult passages in harmonics (sometimes in double stops) and left-hand pizzicato.

As we know well, however, Paganini—although not, we have to recognize, every other violinist—developed a persona that essentially trumped the general principle. He escaped the feminization of the virtuoso function as a consequence of an exotic or Faustian image. His outlandish dress conjured the exotic violin virtuosity of the musical culture referred to at that time by the exoticizing term "Gypsy." His emaciation suggested one who has abandoned normal, earthly life, with the implication of having made a pact with the devil. In his biography of Paganini, François-Joseph Fétis reports, "The extraordinary expression of his face, his livid paleness, his dark and penetrating eye, together with the sardonic smile which occasionally played upon his lips, appeared to the vulgar, and certain diseased minds, unmistakable evidences of satanic origin."[10] Fétis quotes an anecdote told by the virtuoso himself:

> I had played the variations . . . and they produced some effect. One individual . . . affirmed that he saw nothing surprising in my performance, for he had distinctly seen, while I was playing my variations, the devil at my elbow directing my arm and guiding the bow. My resemblance to him was a proof of my origin. He was clothed in red—had horns on his head—and carried his tail between his legs. After so minute a description, you will understand, sir, it was impossible to doubt the fact—hence, many concluded they had discovered the secret of what they termed wonderful feats.[11]

Fétis emphasizes that Paganini took some offense at the idea that he had not come by his abilities through talent and hard work. This provides a good example of the reason to make a distinction between the persona the audience encounters in the music and the biographical composer, as Paganini certainly did. What is important here is that the effect was to counteract the implication that in his music virtuosity reflected a feminine persona. Paganini's persona does not disprove the usual principle that the virtuosic performance is heard as feminine—it rather demonstrates that it is possible to override the gender convention by some kinds of alternative construction.[12]

The Critic and the Composer's Persona— Schumann on Chopin

An interesting work in this regard is Chopin's Variations for Piano and Orchestra, op. 2, on the duet "Là ci darem la mano" from Mozart's *Don Giovanni*. Ostensibly in the feminized genre of the virtuoso variations on an opera melody, this work, in some compositional aspects, might support such gendering of its persona. Its form is not inherently different from many of those that quite clearly assume the persona of the diva. After a fantasy-like exploratory introduction, the theme enters in fairly straightforward fashion. A series of figurational variations follows, and the work concludes in a blaze of free virtuosic fireworks.

Chopin also easily succumbs to biographical gendering as a rather feminine man. His physical frailty, the delicacy of his pianism, his well-known relationship with the powerfully masculinized poet George Sand—all tend to project Chopin as a feminine persona. For this reason it seems especially interesting to interrogate how a masculine persona could be contrived for the "Là ci darem la mano" variations.

Now, one must grant that "Là ci darem la mano" might not, on its own, invoke a female singer. It is, in fact, a duet between Don Giovanni and Zerlina. Chopin does not present it as a duet, though. Thus, generically the variations still belong to the soloist's *Fach*, and thus the presumed persona is that of the *virtuosa*.

An interesting construction of the work's persona occurs, nevertheless, in Robert Schumann's review of the Variations.[13] In this review, appearing in the *Allgemeine musikalische Zeitung* just a few months after Fink's review of Herz that I already cited, Schumann introduced what became a characteristic approach for his writing, the imaginary scene populated with the fictional characters Florestan, Eusebius, and in this case the narrative figure of Julius. Eusebius enters the scene and proclaims, "Hats off, gentlemen—a genius!" In other words, he does not introduce the composer as a virtuoso but as a creative artist. Later, as Florestan describes the music, he concentrates not on the brilliance of the pianism but rather on the sense of the unfolding of a drama, connecting the different variations to episodes in the opera:

Surely the whole is dramatic. . . . Of course, my dear Julius, the speaking parts are Don Giovanni, Zerlina, Leporello, and Masetto. In the theme, Zerlina's reply is drawn amorously enough. The first variation might perhaps be called somewhat elegant and coquettish—in it, the Spanish grandee toys amiably with the peasant maid. . . . The second . . . is . . . much more intimate, comic, and quarrelsome, exactly as though two lovers were chasing each other and laughing more than usual. But in the third—how everything is changed! This is pure moonshine and fairy spell—Masetto watches from afar and curses rather audibly, to be sure, but Don Giovanni is little disturbed. And . . . the fourth—what is your idea of it? Eusebius played it quite clearly—doesn't it jump about saucily and impudently . . . , although the Adagio . . . is in B-flat minor, than which nothing could be more fitting, for it reproaches the Don, as though moralizing, with his misdeeds. It is bold, surely, and beautiful that Leporello listens, laughs, and mocks from behind the shrubbery, . . . and that B-flat major, in full blossom, marks well the moment of the first kiss. Yet all of this is as nothing in comparison with the final movement—is there more wine, Julius?—this is Mozart's whole finale—popping corks and clinking bottles everywhere, in the midst of things Leporello's voice, then the grasping evil spirits in pursuit, the fleeing Don Giovanni—and finally the end, so beautifully soothing, so truly conclusive.[14]

In other words, the persona does not, in Schumann's representation, take the role of the performer but stands as a controlling figure outside the action of the story. Neither a character in the tale nor a virtuosic performer on the stage, the music here comes from a narrative persona who tells a story. In short, Schumann is at pains to establish for Chopin's music his perception of the Romantic voice—perhaps an ersatz Mozart, but in any case a creative mind, a genius, and not a performer at all. The persona behind the music is masculinized as the opera composer, as maestro, rather than feminized as prima donna.

Pianist as Opera Composer—Liszt

Other composers also "masculinized" the virtuosity in operatic arrangements by reconceiving the genre somewhat, as Schumann's review of Chopin does, so that the persona that underlies virtuosity is not modeled on the singer but on the opera composer. We can look, for example, at Liszt, who constructed and framed his operatic transcriptions in ways that largely avoided the vocal persona. Liszt cultivated a strong masculine persona for himself, but I am more interested here in his approach to gendering his virtuosic arrangements of operatic music for the piano. Early in his career, to be sure, we find the thirteen-year-old Liszt composing *Sept variations brillantes sur un thème de Rossini*, and at nineteen he wrote an *Introduction et variations sur une marche du Siège de Corinthe* (notably not based on an aria but a march), but otherwise the explicit identification of pieces as variations disappears (see table 4.1).

Table 4.1. Opera arrangements by Franz Liszt by date and title

1824	Sept variations brillantes sur un thème de Rossini ["Ah! Come nascondere la fiamma vorace" from *Ermione*]
1824	Impromptu brillant sur des thèmes de Rossini et Spontini
1829	Grande fantaisie sur la tyrolienne d l'opéra *La Fiancée de Auber*
1830	Introduction et variations sur une marche du *Siège de Corinthe*
1835	Réminiscenses de *La Juive*
1835–1836	Réminiscenses de *Lucia di Lammermoor*
1835–1836	Grande fantaisie sur des motifs de *Niobe* [from a cavatina, "I tuoi frequenti palpiti" from Pacini's opera]
1836	Réminiscenses des *Puritains* de Bellini
1836–1842	Grande fantaisie sur des thèmes de l'opera *Les Huguenots*
1838–1839	Piece based on melodies from Mercadente's *Il giuramento*
1839–?1842	Fantaisie sur des motifs favoris de l'opéra *La sonnambula*
1840–1848	Réminiscenses de *Lucrezia Borgia*
1841	Réminiscenses de *Norma*
1841	Réminiscenses de *Robert le diable*
1841	Réminiscenses de *Don Juan*
1842	Fantaisie über Motive aus *Figaro* und *Don Juan*
1846	Cavatine de *Robert le diable* [on the cavatina "Robert, toi que j'aime"]
1847	"Spirto gentil" de l'opéra *La favorite*

continued on next page

Table 4.1. Continued.

1847	Concert paraphrase on an operatic theme [from Verdi's *Ernani*]
1847–1848	Drei Stücke aus der Oper *La muette de Portici*
1849–1850	Illustrations du *Prophète*
1855?	*Rigoletto*: paraphrase de concert
1859	Miserere du *Trovatore*
1859	Phantasiestück über Motive aus *Rienzi* "Santo Spirito cavaliere" von Richard Wagner
1859?	*Ernani*: paraphrase de concert
1860	Spinnerlied aus dem *Fliegenden Holländer*
1865	Illustrations de *l'Africaine*
1865–1867	Fantaisie sur l'opéra hongroise *Szép Ilonka*
1867	Les adieux, rêverie sur un motif de l'opéra *Roméo et Juliette*
1867–1868	*Don Carlos*
1882	Réminiscences de *Boccanegra*

Instead of variations there are *Fantaisies* or *Grands Fantaisies* on single themes or groups of themes from, for example, Auber's *La Fiancée*, Pacini's *Niobe* (the aria "I tuoi frequenti palpiti," significantly, for our purpose, known as a tour de force for Giuditta Pasta), Meyerbeer's *Les Hugeunots*, Bellini's *La sonnambula*, and Mosonyi's *Szép Ilonka*. There are *Réminiscences* from Halévy's *La Juive*, Meyerbeer's *Robert le diable*, Donizetti's *Lucia di Lammermoor* and *Lucrezia Borgia*, Bellini's *I Puritani* and *Norma*, and Verdi's *Simon Boccanegra*—not forgetting Mozart's *Don Giovanni*.[15] There are then *Illustrations* from Meyerbeer's *Le Prophète* and *L'Africaine*. There is *Les adieux, rêverie sur un motif de l'opéra Roméo et Juliette*. And finally there are *Paraphrases de concert* on Verdi's *Ernani* and *Rigoletto*. All these cases separate themselves from the model of the simple variation set, because while variations are part of the operatic diva's creative contribution, fantasies on multiple passages from an opera, reminiscences of the opera, and illustrations from an opera are not.[16] Thus Liszt presents these works as anything but a prima donna's vehicle. In their contents and structures, as well as explicitly in their titles, he correspondingly constructs their persona as the masculine composer.

Virtuosity, Gender, and Creative Resistance

To regard virtuosity in the nineteenth century as "empty" or "anti-Romantic" misses an important aspect of musical voice. Listeners certainly did and still do hear the voice of virtuosity as projecting a persona. The failure to recognize and value the virtuosic voice in critical discourse might in fact reflect critics' and historians' gendered perspectives.[17]

As one prominent representation of nineteenth-century virtuosity, the work of the operatic diva thus brings to the fore issues of both gender and the place of the performer. For the instrumental virtuoso—including male players—and composers of variations or arrangements of opera arias, which constituted a considerable repertoire in the period for both public and private settings, such pieces to some extent amounted to an enactment of the persona of the prima donna. In other words, the male performer of aria variations might be regarded as cross-dressing.

Some cases, however, seem deliberately contrived to supersede the diva persona by imposing another through various strategies. In the case of Paganini, this was the cultivation of the idea of the demonic player who derived his ability from supernatural forces. For Chopin's variations on "Là ci darem la mano," not the composer/performer but the critic, specifically Schumann, set up the piano virtuoso as an opera composer, a role strongly gendered masculine. This also applied to cases in which operatic arrangements appear in the form of transcriptions, reminiscences, and the like.

Thought-provoking (or merely provoking) as this sort of gender conventions might be for our understanding of nineteenth-century culture, it also provides an instance of the applicability of the concept of voice in music of that period. It teaches us that virtuosity and the cultural, critical environment in which that virtuosity found meaning were indeed not "anti-Romantic" but genuinely a manifestation of Romantic voice.

Chapter 5

Onstage and Off

Performing Berlioz's *Harold en Italie*

1.

> Oh, thou! in Hellas deem'd of heav'nly birth,
> Muse! form'd or fabled at the minstrel's will!
> Since sham'd full oft by later lyres on earth,
> Mine dares not call thee from thy sacred hill:
> Yet there I've wander'd by thy vaunted rill;
> Yes! sighed o'er Delphi's long-deserted shrine,
> Where, save that feeble fountain, all is still;
> Nor mote my shell awake the weary Nine
> To grace so plain a tale—this lowly lay of mine.

2.

> Whilome in Albion's isle there dwelt a youth,
> Who ne in virtue's ways did take delight;
> But spent his days in riot most uncouth,
> And vexed with mirth the drowsy ear of Night.
> Ah, me! in sooth he was a shameless wight,
> Sore given to revel and ungodly glee;
> Few earthly things found favour in his sight
> Save concubines and carnal companie,
> And flaunting wassailers of high and low degree.

3.

> Childe Harold was he hight:—but whence his name
> And lineage long, it suits me not to say;
> Suffice it, that perchance they were of fame,
> And had been glorious in another day:
> But one sad losel soils a name for aye,
> However mighty in the olden time;
> Nor all that heralds rake from coffin'd clay,
> Nor florid prose, nor honied lines of rhyme
> Can blazon evil deeds, or consecrate a crime.

Thus, to begin, the first three stanzas of the first canto of Byron's *Childe Harold's Pilgrimage*.[1] They launch the verse epic by the convention of calling on the Muse, while, however, modestly accepting that the poet and the poem fall short of deserving to arouse any godly blessing. Next the speaker addresses the reader or listener, introducing the figure of Childe Harold, whose flawed character and reprehensible misbehavior admittedly no elegance of composition can excuse.[2]

The Composer Speaks

The story of Berlioz's composition of *Harold en Italie* is well known.[3] The composer recounts how in 1834 Paganini requested from him a new work to show off a Stradivarius viola. The work was originally intended as a concerto for chorus, orchestra, and solo viola, based on the last moments in the life of Mary, Queen of Scots. It materialized as something quite different.

It was Scottish, however. Some of the music, as we know, Berlioz pilfered from his *Intrata di Rob-Roy MacGregor*, a failure at its first performance in April 1833. Berlioz had withdrawn the work. Nevertheless, he salvaged two melodies from the *Rob Roy* overture as material for the viola piece, where they serve as the main theme associated with the title character and the secondary theme of the first movement's sonata form.

Paganini's concerto turned out to be a "Symphonie en 4 parties avec un alto principal." When the virtuoso saw the score of the first movement, he immediately dismissed it as insufficient to demonstrate his technical prowess. Thus might have ended the sad tale of Berlioz's second symphony. As it turned out, however, the work achieved something of a success. Berlioz included it in his "trunk" repertoire as he traveled across Europe, and while it had performances of very mixed quality and reception, it was far from a failure. The "Pilgrims' March" was a frequent audience favorite. In Brunswick the orchestra's performance of the final movement rocked the hall: "In that scene of the brigands the orchestra became a literal pandemonium; there was something supernatural and terrifying in the frenzy of its energy. . . . You know nothing like it, you others, poets, you are never swept away by such living hurricanes."[4] Paganini never performed the work, but in 1838 he gave Berlioz a free gift of twenty thousand francs in admiration of his music generally.

Berlioz's Harold symphony is in four movements—in that, it is more conventional than his earlier *Symphonie fantastique* and certainly more than his later dramatic symphony on *Roméo et Juliette*, with its operatic numbers and choruses, or the *Grand Symphonie funèbre et triomphale* for military band, strings, and voices. Yet in its use of the solo instrument it is not like either other symphonies or other concertos, and the function of the viola becomes crucial to hearing and understanding the work.

As the basis for the symphony, but, we must note, not as a program, Berlioz turned to Byron, that broody Romantic Scot. Byron and his Childe Harold, specifically in the fourth canto, gave Berlioz the justification for turning to his own memories of travel in Italy during his Prix de Rome term there. The title's allusion to Byron's poem, a long, descriptive travelogue in which the scenes inspire reflective and confessional musings from the young, exiled ne'er-do-well, should provide the appropriate framework for hearing the music.

Berlioz left in his *Mémoires* an account of his idea for the piece that at first seems clear enough, although we shall see that it does not really describe the music quite as precisely as we might wish: "I imagined writing a succession of scenes for the orchestra, in which the solo viola would find itself mixed up like a person more or less active, always preserving its own character; I wished to make the viola, by placing it in the midst of some poetic souvenirs that my wanderings in the Abruzzi left with me, a sort of melancholy dreamer in the genre of Byron's Childe Harold."[5] We can accept, I think, that the work comprises "une suite de scènes" and that these amount to some "poétiques souvenirs" from Berlioz's own peregrinations in the Abruzzi. What he says about the solo viola, which, while behaving in a manner "plus ou moins actif," does not in any sense always maintain its own character, will merit some discussion later.

As he goes on, however, the composer seems to give a different and more convincing sense of where the unchanging character of the melancholy dreamer is heard: ". . . a principal theme (the viola's first melody) recurs throughout the entire work; . . . the melody of Harold is superimposed on the orchestra's other melodies, with which it contrasts in its movement and its character without thereby interrupting the development."[6] In other words, Berlioz is simply inconsistent in this paragraph about whether it is the viola or the theme that represents Harold. This issue in particular is what piques my interest.

The Critics' Puzzle

Berlioz's ambiguity about the figure of Harold and the functions of the theme and the viola has left critics also uncertain. Liszt wrote to Princess Caroline Sayn-Wittgenstein, "There is in this work . . . a characteristic melody for Harold. This melody mingles admirably with the melody of the Pilgrims' Song, with the Serenade of the Abruzzi Mountaineer, and likewise with the Brigands' Orgy—sometimes dominating them, sometimes serving them as support, as relief, or as shading."[7] Liszt assigns the theme to the title character, but he describes its place within the action as notably more engaged than Berlioz suggests. Hugh Macdonald reports Berlioz's first idea: "The novel idea of a viola concerto was due to Paganini, but the even more novel casting of the solo part as a personification of Harold, lost in reverie and contemplation amid diverse scenes of Italian life, was Berlioz's own, borrowing a protagonist from Byron's *Childe Harold* and a choice of scenes from his own recent memories," but he also places the theme as representing the protagonist: "The theme is of perfect classical symmetry, yielding little development, and we are forced to see Harold as an outsider, even though his theme participates in each movement."[8] Kern Holoman has written, "The symbolism, though, is decidedly non-Beethovenian: Chateaubriandesque, rather, as Harold—the physical presence of the violist as well as the part he plays—observes the action from a distance, a splenetic wanderer, perhaps somewhat aloof, whose recurring musical motive is square of form, unobtrusive, studiedly passive."[9] Here at one point the instrument itself appears to represent the figure of Harold, but so does its part, presumably throughout the symphony, and then specifically the theme.

The Music of *Harold*

In its topic, Berlioz's symphony also leads a procession of other interesting nineteenth-century travelogues. Among these—to name just a few obvious ones—we might think of Liszt's *Album d'un voyageur*, later converted to *Années de pèlerinage*, with its own literary references (see the discussion of these collections in chapter 11, especially the observations about the distinction between a simple traveler and the pilgrim on a personal quest for enlightenment, fulfillment, or redemption); Smetana's *Ma Vlast*; and Dvořák's "New World" Symphony.

Berlioz did not follow the precedent of his *Symphonie fantastique* by giving the new symphony a detailed prose program. He titled it *Harold en Italie* and the movements, respectively,

1. Harold in the Mountains, scenes of melancholy, happiness and joy.

2. Pilgrims' March, singing the evening prayer.

3. Serenade of an Abruzzi Mountaineer to His Mistress.

4. Brigands' Orgy, reminiscences [*souvenirs*] of the preceding scenes.

The first movement opens with an introductory double fugue based on a crawling subject and a descending countersubject (mm. 1ff.; example 5.1). Into this enters what will become the leading theme of the entire symphony—which Berlioz called "the Harold theme," and we might as well do the same—first alluded to in the woodwinds (mm. 14–21) and then presented clearly in the solo viola, accompanied by the harp (mm. 38–45; example 5.2), a simple, four-square thing remarkable mostly for its unremarkableness; it might reasonably be described as having the character of, to use Berlioz's own words, "une sorte de rêveur mélancolique." The main body of the movement, a sonata deformation, begins with a motive stated by the solo viola, an idea that takes a few tries to get rolling (mm. 125–38; example 5.3). Berlioz reports that one of the Paris papers reviewed the work, saying, "Ha! ha! ha!—*haro! haro! Harold!*"—the humor of which he did not find amusing.[10] This principal theme, in no way preserving the melancholy dreaminess that Berlioz's description of his idea suggests, rolls

Example 5.1. Berlioz, *Harold en Italie*, mvt. 1, mm. 1–6.

Example 5.2. Berlioz, *Harold en Italie*, mvt. 1, mm. 38–45.

along energetically in G major, the orchestra taking up the music from the solo instrument. A brief transition leads to a surging secondary theme (mm. 173–80; example 5.4), based on D but not set up firmly in that key, so that it sounds more poised on the dominant than in it. Here the viola also seizes on this theme, again contradicting Berlioz's statement that the instrument

Example 5.3. Berlioz, *Harold en Italie*, mvt. 1, mm. 125–38.

Example 5.4. Berlioz, *Harold en Italie*, mvt. 1, mm. 173–80.

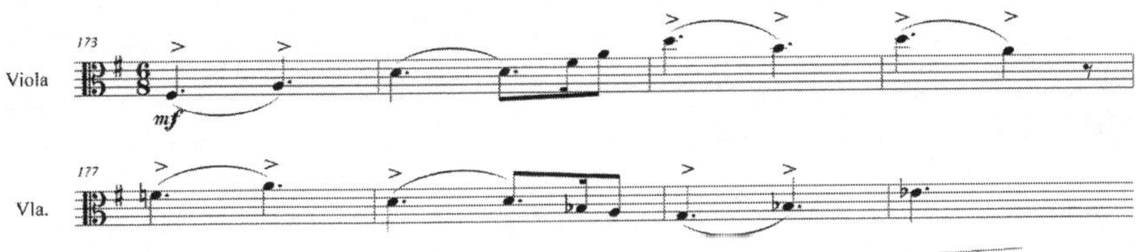

always preserves its character. This theme quickly slips back to the tonic via a first ending and repeat sign, for the repetition of the first part, or then to the dominant of D for the continuation. After development mostly based on the rollicking principal theme, the two themes return in G, although in reverse order.[11] The very long coda (mm. 323–493) reintroduces the Harold theme with further developments of the secondary and principal themes.

The extensive introduction and coda dominate this first movement. The sonata deformation that comprises the body of the movement is so attenuated as to leave the general impression that sonata plot has little importance.[12] As a consequence, the whole becomes more a scenic or characteristic episode than a plotted action. This, as we shall see, continues to be the case throughout the symphony.

The manner of the characteristic here might call to mind some mountainous passages in Childe Harold's voice from Byron's third canto:

72.

> I live not in myself, but I become
> Portion of that around me; and to me,
> High mountains are a feeling, but the hum
> Of human cities torture: . . .

75.

Are not the mountains, waves, and skies, a part
Of me and of my soul, as I of them?
Is not the love of these deep in my heart
With a pure passion? should I not contemn
All objects, if compared with these? and stem
A tide of suffering, rather than forego
Such feelings for the hard and worldly phlegm
Of those whose eyes are only turned below,
Gazing upon the ground, with thoughts which dare not glow?[13]

The function of the viola part here deserves particular attention. It introduces or points out the leading themes, and it continues with the orchestra to convey the musical/pictorial content of the entire movement. Its expressive spirit varies—so by no means representing a melancholy dreamer—as it takes a leading role in the presentation of the mountainous scenery, initially melancholy but then energetic and joyful.

The second and third movements represent scenes not in Byron but related to Berlioz's own experiences in Italy.[14] The second evokes the procession of a group of pilgrims. Recalling his wandering in the Abruzzo mountains, Berlioz writes of "rows of shrines to the Madonna crowning the high hilltops, which in the evening the late reapers follow, singing their litanies, as they are returning from the plains, to the melancholy chiming of the bell from a hidden monastery."[15] The movement belongs to the category of processional movements that also turn up in, for example, symphonies by Beethoven, Mendelssohn, Schumann, Bruckner, and Mahler (and, of course, the "March to the Scaffold" in Berlioz's own *Symphonie fantastique*). The pilgrims walk and sing in a slow 2/4 meter, with a crescendo and diminuendo as they approach and depart. The melody is simple and songlike, although with odd shifts of tonality in some of its phrases, suggesting a sort of Berliozian "tonus peregrinus": the music is in E, but the first phrase cadences on D♯, the next on E, the third on F♯, and the fourth again on E (mm. 16–55; example 5.5).

The overall form is lyrical rather than dramatic. It opens with a brief, amorphous introduction, leading to the procession melody. A return of the Harold theme, the melancholy dreamer, in the viola, clarinet, and horn (mm. 64–101) emerges over the continued plodding, and the song returns. As it concludes, the viola weaves through it in triplets. There follows a new section in which viola solo arpeggios, sul ponticello—and again, incidentally, not in any sense preserving the character that it borrowed at first from the

Example 5.5. Berlioz, *Harold en Italie*, mvt. 2, mm. 16–55.

Harold theme—together with the still-walking bass, accompany the strings in a slow-moving chordal passage with little sense of harmonic function or direction, which Berlioz marked "canto religioso" (example 5.6). The original

Example 5.6. Berlioz, *Harold en Italie*, mvt. 2, mm. 169–84.

song then returns, but gradually softer and more and more fragmented, indicating undoubtedly the last snatches of the tune heard as the pilgrims arrive at their homes and break up.[16]

The specific image employed here and the form, which gives us literal arrival and departure but not plot, again render this movement characteristic rather than dramatic. The function of the viola is first to introduce the theme of Harold into the picture. The contribution of the ponticello arpeggiations to the harmonically free-floating sacred melody—and then in fragments to the end of the movement—does not represent a human figure either active or passive in the scene. Rather, we might hear it as a coloring or quality both twilight-pale and insubstantial, the evocation of a moment when the physical world seems to blur behind a mist, providing access to a spiritual experience.

Movement 3, the Serenade of an Abruzzi Mountaineer to His Mistress, again has something of a link to an episode in Berlioz's *Mémoires*, although the musical details do not correspond at all:

> One night the most peculiar serenade that I had yet heard woke me. A *ragazzo* with vigorous lungs was yelling a love song as loud as he could under the window of his *ragazza*, with the accompaniment of an enormous mandolin, a bagpipe, and a little iron instrument like a triangle, which in the country they call *stimbalo*. His song, or rather shout, consisted of a series of four or five notes in a descending series, and ended, rising again, with a long groan from the leading tone to the tonic, without taking a breath.[17]

In the symphony's third movement we get some rustic winds and drones, but nothing like the roaring voice or descending melodic contour that Berlioz describes.

The design of this movement is quite simple. An introductory galloping passage leads to a songlike English horn solo (example 5.7) in the middle part. At the end of this, the solo viola introduces the Harold theme, and then the horns and woodwinds take up the tune of the serenade, with elaborating commentary in the form of a countermelody in the viola. (Could the viola in this countermelody be letting us in on the reaction of the sweetheart? If so, she merely speaks to herself behind the unopened curtain of her room, and nothing comes of it from the lover's point of view.) The galloping idea

Example 5.7. Berlioz, *Harold en Italie*, mvt. 3, mm. 35–48.

returns, and then a coda brings a Berliozian *réunion de thèmes*, juxtaposing all three elements; here Harold's melody is in the flute, while the viola tracks the song of the departing serenader. Once again the movement belongs to the category of the characteristic—a scenic episode and not a dramatic action. The figures encountered in it are the mountaineer and, momentarily, Harold, both represented by melodic ideas. The viola serves to introduce Harold and at the end to remind us of the serenade.

To conclude this line of observation, it will clarify the point if we leave aside for a moment the famous opening of the finale, returning to it later. First, it will be useful to attend to the main body of that movement, Brigands' Orgy,[18] appropriately "Allegro frenetico," based on a vigorous and often syncopated theme (mm. 119ff.; example 5.8). The viola remains silent through the entire body of the movement (mm. 110–483). Once the form proper begins, it calls on the conventions of sonata form, but in a rather peculiar way. It opens in G minor (m. 119), with B♭ as its contrast key, established by a variant of the principal brigands' theme (m. 164) and reinforced by a new closing theme in B♭ (mm. 178ff.; example 5.9). Development follows, beginning in B♭ minor (m. 201) and lasting about eighty measures. The reprise (starting at m. 281) is peculiar, since it follows as before from G minor to B♭ major (m. 327) rather than closing in the tonic key as expected. This has led some analyses to identify this recapitulation as a written-out repetition of the exposition, as if the movement had no part 2. In that case, the highly unstable passage of development (mm. 201–80) is, in fact, either a sort of closing theme gone wrong or a very long first ending of part 1 of the sonata form. And a good part of it also comes back after the reprise of the themes in G minor and B♭. I hear this latter passage, however, as a coda to the sonata form of the last movement, beginning at B♭ minor, like the passage that I hear as development, but now at last leading to G major (m. 450).

Example 5.8. Berlioz, *Harold en Italie*, mvt. 4, mm. 119–28.

Example 5.9. Berlioz, *Harold en Italie*, mvt. 4, mm. 178–85.

At that point there is an extensive coda, in the G major of the first movement and based on the closing theme of the finale. This coda does not belong exclusively to this movement, however, but rather to the symphony as a whole. It breaks off for a return of the pilgrims—two solo violins and a cello offstage. The viola solo enters at last for what appears to be a failed attempt to find the Harold theme (mm. 494ff.), then simply quits for about the last eighty measures.[19]

Yet again we can appropriately regard the form of the fourth movement, like the preceding ones, as evading dramatization. By failing to bring the proper resolution to the tonic in what ought to be its second half, it declines to become the plotted structure that it promises to be. Once again, all we get is the characteristic. An orgy is not a story.

Not only are the individual movements nondramatic, the entire symphony forms no particular plot either.[20] Nothing directs the events forward in the manner of Beethoven's Fifth Symphony, with its triumphant arrival in C major; the Pastoral Symphony, in which the listener arrives in the country, observes nature and the country folk, and experiences the storm and the thanksgiving afterward; the Ninth Symphony, proceeding from brutal and stubborn struggle through bacchanale and elegiac meditation to the Elysian fulfillment of the finale; or Berlioz's own *Symphonie fantastique*, which is explicitly a story. The *Harold* Symphony merely passes through a succession of distinct but arbitrarily ordered episodes.

Thus, turning back now to the lead-in to the final movement of *Harold en Italie*, it is useful to keep in mind that the preceding episodes form no plot, either within themselves or together. What happens here may look at first like a parallel to the opening of the Ode to Joy, taking up the earlier movements in order and explicitly rejecting them one by one. But, as Mark Evan Bonds has discussed in much greater detail, this is not what Berlioz gives us.[21]

In the present case, what will become the frenetic theme of the main body of the following quasi-sonata form leads off the movement, stopping after eleven measures. In measure 12 comes a quotation of the opening double fugue, the second subject played by the viola, marked in the score "Souvenir de l'introduction." The frenetic theme returns for sixteen bars, leading this time to the viola in a "Souvenir de la marche des pèlerins" (mm. 35–42). And so on in order—or, as we should better say, out of order—through citations by the viola of the mountaineer's serenade (mm. 47–54), the principal theme of the first movement's sonata form (mm. 61–71), and, with the clarinets, a fragmented treatment of the unifying Harold theme.

Now, however tempted we might find ourselves to regard this passage as reflecting what Berlioz knew of Beethoven's Ninth Symphony, which he first heard shortly before composing this music,[22] it does not at all constitute a review of the course of a plotted symphony but merely a collection of remembered fragments from events that bear no necessary chronological relationship to each other. They are isolated moments.

In fact, they are remembrances of experiences in Italy. And evidently, from the returning but not developing appearances of the unifying theme in each movement, this figure represents one present but not engaged in each of them; "Harold was he hight." Far from a Byronic pilgrimage of progressing insight or maturing character, however, the symphony's Harold simply enters each scene momentarily and passes on to another. He is not pursuing a pilgrimage but merely rambling.

In this regard the quotations that open the last movement form a collection of fragments picked up along the way, taken up here, turned over, and set down, but not seized and cast away in the manner of the quotations in Beethoven's Ninth. They are exactly what Berlioz claims: souvenirs from Harold's travels. And as a scrapbook of souvenirs, a traveler's album (to reference Liszt), or even travel memoirs (to reference Berlioz himself), they record personal observations. They do not, however, turn out to have the critical, self-examining quality of *Childe Harold's Pilgrimage*.

Voices in Byron and Berlioz

Yet we still should not give up on pursuing the relationship of *Harold en Italie* to *Childe Harold's Pilgrimage*. Having established that the symphony has no plot, it might seem curious to talk about it in terms of narrativity. Yet we do have an excellent reason to do so. In this connection it will be helpful to think a bit more about Byron's poem.

Much of *Childe Harold's Pilgrimage* represents the observations and musings of Harold as he wanders through Europe, responding to nature and reflecting on history. Byron's Harold stands in the scenes of *Childe Harold's Pilgrimage*, where he engages with those scenes and gives his mind and feeling to them. In fact, most of what we see in Byron's poem we see because Harold points it out to us, describes it, reflects on it, critiques it. In Byron's poem we do not watch the scenes ourselves; rather, we hear Harold telling us what he sees and how it affects him.[23] The figure of Harold in *Harold en Italie*, by contrast, is less affected than this. Harold appears to encounter the mountains, the pilgrims, the singing mountaineer, and the brigands but does not engage with them or experience any character development as a result. We might learn something from the extent of the Harold theme's presence in a movement, but the scenes have more impact on the attentive listener than on the Harold theme, and consequently we ourselves experience more from them than the symphony's title character seems to do. As Ian Gerg puts it, the separation of the Harold theme from the action of the movement means that Harold, whom Gerg identifies as a "virtual observing agent," does not experience "empathic attunement."[24] Curiously, Harold (the theme) is "in" Italy (the music), and yet, in the sense of who is most affected by Italy, we ourselves are Harold.[25] This makes for an unexpected understanding of Berlioz's chosen title. To the extent that the recurring theme stands farther outside the music, the listener will feel more like a participant than merely like a spectator observing a tone painting. Surely it explains our interest in the music as more than trivial sound effects.

Moreover, and significantly, we must note that Harold's voice is not the narrative voice of Byron's poem. As we heard at the beginning, Byron created a narrative persona, one who introduces Harold to us but does not at all enter into the scenes. A few passages from canto 3 will represent this narrator's presence in later parts of the poem:

8.

> Something too much of this:—but now 'tis past,
> And the spell closes with its silent seal.
> Long-absent HAROLD reappears at last;
> He of the breast which fain no more would feel,
> Wrung with the wounds which kill not, but ne'er heal; . . .

16.

> Self-exiled Harold wanders forth again,
> With naught of hope left, but with less of gloom;
> The very knowledge that he lived in vain,
> That all was over on this side the tomb,
> Had made Despair a smilingness assume,
> Which, though 'twere wild,—as on the plundered wreck
> When mariners would madly meet their doom
> With draughts intemperate on the sinking deck,—
> Did yet inspire a cheer, which he forbore to check.

52.

> Thus Harold inly said, and pass'd along,
> Yet not insensibly to all which here
> Awoke the jocund birds to early song
> In glens which might have made even exile dear:
> Though on his brow were graven lines austere,
> And tranquil sternness which had ta'en the place
> Of feelings fierier far but less severe,
> Joy was not always absent from his face,
> But o'er it in such scenes would steal with transient trace.[26]

In each of these passages, Harold appears within the scene, described in a narrative by another observer, the poet who first introduced him in the opening stanzas. This narrative voice stands outside the scene or the action, never present in it but only reporting. This makes explicit three levels: in stanza 52, the birds that sing in the glens; Harold, who listens to and feels affected by them; and the poet, who reports Harold's progress and his transient joy in contrast to his usually austere and stern state of mind.

In *Harold en Italie* the orchestra enacts what the traveler observes. The "Harold" theme locates him in each scene.[27] Berlioz's conception works like Byron's poem in those senses. Neither orchestra nor "Harold" theme represents the narrative persona. In fact, that role falls to the viola, which, as Berlioz conceived the work, operates clearly apart from the orchestra. Significantly, too, the harp is closely connected to the viola soloist. At the viola's first entrance, its melody is introduced and accompanied by the harp. We have here an unmistakable representation of the poet's opening invocation of the Muse, in which he explicitly referred to his lyre. The two instruments do not always maintain this relationship through the piece, but the effect here is clearly to establish the viola as a distinct presence, the presence of the poet/singer.

The composer's instruction for the staging of the performance adds an unmistakable visual cue to the presence of this Romantic voice in the work. For the viola, "the performer must be placed on the front of the stage, near the public and isolated from the orchestra," and for the harp, "the harp should be placed near the solo viola."[28] The location of the solo viola and the harp together and apart from the orchestra reinforces the explicitly multilayered nature of the work's discourse. Unfortunately, in most performances the viola soloist simply stands more or less where any concerto soloist would, on the conductor's immediate left, hip to the concertmaster's music stand. The harp tends to be pushed a little forward, in among the violins, but tentatively so. Performers should take Berlioz at his word and place the viola away from the orchestra, an entirely distinct voice. The clearest arrangement would put the viola and harp together, far out in the down-right corner of the stage and noticeably closer to the audience than the first violins—that is, on the audience's left and outside the proscenium arch, so that the sound comes from a different direction and the concertgoer cannot possibly miss Berlioz's idea that the viola represents a distinct voice that sets and interprets the scene.

Like Byron's narrator, the viola introduces the figure of Harold, and it recounts from the outside the traveler's own observations and thoughts. Narratologically, it constitutes a separate *plane of discourse*, one that sometimes intersects the plane where Harold and his situations are located. This way of regarding the different modes of discourse proposes an alternative to "levels" in order to imagine them as not merely parallel and always separated by a uniform distance.[29] Berlioz's linking of his symphony to *Childe Harold's Pilgrimage* is especially justified in this sense.[30]

The musical narrativity of *Harold en Italie* is complexly multidimensional. Unfortunately, as we learned earlier, even Berlioz did not describe consistently the different roles in his music of the Harold theme and the viola. And it is not possible to explain the viola's specific narrative functions by reference to *Childe Harold's Pilgrimage*. Byron's narrative persona does not—really, cannot—engage with Childe Harold's voice in the way that Berlioz's viola engages with Harold's theme and the musical situations in which it appears, particularly in simultaneous counterpoints. The narrator in *Childe Harold's Pilgrimage* does not do things like the viola does, for example in picking over souvenirs from the protagonist's travels and holding them up one by one as mementos. But that should not trouble us. We know that the symphony's scenes and episodes themselves are not tied to those in Byron's poem, and Berlioz's traveler does not appear to engage in the historical reflections, the political philosophizing, or the intense soul-searching that Byron's pilgrim does.

There remains another way in which Berlioz's narrative contrasts with Byron's, and it has to do with what Mieke Bal calls focalization.[31] As she reminds us, a narrative always has a focalizer, through whose eyes (or other senses, or mind) the narratee's information comes. Although the narrator's voice might focalize the narrative, the narrator not uncommonly reports what a character notices, and in such a case the character, not the narrator, is the focalizer. Bal thus distinguishes between character-based focalizers and external focalizers.

It should be clear that in Byron's *Childe Harold's Pilgrimage* Harold is nearly always the focalizer. We know Harold because of what he observes and what he feels and thinks. We see mountains because Harold sees them, and "high mountains are a feeling" for us because they are a feeling for Harold. Even when the narrator comments on Harold, the places on the pilgrimage are revealed through Harold's senses and responses. The narrator mentions the "jocund birds" in the "glens which might have made even exile dear," but it is Harold who focalizes them, as the transient trace of joy steals over his face, not the narrator's.

The situation is reversed in *Harold en Italie*. The theme that represents Harold does not focalize the scenes at all. When it enters, it is merely juxtaposed with the mountains or the pilgrims or the mountaineer's serenade. The Harold melody engages at times more and at times less intimately in the musical texture. In itself, however, it seems to remain untouched by them; no awe at the sublime peaks or joy at the waking birds alters it. Nor does it affect our perception of the rest of the music. If it were simply omitted, we could probably enjoy Italy perfectly well without Harold.

But this is not true of the viola, acting in its narrative function. The viola directs our attention and colors our view. For example, in the first movement, the main theme of the Allegro comes to us by a deliberate device in the viola: "Now look. . . . Look at this. . . . Now look at this here. . . . Here at last is the rollicking theme of the piece." In the middle of the pilgrims' procession the scrimmy effect of vision is the result of the viola ponticello arpeggios. This focalization is particularly effective in the codas of the movements. As the pilgrims disappear, the viola's arpeggios show the last blur of the fading twilight (mm. 327–32). At the end of the serenade the viola tracks the departure of the dejected swain (mm. 168–208). At the symphony's end the viola offers the last glimpses of the figure of Harold (mm. 491–501).

In the end, it is worth remembering, despite Berlioz's own inconsistencies in describing *Harold en Italie*, that in late-eighteenth- and nineteenth-century dramatic and narrative music, except for a few naive instances, it is themes, not instruments, that have—or, better, constitute—characters. Harmonic instability and stability lend music the contours of tension and resolution that can enable plot to unfold. Rhythmic activity, motivic fragmentations, textural juxtapositions, and the like make up musical actions. Instruments, by contrast, *present* the actions and color the scenes. Explicitly in the case of *Harold en Italie*, the scoring—specifically, in the use of the solo viola—creates the narrative persona.

It is this distinction between Harold as a figure in each scene, indicated by the theme, and the narrative presentation, embodied in the viola, that critics generally overlook.[32] Edward T. Cone, who became the pioneer of musical narratology, wrote in 1971, "This symphony really has two *idées fixes*—Harold's theme, and the solo viola itself. While the former undergoes little transformation (at least until the last movement) and represents a fixed point of view, so to speak, from which the varied musical events can be apprehended, the latter provides a highly flexible comment on the action—sometimes coinciding with the theme, sometimes invoking other melodic ideas, sometimes quite free. No doubt it is from the interaction of these two that the character of the hero is to be inferred."[33] This comes very close to locating the narrative voice on a separate plane from the character Harold, but here even Cone did not quite arrive at that essential distinction.

Ian Gerg takes a different approach to the relationship between the Harold theme and the viola: "the *narrating* Harold is not literally represented by the viola. Instead the presence of the viola represents moments when narrating agent Harold—the virtual observing agent—more directly injects himself into the musical story."[34] This somewhat distinguishes the viola from the Harold theme, but it has the complicated effect of placing the instrument in a conceptual interstice between the musical enactment of the scene (in this case the pilgrims' march) and the musical representation of Harold. Gerg's hearing makes Harold both agent and narrator throughout the symphony in general, while he asserts that the viola's function is to position Harold, so that it has the effect of making Harold both less an observing agent and less a narrator. Gerg's point seems reasonable from the single passage that he examines, measures 54–69 of the second movement, where the viola (Gerg's music example does not show that it is doubled by clarinet and horn) overlays the Harold theme on the pilgrims' march, but for the work in general it ignores the vast preponderance of the viola's music, which does not consist of the Harold theme, neglects the multiple appearances of the Harold theme in the orchestra, and disregards the crucial effect of Berlioz's placement of the solo instrument away from the orchestral action.

Another approach to the nature of narrative and the figure of Harold in *Harold en Italie* is that of Robert Hatten, who identifies a function that he identifies as "self-narratizing virtual agent," something like a musical, virtual equivalent of a first-person narrator in a work of literature.[35] This makes sense fundamentally because Harold represents a level of discourse distinct from the scenic body of the orchestral music. From this viewpoint we would imagine that Harold narrates each episode, including himself in it. Further, as Hatten suggests, we might imagine that "his impressions suggest a level of evaluative distance." It is difficult to conceptualize how we can claim to know the impressions experienced by a virtual agent, however, even a self-narratizing one. Hatten (like Gerg, and with reference to the same specific passage, but including the complete scoring of the theme for clarinet, horn, and viola) describes the degree to which the Harold theme seems to be close to or participating in the action, that is, to what extent the theme operates in the same level of discourse as the rest of the musical action. This is not quite the same thing, though, as having impressions of that action. Clearly, the Harold theme is woven into the texture of different passages in different ways, just as Harold is in the scenes of *Childe Harold's Pilgrimage*, but that reflects something like the distinction between participation and merely by-standing, or perhaps between foreground and background, in a scene. Again, however, the *Harold* Symphony's governing distinction in level of discourse, the spatial separation of the viola and harp from the orchestra, gets lost in the interpretation. Although Hatten begins by stating that "Harold is identified as a virtual agent in the music by means of his association with the solo viola and its signature theme," the role of the viola disappears in the remainder of his discussion. Yet the special feature of Byron's poem that Berlioz emulated in his symphony—the feature that makes *Harold en Italie* worth a chapter to itself—is precisely the multiple layering that places the main symphonic activity in one plane, the observable and nameable figure of Harold in another intersecting plane, and the viola as the representation of a narrator in yet another.

We should not seek too hard for direct parallels between Berlioz's work and Byron's. Though both occur in Italian locales, the episodes in the two works are not the same. Though they share some character traits, the figure of Berlioz's visitor to Italy is not Byron's Childe Harold. And the narrative personas of the two works do not resemble each other by relating to the rest of the work in precisely the same manner, which would be unreasonable in any case. In fact, the distinctive aspect of the viola's function in *Harold en Italie* is that it relates to the thematic and textural activity of the work as if on a separate plane intersecting the orchestra's recounting and the scenes themselves as from another dimension.[36] This represents a special potentiality in music, possibly more fruitful in our art than any other.

But if we do not look for artificial and really impossible parallels, we can see how the relationship suggested by Berlioz's choice of title for his symphony illuminates his work's reliance on complex intersections of discourse established in the music. A narratological treatment does enrich our understanding of what is going on in *Harold en Italie*.

Chapter 6

The Voice and the Listener

Applying Mendelssohn's Aesthetics

The Idea of Songs Without Words

Mendelssohn's songs without words raise provocative questions about musical aesthetics and particularly the aesthetics of musical voice, questions that repeatedly engaged the composer himself.[1] The oxymoronic genre designation suggests a fictive vocal song and singer as well as a potential but always only implicit poetic text. Consequently, these pieces generated an intriguing line of thinking and writing about the relationship between music and words, and thus they also raise issues about speakers and listeners.

Like the vocal song, the song without words stands outside the governing plot-based principle in Enlightenment instrumental music and the specifically narrative aesthetic of Romanticism. Because it is not a dramatically structured genre, the voice in the music is not a narrator but a lyric persona. Mendelssohn's songs without words fall into the broad category of the character piece, an instrumental music equivalent of the lyric poem.[2] Although they represent the character piece in a general sense, the songs without words differ significantly from the character pieces of both their Baroque predecessors (for example, the named pieces in the keyboard *ordres* of François Couperin) and the cycles of pieces that Schumann composed at about the same time. Baroque character pieces operated on the aesthetic assumption that they evoked affects derived from or consistent with their topics. Mendelssohn took a very different aesthetic position. At the same time, his songs without words do not join to form plotted cycles in the manner of Schumann's collections. They certainly represent character, but they go farther—they also imply a speaking character in the persona of the lyric ego of the fictive singer of the song.

In the mid-1820s, Mendelssohn composed piano character pieces, publishing in 1827 a set explicitly titled *Sieben Characterstücke*, op. 7. They manifest the young composer's mastery not of lyric expression but of counterpoint. Numbers 3 and 5 are actual fugues, while some of the others (at least 1, 2, and 4) take much of their pianism audibly from Bach's inventions and sinfonias or preludes. They lay claim to the title of "character pieces" by their headings, which name specific affects: (1) *Sanft und mit Empfindung* (Quiet and with feeling), (2) *Mit heftiger Bewegung* (With vigorous motion), (3) *Kräftig und feurig* (Powerful and fiery), (4) *Schnell und beweglich* (Fast and animated), (5) *Ernst und mit steigende Lebhaftigkeit* (Serious and with increasing animation), (6) *Sehnsüchtig* (Longingly), (7) *Leicht und luftig* (Light and airy). All these pieces take instrumental forms. Aside from the fugues and the invention-like number 4, the rest of the forms are binary. The final piece, a fine example of the Mendelssohn elf-scherzo style (closely contemporary with and in the same key as the overture to *A Midsummer Night's Dream*), clearly employs sonata form.

In 1828, as a birthday gift for his sister Fanny, Mendelssohn wrote his first piano song, which bore the title *Lied*, as would continue to be the case for such pieces later in his oeuvre. We now casually categorize these piano songs as "character pieces," but given his op. 7 as the immediate background for his first work in the new style, the composer likely intended to distinguish between the genres *Characterstück* and piano *Lied*. In both the melody-and-accompaniment texture and the avoidance of instrumental forms, the songs are lyrical rather than instrumental. More intriguingly, the title *Lied* both indicates the vocal quality of the melodic style and implies a poetic text, despite Mendelssohn's offering nothing like the paratextual indications of expressive content that he gave to the character pieces of op. 7. Titling a piano piece "A Song," as Mendelssohn did his second such piece, composed on his first visit to London for the daughter of an English friend (published later as *Lied ohne Worte*, op. 19, no. 4, MWV U 73), evokes for the music a fictive context in which there is poetic text and a voice. Neither poem nor singer appears in the score, but they should be no less fully present to the listener's imagination than the fairies in the *Midsummer Night's Dream* overture.

Schumann made a remarkable observation about Mendelssohn's songs without words in his review of Mendelssohn's second book of such pieces (op. 30). Schumann quite explicitly constructed out of the actual person of his reader a persona from whom the music should be perceived to stem. He imagines himself, any of his readers, or Mendelssohn as the pianist in a moment of inspiration at the keyboard:

Who has never sat in the twilight hour at the upright piano (a grand piano seems already too aristocratic) and in the midst of improvising unconsciously begun to sing along a gentle melody? If one were able to join the cantilena to the accompaniment in the hands alone, and most of all, if one were a Mendelssohn, the most beautiful song without words would emerge therefrom. Still more easily, if one were first to compose a text and then delete the words and thus give it to the world. That would not be right, however, but a kind of deception. One would then have to propose a test of the precision of musical expression of feeling, and induce the poet whose words one suppressed to underlay a new text to the composition of his poem. If the latter instance coincided with the former one, it would be a demonstration of the reliability of musical expression. To our songs. One perceives them as clearly as the sunlight. In sincerity and beauty of feeling the first almost equals the one in E major in the first volume, though that one flows from closer to the original source. Florestan said, "The one who has sung such a song can expect a long life, both while alive and after death; I believe it is my favorite." The two-voice accompaniment in the inner parts later here and there becomes one-voiced, whereby it avoids monotony. (That last statement sounds almost like a self-contradiction.) The second song reminds me of "Jägers Abendlied" by Goethe: "Im Felde schleich' ich still und wild, gespannt mein Feuerrohr, etc.," and its delicate, misty structure equals that of the poet. The third seems to me less significant and almost like a round in a family scene by La Fontaine, but it is pure, unadulterated wine that goes around the table, even though it is not the most full-bodied and rarest. I find the fourth especially charming, a bit sad and introspective, but in the distance it speaks hope and home. In the French edition, in all the pieces but particularly in this one, there are significant departures from the German edition, which don't appear to belong to Mendelssohn.—The next bears something undecided in its character, both in form and rhythm, and it has a corresponding effect. The last, a Venetian barcarolle, closes out the whole softly and gently. So enjoy again something from this noble spirit![3]

Schumann starts by proposing that the lyric voice might represent any of the readers of his review or the listeners to the songs without words. Later that persona takes on the figure of a fictive Mendelssohn—namely, the Mendelssohn whom Schumann envisaged as F. Meritis. Presciently, as we shall see, Schumann regarded the genre of textless song as raising the question of how effectively music alone can express a feeling.

Mendelssohn, to be sure, never imagined himself—that is, "FMB"—as the persona for his songs without words. Indeed, he formulated a striking way of understanding music, identifying the persona in a perhaps unexpected way. Marc André Souchay, a relative of Mendelssohn's wife, Cécile, wrote to the composer in 1842, asking whether he had rightly identified the emotions expressed in some of the songs without words. He suggested specific poetic ideas that he believed might lie behind each song.

> The most wonderful piano pieces that I know have for years been your *Songs Without Words*. Even when I was still a child, I found in them such distinctive feeling and penetrating emotion that they became my favorite of all piano pieces. But this deep feeling, which emerged long ago, has become ever greater, and now that I have formulated for myself a definite idea for each of these masterful works—now they give me twice the pleasure; my earlier love and fondness for them have become complete enthusiasm.
>
> Of course, I have often been laughed at for my fantastic ideas, even by people whom I had to acknowledge and honor as practicing musicians—for example, my current teacher here, the Court Chamber-musician Deichert, who will hear nothing of ideas, but only of notes! But that cannot be correct; I cannot imagine that there is no poem behind these masterful paintings. I beg you, noble sir, not to take it as arrogance if I dare to share my opinion openly with you, but rather to seek the reason for my daring in my extraordinary veneration for you and in my eagerness. I believe it would not be incorrect to say that the various meanings of the songs could perhaps be the following:

Vol. 1 [op. 19b]: no. 1 [MWV U 86], resignation; no. 2 [MWV U 80], melancholy; no. 3 [MWV U 89], scene of a *par-force* hunt; no. 4 [MWV U 73], praise of the goodness of God; no. 6 [MWV U 78], Venetian gondolier-song. *Vol. 2* [op. 30]: no. 1 [MWV U 103], depiction of a devout and thankful person who has been sought after; no. 2 [MWV U 77], hunting scene; no. 4 [MWV U 98], strong desire to go out into the world; no. 5 [MWV U 97], lullaby; no. 6 [MWV U 110], Venetian gondolier-song. *Vol. 3* [op. 38]: no. 1 [MWV U 121], boundless but unrequited love, which therefore turns into longing, pain, sadness, and despair, but always becomes peaceful again; no. 2 [MWV U 115], anxious expectation (alternating longing, anxiety, and pain); no. 3 [MWV U 107], love song; no. 4 [MWV U 120], contentment; no. 5 [MWV U 137], despair; no. 6 [MWV U 119], duet. *Vol. 4* [op. 53]: no. 2 [MWV U 109], longing; no. 3 [MWV U 144], despair; no. 5 [MWV U 153], warlike folk-song.[4]

Mendelssohn's reply has become one of his most often quoted letters, though some of its implications have not generally been fully understood:

[Words] seem to me so ambiguous, so vague, so easily misunderstood in comparison to a piece of genuine music, which fills one's soul with a thousand better things than words. That brings me to the opposite point of view from the opinion of your present teacher, who wants to know merely about pretty tones and nothing of ideas. What a piece of music that I love expresses to me are not thoughts that are too vague to be contained in words, but rather *too precise*.

Thus I find in all attempts to express these thoughts something right but also in all of them something unsatisfactory, not universal, and so it seems to me with yours, too. That is not your fault, however, but rather the fault of the words, which cannot do any better. If you ask me what I was thinking with regard to it, I tell you: just the song, as it stands. And should I also have had a certain word or certain words in mind in the case of one or another of them, then I could tell them to no other person, because the word does not mean to one person what it means to another, because only the song can say the same thing to one, arouse the same feeling in him, as in another—a feeling that does not, however, express itself by means of the same words. Resignation, melancholy, the praise of God, *par force* hunt—one person will not think of these things in the same way that another does; for one resignation will be what melancholy is to another; the third cannot formulate a true, lively impression from either word. Indeed, if a person is by nature a true, avid hunter, then for him the praise of God and the *par force* hunt would come to pretty much the same thing, and for him the sound of the horn would be effectively and genuinely the true praise of God. We would hear nothing in it except the *par force* hunt, and however much we might go round and round with him about it, we would never get anywhere. The word remains ambiguous, and we would still both understand the music correctly.[5]

Commentators have always recognized Mendelssohn's main point here. He states his belief that the ideas and feelings that music expresses are both stronger and more specific than ideas and feelings that words can communicate. While his assertion responds directly to Souchay's letter, the composer might also have recalled the experiment proposed in Schumann's review. Mendelssohn claims that a true understanding of a musical work can never be captured in words. Yet he goes farther, insisting that any attempt to convey musical meaning in words is bound to fail. In an obvious way, Mendelssohn's position is undeniable, and the treatment of the songs without words in later publications provides clear enough evidence. Table 6.1 compares the characterizations that Souchay proposed for the songs without words in the first four opus collections and the titles assigned to them in three representative English-language publications.[6]

The English titles reflect a more or less consistent tradition, representing mostly duplications or synonyms. Some degree of variation among them appears in op. 30, no. 4, MWV U 98 ("The estray," "The misguided one," "The wanderer") and op. 53, no. 5, MWV U 153 ("Song of triumph," "Folksong"), but on the whole it seems apparent that they arise from a common source. They are not entirely inconsistent with Souchay's characterizations. Mendelssohn probably had in mind precisely the observation that, for instance with op. 19, no. 1, MWV U 86, Souchay's suggestion, "resignation," seems no more or less valid than alternatives such as "sweet remembrance." Likewise, to characterize one's response to the emotional

Table 6.1. Comparison of characterizations for songs without words for opp. 19b, 30, 38, and 53

Opus number, MWV	Souchay	Gilson (ca. 1885)	Ditson/Goetschius	Schirmer/Sternberg
Op. 19, no. 1, MWV U 86	Resignation	Sweet souvenir	Fond memories	Sweet remembrance
Op. 19, no. 2, MWV U 80	Melancholy	Regret	Regrets	Regrets
Op. 19, no. 3, MWV U 89	Scene of a *par-force* hunt	Hunting song	Hunting song	Hunting-song
Op. 19, no. 4, MWV U 73	Praise of the goodness of God	Confidence	Confidence	Confidence
Op. 19, no. 6, MWV U 78	Venetian gondolier-song	Venetian barcarolle	First Venetian gondola song	Venetian boat-song no. 1
Op. 30, no. 1, MWV U 103	Depiction of a devout and thankful person who has been sought after	Contemplation	Contemplation	Contemplation
Op. 30, no. 2, MWV U 77	Hunting scene	Without repose	Without repose	Unrest
Op. 30, no. 4, MWV U 98	Strong desire to go out into the world	The estray	The misguided one	The wanderer
Op. 30, no. 5, MWV U 97	Lullaby	The brook	The brook	The brook
Op. 30, no. 6, MWV U 110	Venetian gondolier-song	Second barcarolle	Second Venetian gondola song	Venetian boat-song no. 2

continued on next page

Table 6.1. Continued.

Opus number, MWV	Souchay	Gilson (ca. 1885)	Ditson/Goetschius	Schirmer/Sternberg
Op. 38, no. 1, MWV U 121	Boundless but unrequited love, which therefore turns into longing, pain, sadness, and despair, but always becomes peaceful again	The evening star	The evening star	The evening star
Op. 38, no. 2, MWV U 115	Anxious expectation (alternating longing, anxiety, and pain)	Lost happiness	Lost happiness	Lost happiness
Op. 38, no. 3, MWV U 107	Love song	The poet's harp	The poet's harp	The poet's harp
Op. 38, no. 4, MWV U 120	Contentment	Hope	Hope	Hope
Op. 38, no. 5, MWV U 137	Despair	Passion	Appassionata	Passion
Op. 38, no. 6, MWV U 119	Duet	Duetto	Duet	Duet
Op. 53, no. 2, MWV U 109	Longing	The fleecy cloud	The cloud	The fleecy cloud[s]
Op. 53, no. 3, MWV U 144	Despair	Agitation	Presto agitato	Agitation
Op. 53, no. 5, MWV U 153	Warlike folk-song	Song of triumph	Folksong	Folk-song

content of the next piece, op. 19, no. 2, MWV U 80, as either "melancholy" or "regret" could be convincing. Mendelssohn asserts that the differences here lie not in the listener's feeling, because that must be precisely what the music conveys, but in the words one chooses to express that feeling. We can accept the differing verbal responses in such instances easily enough. In other cases, however, the characterizations differ so sharply that they justify Mendelssohn's resistance to the entire enterprise. He would assert that the inconsistent characterizations in the case of "lullaby" and "the brook" for op. 30, no. 5, MWV U 97, both reflect the same feeling despite their very different mental images. For some listeners, "the evening star" must convey the same feeling that Souchay responds to by the description "boundless but unrequited love, which therefore turns into longing, pain, sadness, and despair, but always becomes peaceful again."

We might also take the opportunity to compare Souchay's characterizations of the op. 30 songs without words to those that Schumann gave in his review. For the first piece, Schumann wrote in Florestan's voice, "The one who has sung such a song can expect a long life, both while alive and after death," an evocation not, perhaps, so very different from Souchay's "depiction of a devout and thankful person who has been sought after." Schumann compared the second to Goethe's poem "Im Felde schleich' ich still und wild," while Souchay understood it, not altogether differently, to reflect melancholy. The two differ much more about the third piece, Schumann comparing it to "a round in a family scene by La Fontaine" and Souchay a "scene of a *par-force* hunt." For the fourth, they hear a desire to go in opposite directions: Schumann, "a bit sad and introspective, but in the distance it speaks hope and home"; Souchay, "strong desire to go out into the world." Schumann hears the fifth song as having "something undecided in its character," while Souchay calls it a lullaby. Both agree, of course, that the final piece is a gondolier song.

In such cases each of the listeners might find another's verbal response mystifying, but for Mendelssohn the problem stems not from indefiniteness in the music but rather from the fact that "the word does not mean to one person what it means to another, because only the song can say the same thing to one, arouse the same feeling in him, as in another—a feeling that does not, however, express itself by means of the same words," and "however much we might go round and round with him about it, we would never get anywhere."

Mendelssohn only rarely gave titles to the songs without words. In most of his manuscripts he headed them *Lied,* more seldom *Ein Lied ohne*

Worte. He did provide titles for a few, but rather than expressing the pieces' feelings, these identify subgenres.[7] They include

- "Auf einer Gondel" (op. 19b, no. 6, MWV U 78, "On a Gondola" in the engraver's copy for Novello and "Venetianisches Gondellied" in the first edition); "Gondolierlied" and "Venetianisches Gondellied" (op. 30, no. 6, MWV U 110); "Lied auf einer Gondel" (op. posth. in A major [MWV U 136]); "Gondellied" (op. 53, no. 3, MWV U 144);[8] "Gondellied" and "Venetianisches Gondellied" (op. 62, no. 5, MWV U 151, "Venetian Barcarolle" in four-hand arrangement for Queen Victoria and Prince Albert);

- "Anderes Abendlied" (op. 53, no. 4, MWV U 114, in an album copy for Ignaz Moscheles with reference to that album's immediately preceding vocal "Abendlied," i.e., "Auf Flügeln des Gesanges");

- "Duett ohne Worte" (op. 38, no. 6, MWV U 119);

- "Volkslied" (op. 53, no. 5, MWV U 153);

- "Frühlingslied" (op. 62, no. 6, MWV U 161, indicated on a list of the complete songs without words in a printing from the original plates of op. 19b but not used as a heading for the actual music in the print);

- "Reiter-Lied" (op. posth. in D minor, MWV U 187); and

- "Kinderstück" (op. 102, nos. 3 and 5, MWV U 195, U 194, published posthumously as Lieder ohne Worte; in Schirmer edition titled "Tarantella" and "The Joyous Peasant," respectively).

Mendelssohn also seems to have acknowledged in his letter to Souchay that we could all recognize the genre of a hunting song. Notably, the title "Funeral March" (Trauermarsch), op. 62, no. 3, MWV U 177, does not stem from Mendelssohn himself, but genre identification and implicit expressive content are obvious—so obvious, in fact, that Ignaz Moscheles transcribed it for wind band, and it was used at Mendelssohn's funeral in Leipzig on November 7, 1847.[9]

As important to Mendelssohn's aesthetic as the pointlessness of using words to communicate about music is the belief that the idea or meaning expressed in music is identical for every listener. The content of the music is immanent in it, and thus, in the composer's aesthetic conception, the listener must experience the emotion directly as her or his own. That Mendelssohn credited each listener with a true understanding of the work comes through clearly in a letter to Josephine von Miller, regarding an unpublished piano song that he had written out for her (MWV U 88):

> You want to know from me words to the little song in A major that I left behind with you. But how could I begin to discover such things for it? For this is exactly the main issue with such a song without words, that each person thinks of one's own words and one's own sense in it and sets it for oneself with one's own words. I have indeed done this, too, but only very disjointedly, here and there just one word on one note, then again a cluster of notes without any words, then again words with no sense—and that I may certainly not write for you in such a fashion, particularly when it properly achieves the sense. Therefore just discover the verses for yourself; I certainly know that you understand the meaning, even if you deny it or, to put it in your words, "despite all modesty," and if you should not know it, then the entire song is useless and unsuccessful. I would then promise solemnly to bring you a better one this fall, that would articulate its state of mind more clearly than this one perhaps does.[10]

Mendelssohn refused to provide words for the piece, but he did not discourage Fräulein von Miller from finding words of her own.[11] John Michael Cooper perhaps takes too seriously Mendelssohn's statement here as sincere encouragement to von Miller to formulate a verbal text for the music, but the composer certainly allowed her to go ahead and do so, although clearly only for herself. He believed that she would understand the music, and undoubtedly he would hope this for every listener. We should notice that in suggesting to her that she should find her own verses to the song, he slips neatly from stating his confidence that she understands (*verstehen*) the piece to saying that if she does not know (*wissen*) the song's meaning (*Bedeutung*) or, as earlier in the discussion, its sense (*Sinn*), then the music must have failed. To succeed, the song should clearly speak its state of mind (*seine Stimmung aussprechen*). Importantly, Mendelssohn never states that the music's goal should convey to the listener the composer's, or anyone else's, thoughts or feelings. If we take him at his word, his ideal is always that *the music articulates* something that *the listener knows.*

Because the music actually articulates something that the hearer knows, then as an inevitable consequence, when one truly hears a piece, one must subconsciously or fictively be identifying oneself as the lyric persona in the music of the song. Verbal responses, then, constitute reflections, although inadequate ones, of a listener's own thought or emotion, determined by the music, and in the aesthetic sense the actual listener becomes the fictive singer of the (wordless) song, experiencing her or his own poetic moment. So perhaps Schumann's fantasy was not so far wrong—the idea that one understands Mendelssohn's songs without words in imagining one's own words is perfectly consistent with Mendelssohn's aesthetic claims.

Frieder Reininghaus aptly noted that a song without words represents an intimate, personal moment of musical experience. In discussing the "Funeral March," op. 62, no. 3, MWV U 177, he remarked that although the music invokes an orchestral or wind-band scoring, it is nevertheless scored for an intensely individual setting. He observed, and this applies to all Mendelssohn's songs without words, that the piece is "completely individualized for the pianist alone, for a hermetically closed off, private sphere. To be sure, Mendelssohn's piano work is speechless in a conceptual sense; nevertheless, it enables [*vermag*, perhaps even in the sense of inducing] discourse."[12] The expressive content of the music arises in the individual playing and hearing the song, in the absence of or even disregarding anyone else. The music must come as the utterance of the one who experiences it.

Experiencing Voice in a Song Without Words

If in the personal experience of a song without words the listener (or the domestic piano player in Schumann's scenario) knows precisely what the music expresses and experiences it as her or his own feeling, and if we acknowledge at the same time the impossibility of capturing that content in words, how might we deal with that music and that experience of feeling? The following discussion takes as an example the Song Without Words op. 53, no. 2, MWV U 109, characterized by Souchay as "longing," in the English publications titled "The Cloud" or "The Fleecy Cloud(s)," and in at least one modern compact-disc release titled "Widmung"[13] (dedication; Mendelssohn sent the autograph score to Clara Schumann). I examine closely the piece's specific expressive elements for the player and listener, but I take care to avoid verbal translation, characterization, or interpretation of that expression. I aim to bring to the fore the way in which one exemplary song without words, modest yet meaning-filled, manifests what Mendelssohn identifies as its sense (*Sinn*). In terms of approach, the nature of the relationship of specific musical features to the sense of any piece could be demonstrated equally well by other songs without words or, really, any musical work.

This suggests a sort of phenomenological approach to analysis, following the piece's expressive materials through our experience. I attend to the course of the music from beginning to end rather than, as one might, diagramming the overall structure of the piece to show its form or plot. At the same time, I mean to offer more than a meaningless list of musical details. My intention is to demonstrate how we might follow the aspects of the piece that determine the sense (*Sinn*) that we will find one knows (*weisst*) in the music or—to say the same thing in another way—how the twilight extemporization that Schumann imagines generates expressive content.

To begin, the first four measures plus the downbeat of measure 5 (example 6.1) simply play through a basic harmonic framework of chord functions in E♭: I—I6—ii7—V7—I. In itself this progression is expressively neutral. Rhythmically, however, starting at the opening beat the accompaniment of repeated-chord triplets at an allegro tempo requires the pianist to generate, and therefore express, persistent energy. The melody unfolds in duplet motion rather than triplets, so that the accompaniment rhythm drops into the background as a rapidly pulsing vibration but not the prominent rhythmic subdivision. The melodic line proceeds (i.e., Schumann's player conducts it) over the harmonic progression by outlining the triads, enriching them with various nonchord tones. Over the E♭ in the first two measures the melody ascends from G4 through B♭4 to E♭5. The triadic outline is

Example 6.1. Mendelssohn, *Lied ohne Worte*, op. 53, no. 2, MWV U 109, mm. 1–5.

filled in by successive passing tones, first sliding chromatically through A♭4 and A♮4, then stepping diatonically through C5 and D5. The ascent thus accelerates over the melody's first measure and a half. A natural crescendo supports this melodic gesture. The phrase reaches its climax at the start of measure 3, an appoggiatura G5, sforzando and tenuto, above the F-minor seventh chord. The player feels this first nonadjacent melody note as the skip from her third finger on E♭ to her fifth on G as she reaches both the limit of her hand and the peak of the phrase. The listener would note with some degree of surprise the melodic "overshot" as the line skips to the G5 rather than proceeding by step, as might naturally be expected, from E♭5 to F5. The appoggiatura's resolution redirects the line downward linearly, with a decrescendo to the phrase's end. The melody passes through chord tones F5 and E♭5 and the nonchord tone D5 over the ii7 harmony. Against the V7 in measure 4, accented nonchord tones come at the beginning of each beat: C5 is an appoggiatura or accented passing tone to B♭4, A♮4 is an accented chromatic passing tone to A♭4 (the counterpart to its direction in measure 1), and, still more intensely, C5 is a free nonchord tone before A♭4 returns,[14] slipping back to G4, now *piano*, on the downbeat of measure 5, the third of the tonic harmony as at its initial iteration. The emotive content of this first phrase comes from the combination of the grounded harmony in a straightforward progression in E♭, the melody's rhythmic independence from the accompaniment's quicker pulsations, the arching melodic and corresponding dynamic contour, the shift from chromatic to diatonic motion, and the thrill of the overshot to the appoggiatura G5 at the climax and the abating descent, as well as the stressed nonchord tones, both the paired passing tones in the ascent and the various types of dissonance in the descent. The player will feel the expressive content of the phrase in the energy necessary to animate the pulsing accompaniment, the rhythmic separation of her right hand from that pulse, and the comfortable way that the melodic line accommodates her hand in closed positions.

The next phrase (example 6.2) introduces a change of style and expression. In the right hand comes a leap from G4 to E♭5 with three iterations

Example 6.2. Mendelssohn, *Lied ohne Worte*, op. 53, no. 2, MWV U 109, mm. 5b–10.

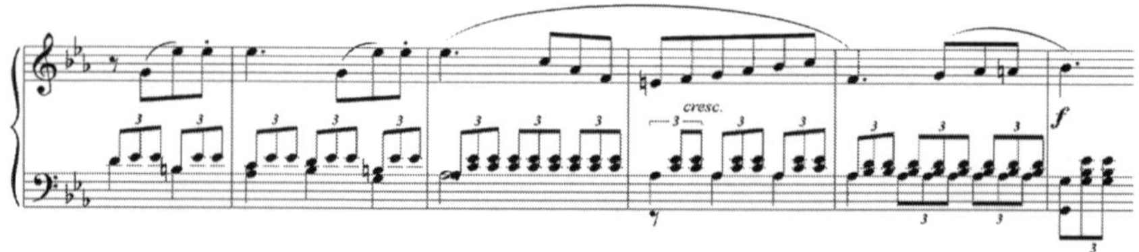

of the upper note, and this static motive is repeated (suggesting indecision, a reflective pause, or even emphasis) before the melody continues. Meanwhile, the harmonic rhythm moves more quickly than the pace of a single chord per measure that has dominated up to this point, while a changing-tone motion in the lowest voice underlines the descent from E♭ through C minor to A♭. It rests on the subdominant and ii $^6_5$ for two measures, changing to V $^4_2$ as the bass maintains the pitch A♭3. In measures 7 and 8, the right hand outlines the F-minor seventh, first as an arpeggiated descent from E♭5 to F4, then with a crescendo through a scalar ascent with nonchord tones on the beats, recalling the accented dissonances in measure 4 but now taking the opposite melodic and dynamic direction, thus inverting the arch formed by the melody of the first four measures. The rhythmic sensation between the hands and the comfortable hand positions resemble those in the opening measures, so that the general expressive content both complements and contrasts with the start of the piece.

The opening of the song returns in measures 10–15, which repeat measures 2–7 with only a slight alteration (D♭4 rather than D♮4 in the left hand in measures 13–14, leaning more toward the subdominant). The end of this phrase introduces a strong conclusion to the first part of the piece. At measure 16, the music condenses the ii $^6_5$ and V7 from measures 8–9, and then measures 18–19 present a cadential progression through vi, IV, and ii in two-beat groupings (each harmony intensified by a preceding applied dominant), producing a hemiola that increases the rate of harmonic motion (example 6.3). A descending melodic sequence in four-eighth-note groupings matches the harmonic acceleration. In this sequential pattern, appoggiaturas fall regularly on the first eighth note of each group of four, producing a harmonic accent that strengthens the hemiola. The melodic patterns lie comfortably under the player's fingers (4 3 2 1 4 3 2 1 . . .). At measure 20, the accompaniment's triplet and the melody's duplets give way to a simple, chorale-style cadence on E♭ at measure 21.

Example 6.3. Mendelssohn, *Lied ohne Worte*, op. 53, no. 2, MWV U 109, mm. 17–21.

This passage brings together the elements that determine the sense of the piece as a whole, producing its expressive content, unnameable as that must be—and, it should be emphasized, unnamed here. The player or listener experiences the coalescence of the fluent pianistic idiom, rhythmic juxtapositions, simple and forward-directed harmonic and melodic motion, rising and falling gestures supported by reinforcing dynamics, and prominent strong-beat dissonances in the melody.

As the song continues, these features persist, along with additional ones. Rather than rehearse the continuing elements in itemized detail, we can highlight some new developments. First, at the second half of measure 21 the left hand assumes an active part in presenting the melodic material, creating a dialogue with the right hand. Measures 23–29 unfold over F3, the root of ii and V/V in the song's tonic E♭ (example 6.4). Particularly remarkable are the nonchord tones in measures 26–28, where the right hand plays a pianistically comfortable sequential pattern descending by thirds. This begins in measure 26 with pitches entirely dissonant against the F-minor triad: B♭5 G♭5 E♭5 D♭5. As the sequence descends, the dissonances become fewer—in measure 27, G♭5 E♭5 C5 B♭4, where the C is a chord tone; and in measure 28, E♭5 C5 A♭4 G♭4, with both C and A♭ members of the triad. The minor mode then takes over, leading to cadences in E♭ minor at measure 33 and A♭ minor in 41. The music then idles in E♭ minor on a $^6_4$ over B♭ embellished or, perhaps better, deferred by the iv6, after which diminished sevenths on A and D lead in the reprise of the opening at measure 50. Problematic as it would seem to claim—or even try—to discover a verbal characterization of the first twenty measures of the song, the next thirty have elaborated and intensified the feeling.

The piece's opening returns, dolce, leading into measure 50. Instead of recapitulating the first part completely, the music elides away measures 8–15. The sixteen-measure coda relies on only ii (or V/V), V, and I harmonies.

Example 6.4. Mendelssohn, *Lied ohne Worte*, op. 53, no. 2, MWV U 109, mm. 26–29.

The three-eighth-note lead-in gestures in the left hand duet with a narrow-range, mostly quarter-note melody in the right. The melodic activity then decelerates and collapses onto a repetitious figure of E♭4 embellished by changing notes F4 and D4, except that its last iteration substitutes for the F4 an unexpected bit of energy: a dotted-eighth/sixteenth-note rhythm and leap to A♭4. Whereas the middle of the piece brought intensification, the coda offers a reduction of intensity in both melody and harmony.

The final tonic chord arrives in measure 73 (example 6.5). Here the song's opening ascent appears for a final time, supported by the constant root-position E♭ chord. At the peak of the phrase, the fifth-finger G5, which constituted the characteristic dissonant appoggiatura of measure 3 and each of its subsequent occurrences, now becomes a chord tone, the third of the tonic triad. No longer requiring resolution, it sustains for two measures while the pulses of the triad in the left hand slow from triplets to full beats, notated as eighth notes separated by eighth rests, although with the damper pedal depressed. At the last note of the piece the right hand drops from G5 to E♭5, supported only by E♭2 in the bass, still with the tonic triad (and the high G5?) kept reverberating by the pedal, under a fermata. We may presume that fictive extemporizing pianist at twilight—unlike a performer who would need to go on to another piece on a recital program, and where there is no audience expecting to applaud—could continue the fermata as long as the sound lasts, and perhaps even beyond that.

A variety of style features combine to make Mendelssohn's *Lied* in E♭ meaningful—*Sinnvoll*, if you will. In Mendelssohn's thinking, the sense of the music is both precise and unmistakable, and the player or listener must know its inherently explicit meaning. To exactly the extent that the music expresses its content unmistakably, however, it inevitably resists translation or even paraphrase in words. Performing and perceiving this piece should make obvious how vague and inadequate are titles such as "longing" or "the fleecy clouds."

Example 6.5. Mendelssohn, *Lied ohne Worte*, op. 53, no. 2, MWV U 109, mm. 73–77.

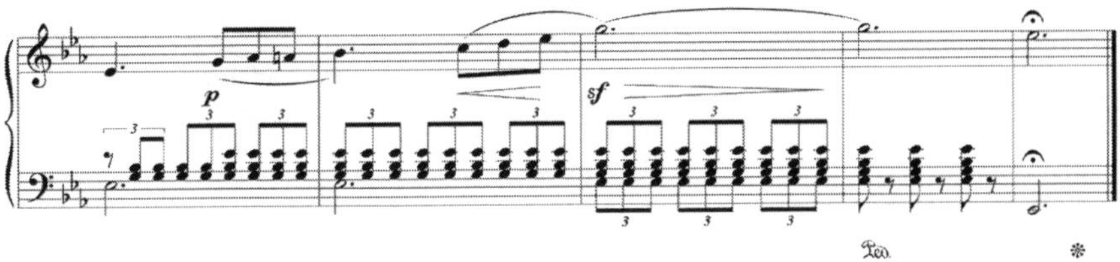

Further Observations About Music and Words

Mendelssohn accepted, albeit with some ambivalence, that listeners would respond with their own words to the feelings that the music expresses—that is, the feelings that the listeners perceive. The songs were without words, but their listeners certainly were not. Souchay's characterizations and the verses that Josephine von Miller might have made for the pieces form only a small part of the evidence for this. Christa Jost lists six published sets of selections from Mendelssohn's songs without words *with* words, stretching from 1842 to 1900, and discusses a vocal quartet setting in English based on op. 62, no. 4, MWV U 175, by Charles A. C. Wilson. R. Larry Todd also describes several instances in which anonymous poets added words to Mendelssohn's songs without them. He even left some abortive attempts of his own.[15] These settings strikingly validate Mendelssohn's judgment—they represent individuals' sincere responses to his pieces, but none comes close to an adequate expression of its meaning. John Michael Cooper proposes that it was in fact the inadequacy of the first set of published text versions of his songs without words, that of Karl Christern, who added poetically unsatisfactory poems to the music, that led Mendelssohn to adopt the position of discouraging such attempts.[16]

We know from his own admission that Mendelssohn himself engaged in such impositions of words on the piano songs. His remark in the letter to Josephine von Miller that "I have indeed done this, too, but only very disjointedly, here and there just one word on one note, then again a cluster of notes without any words, then again words with no sense" suggests only isolated jottings, however, and not any serious attempt to create a singable text, nor, as he mentions, anything that he might have shared with anyone else. A remark from Fanny Hensel to Felix in a letter of September 7, 1838, indicates that the two tried this sort of thing when they were quite young:

> Dear Felix, when the words are removed from vocal songs in order to use them as concert pieces, that is a true counterpart to the experiment of underlaying words to your instrumental songs, the other half of a looking-glass world. . . . Now should one not possess an enormous opinion of oneself (no, one shouldn't), when one sees the games with which we occupied our time as half children now reinvented by the grand talents and used as fodder for the public?[17]

(It is conceivable that Fanny's "we" refers not only to herself and Felix but also to a common diversion of children generally, who often make up words to tunes.)

An intriguing draft by Mendelssohn of a brief piano andante in A major, MWV U 76, is preserved in the composer's *Nachlass*, dated June 13, 1830, which he then copied into a letter that he sent to Fanny the next day, referring to it there as a "Lied" (example 6.6).[18] After the end of the draft and its date there appear four brief lines of text:

Wende ab
Wohl muß ich sein so ferne,
Wohl seh ich sie so gerne,
doch Alles

"Turn away / I must indeed be distant / I would so like to see her / But everything . . ."

Jost and Cooper suggest that these lines represent an incomplete attempt by Mendelssohn to write a poem to go with the music, and Cooper shows

Example 6.6. Mendelssohn, Andante, MWV U 76, Mendelssohn-*Nachlass*, 18:9.

how the diction of the words might correspond to some of the phrases of the melody.[19] If the intention were to create a vocal song, however, the likely place to enter the words would have been above the staff rather than separately at the end of the draft. Instead, they might have been intended to respond to the spirit of the music, in the manner of Souchay's attempts. The experience of being parted from a loved one is explicit in the letter from Felix to Fanny: "I would like to be with you and see you and tell you something, but that is impossible. So I have written out a song for you, as I would like to and mean to; in doing so I thought of you, and it made me feel very tender."[20] If Cooper is correct that Mendelssohn's strong rejection of the idea of imposing words on his piano songs emerged only a decade later, then it is reasonable to take this manuscript as evidence that he had not yet developed that aversion. Even though not intended to be sung, the words might seem a credible response to the feeling in the piece. The overall character arises from the andante tempo, the shading toward B minor, the textural evocation of the choral *Volkslied,* some post-horn-like successions of triads, sighing suspensions, and perhaps most of all the fading of dynamics, tempo, and harmony on the open-ended half-cadence. The unfinished thought at the end of Mendelssohn's inscription ("doch Alles . . .") does not fit the rhythm of the music at the end of the piece closely enough to be sung to the last phrase, but it shares its incompleteness.

Jost and Todd also discuss one instance in which Mendelssohn himself engaged in the transformation of a song without words into one with words.[21] In 1836 Mendelssohn composed a piano Lied in F-sharp minor, which was not included in any of his published books of songs without words. In 1844 the composer's close friend Carl Klingemann worked with him to adapt the music into a vocal duet, published as the "Herbstlied," op. 63, no. 4, MWV J 11. Todd shows how the imagery and sense of the text developed over the process of revision to intensify the idea of the passing of the seasons as a metaphor for the experience of loss and longing.[22] We might speculate that the changes to the text represent attempts to bring the poetry closer to capturing the precise content of the music, although it seems more likely that the revisions were intended simply to create a better poem.

These textings of songs without words raise another issue, the relationship of music and words in vocal songs. Despite the usual compositional chronology by which songs are created, in which the poem preexists the music, so that we are accustomed to thinking of the music as setting the words, in the Mendelssohnian aesthetic the song should be experienced as a case of feeling, determined by the music, that evokes the song's words as one compelling verbal response. The implication of Mendelssohn's position is that the song composer succeeds by reading poetry in a way that grasps the underlying feeling that motivated a poem and discovering music that constitutes that inspiring feeling. Mendelssohn captured this view of the song composer's role in a letter on January 2, 1831, to Klingemann, who wrote the poems for several of Mendelssohn's vocal Lieder: "With your words I have the special feeling that I do not need to *create* any music; it is as if I read it [the music] between the lines [of the poem], and as though it were already standing before me."[23]

This has equal significance for the singer, for if the music does constitute the feeling, then it must do so for the singer, and the singer therefore represents a lyric speaker who responds to the emotive content of the music by singing the words. The song's persona, as embodied in the singer, is one who experiences a feeling precisely and immediately, through music rather than through poetry, and whose thoughts and ideas arising from that feeling are responded to in words. This is why the singer must never begin to sing without first hearing the music genuinely and deeply—the music constitutes the feeling that motivates the singing.

The aesthetic premise, although it arose from the idiosyncratic genre of songs without words, extends beyond those pieces and the companion genre of the vocal song. The fact that in music listeners experience feeling in the most direct way must apply to all other works, as well. We should certainly approach all of Mendelssohn's music from this perspective.[24] The performer of any vocal work ought to hear and feel the music in such a way as to become the fictive poetic speaker whose words that music generates. This applies as much to performing the role of Elijah in Mendelssohn's oratorio as to the singing of his most modest Lied. Even choral singers ought to understand their role in this way. For listeners, likewise, the feeling in the music of any vocal work must be heard as their own, shared with the singer, whose words are the particular response shared at that moment.

Mendelssohn's aesthetic stance applies to all instrumental works, as well. The music of a Mendelssohn symphony or piano trio forms just as valid an instance of music that "expresses . . . not thoughts that are too *vague* to be contained in words, but rather too *precise*." Because music "says the same thing to one, arouses the same feeling in him, as in another," any listener who grasps the music should have the experience of becoming fictively the narrative voice of the plotted work. At the same time, however, because the feeling "does not, however, express itself by means of the same words," any effort to characterize the content of an instrumental work is limited by the fact that the music embodies its ideas and feelings perfectly clearly, while words can only constitute vague attempts at individual responses to those ideas and feelings.

For one who can accept Mendelssohn's aesthetic premise, this principle would govern not only Mendelssohn's works but those of any composer. The skeptic might object on the grounds that we should apply different aesthetic presuppositions to different music. Mendelssohn would disagree, however. The composer wrote to Souchay not just about the songs without words or about his own music. He claimed to be writing about "what *a piece of music that I love* expresses to me" (italics added). Nevertheless, he could not name, except in the music itself, the content that the piece expresses. Johann Peter Lyser, who tried to propose words for some of Mendelssohn's songs without words, perhaps put it best: "I soon perceived that Mendelssohn's songs without words would more correctly be described as '*feelings for which there are no words.*'"[25] This truth must frustrate any listener who would share Marc André Souchay's wish for verbal elucidation, but Mendelssohn assures us that as listeners we experience the feelings in the music directly as our own. Any perceptive listener would "still understand the music correctly," as he wrote to Souchay, or would "know" the music in its meaning or sense, as he wrote to Josephine von Miller. There is no separation, then, between narratee and narrator, between the actual hearer and the fictive speaker.

Chapter 7

The Poet Speaks in the Song Cycle
Schumann's Eichendorff *Liederkreis*

Constructing Schumann's Eichendorff Cycle

Like Schubert's Heine song cycle discussed in chapter 3, Schumann's Eichendorff *Liederkreis* also manifests an absence of chronological continuity. Unlike
Schubert with Heine's *Heimkehr* poems, however, Schumann chose poems
that Eichendorff never intended as related in any way. They intermingle
texts of which some had appeared as embedded songs within various of
Eichendorff's novels and others as independent single lyrics. The texts were
treated as entirely independent entities and organized by Eichendorff's friend
the literary historian Adolf Schöll, who compiled them within various categories, without regard to their original contexts, in the *Gedichte von Joseph
Freiherr von Eichendorff*.[1] Clara Schumann copied them, presumably with
input from Robert, from that publication into a collection of poems for use
as song texts, although Schumann would already have known at least some
of these texts from his earlier reading of Eichendorff's novels.[2]

Since the songs do not follow any sequence within the poet's work,
there is no question of an order based on the literary sources. Schumann did
manipulate the succession of the songs, however, during an extended creative
process from the copying of the poems in the order in which they occurred
in the Eichendorff/Schöll collection, to the actual order of composing the
songs, to a first publication in 1842, and finally to the second edition in
1850. Schumann's obviously intentional placement of the songs disallows the
kind of reorganization that critics have applied to Schubert's Heine Lieder.

Yet the plan unfolds no story line or causal connections. Indeed, between the two published editions of Schumann's *Liederkreis* the textual and musical content changed, because the composer replaced the opening song of the 1842 version, "Der frohe Wandersmann," with a different one that he had composed along with the others but then left aside until 1850, "In der Fremde (I)."[3] To the extent that critics find reason in the poetic sequence, this appears to be limited to a general pair of trajectories dividing the twelve songs into two arcs of six each, grouped around contrasting moods: first, melancholy that yields to happy anticipation; second, a troubled mind eventually replaced by ecstatic fulfillment. The texts of op. 39 are replete with recurring images—night (and moon and stars), twilight, forest, birdsong, garden, castle, wedding, solitude—but these fill Eichendorff's poetry and that of his contemporaries, so it is difficult to argue that they constitute distinctively unifying themes for this cycle.[4]

Unlike the case of Schubert's Heine songs, we have the authority of Schumann's title itself to confirm that the *Liederkreis von Joseph Freiherrn von Eichendorff*, op. 39, is a bona fide cycle. John Daverio included op. 39 among the works by which he considered Schumann to have "established the ideal type" of the song cycle.[5] How we should understand the title remains an open question, however. David Ferris's observation "it is a question of how the ambiguous status of the song leads us to expect and ever yearn for the context of a larger whole within which we can make definitive sense of it" applies to the status of songs and cycles in general, and certainly to this work.[6] As Benedict Taylor notes, "The reception of Schumann's *Liederkreis* reveals how much the desire for coherence is ingrained in our expectations of narrative and psychological identity."[7] In this regard the location and identity of the lyric voice become central.

As mentioned earlier, some degree of poetic coherence among the twelve poems that Robert chose, presumably with direct help from Clara, who copied them into a book of texts to be set as songs, arises from the recurring ideas and images spread across them. More than one commentator has observed, however, that the symbolic network that pervades the poetry is shared by German Romantic lyric poetry in general, and especially throughout the poems of Eichendorff. As we have already noted, Jürgen Thym suggests that the topics in these songs are so typical that their recurrences might, in fact, not signify much.[8] Schumann's chosen poems bring this network to such a density, though, that it draws attention to itself. Wilhelm Killmayer condenses the characteristic Eichendorffian themes humorously into a single run-on sentence: "He luxuriates in a journeyman's happiness, in which, with a cheerful eye on a jolly journey in the fresh air, he gets mixed up in an antique affair of the nobility, where, in the moon's glow in the valley, he sees an old castle lying, in whose garden, full of roses, white and red, his beloved seems to be waiting for him, although she is dead, and the nightingales want to tell him something of the beautiful ancient time."[9] Yet the very conspicuousness of the type that Schumann draws together in his chosen poems—though not in such a tongue-in-cheek fashion—helps to create cyclical coherence.

Without developing any schematic, thoroughgoing, formal structure, op. 39 nevertheless incorporates plenty of musical markers of cyclicity for previous commentators who have placed such evidence ahead of the question of the work's voice, or even of the poetic content itself. Harmonically, the twelve songs connect by both close relationships between adjacent numbers and a palindromic design of the first three and last three keys. Table 7.1 shows only the closest relationships—parallel major/minor, dominant and subdominant. Only "Die Stille" relates more distantly to its neighbors, as a third relation appearing parenthetically between two songs in the same key. The palindromic beginning and ending encourage the analyst to consider

Table 7.1. Some tonal relationships in Schumann's Eichendorff *Liederkreis*

Song	Key	Close adjacent relationships	Partial palindromic design
In der Fremde (I)	f♯		Parallel key to no. 12
Intermezzo	A	Relative major of no. 1	Same key as no. 11
Waldesgespräch	E	Dominant of no. 2	Parallel key to no. 10
Die Stille	G		
Mondnacht	E	Return to key of no. 3	
Schöne Fremde	B	Dominant of nos. 5, 7	
Auf einer Burg	e	Ends on E major, dominant of no. 8	
In der Fremde (II)	a	Subdominant to no. 7	
Wehmuth	E	Dominant of no. 8	
Zwielicht	e	Parallel key to no. 9	Parallel key to no. 3
Im Walde	A	Subdominant major to no. 10	Same key as no. 2
Frühlingsnacht	F♯		Parallel key to no. 1

the implication that the concept of cycle at least applies to the twelve songs in the sense of a circular tonal plan that departs from and returns along partly the same path to F♯. The central six songs do not abide by that simple schema, but instead they center to some extent on E—the major and minor forms of that key, the dominant of both (B), and the relative major (G) and subdominant (a) of the minor.

In addition to the apparent harmonic plan, several analyses have demonstrated that one might easily identify recurring melodic motives linking certain songs.[10] One of these, a rising and falling fifth, belongs mainly to the piano part. It emerges in the first song (mm. 10–11) as a rising and falling fifth, B4 – F♯5 – B4. In no. 2, the same interval, rising but not falling back, is the first sound in the treble staff in the piano. The falling fifth sounds prominently in the bass in no. 5 (see mm. 10–13, B3 – E3 and B2 – E2, and the parallel positions in later stanzas). In no. 6, the rising and falling motive occurs as both a fourth and a fifth: A♯4 – D♯5 – A♯4 (mm. 1, 7, 11), F♯4 – C♯5 – F♯4 (mm. 4, 13, 18), and at the original pitches B4 – F♯5 – B4 (m. 20). At the end of the song, it expands to a sixth, F♯4 – D♯5 – F♯4 (mm. 24, 26, 28) and two octaves lower in the penultimate bar (m. 29). Along the way it develops into a rising leap of a sixth answered by a scalar descent, B4 – G♯5 – F♯5 – E5 – D♯5 – C♯5 – B4 (mm. 21–22 in unison between piano and voice; example 7.1).

Example 7.1. Schumann, Eichendorff *Liederkreis,* unifying motivic gestures in piano parts.

Example 7.1a. No. 1, "In der Fremde," piano, mm. 10–11.

Example 7.1b. No. 2, "Intermezzo," piano, mm. 1–5.

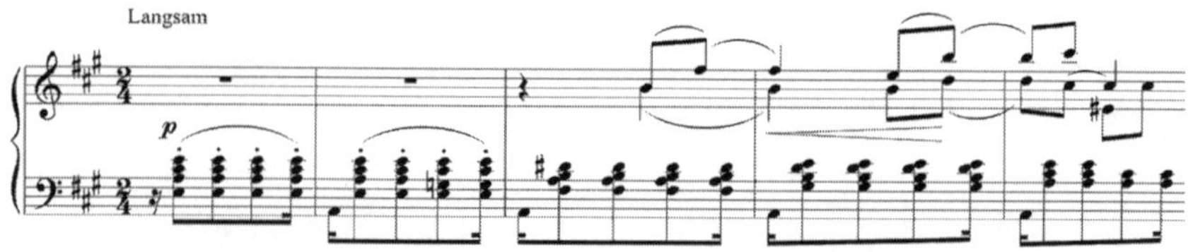

Example 7.1c. No. 5, "Mondnacht," piano, mm. 10–13.

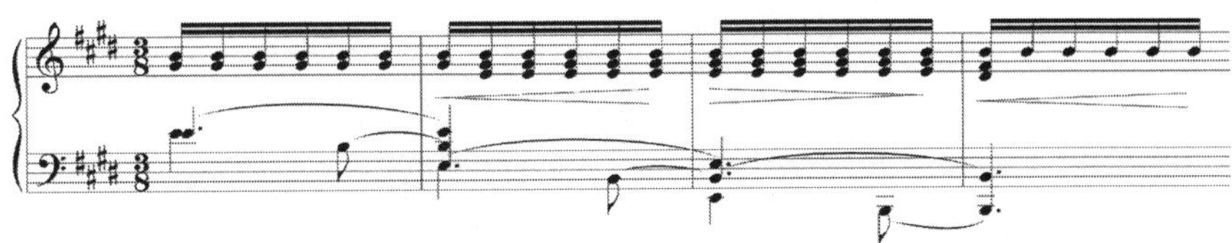

Example 7.1d. No. 6, "Schöne Fremde," piano, mm. 1–7, 20–30.

Eventually, this last form, leaping and then descending by step, recurs in the piano part of the last song, with the opening leap appearing as a fourth (A♯4 – D♯5 etc. in mm. 10 and 12), a seventh (C♯5 – B5 etc. in m. 24), and a fifth (C♯3 – G♯3 etc. in mm. 26 and 28).

Example 7.1d. Continued.

At least one vocal motive emerges clearly, connecting songs nos. 7 and 8, in both cases with piano support. This motive would govern the melodic design of each song, even if one considered each one singly. As it appears directly at the beginnings of the two songs consecutively, it is unmistakable. In both melodies the vocal line drops a fifth (perhaps connecting this motive to the piano motive previously discussed) from a dotted note in duple meter,

Example 7.2. Schumann, motivic connection between nos. 6 and 7.

Example 7.2a. No. 7, "Auf einer Burg," voice, mm. 1–2.

Example 7.2b. No. 8, "In der Fremde," voice, mm. 1–3.

pauses for note repetition on the lower pitch, and then ascends by steps to the third scale degree in the minor key (example 7.2).[11]

It should go without saying that all these tonal and melodic features, which analysts accurately perceive, in themselves would support an argument for the cyclicity of the *Liederkreis* only by way of mere musical artifice rather than by poetic content. As was the case with Schubert's Heine songs, we should rather regard these observations as potentially useful supporting evidence for a stronger argument based on the expressive content and the voice that actually make the work coherent.

The Plotless *Liederkreis*

Despite the recurrent poetic topics and musical devices that contribute to its unity, the Eichendorff *Liederkreis* undeniably lacks a compelling through line, even a nonchronologically presented story as in Schubert's Heine cycle. The poems derive no chronological sense from Eichendorff, as we have observed, but neither did Schumann impose any. Nothing except the fact that in a performance a single singer would perform them all even suggests that they all represent the experiences and expressions of just one person; in fact, "Waldesgespräch" explicitly enacts an encounter between two speakers. Taylor argues, "Paradoxically, however, it is in the very absence of a clear plot—but with the continual insinuation that there might be one, or should be one, and that a meaningful narrative coherence is what the characters, and the reader or listener, are struggling to find—that Schumann's work approaches Eichendorff's wider aesthetic," and he hears this as "homologous to the presentation of Eichendorff's favorite themes of confusion and phantasmagorical enticement."[12] As we observed earlier, some commentators have noted that the twelve songs are grouped into two sets of six each, which, in spite of some reordering within each half dozen between composition and publication, culminate in an expression of hopefulness in "Schöne Fremde," no. 6, and in passionate rejoicing at the achievement of happy love in "Frühlingsnacht," no. 12.[13] Nothing generates any impression of causation through either half of this subdivided trajectory, however.[14]

Nor do the texts of the poems form a sensible circular course of events. If anything, the speaker of the first song, "In der Fremde (I)" (Aus der Heimat hinter den Blitzen roth), looks sadly backward at the end of a life—"Vater und Mutter sind lange todt. . . . da ruhe ich auch . . . und Keiner kennt mich noch hier" (Father and mother are long dead. . . . I, too, shall rest . . . and no one knows me here any longer). Yet if the songs have any overall direction toward no. 12, they lead to fulfillment and rejoicing—"und die Nachtigallen schlagen's: 'Sie ist deine, sie ist dein!'" (and the nightingales proclaim it: "She is your own, she is yours!"). Schumann's first published version in 1842 ameliorated this particular logical problem by omitting "In der Fremde (I)" and opening with the separately composed "Der frohe Wandersmann," in which the speaker sets out on the typical journey of German Romantic *Wanderlieder* cycles, looking forward rather than backward. That does not counteract the failure of the successive songs to trace any progressive arc. It also makes for a less challenging and, in the end, less interesting work. Most of the discussion here will deal with the final version of 1850, which dropped "Der frohe Wandersmann" and set "In der Fremde (I)" at the start.

The problem for understanding the unity of the Eichendorff songs, consequently, becomes one of finding the governing voice in the context of the nonchronological ordering of the twelve songs. That is to say, the coherence of the *Liederkreis* depends on our understanding them as presented by a single voice. This project has vexed critics in the past. Benedict Taylor suggests, "There is no consistent subject or persona across Schumann's songs, *at least on the surface*" (italics added).[15] David Ferris asserts, "There is no single narrator who speaks throughout the cycle. The narrative point of view shifts from one poem to another, and there is no sense that they are each describing parts of the same story. What Schumann creates in this cycle is a kind of collective narrative voice, which relates various aspects of a shared experience."[16] One might agree with the first two sentences here, but I find the imposition of the idea of a "collective narrative voice" an artificial solution. Andrew Weaver treats each song as having its own narrator but asserts that the songs all share the same telos—here, the desire to transcend the material world.[17] In the end, though, this suggests not much more than the trivial observation that a cultural group shared a common literary ideal. This could, however, be said of a recital of selected nineteenth-century songs by several composers, so it hardly contributes to justifying the claim that the Eichendorff songs constitute a cycle.[18]

In the end, I find it inescapable that to justify the integrity of a cycle we must recognize a distinct, unitary persona based in the work itself. Since this cycle does not follow a narrative trajectory, the voice must be that of a lyric ego rather than a narrator. Nevertheless, Schumann does convincingly establish a consistent subject for the cycle by placing "In der Fremde (I)" ("Aus der Heimat hinter den Blitzenroth") at the start.

> Aus der Heimat hinter den Blitzen rot
> Da kommen die Wolken her,
> Aber Vater und Mutter sind lange tot,
> Es kennt mich dort keiner mehr.
>
> Wie bald, ach wie bald kommt die stille Zeit,
> Da ruhe ich auch, und über mir
> Rauscht die schöne Waldeinsamkeit,
> Und keiner kennt mich mehr hier.

> "From my homeland behind the red lightning, clouds are coming, but my father and mother are long dead, no one there knows me anymore. How soon, ah, how soon the silent time is coming, when I, too, rest, and over me, the beautiful forest loneliness rustles, and no one here knows me anymore."

In this way, the opening song of Schumann's cycle has the same function as Schubert's "Der Atlas" in his Heine songs, discussed in chapter 3. Here the speaker of the Eichendorff *Liederkreis* introduces himself (or possibly herself),[19] reflecting on the observation of nature in the clouds, lightning, and forest; on the loss of parents and former friends; and on the speaker's own approaching death.[20] None of the other eleven songs takes this kind of perspective. For example, no. 2 ("Intermezzo") is mostly about the hearer, no. 3 ("Waldesgespräch") enacts a dialogue, no. 7 ("Auf einer Burg") is entirely in third person, no. 10 ("Zwielicht") counsels the listener in second person. The songs that do focus on their speaker's own feelings generally reflect only a momentary response to an observation of nature. A possible exception is no. 9 ("Wehmut"), but it does not suggest the life's experience that no. 1 does. It is worth noting that the alternative first song, "Der frohe Wandersmann," might also be considered to have set up the identity of a lyric persona (in that case, definitely male), but it promises a story-based continuation for a *Wanderlied* cycle, which the following songs fail to fulfill. This must surely account sufficiently for Schumann's later rejection of that song and return to "In der Fremde (I)."[21]

Immediately with the text of the second song the listener recognizes the work's lack of chronology in the order of the songs' appearance. The move to something that amounts to a love letter might belong to the character of a speaker who has just been contemplating death, but if so, then it is more likely as a flashback than a continuation of the action. The third song, which takes place entirely between two other speakers, can only be a recitation of a fictional exchange between the actors in a folk legend, not a personal lyric. Songs 4–6 might form a little group, linked as they are by images of flying and the night sky,[22] conceivably flashbacks to the early life of the speaker of no. 1, but by this time likely just heard as collected lyric expressions, not even necessarily all representing the same person's experience, and these bring the group of six to its close. The following six songs, until the last, are all more pessimistic and haunting, but they do not center on a single storyline or speaker. The final song expresses the ecstasy of love—clearly not the outcome of the songs leading up to it and equally not connected by any evident causality to the opening song and its speaker.[23]

What, then, could unify such a miscellany of lyrics? David Ferris offers the idea that the assemblage of the songs in a composite work gives them meaning simply in the sense that together they provide a context for them all: "The cycle . . . is a particular kind of collection, . . . composed of pieces whose forms tend to be fragmentary and whose meaning tends to be obscure. The cycle does not create the overarching unity that provides such pieces with completion and clarity but is itself discontinuous and open-ended. The context that the cycle sets up is provocative; it implies structural connection and hints at larger meaning, but it never makes them explicit or definitive."[24] Ferris also makes the useful historical observation that such a collation would appeal to the same aesthetic sensibility that August Wilhelm

Schlegel espoused in favoring sketches and series of sketches over finished paintings because of the way in which they engage the viewer's imagination. The sketches would take meaning from the larger work—which, however, would not itself be complete and self-contained.[25] Lyric poems and songs based on them might also be comparable to literary fragments of the type promulgated by Friedrich Schlegel, which, as Ferris remarks, were also always published in collections.[26] Such gatherings of fragments would generally have a single author or perhaps a shared topic, which provided some conceptual unity. Likewise, Friedrich Schlegel describes the novel as a composite work comprising heterogeneous genres: "Indeed, I cannot conceive of a novel that does not intermingle narrative, song, and other forms." For Schlegel what holds the novel together is a "spiritual center point" (*geistigen Zentralpunkt*).[27] The same applies to the *Liederkreis*. We could easily think of op. 39 as a similar intermingling of genres: confessional, lyric, dramatic, descriptive, narrative. A narratological approach to discovering its center will, of course, seek out the voice that the composite work adopts or creates.

Given the world-weary mood established at the start, we can sensibly hear the remainder as something like a personal anthology—a gathering of memories, observations, and reflections; a legend; and even a proverb ("Zwielicht"). The speaker of "In der Fremde (I)" assumes a high degree of authority, based on both the position of the poem and the personality whom we encounter in it. This is someone with poems to share, who invites us to hear the following statements as we would the anecdotes, letters, musings, tales, and wisdom of an elder.[28] Thus each individual song can have its own lyric voice, quoted by the initial speaker, while the first poem acts as the center, more than as the beginning, of the whole.

From the point of view of harmony, the same sort of relationship applies. The opening song, "In der Fremde (I)," is in F♯ minor, and the last, "Frühlingsnacht," in F♯ major. The remaining keys are all taken from the sharp side; only no. 8, the second song in the cycle titled "In der Fremde" ("Ich hör' die Bächlein rauschen," in A minor), and no. 7, "Auf einer Burg" (which invokes the Phrygian mode), have no sharps, although they both end on tonic major chords. No. 4, "Die Stille," is in G major. No song is in D major or B minor (i.e., with two sharps). The range from no sharps or flats to six occupies the entire sharp side of the tonal spectrum, and although in itself it might not seem to produce musical unity, it is suggestive.

As noted earlier, the keys array themselves in an order that begins and ends as a palindrome. It also establishes some close tonal connections between adjacent songs, which is, of course, inevitable with a collection of pieces representing a limited span of keys. We can view this in another way, keeping in mind the principle that we have applied to the texts. To hear how the cycle establishes harmonic unity for the twelve songs, we should start with the first, "In der Fremde (I)." Its key of F♯ minor, firmly fixed in the song's first strophe of four text lines, opens up emphasis on the closely related harmonies of A, E, and B in the first three lines of its second strophe, leading back to F♯ minor. This therefore introduces almost the entire harmonic scope of the twelve songs. Only the key of G is missing—but, strikingly, the song's final line and the postlude provide even that, in the form of the Neapolitan triad outlined in the melody over the F♯ tonic pedal.[29]

To put this another way, the first song, like the first poem, occupies the center point and not one end of a linear trajectory. From the point of view of musical structure this would of course be true of the beginning of any tonal musical work. But it does more than that. It also sets up the positions in which the other numbers range around it. And the remarkable appearance at the song's end of the Neapolitan G major, which is not such a closely related harmony, clinches this function.

At this point we should reflect on the meaning of the German word *Kreis*. Michael Musgrave, who represents what has undoubtedly been the most common assumption about the meaning of the word, translates *Liederkreis* as "literally, a song circle."[30] This image might apply better to a cycle such as *Dichterliebe*, in which the keys partly proceed along the circle of fifths, although with some loops and ellipses. This is not the only, or even the most compelling, way to understand the German word, which we might read equally "literally" as "song orbit." When Schumann chose it for the Eichendorff *Liederkreis*, he might not have had in mind the image of a continuous circle, with the successive songs positioned along the circumference. Instead, the idea here seems closer to the concept of orbit, in which the poems and songs occupy places variously closer and farther but always related by gravitational attraction to the cycle's "spiritual center point." In this sense, the *Liederkreis* also resembles a person's circle of friends—each one in some way connected to and standing at a unique distance from the person at the center. The songs relate in just this way to the poetic and musical persona of the first one.

We should now be able to approach the identity of the persona of the cycle. We have discovered that the speaker of the whole introduces himself in the first song. He finds himself far from home and the comforts of family, isolated in society, sensitive to the atmospheric and scenic environment, and weary with the world. Both textually and harmonically, we learn from the first song and the rest of the cycle that the persona encompasses or projects different situations, including some near and others more distant. Melodically, the song introduces a motivic connection that recurs through the ones that follow, without any particular symbolic consistency but rather like a signature, or perhaps merely an inadvertent fingerprint. Over the course of the twelve songs, we find this persona expressing individual feeling (but, importantly, the feeling might belong to the song's speaker and not the cycle's persona); moved by birds, forest, night and the moon, and so on; recounting legends; and offering wisdom. This is, in its essence, the voice of a late Romantic poet, no longer innocent but with a vivid memory of naïveté, conscious of the medieval past, owner of folk legend, both wise and vulnerable to profound emotion.[31]

Schumann's contemporaries recognized this—both about him in general and particularly in relation to the Eichendorff *Liederkreis*. Franz Brendel wrote, "Schumann is a Romantic—it is primarily in this that the explanation lies for the just-mentioned old German naïveté—and his orbit of feeling [*Empfindungskreis*] is therefore very closely related with that which the poets of our Romantic School have opened up. The fantastic opulence that they dreamed of, Schumann has presented musically in the *Liederkreis von Eichendorff*."[32] One might argue that this Schumann whom Brendel acclaims in the Eichendorff cycle constitutes not a lyric persona but instead the figure Wayne Booth identifies in discussing novels as the "implied author."[33] As a matter of fact, any set of songs forming an opus that does not qualify as a cycle will have an implied author in Booth's sense of a "second self" or even "official scribe" who emerges in the real author's writing of the work. For nineteenth-century song collections, this typically means that the implied author (or implied composer) acts as a poet, in the generalized sense that Daverio describes, when he asserts that the song cycle manifests Schumann's assumption for himself of "the role of the poet," arriving at this point primarily from the composer's creative act, but in a generic sense that would not distinguish this case from many others: "Responsible for the selection, arrangement, and setting of a group of texts so that together they constitute a coherent musical and literary whole, the composer of a song cycle functions no less as poet."[34]

This would also apply to the *Myrthen*, op. 25, which Schumann called a *Liederkreis* but which includes poems by numerous authors. The selection of texts does not just biographically (and trivially) represent the composer Robert Schumann as a poet but fictively (and aesthetically) constructs a lyric persona as the gatherer and arranger of a bridal garland (*Kranz*). In that sense, the opus constitutes a cycle because of its fictive construction as not merely but literally an anthology—that is, from the Greek ἀνθολόγιον, meaning a gathering of flowers.

As a counterexample, in which the songs of a set present clearly individual lyric personas, we can take Schumann's collection of *Drei Gedichte* by Emanuel Geibel, op. 30. Here the songs' titles identify the speakers respectively as "Der Knabe mit dem Wunderhorn," "Der Page," and "Der Hidalgo," and their music gives them distinctive voices. For such a set we can certainly imagine an implied author, but not a unified lyric voice. In fact, Brendel, in the paragraph immediately following the one just quoted, turns to Schumann's op. 30 Geibel songs as an instance in which the composer reveals himself less profoundly ("zeigt sich der Componist minder tief"). This surely reflects the listener's experience in op. 30 of an implied author rather than a pervasive lyric persona. The way in which the first song of the Eichendorff *Liederkreis* represents a self-introduction on the part of the lyric "ich," however, identifies the speaker of that song as the central lyric voice, whom the listener should discern as the overriding persona for all the songs in the cycle.

As was the case for Schubert's six Heine settings, discussed in chapter 3, the voice of Schumann's Eichendorff songs does not belong to the same time or class as the singer in a cycle of *Wanderlieder* such as Schubert's two Wilhelm Müller cycles. This surely gives us the best explanation for Schumann's replacement of the naive and rustic character of "Der frohe Wandersmann," which opened the original version of the Eichendorff *Liederkreis*, with the world-weary speaker of "In der Fremde (I)." To the extent that songs in op. 39 apply a folklike style to texts that suggest the outdoors, they employ a borrowed idiom, artistically adapted as quasi-quotations or as cultural references. Like the persona of Schubert's Heine songs, therefore, that of Schumann's *Liederkreis* represents the generation of the midcentury and its urbane, sophisticated culture. These voices and their functions in the song cycles are very different, however: while Schubert's Atlas/Doppelgänger repeats his own unhappy biography, Schumann's speaker centers an orbit of Romantic poetic moments.

Excursus: The Listener

Taylor intriguingly observes that in the texts extracted from Eichendorff's novel *Ahnung und Gegenwart* that Schumann included in his op. 39, "The poems are all linked through being heard by a single protagonist, in this case the novel's central figure, Friedrich (we might say that the listener is invited to occupy his subject position)."[35] From this point of view we might ponder the cyclicity of the Eichendorff *Liederkreis* as arising not from its single speaking voice but from its assumption of an individual narratee. We would then imagine ourselves as song-cycle listeners to stand inside a composite work not unlike a novel, which, as we have seen, Schlegel described as a mixture of genres.

Ferris, in the context of his discussion of the cycle as a collation of fragments, asserts that it is "provocative" and "hints at larger meanings."[36] Because the *Liederkreis* teases the hearer and poses the challenge to pursue actively a significance beyond the individual song as isolated fragmentary lyric moment, the listener becomes a narratee. This, in turn, forces an assumption that the work as a whole has a unitary voice encompassing any individual lyric voices within it.

This foregrounding of the listener's presence in the cycle raises again the concept of *Kreis* as orbit. The attentive listener experiences the effective gravitational force of the work's persona. In this sense, when we engage with the cycle, we join the orbit of the governing persona (in op. 39 identified with the speaker of the first song), along with the lyric voices of the individual songs, the composer, the performers, and other listeners. We might say that the work's title or genre name draws together all its interlocutors—both fictive and real—to participate in a common activity, in the same sense as we would apply the concept to other shared activities, such as a quilting circle or literature circle. It draws us, too, into the lyric persona's "song-circle"—in other words, Lieder-Kreis!

Chapter 8

Feminine Voices in Instrumental Music

"Sonate que me veux-tu?"

Music history no longer distinguishes—if it ever truly did—between so-called "absolute" and "programmatic" instrumental music. The first explicit use of the term *absolute music* comes from Wagner in 1846, as part of an essay on Beethoven's Ninth Symphony. In that context, Wagner regarded such music as empty and meaningless. In fact, he subsequently denied that any such thing existed at all. Responding to Wagner, Eduard Hanslick made much of absolute music, treating it as a pure and ineffable form of art. He did not, however, treat music as a type of creation somehow so abstract that it could be intelligible only to dispassionate analysis.[1]

Music without texts or suggestive titles nevertheless carries meanings beyond the mere configurations of the notes, meanings that derive from the references attached to instrumentation, social functions, cultural conventions, and many other sources. No nineteenth-century music is absolute in the sense of being merely organized sound. We might indeed say that music consists of "tones organized in time," but only if by that we mean that all works arise from their times and embody ideas that belong to their historical contexts.

This chapter considers two works from the 1840s that take different approaches to sonata form, arriving at different deformations that we can read as feminist plots. In order to clarify their idiosyncrasies, we can remind ourselves briefly here that the most common plot of a large sonata movement, as codified in the first part of the nineteenth century,[2] employed its harmonic plan to create a stable point of departure, a move to a heightened level of tension, a period of conflict and rising stress, a moment of climax leading to resolution, and an extended dénouement. This plan of tensions is expressed or enacted by themes that possess identifiable character: serious or comic, military, songlike, dancing, and so on. In the course of a piece's structure, the thematic materials undergo processes of contrast, departure and return, disintegration and reintegration, and reassembling in a resolved position (the tonic key) at the end. This is why we hear the form as a dramatic action or plot.[3] (For a detailed, technical representation, see table 2.1.)

From at least the 1840s, and notably in some recent feminist scholarship, the form has carried implications that represent a compelling instance of the embeddedness of cultural meaning in nonprogrammatic music. For the clearest presentation of this thinking in the mid-nineteenth century, we can turn to the formulation by A. B. Marx in 1845 of the idea of a "masculine" first theme and "feminine" second theme as the ruling convention in descriptions of sonata form. Marx's description of this model, the most influential for the period, reads,

> In this pair of themes . . . the main theme is the foremost, thus distinguished by greater freshness and energy—consequently the more energetic, marked, absolutely formed . . . , the governing and determining one. The secondary theme, on the other hand, is created after the primary theme's energetic confirmation, serving for contrast, dependent on and determined by the preceding one, and in consequence of its nature the gentler one, framed more flexibly than markedly, the feminine in comparison to the preceding masculine. Precisely in this sense is each of the two themes different from the other, and only together do they comprise something higher, more complete.[4]

Table 8.1 outlines the most common and presumptive version of the form for large nineteenth-century sonata movements in general, the version that Sonata Theory classifies as "Type 3," showing the positioning of the conventional gendered thematic character types.

Critics in the late twentieth century found the normative sonata plot inherently grounded in masculine assumptions and a symbol of the hegemonic domination of the male over the female in nineteenth-century European culture. The masculine character is assumed to be the main protagonist, undergoing stress and tension but emerging triumphant and as stable as he began. The feminine character is presented as secondary, initially located in

Table 8.1. Sonata form as plot, including conventional gendering of thematic characters

Part I	Section 1	**Theme/character:** Theme(s) associated with principal key (P); masculine character **Harmony/plot contour:** Home key; stable situation, followed by increasing tension
(Part I continued)	Section 2	**Theme/character:** Theme(s) associated with secondary key (S); feminine character **Harmony/plot contour:** Contrast key; tension
Part II	Section 3	**Theme/character:** P (masculine character) and/or S (feminine character) **Harmony/plot contour:** Unstable; rising action to climax
(Part II continued)	Section 4	**Theme/character:** P (masculine character), S (feminine character) **Harmony/plot contour:** Home key; resolution and reestablished stability

a place of irresolution and fulfilled only by joining the position reasserted by the dominant masculine.[5]

With this paradigm in mind, I turn in the following discussion to two works by important pianists, Fanny Hensel's Piano Trio in D Minor, op. 11, and Frédéric Chopin's Piano Sonata in B Minor, op. 58. Each of these pieces engages the dominant assumptions about the sonata in their decade in a way that challenges the conventions, creating different narratives that, in their respective ways, reveal feminist counterplots.

Hensel and the Heroic Feminine

Fanny Hensel's Piano Trio in D Minor, op. 11, serves as a good example of a work that might casually be classified as "absolute" music but that demonstrates the inappropriateness of such a categorization. It constitutes an ideal case study for the discussion of narrativity in music that has no explicit extramusical content, for the composer left no direct paratextual clues to its meaning. Nevertheless, it turns out to recount a particular type of feminist plot.

The work was written not long before the composer's death, in 1846 and 1847, and was intended for the birthday of her younger sister, Rebecka, on April 11, 1847. It has for several decades stood as a primary representative of Hensel's mastery of composition. As her largest and most complex nontexted and nonprogrammatic work, it has provided her biographers and analysts their most compelling example of her genius in instrumental ensemble music. Treatments of the work generally resolve themselves into analyses that reach such conclusions as that Fanny was a brilliant composer (comparable to her brother Felix), that she had her own approaches to style (not merely parallel to her brother's), or that she engaged in close compositional dialogue with her brother.

Granting all those observations, the Trio further merits narratological interpretation in its own right, for it manifests an intrinsically interesting narrative conception. We must, of course, resist hearing the work as merely autobiographical or meaningless except as some personal revelation of Hensel herself. Nevertheless, the work both adopts feminine narrative positions and exemplifies feminism in its plot. Its narrative voice emerges not only from the social contexts of bourgeois Europe in the first half of the nineteenth century but also from the Trio's family history. The inner movements' genres, a religious andante and a Lied, impose a feminine cultural and domestic narratorial identity. The work's history—as a birthday tribute from sister to sister—reveals a female addressee. Internally, the Trio's plot constitutes an unmistakable demonstration of how a composer can work with and against the period's gender-coded conventions of sonata plot and multimovement design to create a feminist narrative.

The Trio's special character in its content and its plot design both merit more critical interpretation than they have so far received. Even the composer's enthusiastic biographer Françoise Tillard described the work as "not especially original in form,"[6] a judgment that, as will become clear, simply does not hold up, if we listen closely to the music. But the Trio was not always heard as lacking originality. An anonymous critic writing in the *Neue Berliner Musik Zeitung* at the time the Trio was published (shortly after the composer's death) proclaimed, "We [find] in this Trio broad, sweeping foundations that build themselves up through stormy waves into a marvelous edifice. In this respect the first movement is a masterpiece, and the Trio most highly original."[7] R. Larry Todd, in his 2010 biography of Hensel, expressed the view that the Trio, like others of her mature works, demonstrates greater spontaneity than the music of her brother.[8]

What interests me in the Trio is first of all how the relationship that develops between the themes over the course of the first movement unfolds an unconventional sonata plot. The piece opens Allegro molto vivace in D minor, clearly enough with a strong, masculine passage for violin and cello in a powerful unison over an energetic, almost roaring piano accompaniment (P; example 8.1). Markus Waldura characterizes Hensel's approach to the construction of the theme as more boldly Beethovenian than lyrically Mendelssohnian in its open-ended unfolding out of a series of contrasting motives.[9] After some heightening of tension in the transitional passage, the secondary key, F major, brings a lovely, recognizably feminine contrast. The markers of the feminine in this theme are both its lyricism—Hensel marked the passage "cantabile"—and the fact that it is expressed in dialogue between cello and violin (S; example 8.2). Here I am unable to concur with Suzanne Cusick, for whom the presence of melodic leaps makes the secondary theme seem masculine:

> Nor do [*sic*] the nature of the themes seem promising candidates for the kinds of readings of sonata form as gendered discourse that Marcia Citron and Susan McClary have essayed: the second theme is not very different from the first, and is certainly no less angular, leaping, stylistically "masculine." At best one might argue that the presence of a second "masculine" theme where a "feminine" one ought to have been (according to Hensel's contemporary A. B. Marx) construes the discourse as having no room for the feminine (or no room for the feminine side of an actual woman composer's thought). But the similarity of themes could as easily be explained as a manifestation of Hensel's concern for organic unity, a concern revealed in countless details of this work.[10]

Despite its leaps, however, the secondary theme clearly contrasts with the primary one. The dotted quarter and eighth notes in example 8.1 aggressively kick the line in P up from A to D, and the subsequent return to A means that the leap of the sixth to F demands the immediate output of more energy. The dotted half and quarter notes in example 8.2, by contrast, give the long notes of S a chance to expand lyrically to the upward skip, and the gradual ascent from C through C♯ to D before the rise to B♭ gives the phrase a less muscular and more graceful character. Likewise, at phrase

Example 8.1. Hensel, Piano Trio in D Minor, op. 11, mvt. 1, mm. 1–9.

endings, the upward-pressing semitones in the principal theme at measures 7 and 9 convey a clearly more forceful effect than the secondary theme's relaxation from F to E in measures 61 and 65. The very extent to which the themes resemble each other should draw attention to their differences. One might say (although I emphatically would not want to propose any sort of biographical reading) that they relate as male and female siblings. Closing material, made up of a long, descending musical line, ends this plot's exposition.

Example 8.2. Hensel, Piano Trio in D Minor, op. 11, mvt. 1, mm. 58–65.

During the course of the movement's development in section 3, the principal theme (with its masculine character) is fragmented and pressed through a series of key areas, starting softly and building through a long crescendo and then a decline. The secondary theme (or character) follows in turn, in two fairly distant areas, the major third above the tonic (F♯) and the major third below (B♭), now given a new treatment, con espressione and quite agitated.

It is in the dénouement that the movement takes its surprising turn. The masculine material brings back the tonic key, as we expect, and then the appearance of the feminine second theme is set up in quite the normal fashion. When S arrives, however, it does not merely return accommodated to the key of the masculine theme. The feminine theme—that is, character—seizes control of the action (example 8.3). Although still the same lyrical melody, the S theme is now fortissimo, in unison for violin and cello, bold and assertive, presenting the key of D major not as the sweetening of the minor-key home of the masculine theme but as the ideal optimistic counterpart to the masculine intensity of the character of the principal theme.

Example 8.3. Hensel, Piano Trio in D Minor, op. 11, mvt. 4, mm. 298–305.

Should we read this plot as feminist? Cusick, whose feminist credentials are beyond doubt, did not see her way to such an interpretation, writing, "Indeed, as I think many feminist critics have found, formal and tonal analysis by themselves seem not to reveal anything much about the gender of composers, or their experience of difference."[11] Hensel, however, experienced musical works that explored the difference of masculine and feminine themes and characters in explicitly gender-based plots. James Hepokoski points out the powerful influence of the overtures to Weber's *Der Freischütz* (premiered in Berlin in 1821) and Wagner's *Der fliegende Holländer* (1843), in each of which the apotheosis-like return of the feminine S theme programmatically represents the redemptive role of the woman in the opera's plot. He suggests that movements built on the model of the latter can even be interpreted, from the perspective of recognizing masculine hegemony, "as a formula facilitating the production of a masculine erotic fantasy—hyperbolically projecting an encounter with and appropriation of the sexually desirable" and cites Strauss's *Don Juan* as a later instance of the type.[12] The first movement of Hensel's Trio constitutes a significantly different case. It does not reflect any operatic or programmatic story, and we must therefore take it on its own terms. The themes present gendered characters, P as masculine and S as feminine, and there is an apotheosis for the feminine character at the end. Unlike in the Weber and Wagner examples or Strauss's tone poem, however, we have no paratextual reason to interpret the late manifestation of the feminine character in the Trio as having redeemed the masculine or as the object of male desire. This movement unfolds a plot in which the feminine S ultimately achieves unforeseen strength and controls its part of the dénouement on equal terms with the masculine character in its part.

A feminist plot certainly does not necessarily mean anything about "the gender of composers," as Cusick points out, but it obviously requires some experience of difference, because such experience includes insight into cultural or social conceptions of gender. Although Hensel once wrote to her brother, "I'm no *femme libre* . . . ,"[13] this movement certainly offers a vivid portrayal of one sort of liberation of the feminine character. The movement enacts a plot in which at its first appearance the feminine behaves in "proper," decorous fashion. At the resolution, however, this character reappears proud and strong, resolved to the tonic of the main theme but at the same time assertively transfiguring it, so that it becomes clear that she will not slip subserviently into the role of accommodating the governing attitude of that masculine environment, and in fact takes over the whole. Whereas heroism is usually associated with masculine values, here it is revealed to be a character trait of the feminine theme within this plot.

A Woman's World

The Trio also includes markers of more conventional femininity. The second movement is an Andante espressivo that belongs to the "religious adagio" type. It adopts a straightforward symmetrical ternary form. The third movement is headed "Lied—Allegretto." Commentators always note the resemblance of its lyrical melody to the *romanza*-style aria "If with all your hearts ye truly seek me," from Hensel's brother's oratorio *Elijah*, and it is certainly more songlike than instrumental in nature. In form, it also follows the conventions of the Lied, unfolding as a quasi-strophic series of variations, featuring each of the instruments in turn. Larry Todd notes that Felix played through the oratorio for Fanny at the piano a few months before she composed the

Trio. He thinks of the *Elijah* reference as "a response to or extemporized contemplation of her brother's music." He continues,

> If the subject of Fanny's trio is her musical relationship with Felix, the composition nevertheless contains powerfully expressive music and shows the hand of a musician now comfortably engaged with issues of large-scale form and structure. The many allusions to Felix's music do not so much betray a lack of originality as offer an enriching layer of complexity. . . . For all the intensity of the siblings' relationship, and the masquerading, Schumannesque exchanges between them, Fanny still succeeded in finding her own creative space and in eclipsing the limitation of her miniature Lieder and character pieces for piano.[14]

Todd deals with the framing of the restrained interior movements in contrast to the assertive outer ones by relating them to Hensel's personal and artistic experience: "Taken as a whole, the Trio juxtaposes extroverted outer movements conceived as musical drama with introverted, poetic movements, and establishes an opposition between the dramatic and lyrical, the public and private that Fanny confronted as a professional musician in the waning days of her life."[15] This also resonates with gender differences in the middle of the nineteenth century in general, however, so we must not read this as making a claim uniquely about Fanny Hensel or in any sense as justifying an autobiographical reading of the Trio. In bourgeois families of the time, the maintaining of religious observance and the upbringing of children, represented here by the religious spirit of the second movement, and the cultivation of music in domestic circles, represented by the Lied, typically fell among women's responsibilities. In that sense, although the Trio is not about Fanny Hensel's life, it invokes the lives and activities of women generally in her time and social environment. As I noted earlier, from the historian's point of view music does consist of tones organized in time in one sense—not in some sense of "absolute music" organized in time in the abstract, however, but in the sense that each work is a product of the time in which it is composed.

The fourth movement returns to a bolder, more assertive style. It opens in D minor with a languid, quasi-improvisatory passage featuring something like the lassú passage that opens a Hungarian csárdás, a genre that became very popular in the bourgeois salons of Western Europe in the 1830s and 1840s. This accelerates into a lively fiddle tune like a csárdás's friss. These ideas serve as the thematic material for the body of the movement. At the end, however, and completely unexpectedly, the secondary theme of the first movement returns, in its heroic manner in D major. The plot of the Trio is even more comprehensively feminist than the contemporary listener—or we—would have anticipated. In fact, this is the only theme that moves outside the action of a single movement, and therefore we are forced to regard this recognizably—but not by any means stereotypically—"feminine" theme as the unifying, central, predominant theme of the work. There can be no doubt about the identity of the controlling character in this unusual story: it is the feminine S theme. And its place in the plot of the Trio as a whole, not just of the first movement, is clearly heroic.

Romantic Voice in the Trio

Before we finish with our observations about Hensel's Trio, it is worth considering the identities of the *narrative persona* and the *implied composer*.[16] Largely, this work is not pushy about the narrative position; the narrator does not intrude audibly and disrupt the action, as in, for example, some of Beethoven's most explicitly narrative works (think of the opening of the finale of the Ninth Symphony or the first movement of the "Tempest" Sonata, already discussed in chapter 2). Based solely on our observations of genre and technique, we can form an interesting picture of the implied composer for this work. That figure would not be identical with Hensel at her writing desk, of course, as we noted in chapter 1. It stands beside the significant internal musical evidence of the Trio's narrative persona that we have already observed, revealed through internal musical features: the thematic characters; harmonic plot; textures; allusions to domestic, sacred, and exotic musics; and so on. The performance demands a high level of pianism so prominently that we must certainly hear the pianist behind the music, and in that sense it is reasonable to understand that we are hearing the implied composer as virtuosa. Because the internal movements are a religious adagio and a Lied or song, we might extrapolate that there is some bent toward interests in the spiritual and in domestic music making, and the nineteenth century would certainly have feminized those spheres. Thus, not only is it appropriate to take the character within the plot as feminine, but, despite Cusick's entirely appropriate caution that "formal and tonal analysis" do not reveal anything about "the gender of *composers*,"[17] it would not be wrong hear that the music constructs the *implied composer* as well as the narrator position as a woman's position.

In the reception of works by women, critics almost invariably construct interpretations based on their knowledge that the composer was a woman. This reflects the underlying historical cultural fact that composing, especially of multimovement instrumental works, was typically a male enterprise. Consequently, in real experience a female narrative persona is not constructed exclusively inside the music. For example, an early review of a performance of the Hensel Trio in Boston noted that the work was remarkable "particularly . . . as the production of a woman, in a sphere of Art which woman has so seldom entered." It notes that she was Felix Mendelssohn's sister and the wife of the Prussian court painter Wilhelm Hensel. The writer goes on to impose an implicit assumption and gender-based (or, perhaps better, gender-biased) demand on the piece: "The Trio we cannot regard as solving the question whether the genius for musical *creativity* is among the attributes of woman; but it is certainly a fine Trio; full of interest and beauty." The review does not actually analyze the music in any detail, and it is a matter of conjecture whether its ultimate judgment on the Trio should be taken as suggesting merely surprise that it seems so masculine or actually recognizing its plot of liberated feminism: "The most striking thing about it is that it is so vigorous, so full of fire, especially in the first and last movements. . . . The Trio nowhere sinks into weak or morbid sentiment; in sustained strength, indeed, it exceeds some favorite productions of her brother." Finally, "It is a difficult piece to execute, and shows musician-like resources, invention, treatment, skill in modulation, and knowledge of the capacities of string instruments, to a degree that one would hardly credit who had not heard."[18] In fact, to put it another way, the reviewer seems to have the same experience with the feminine narrative persona as the plot has with the feminine character within the work—the discovery of impressive, even if unexpected, boldness and self-assurance.

What we need to avoid, at all costs, is the idea that the Trio is an attempt at autobiography. The major-key theme of the first movement is not to be understood as representing Hensel herself, nor are the events of the music supposed to correspond to her life. That would be to fall into the (auto)biographical fallacy. As I have already emphasized, although all authors draw on their own experience, they do not explicitly recount the facts of their own histories in their art. Further, as we do not interpret the leading character in the Trio's plot as a representation of the composer, we should also not regard the narrative persona or the implied composer presenting this feminist plot as identical with Fanny Hensel, for, as we have seen, narrators and implied authors are as much created as are the themes' characters. The factors that make the theme, the narrator, and the implied composer female do not depend on Hensel's gender. They would be female even if composed by a man. Our next example compellingly demonstrates this.

Constructing Chopin's Sonata in B Minor

Like the first movement of Hensel's Piano Trio, Chopin's B-Minor Piano Sonata, op. 58, problematizes the dramatic plot conventions of sonata form. In addition, it should disabuse us of the (auto)biographical fallacy for good, because it comes from a Romantic voice that is obviously fictitious. It thus presents a hermeneutic challenge, but at the same time it also offers a methodological model. The movement opens two lines of interpretation, one dramatic and yielding a gendered interpretation of character and plot, the other narrative and producing a particular identification of the voice in the work.

We may begin by situating the Sonata both in Chopin's life and in the history of the sonata as genre and form. We can place the first movement of the Chopin Sonata next to the model for the understanding of sonata form as it was established at the time of the composition of this piece and show how the work treats the form. We can read this movement as a discourse of different layers, distinguishing how those layers speak and what they say. Finally, we might give a particular name to the movement's narrative persona.

The sonata was composed in 1844, during a difficult period in the composer's life. At the age of thirty-four, he was suffering from ill health and from the news of his father's death. He found it difficult to work. Indeed, the B-Minor Sonata was his only composition completed during that year. It is tempting to search the sonata's music itself for evidence of these personal physical and emotional experiences. Yet it might also be worth considering that the near-hiatus in his output arose from specifically artistic issues that concerned the composer, which had to be worked out before he felt comfortable proceeding to a new stage of artistic development. The music does not reveal the composer's biography, but his work certainly occupies a place as a biographical fact in his life story.

The sonata genre holds a problematic place in Chopin's oeuvre. In contrast to his more characteristic virtuoso and salon pieces, the genre seems somehow inimical to the composer. Confronted with the B-Minor Sonata, therefore, one is not surprised that the first movement has presented difficulties for analysis and interpretation.[19] Critics have often suggested that

Chopin's treatment of sonata form is not very convincing. Paul Egert, in his study of the composer, praised the sonata in general but held reservations about the first movement: "A more 'combined' piece is Chopin's B-Minor Sonata; the ideas flow in such profusion that symphonic working-out of thematic development is forced into the background; . . . nevertheless, in view of the elegant second, songlike third, and dramatic final movement with its course toward greatness, this piano piece will always be able to hold its place among the first-rank piano pieces of the last century."[20] Vincent d'Indy had no patience with the piece at all. He found that it represented "the *pianistic* style, a style whose effects have been and still are deplorable from several points of view." And as for the first movement,

> Every spirit of construction and of coordination of ideas is unhappily absent from it; . . . truly the homework assignment of a pupil determined to create here a development because that is the usual thing; but all logic is jealously banished from it. [And as for a recapitulation, it is] very nearly nonexistent, because the best element, theme A, by an inexplicable omission, does not reappear there: . . . [The movement is a] childish sketch that leaves us very far from the monuments of order and harmony so justifiably admired in the works of Bach and of Beethoven.[21]

Some, to be sure, have come to the movement's defense. In a close and sympathetic analysis of the movement in 1922, Hugo Leichtentritt demonstrated that the principal and secondary themes can be played simultaneously in counterpoint (a relationship that does not appear in the piece itself) if one makes only subtle changes in the music. He further showed that the second theme might be evolved from the first through an intermediate-stage melody that has some traits in common with each—a missing link, however, that is certainly missing.[22] The intention of such analysis is formalist, depending on the presupposition that structural unity is the basis of musical value. The flaw in such an argument is obvious—the unities identified by the analysis are not, in fact, manifest in the work. We shall have to find in our experience of the music more interest than that and meaning of another kind.

The sonata as a genre forms a relatively small part of Chopin's oeuvre, as it did the oeuvres of most nineteenth-century composers. By the mid-1840s the genre conspicuously stood as a holdover from the previous century—and its form had largely become codified by writers who looked back to models from the Viennese masters up to the period of Beethoven and Schubert. Few sonatas were composed by any of the leading Romantics after the 1820s, and those either were likely to be regarded as "academic" works or were subsumed into a multimovement cyclical, programmatic design. Charles Rosen observes that by the middle of the nineteenth century,

> The attempt to open up the sonata took two basically related directions:
>
> 1. The cyclical sonata in which each movement is based on a transformation of the themes of the others. . . .
>
> 2. The combination of a one-movement and four-movement structure into one amalgam. . . .
>
> . . . The form was . . . no longer a free development of stylistic principles, but an attempt to reach greatness by imitation of classical models. The results, at their best, attain a noble, expansive, relaxed, and academic beauty unattainable (and unsought for) in the late eighteenth century.[23]

But Chopin's nonprogrammatic sonata does not, in fact, follow a cyclical or amalgamated design, nor does it seem attributable to backward-looking academicism. (And Rosen has nothing to say about it in his large study of Romanticism, though that book is substantially centered on Chopin.)

The first movement of Chopin's op. 58 Sonata differs from the standard plot in a significant way. Rather than the most familiar Type 3 sonata form, it adopts a deformation of Type 2 (see tables 8.2a and 8.2b).[24] This form, employing a "balanced" rather than "rounded" handling of the binary structure, was not uncommon in the mid-eighteenth century, but it became much rarer in substantial movements by the end of the century and had its most significant instances in Chopin's sonatas. The default design—against which critics measured the completeness and maturity of movement forms—had become Type 3. From the quotations we have just observed, we can see that for later critics of Chopin's work in the late nineteenth and early twentieth centuries this seemed a weak option. Especially d'Indy's objection that by an "inexplicable omission" a recapitulation of the P theme is missing and his condemnation of the first movement of Chopin's op. 58 as "childish" make this clear.

Table 8.2a. Form of Chopin, Piano Sonata in B Minor, first movement—themes and harmony

Part I	Section 1 (mm. 1–40)	**mm. 1–7:** theme—P; harmony—b:–e: **mm. 8–16:** melodic extension; sequential harmony **mm. 17–22:** theme—1T; harmony—B♭ g **mm. 23–30:** theme—2T; harmony—D$_4^6$ E♭ **mm. 31–40:** transition; to D:V
(Part I continued)	Section 2 (mm. 41–91)	**mm. 41–55:** theme—1S; harmony—D **mm. 56–65:** theme—2S; harmony—f♯–D **mm. 66–75:** theme—3S; harmony—D **mm. 76–83:** theme—1K; harmony—D **mm. 84–91:** theme—2K; harmony—D
Part II	Section 3 (mm. 92–149)	**mm. 92–109:** theme—K+P; harmony—(b) **mm. 110–18:** theme—P; harmony—(c) **mm. 119–36:** theme—2S; harmony—D♭, E♭ **mm. 137–41:** theme—1T; harmony—g♯ **mm. 142–49:** retransition; harmony—b$_4^6$ to B:V
(Part II continued)	Section 4 (mm. 149–204)	**mm. 149–65:** theme—1S; harmony—B: **mm. 166–75:** theme—2S; harmony—d♯–B **mm. 176–85:** theme—3S; harmony—B **mm. 186–93:** theme—1K; harmony—B **mm. 194–97:** theme—2K; harmony—B **mm. 198–204:** coda; harmony—B

Table 8.2b. Form of Chopin, Piano Sonata in B Minor, first movement—abbreviated

Part I	Section 1 (mm. 1–40)	**Theme/character:** Theme associated with principal key (P)/masculine character **Harmony/plot contour:** B minor, followed by increasing tension
(Part I continued)	Section 2 (mm. 41–91)	**Theme/character:** Theme(s) associated with secondary key (1S, etc.)/feminine character **Harmony/plot contour:** D major
Part II	Section 3 (mm. 92–150)	**Theme/character:** P disintegrating, 2S **Harmony/plot contour:** Unstable
(Part II continued)	Section 4 (mm. 151–204)	**Theme/character:** 1S, etc. **Harmony/plot contour:** B major

The movement opens with a theme in the tonic, B minor, that is motivic in structure and bold in character (P; example 8.4), a standard enough opening gambit. After a transition (via B-flat and D minor), the relative key, D major, is introduced by a contrasting theme in lyrical style (1S; example 8.5), followed by further secondary and closing themes (2S, 3S, 1K, 2K). The development section begins with unstable references to the principal-key thematic material, with which it eventually dispenses in favor of clear and stable statements of 2S in D-flat and E-flat before the retransition. At the return of B as tonic, the mode is major and the material is limited to that associated in the exposition with the secondary key. The "principal" thematic material is never restored or resolved (as d'Indy pointed out as one of his reasons for dismissing the work).

The Type 2 form is one among the possible options of first-movement form, but simply to describe this movement's various sections and themes,

Example 8.4. Chopin, Sonata in B Minor, op. 58, mvt. 1, mm. 1–8.

Example 8.5. Chopin, Sonata in B Minor, op. 58, mvt. 1, mm. 41–44.

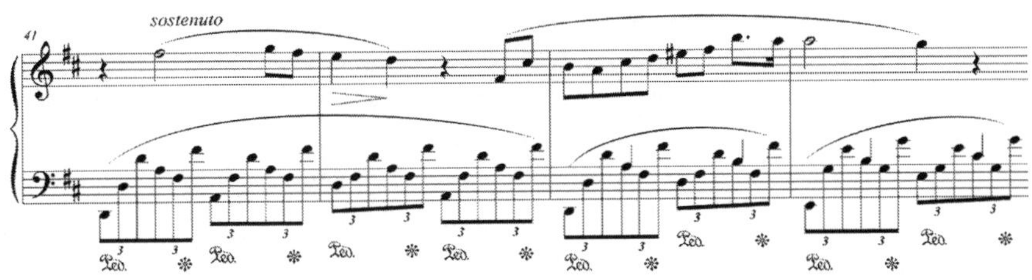

trace the harmonic course of the music, identify the formal functions of the successive passages, and thereby classify the movement accurately would be to overlook the special significance of the form for its plot. The movement follows a storyline in which the first character (theme P) is transported to an unstable environment, subjected to dis-integrating forces, and then abandoned. The other characters, meanwhile, are introduced in a contrasting environment, and one (2S) is relocated to a couple of other places, but for them nothing that happens seems to raise the stakes very much. If we listen to sonata form anticipating a dramatically conceived plot structure in which themes identified by their characters, and most expectedly the bold leading character of the plot's opening, pass through conflict and crisis to achieve resolution and dénouement—the conventional Type 3 model—we would find ourselves agreeing with the Sonata's early critics that in this movement the dramatic plan seems to have some self-evident plot flaws.

To interpret the movement sympathetically, we can hear it as a strikingly feminist story. The reception history of the Chopin B-Minor Sonata obviously identified its themes in gender-coded terms.[25] D'Indy described the principal theme as characterized by "noblesse" and "qualités *symphoniques*," while he regarded the second as "séduisante" and made worse by its ornamental nature.[26] Leichtentritt called attention to the first theme's "energy" and "determination" and wrote that the second melody "lulls itself aloft."[27] Ursula Dammeier-Kirpal distinguishes the first theme as characterized by "determination and clarity," the second as "peaceful, songlike" and eventually proceeding into "ever more abundant adornment."[28]

As we have seen, the plot of the B-Minor Sonata clearly does not operate according to the Type 3 model, in which stability is restored by the tonic return of a masculine-gendered P theme; rather, it undercuts that model. The masculine character, determined to fulfill the plan of violent adventure for which its nature predestines it, succumbs to these very stresses. The feminine character, on the other hand, maintains a noncombative nature, avoids the self-destructive tensions of development, and emerges in control of the tonal center, still in possession of its stable character, at the resolution. This is the old, oppressive, masculine-hegemonic sonata form reconceived. It comprehends the nature of the conventional plot structure, but it tells a different story: masculine character and aggressive behavior fail, and feminine patience and self-possession succeed.

In a broader sense, the plot here is about the self-destructiveness of a "will to power" and the success of self-possession and the refusal to engage in conflict and crisis. It is an argument against the principle of the conventional plot itself. This story makes the case that the masculine must sometime extinguish itself through the type of activity it embraces, while feminine character and behavior need neither produce nor fall victim to such conflict. In short, Chopin's movement reflects a feminist reconception of sonata form, not in the manner of Hensel's Piano Trio, in which the feminine character seizes a strong position, but offering an alternative plot to the "heroic" model of struggle and victory. In his discussion of gender in the themes and structures of sonata-form movements, James Hepokoski concludes insightfully that

> varying realizations abound . . . no single mode of interpretation can solve our hermeneutic problems. The whole topic of the sonata as an instrument for the construction of gender—that is, for the explicit articulation of different, socially normative gender roles—needs far more investigation. From the point of Marx and early Wagner onward, however, the concept of the sonata, along with its potential for gender articulation, continued to split into numerous subtypes and deformational patterns. Each needs to be addressed on an individual basis—hopefully, in a manner as unimpaired as possible by the narrative agendas of our own ideological preconceptions.[29]

Thus Hensel's and Chopin's plots may promulgate very different but equally valid feminist positions.

Fictive Romantic Voice in Chopin's Sonata

Further, however, the movement should be heard as feminist not merely in its plot but in its narrative voice. We return to the definition by Scholes and Kellogg: "By narrative we mean all those literary works which are distinguished by two characteristics: the presence of a story and a story-teller. A drama is a story without a story-teller. . . . For writing to be narrative no more and no less than a teller and a tale are required."[30] Chopin's sonata is narrative because its action forms a plot and because it reveals a distinct narrative subjectivity, a recognizable persona behind the story.

Up to the point we reached a moment ago, we have discussed the movement as plotted—we have heard it as a drama. But we must not miss the fact that the listener is supposed to recognize about this movement both that it begins by enacting a recognizable sonata-form strategy and that this Type 2 sonata plot is employed in order to represent a particular kind of meaning. Significantly, the movement is not the Type 3 sonata form that dominated the mid- and late-nineteenth-century repertoire—at least, in its reception history critics found it difficult to allow it a place as an example of the conventions they understood to attach to that form. In fact, by the way in which it plays with expectations of sonata form as heroic plot, this movement turns out to be *about* the contemporary plot conventions of sonata form. Andrew Davis suggests a similar idea, making the sonata an instance of the Romantic treatment that "neither ignores nor conforms to Classical precedents; it *uses* the generic conventions as a backdrop against which to pursue a vigorous expressive discourse in contemporary Romantic values."[31] Enough of the sonata plot is enacted to make the form its main content, but, as the movement proceeds, the action becomes not that of conventional Type 3 sonata form but one that works out a Type 2 sonata plot in a way that represents a moral alternative.

In brief, this piece must be understood as taking place on two levels of discourse—the action of something that engages with sonata form and the treatment of sonata form from a particular point of view. Thus the title itself may be understood not simply as a genre identification but as a statement that the piece is about "sonata," a narration that critiques dominant narrative assumptions of heroic plot. In this sense, the movement is not simply narrative but metanarrative.[32]

Two recent analyses of works by Chopin have proposed something of this sort. In a 2004 article on Chopin's Fourth Ballade,[33] Michael Klein sets up an opposition between static and active themes or passages, interpreting one type as representing the past and the other the present, one as lyric and the other as narrative. Klein proposes that music can unfold a logical sequence of expressive states, which is to say that it can be plotted, although not as actions carried out by actors. In the Fourth Ballade (as in the First) the plot unfolds as a succession of appearances of an initially more modest internal, lyric theme, culminating in its apotheosis in an enriched manifestation. Klein reads lyric passages, however, as static and evocative, while he calls active and modulatory passages narrative. Action, in this model, is something that a narrator performs by imposing modulatory motion on the music. Musical characters seem inert images taken from the past, lacking volition or function, led from one moment to another or presented in one static manifestation after another by the intentional control exerted in the present by means of energetic, nonthematic passages. In other words, there is no action to be followed in a plot except that of a manipulative fictive narrator as deus ex machina, stringing together otherwise isolated expressive states. By this means, Klein solves the problem of finding evidence of the narrator as well as answering the skeptics who argue that music cannot be narrative because it has no past tense. When a piece is narrative, some of the music is, in effect, remembered from an imaginary past, as if it had been scrapbooked, and narrativity in the present could be asserted by the movement of turning the pages.

Andrew Davis deals with the issue of time specifically in his discussions of Chopin's B-Minor Sonata.[34] Davis makes a distinction between "temporal" and "atemporal" music, by which he contrasts passages that contribute to the direction and pace of a normative sonata movement with those nonthematic passages heard as parenthetical interpolations or divergences in that progress. For Davis,

> The temporal elements in the sonata will often include its principal rotational modules . . . , normatively presented—that is, sounded in the normative chronological order and at the normative narrative-rhythmic pace, such that story time (understood now as sonata-story time: the time passing within the world of the sonata) and narrative time (the time in which the sonata is conveyed aurally to the listener) can be understood as coinciding. When such norms and expectations are disturbed by certain types of *rhetorical gestures* comprising expressively *marked* discontinuities or other disruptions that encroach on the music's normative, forward-vectored flow, that music can signify a shift outside the first narrative and into an atemporal stream.[35]

He demonstrates the distinction in digressive passages in the B-Minor Sonata's first movement, which veers—in ways not at all atypical for Chopin—through quite distant keys on the way to the usual goals in a sonata plot. Davis treats the movement as revealing a narrative presence, but the "narrator" that he identifies is generically a composer, engaging with the same issues of structure dealt with by any nineteenth-century sonata composer. His discussion does not attempt to come to grips with either the personality or cultural assumptions that I deal with here.

One difficulty with Klein's and Davis's time-based arguments for the revelation of narrativity in music is that both depend on the analyst's definition of what in a movement constitutes fundamental action and what does not. There are pieces in which levels of discourse obviously can be heard as distinct in voice from surrounding music—as we saw in chapter 2, the first movement of Beethoven's "Tempest" Sonata serves as a *locus topicus*—but in default of such an in-your-face moment, we will more constructively listen to a movement as unfolding continuously in a developing plot. Shifts between contrasting characters and alternations between momentarily static and increasingly driven activity make up the ebb and flow of activity in any interesting plot. If we hear all the moments of a given style in a piece as something like quotations or static snapshots from the past, as Klein implies, strung together like someone's reminiscences, even following some kind of logic, and we hear others in more active styles as disengaged from action, that does not constitute narrativity. If, as in Davis's approach, only some bare, normative path through a Type 2 sonata movement (in the case of Chopin's Sonata) counts as the temporal plot for the work—an analytically extrapolated sonata conformation rather than deformation—and the rest as atemporal digressions imposed from outside, then the sense of an actual distinctive or recognizable plot disappears altogether.

Although both Klein and Davis offer detailed and perceptive close analyses of Chopin's music, the arguments by which they claim to identify the narrativity in the works are not necessarily convincing. In both cases the analysts seek to demonstrate narrativity by showing that the music makes it audible, as if we had to hear the narrative gears grinding, to become distracted from following a plot by the artifice of narrative manipulation, in order for the music to be narrative. Ultimately, these methods do not anyway approach the aim of this book, to become acquainted with the personalities who express themselves in the music. Romantic voices in music do not need to intrude audibly into their own discourse. We come to know them in various ways, not necessarily by hearing them in the tones. We do not have to pick them out by analyses that extract the contrasts, the detours, and consequently the interest from musical plots in order to leave a residue of a narrator.

It is worth pursuing another approach to a narratological reading of Chopin's Sonata. Scholes and Kellogg have this to say about plot: "Plot can be defined as the dynamic, sequential element in narrative literature. Insofar as character, or any other element in narrative, becomes dynamic, it is part of the plot."[36] Thus, one way to locate a narrative voice is by setting dynamic and nondynamic elements apart on different levels within the discourse.[37] One might argue that not only does this sonata's principal theme find its destruction in its dynamic activity, the secondary theme also remains conspicuously not dynamic at all. To the extent that the initial secondary theme partly stands outside the plot, then, it serves not only as part of the action but also to reveal its meaning. As Hayden White has suggested, narrative embodies a moral viewpoint,[38] and certainly we have observed that this is the case in the Chopin sonata movement. Moreover, the secondary theme, which draws attention to the moral of the action, assumes functions of both character and narrative persona.

It is at this point that we recognize an individual subjectivity at work. And we can find a more precise acquaintance with this individual. This movement's persona is, in Wayne Booth's classification, a "dramatized narrator" and, in Mieke Bal's terminology, a "character-bound narrator."[39] As a consequence, we are justified in looking to the music itself to identify this narrator—that is, to specify the persona's character. So far we know one thing about the narrator: she is certainly identified, by lyrical musical style and by position within the narrative, as female.

Fictional Chopin

This narrative voice has an even more specific identity, however. The voice of lyric pianism here is one that listeners can identify easily, for it must inevitably be understood as the voice of Chopin—that is to say, of a fictive persona of Chopin that listeners familiar with Chopin's music automatically identify. At the arrival of the D-major theme, the listener almost certainly thinks, "Ah! That really is Chopin." The movement's reception history leaves no doubt. In reviewing the sonata at its first publication, the *Allgemeine musikalische Zeitung* described the second theme as "a genuinely Chopinesque songlike cantabile supported by triplets."[40] The critic of the *Neue Zeitschrift für Musik* stressed that it possesses "in its expression . . . certain peculiarities that, while they differ very strikingly from the conventional, are recognizable at first glance. . . . [This sonata] *is by Chopin*."[41] D'Indy, in describing the inadequacy of the secondary theme for a sonata movement, complains that "this defect is frequent enough with Chopin. . . . He falls back on those Italian turns of phrase, imprinted with the style of the theaters and salons of his time."[42] Adolf Weissmann asks rhetorically, "Do we not listen now, enchanted once again, to Chopin the cantilena-singer?"[43] Dammeier-Kirpal, even in a discussion that is almost completely formalistic, could not resist pointing out that this is "a genuinely Chopinian melody."[44] Certainly this would have been evident for listeners in the music's primary milieu, the

Parisian salon of the 1840s,[45] in which the audience knew Chopin firsthand and heard this playing explicitly as the expression of Chopin's voice among the conversation of other, equally familiar ones. The recognizability of this voice enabled Schumann's music to introduce Chopin as a character in *Carnaval*; the intertextual reference it makes to Chopin's most personal and recognizable style cannot be missed.

The style is unmistakably that of the nocturne. Andrew Davis alludes to this in his article "Mixed Genres and Narrativity in Chopin's B-Minor Sonata,"[46] but only in a single quick reference at the end of his discussion. There are two important aspects of this observation worth developing. The first is that the nocturne as a genre was gendered as feminine in the 1830s and 1840s. Jeffrey Kallberg explores this issue with ample quotations from critics of the period.[47] It is therefore not only the style features of the D-major theme that make it gendered but the recognition of the genre. The second significant point is that the nocturne is a lyric genre, and like a lyric poem we understand it as presenting the personal experience of the "lyric I." That means that the "dramatized narrator," whom we recognize as a fictive "Chopin" persona, speaks in the revelatory first person at that moment. One would call a passage such as the secondary theme in the B-Minor Sonata "Chopinesque," no matter who had composed it. By 1844 the composer of the sonata could only have understood that "Chopin" was inscribed in the work. It is as direct a naming of the dramatized narrator as in *Moby-Dick*. It says with absolute clarity, "Call me Chopin." More recently, Wayne Petty finds that the Trio of the third-movement Funeral March of Chopin's Piano Sonata in B♭ Minor, op. 35, "stations a distinctly Chopinesque voice antithetically to what comes before," and Michael Klein asserts that "we might identify the nocturne as a metaphor for Chopin's own subjectivity, as if he has written himself into the narrative as a musical persona."[48]

Let us reiterate, though, that a narrative presented in first person is not delivered in the voice of the author/composer as writer but rather in that of the persona that she or he constructs. It is not "Chopin himself"—a Parisian man, thirty-four years old, in failing health and mourning the recent death of his father in his native Poland—who is the persona here. It is the narrator-Chopin, a fictive persona, specifically inscribed in this sonata movement for this sonata movement.[49] The movement itself helps to foreground this point, for we have recognized two things about the first-person-narrative S theme—it names itself "Chopin," but it is also female. This is not at all to say that the biographical composer himself was an effeminate man; it simply—but crucially—means that the listener should understand the fictive narrator "Chopin" to be a woman. If we are tempted to confuse the composer who wrote the sonata with the narrative persona in this case, that is, to fall into the biographical fallacy, we have only to remind ourselves that the narrative voice we hear can only reasonably be recognized as the entirely fictive "Chopin herself." This persona has no pulmonary diseases, no deceased parents. "Chopin herself" does, however, have a unique character, a plot to unfold, and a moral position to unfold in it.[50]

In summary, the first movement of the B-Minor Sonata may be described as narrative in the sense that it both enacts plotted form and, on another level of discourse, simultaneously offers a personal—or better, a persōnal—view of conventional plot. The narrative persona—and it is a Chopin persona—rejects the dramatic drive of sonata form and instead tells a story that resolves in favor of a feminist moral. In composing the B-Minor Sonata, Chopin explicitly engaged an artistic issue of Romantic music, working out a statement in musical terms. Little wonder, then, that such a crucial and profound effort represents a single product of a long period of musical thought in the composer's development.

Chapter 9

Finding a Voice in the Symphony

Quotation in Schumann's Symphony in C, Op. 61

Historical Context and Musical Content

Schumann's C-Major Symphony, op. 61, presents intriguing problems of interpretation. Widely admired in the nineteenth century because of its perceived metaphysical content, it became less so in the twentieth, at least until recently, because structuralist and positivist analysis could not easily account for it.[1] Both its form and its content confront the listener and musicologist with unexpected challenges.

Schumann's work on the Symphony took place between December 1845 and October 1846. He may have had some idea of taking on a symphony project as early as September 1845, when he remarked cryptically at the end of a letter to Mendelssohn, "For several days a lot of drumming and trumpeting has been going on in me (trumpets in C); I don't know what will come of that."[2] Apparently in part as a reaction to hearing a performance of Schubert's "Great C-Major" Symphony, Schumann started late that year to work in earnest. He began sketching on December 12, 1845, and the draft of the whole work was practically complete on December 28.[3] He started to orchestrate the Symphony on February 12, 1846, but he could work only slowly because he was bothered by severe tinnitus. He completed the score on October 19. Mendelssohn conducted the Symphony's premiere on November 5, 1846, in the Leipzig Gewandhaus, but the performance was not particularly successful.[4] The second performance, which took place on November 16, met a warmer response. The Symphony was published in 1847.

A number of leading scholars have discussed this symphony, and each has contributed particular insights into the work.[5] The present essay approaches the work from a narratological viewpoint, opening up a new interpretation of both its form and its content.

The plot trajectory of the Symphony as a whole presents some curious features, which should serve as clues to interpretation. As Anthony Newcomb points out, it belongs to the "end-accented" or "heroic" plot archetype, established by Beethoven's Fifth and Ninth Symphonies. In such works, the progress from the minor mode to the major at the end invokes a plot in which struggle leads to victory, or suffering to healing or redemption. Despite its presumptive modality, the C major of Schumann's Second Symphony is darkly shaded by the minor through its first three movements. As a result, it resembles Beethoven's Fifth on the large scale, C minor superseded by C major in the final movement.[6]

The first movement opens with a notably serious introduction, sostenuto assai, which leads to an allegro sonata form in C major. From the start the major mode sounds attenuated, however, because of the strong presence of E♭, heard already in the first measure (as D♯4 in the violins). The key of E♭ also significantly inflects the movement's plot line, appearing in the place of the secondary key at section 2 instead of the expected modulation from C to G; the eleven measures of stable E♭ are followed by just fourteen measures of closing material in the dominant area, so that C minor becomes as important as C major in representing the movement's tonic.

The Scherzo likewise features C minor. The movement opens on an F♯ diminished seventh with A in the bass and E♭ prominently in the top voice at the first downbeat. As in the first movement, the dominant arrives (m. 12) by way of a move through E♭ (m. 8). The Scherzo emphasizes the flat-key side throughout, even after the music has established C major (and this emphasis includes the middle of the G-major first Trio, mm. 122–30 in B♭).

The Adagio espressivo third movement is explicitly in C minor. It features a pathopoeic theme that begins with a minor-sixth leap from G4 to E♭5, followed by the highly expressive diminished-fourth descent to B♮4. At the movement's conclusion, despite a key signature change to C major, the penultimate cadential harmony is not the dominant but the fully diminished seventh chord with A♭ in the bass rather than the dominant G.

The fourth movement begins with a tremendous acclamation in C major, with a momentary brightening by way of the tonicization of G (mm. 4–8), so that any minor shading is abruptly obliterated. The tendency of E♭

to intervene in the modulatory scheme from tonic to dominant is nowhere to be heard. Aside from a couple of very passing B♭s (as V7 of IV, mm. 32 and 38) there is hardly a flat to be found in the first hundred measures and more of the movement. The flat-side harmonies in the development add warmth rather than darkening the expressive content. The ending is governed by C major. Newcomb's detailed description interprets the final passage as representing not merely victory, in the fulfilling harmonic arrival, but reconciliation, specifically in the way in which the thematic/motivic oppositions set up at the start of the Symphony and tracked over its entire course ultimately reach a resolution.[7]

Heroic Narrative, Not Autobiography

This overarching trajectory in the Symphony from half-darkness to light constitutes the essence of its plot. Also notably, the work sets up a single leading character that dominates the whole. As we have established, character in Enlightenment and Romantic music is embodied in rhythmic/melodic thematic material. Newcomb points out that the opening measures of the introduction establish thematic material that pervades the course of the Symphony, even as it grows and changes. The brass fanfare, with its dotted rhythms and leaps of fifth and fourth, is juxtaposed to the simultaneous crawling line in the strings, marked by smooth rhythmic flow and step-wise, even chromatic, motion—a sort of dual character, like Florestan and Eusebius. The extreme contrasts between the component elements of this theme make it almost inevitable that whatever material follows will appear as a development out of some aspect of the character of the opening. As the music's plot unfolds, new ideas arise out of existing ones, so that we hear not merely intermittent cyclic thematic resemblances but organic character development.[8]

Although the Symphony is ostensibly a work of absolute music, we would misrepresent it by the sort of analysis that focuses on the details of pitch configurations and intricacies of structure rather than thematic character and dramatic plot. The music's progress in both harmonic plot and thematic character, and the idiosyncratic treatment of the conventions of sonata form and symphonic plan, unfolds a clearly intentional plot. In his 1850 article on the work, Ernst Gottschald described the Symphony as presenting "the *victorious* striving of the particular individuality for the most sincere fusion with spiritual universality, in which all the egoistic limits,

limits that divided individual spirits from each other, are annihilated, so that [those spirits] love each other as equals, for they live in the realm of liberty, equality, and fraternity."[9] We shall return to this very perceptive and provocative interpretation.

Commentators have frequently fallen into the trap of treating the Symphony's principal character as a representation of the composer. Gottschald identifies the work's "particular individuality" as representing "the composer's personality, still caught up in a strange isolation."[10] Michael Steinberg argues that Schumann's persona emerges most explicitly in the third movement.[11] Others have also succumbed to the temptation to make Schumann the protagonist of the narrative, citing some comments that the composer himself made about his health during the Symphony's composition. Schumann experienced a nervous breakdown in August 1845. He was still recuperating in December, at the time when he drafted the Symphony. Further, as mentioned earlier, during the work's orchestration he had trouble with the ringing in his ears that presaged his eventual neurological crisis. On November 26, 1849, three years after the completion of the Symphony, Schumann wrote to the Hamburg music director Georg Dietrich Otten, "I wrote the Symphony in December 1845, still half sick; it seems to me that one would have to hear this in it. Only in the last movement did I begin to feel myself again; actually, I became better only after finishing the whole work. But otherwise, as I say, it recalls to me a dark time."[12] This might tempt us to imagine that the Symphony's plot represents a specific experience in the composer's own life. Newcomb writes, "Although the plot archetype of a particular work may have no connection with the life of the composer, that of op. 61 had an autobiographical dimension. The struggle in the symphony from suffering to healing and redemption seems also to have been Schumann's own."[13]

Nevertheless, we should determinedly avoid falling into the biographical fallacy—or more appropriately the (auto)biographical fallacy. Interpreting a work of art as portraying its creator's life or an episode in the artist's experience trivializes the artistic creation. As I have emphasized throughout the preceding chapters, it demotes a work to the petty function of personal diary keeping, and it makes the listener a sort of voyeur.

Schumann's letter to Otten does not, in fact, justify such an interpretation. Schumann clearly states that he "actually . . . became better only *after* finishing the whole work" (emphasis added). The letter does not assert that the Symphony represents the composer's experience of illness and recovery in late 1845 and early 1846; rather, it simply says, "it recalls to me a dark time." Insofar as the plot archetype belongs to the class of those that proceed from struggle to victory or suffering to healing or redemption, it does not represent the course of Schumann's health at all.[14] More sensible, indeed, would be simply to regard Schumann's illness and recovery, or anyone else's, as representing a trivial instance of the plot paradigm.

Nevertheless, recognition of the plot archetype here is clearly compelling on the basis of the documents and the music itself. As we have observed, the first reviewers perceived the Symphony's narrative contour. Schumann validated this view, writing to Taubert on March 3, 1847, a few months after the Symphony's completion and first performances, that the work was "as a whole a dark piece,—only in the last part do a couple of friendly beams break through."[15] The plot in the Symphony no doubt embodies heroic struggle leading to victory or suffering leading to redemption.[16] The protagonist is not, however, the ailing and recovering composer.

Intertextual References

Having established the C-Major Symphony's plot in terms of tonality and thematic characters, we must now turn our attention to the work's most peculiar and important aspect. Schumann's Symphony famously contains a number of explicit citations and allusions to other music. Some of these are so conspicuous that they have received extensive discussion, others have been noted but deserve new attention, and some have been overlooked. Taken together, they contribute significantly to an understanding of the Symphony's meaning.

Intertextuality is a complicated concept, by nature impossible to pin down, but this chapter depends only on intertextual connections of a straightforward sort.[17] Its argument accepts as axiomatic the understanding that texts inevitably refer to or reflect numerous other texts, and therefore the meanings of texts depend on each other. Some intertextual references come from the self-conscious intentions of composers; some arise, perhaps subconsciously, from the music they know or the conventions of genre and style within which they work. Some intertextual references emerge from our readings or hearings of texts, determined by our own knowledge and assumptions. In this chapter, the intertextual references in the Schumann C-Major Symphony include both the composer's models of structure—for example, the conventions of symphonies in his time and especially the symphonies of Beethoven—and quotations from, citations of, and allusions to music in Schumann's repertorial experience. For that reason, we can have confidence that they arise from the work's historical context and we do not impose them arbitrarily. The line of thinking here does depend on us to approach the music bidirectionally, however, in the sense that we want to know the work's Romantic voice by means of the field of references that we can perceive in the music, and therefore we take it as given that the Romantic voice must know and, in fact, intend those references. Although this manner of reading would not apply universally to all investigations of any texts, this Symphony steers us into it, as will immediately become clear.

The Symphony opens, as mentioned earlier, with double motivic material, a brass fanfare and a sinuous line in the strings. The fanfare self-evidently refers to the slow introduction of Haydn's "London" Symphony, No. 104 in D Major, from which it adopts the dotted rhythm and the successive leaps from the first scale degree, up a fifth and then down a fourth. Critics have not failed to notice the reference. R. Larry Todd, unlike other listeners, qualifies the allusion as *apparent* (his italics) but expresses skepticism about whether Schumann intended it. He points out that fourths and fifths are part of the idiom of the symphony as a genre. He also proposes that the dynamic difference—Schumann's fanfare is played *piano*—means that the later work does not "evoke the magisterial" quality of the earlier one.[18] I would argue that to recall a distant sound as a sort of echo precisely conveys the concept of evocation. To copy it *forte*—that is, more literally—would be repeating Haydn's symphony rather than evoking it, and Schumann had in mind that listeners should recognize the reference but not mistake the work that they are hearing. Also like Haydn's symphony's opening, Schumann's sets off the leaping fanfare by contrast to stepwise material in a middle range. In Haydn's case (example 9.1a), the bold, tutti opening (mm. 1–2) is balanced by two iterations of a soft, chordal progression from i6 to V_2^4 in the strings (mm. 3–4). Schumann accomplishes a similar effect by playing the brass fanfare simultaneously with the strings in parallel thirteenths (example 9.1b).

The Scherzo also refers to previous music. The opening harmony, spelled as the diminished seventh on F♯ over A in the bass, suggests the tutti blast at the opening of the Wedding March in Mendelssohn's incidental music to *A Midsummer Night's Dream*. Mendelssohn's harmony, also launching a movement in C, is the half-diminished seventh on F♯ over A in the bass. Again, the use of an approximate rather than a literal citation serves to connect Schumann's music to Mendelssohn's but also to establish reference

Example 9.1a. Haydn, Symphony No. 104 in D, mvt. 1, mm. 1–4.

Example 9.1b. Schumann, Symphony in C, op. 61, mvt. 1, mm. 1–4.

rather than mere quotation. Later in the Scherzo is another instance, when in the course of the Trio II the violins' melody twice spells out the notes B-A-C-H, the second time in rhythmic augmentation as a sort of cantus firmus over contrapuntal parts in the lower instruments (mm. 230–32, 257–62). Between these statements is a passage for woodwinds over a quicker, steady viola line, which seems unmistakably to recall the walking or running bass texture of Baroque music (mm. 239–54). If the explicit spelling out of Bach's name eluded a first-time listener, the suggestion of a sort of stile antico probably would not.

Historical allusions continue in the Adagio. Listeners since Brahms have noted a similarity between the melody of the symphony's slow movement and the opening of the trio sonata in the *Musical Offering*.[19] Ingeborg Maass hears it as allusion to a Baroque *Affecttypus*,[20] and indeed this theme is an example of a Baroque figure, *pathopoeia*, embodied in the leap up of the minor sixth (G4 to E♭5), followed by the highly expressive diminished fourth descent (to B♮4), and resolution up by a semitone (example 9.2). Linda Correll Roesner, crediting Bernhard Appel,[21] points out the resemblance of this theme to the melody of the soprano aria "Seufzer, Tränen" in Bach's cantata *Ich hatte viel Bekümmernis* (BWV 21), which, however,

Example 9.2a. Bach, *Musical Offering*, Sonata, mvt. 3, mm. 1–2.

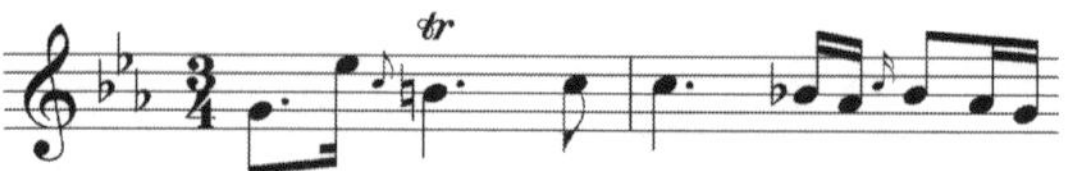

Example 9.2b. Schumann, Symphony in C, op. 61, mvt. 3, mm. 1–4.

does not begin with the ascending minor sixth but the complementary descending major third. We might rather agree with John Daverio that the melody resembles the theme of the aria "Erbarme dich" in the *St. Matthew Passion*.[22] In fact, we could well say that the theme refers to any or all of these examples in Bach's oeuvre, or at least to a recognizable affective figure that Schumann and the informed contemporary listener would most likely have associated with Bach's music.

The passage in the Adagio that begins at measure 62 also suggests the Baroque texture of melody against a motoric or walking bass. It opens by establishing constant sixteenth-note motion in the second violin part, which turns out to be the walking part, against which the first violins and clarinet play a descending melody in syncopated eighth-note values, giving the effect of a cantus firmus. The texture continues, with the roles reassigned every few measures but always with the descending line at least doubled—in measures 69–73 played by the violins in octaves with a bassoon doubling the second violins, and as the line descends to the point where the violins have to play in unison, the oboe takes the higher octave. The listener naturally recognizes the texture as a reference to the era of Bach. It also constitutes another intertextual allusion, which we will return to shortly.

Several citations turn up in the finale, within section 4 of the form—that is, what, if the music recapitulated, would be the recapitulation. The return of C major is prepared by a fortissimo and sforzato dominant seventh chord, followed by a rest with a fermata. Then, in the home key and in place of a thematic return, comes one of the best-known quotations in the Symphony, the first phrase of the sixth song in Beethoven's

An die ferne Geliebte, "Nimm sie hin den, diese Lieder" (example 9.3), in a passage that Newcomb aptly characterizes as expressing "serene confidence" after the achievement of redemption or victory in this finale.[23] The placement of this melody forces the listener to notice it, set up as it is by the preceding dominant, and just where one knows to expect a thematic recapitulation. At least as explicitly as the Haydn citation at the Symphony's opening and as the reference to Bach's music at the opening of the slow movement (and B-A-C-H in the scherzo), it draws Beethoven into the constellation.

One citation that might be arguable occurs in the Symphony's finale at measure 445, where the trombones introduce a new, isolated melodic gesture. The resemblance is to Mendelssohn's *Lobgesang*, no. 10, measures 87ff. (the fugue on the text "Danket dem Herrn"; example 9.4). The general contour—a leap of a fourth followed, beginning with a dotted rhythm, by a scalar descent through whole tone, semitone, whole tone, and so on—might, however, seem sufficiently generic to make us doubt the deliberateness of this possible connection. Moreover, the tempos are somewhat different. A resemblance such as this could well be dismissed as coincidental, but the accumulation of citations by this time suggests that any newly introduced, sharply profiled, and isolated melodic/rhythmic idea should come across as a reference.

So, we can proceed to yet another instance, which appears a bit later in Schumann's finale (mm. 544–51). The reference here should be unmistakable; it recalls the choral finale of Beethoven's Ninth Symphony, at the words "Alle Menschen, alle Menschen . . . werden Brüder" (mm.

Example 9.3a. Beethoven, *An die ferne Geliebte*, no. 6, mm. 9–10.

Example 9.3b. Schumann, Symphony in C, op. 61, mvt. 4, mm. 394–97.

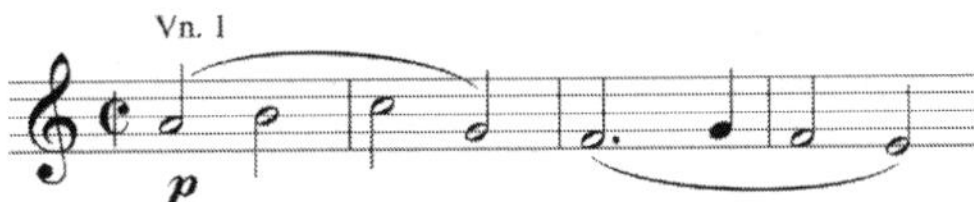

Example 9.4a. Mendelssohn, *Lobgesang*, op. 52, mvt. 10, mm. 87–90.

Example 9.4b. Schumann, Symphony in C, op. 61, mvt. 4, mm. 445–52.

806–11; example 9.5). The melodic, harmonic, and rhythmic features make Schumann's passage a clear imitation of Beethoven's.

Strikingly, given the list of cited composers so far, we have not mentioned Mozart, who by now must seem a conspicuous omission from the pantheon of German composers whose music Schumann invokes. He does have a place in Schumann's Symphony, however, and indeed the

Example 9.5a. Beethoven, Symphony No. 9, mvt. 4, mm. 806–11.

Example 9.5b. Schumann, Symphony in C, op. 61, mvt. 4, mm. 544–51.

Mozart citation offers a key to interpreting all the others in the work. The citation is the same passage in Schumann's Adagio that we have already noticed as an instance of Baroque-style walking-bass texture, but now I would like to suggest hearing it as a reference to *The Magic Flute* (example 9.6). This is a citation that scholars have occasionally noted, but one that I believe has not been drawn closely enough into interpretations of the Symphony.[24] Both Mozart's passage and Schumann's are in C minor, both feature a walking bass that accompanies descending melodic lines syncopated so that they move off the beat. At the opening of Mozart's section, the melodic material does not sound in octaves, but it is split between parts at the interval of a sixth, so that the effect of Schumann's passage resembles it strongly. Moreover, when the voices enter, they do sing in parallel octaves.

Example 9.6a. Mozart, *Die Zauberflöte*, act 2 finale, mm. 196–207.

Example 9.6b. Schumann, Symphony in C, op. 61, mvt. 3, mm. 62–74.

There is one composer whose symphonic work somewhat surprisingly does not seem to be cited in Schumann's C-Major Symphony: Schubert. Schumann had played a crucial role in the recovery of Schubert's symphony in 1839, and he had heard it performed just before beginning work on his own C-Major Symphony. In fact, it might seem remarkable that Schumann's Symphony shares little with Schubert's other than their common key. Jon Finson notes that the finales of both composers' C-major symphonies feature insistent dotted rhythms in their main themes, but this similarity (Finson finds it the only one between the two symphonies) does not rise to the level of a specific citation.[25] A sharp-eared listener might yet discover a reference. It is possible, though, that Schumann regarded Schubert as more important as a Lied composer than as a symphonist, or his symphonic compositions as still insufficiently established in the repertoire to make a quotation appropriate for his purposes.

Clearly, the issue of influence must have contributed importantly to Schumann's creative imagination as he composed this work. This would be true for any composer writing a symphony in the decades following Beethoven. The observation that Schumann's C-Major Symphony deals consciously with the symphonic tradition is by no means new. Arnfried Edler noted that the choice of the key of C taken together with Schumann's assertion to his Dutch admirer Verhulst that his Symphony would be a "rechte Jupiter" indicates that in his creative imagination Mozart's K. 551 held a place in its heritage.[26] Edler goes even further in regard to the significance of the reference to Haydn's Symphony No. 104, describing it as "the symphonic tradition itself, represented by the Haydn citation."[27] As Ludwig Finscher succinctly put it, in this symphony "the idea of musical work itself becomes thematicized—there is hardly another symphony before Brahms, in which substantive and structural unification is wrestled with so rigorously and so strenuously as here, and hardly any in which at the same time the idea of musical work is set up with such historical depth."[28]

We often think of the anxiety of influence as an issue for composers after Beethoven, and Schumann certainly regarded Beethoven as the looming predecessor who could raise the anxiety of his successors. Mark Evan Bonds's insightful study of the Beethoven problem in general, for example, demonstrates how different composers' symphonic works in the nineteenth century come to grips with his awe-inspiring legacy. Bonds focuses on Berlioz, Mendelssohn, Schumann (the D-Minor Symphony rather than the C-Major), Brahms, and Mahler.[29] Here, though, Schumann dealt with the "anxiety of influence" not by avoiding it but by acknowledging and even embracing it, radically foregrounding intertextuality in this Symphony. This observation merits closer consideration, drawing together now the Symphony's plot and the allusions.

Form and Meaning

The citations, combined with the shape and nature of the plot established earlier, determine the narrative voice for the C-Major Symphony. Unmistakably, by means of its multiplicity of citations and allusions, the narrative voice of the work claims a particular identity. As we hear it, we must recognize that the Symphony's narrative persona is familiar with, and even particularly conscious of, the leading contributors to the German musical tradition from the time of Bach to the 1840s. The motivation for the Symphony as well as the plot itself must be understood within the purview of the symphon-ist's narrative position. The impulse to express the heroic plot issues from self-conscious concern with the symphonic tradition. The struggle and ful-fillment represented in the work relate directly to the narrator-symphonist's musical experience. The symphonist persona responds to the anxiety of influence both by narrating the plot contour "through suffering to joy"[30] and by bringing the composers of the tradition explicitly into the musical text. This makes for a much more interesting narrative interpretation than regarding the C-Major Symphony as merely an autobiographical account of the composer's illness and recovering health.

Furthermore, one citation in particular offers explicit insight into the symphony's plot. The reference to Mozart's *Magic Flute*, together with a neglected remark in Schumann's correspondence, reveals what might have been Schumann's own conception of the meaning of the heroic plot in this symphony—the striving for a position in history. The remark comes in a letter from Schumann to Joseph Fischof on November 23, 1846, where Schumann wrote that the music was "etwas geharnischt."[31] The word *gehar-nischt*, which describes a knight girt in armor, is a peculiar one, the German idiom suggesting the expression of some sort of belligerent attitude. One might think that the narrator-symphonist intends to confront and do battle with his predecessors in the great German musical tradition.

But this is not quite right. Probably, the reader will already have recognized the intertextual connection with undoubtedly the most famous occurrence of the word *geharnischt* in the history of music—the "zwei geharnischte Männer" in the trial scene at the climax of *The Magic Flute*.[32] It is hard to imagine that Schumann did not think of this reference when he wrote the word, and the musical reference strengthens the connection. What then does it signify? Here is what the two Armed Men sing:

Der, welcher wandelt diese Straße voll Beschwerden
wird rein durch Feuer, Wasser, Luft, und Erden;
wenn er des Todes Schrecken überwinden kann,
schwingt er sich aus der Erde Himmel an.
Erleuchtet wird er dann im Stande sein,
sich den Mysterien der Isis ganz zu weih'n.

("He who wanders this path full of burdens, becomes pure by fire, water, air, and earth; if he can conquer the fear of death, he ascends from earth to heaven. Enlightened, he will then be in a position to dedicate himself completely to the mysteries of Isis.")

We could not ask for a clearer formulation of the plot archetype that Schumann's C-Major Symphony unfolds. The story does not have to do with sickness and recovered health but with trials passed to earn admission into the company of the enlightened. As a plot archetype, as well as in the action of the opera, the passage expresses a sort of moral ideal.[33]

Later commentators who have framed the symphony as a diaristic recounting of Schumann's illness in 1845 have done so based on the plot contour and Schumann's remarks in his letters, overlooking the explicit content of the music. Reviewers who described the C-Major Symphony in the first few years after its appearance, hearing it in its own terms and undistracted by Schumann's correspondence, did, however, understand that it enacted a story of striving and achievement. Reviewing the score's first edition, Alfred Dörffel wrote in 1848, "The music is none such as is discovered by the lucky grasp of the genius; it is one attained [by effort] and has behind it a great world view, a great life."[34] In a lengthy response to Dörffel, Gottschald, without noting the allusion to *The Magic Flute* or the text sung by the "geharnischte Männer," referred to the "most profound soul, which endures firmly and without trembling the trial by fire of the 'forms.'"[35] As we noted earlier, Gottschald suggested that the work's "Grundidee" was "the *victorious* striving of the particular individuality for its most sincere fusion with spiritual universality, in which all egoistic limits, limits that divided individual spirits from each other, are annihilated, so that [those spirits] love each other as equals, for they live in the realm of liberty, equality, and fraternity."[36] Dörffel and Gottschald each capture both the process of trials and attainment and the fulfillment in the arrival at greatness and spiritual community.

Franz Brendel, reviewing the Symphony's second performance, stressed the Symphony's universality and objectivity (i.e., in contradistinction to Schumann's highly personal expression in his earlier works), an idea that also pervaded Dörffel's and Gottschald's comments: "If in the works of Schumann's first period the fantastic dominated, then here it is the plastic, objective stamp of the thoughts, mediated by his contrapuntal studies, a direction that characterizes the works of his second period generally."[37] This perception of the universalizing affirmation of the Symphony reveals far more significance than does the comparatively trivializing idea of the music as a programmatic rehearsing of an autobiographical episode.

Approaching the Symphony narratologically, bringing together both harmonic direction and thematic content, both plot and voice, thus brings us closer to the core of Schumann's symphony. The integration of these elements also permits a compelling interpretation that speaks at multiple levels: most generally as a statement about heroic action and Elysian arrival, as a reflection of the anxiety of influence felt by composers continuing the tradition after Beethoven, and, yes, specifically in regard to Schumann himself, but not in regard to his health.

The (auto)biographical fallacy may be avoided by observing, as the composer himself did, that the narrative persona of the Symphony is not Schumann but a voice with experience of struggle and recovery, the symphony as genre, and German musical heritage. The citations that occupy such a considerable amount of the music ought to direct the listener clearly enough to recognize this. Reynolds points out that for nineteenth-century composers the B-A-C-H motive "gained symbolic status, a change that followed inevitably from the cultural progression that replaced the image of Bach the Leipzig cantor with one of him as source of German musical nationalism."[38] This extends to the reference to Bach's music in the theme of the slow movement and the employment of the Baroque walking bass in both the Scherzo and Adagio. As for the references to later works, Newcomb noted that the Symphony's opening allusion to Haydn "proclaims as effectively as a poetic preamble one quite specific program: Schumann's courageous and ambitious decision to measure for the first time his particular methods and abilities against the overwhelmingly, even terrifyingly prestigious tradition of the Viennese Classical symphony—a tradition that for Schumann meant Haydn, Mozart, Beethoven, and Schubert's Great C-Major Symphony."[39] More generally, the citations of and allusions to nonsymphonic works, including the Beethoven song from *An die ferne Geliebte* and the chorale in the finale of *The Magic Flute*, situate the Symphony among the entire repertoire of German musical heritage.

Nevertheless, the panoply of allusions does not render Schumann anonymous or external to the Symphony. There is yet one further and very telling quotation that we must take into consideration. Near the end of the development section of the fourth movement, Schumann actually places himself into the work, and in a remarkable way. As Gerd Nauhaus was perhaps first to point out,[40] at measures 343–49 the Symphony's finale quotes measures 131–35 of the last fugue in Schumann's Six Fugues on the Name B-A-C-H, op. 60, the opus number immediately preceding the C-Major Symphony, a composition that had occupied the composer for much of the year 1845 (example 9.7). By adding this Schumann reference to those to Bach, Haydn, Mozart, Beethoven, and Mendelssohn, the Symphony adds Schumann to the list of canonical composers in the German tradition. Significantly, the passage quoted here is not a characteristic passage from Schumann's oeuvre, such as one of his piano pieces of the 1830s or the songs of 1840. Instead, it is particularly the Schumann who looks back to Bach. The Symphony thus asserts that the composer wins through to the status of greatness in the tradition of German music, not in the idiosyncrasies of his personal style but specifically in acknowledging the heritage of his forebears.

To finish, therefore, let us return again to the plot and the allusions and reconsider in that context Gottschald's formulation along with the quotations of Mozart's *Magic Flute* and Beethoven's Ninth Symphony. As Gottschald explained, the overall achievement of the plot, culminating in the Symphony's finale, is the "attainment" of "spiritual universality," where individual spirits "live in the realm of liberty, equality, and fraternity." Tamino in Schikaneder and Mozart's opera, too, achieves induction into the realm of the enlightened, and for Beethoven the hero earns entrance to an Elysium where, indeed, "all men become brothers." In the final analysis, symphonic engagement with the challenges of the great composers justifies a claim to admission into the community that by the 1840s the narrator-symphonist

Example 9.7a. Schumann, Six Fugues on the Name BACH, no. 6, mm. 130–35.

Example 9.7b. Schumann, Symphony in C, op. 61, mvt. 4, mm. 343–49.

understood as the canon of great German music, a canon that began, both in history and in Schumann's inspiration for the C-Major Symphony, with Bach and that now extended through Haydn, Mozart, and Beethoven to the present of Mendelssohn and to Schumann himself.

Chapter 10

Traveler and Pilgrim

Epigram and "Vallée d'Obermann" from Liszt's *Années de pèlerinage*

A Brief History of "Vallée d'Obermann"

"Que veux-je? que suis-je?" These questions stand at the beginning of the epigram Liszt used as preface to "Vallée d'Obermann." They represent, to be sure, essential ponderings for all Romantics: "What do I want? What am I?" For the consideration of narrativity in music, they might address listeners with a challenge, asking us to identify the voice behind the piece.

The original self-questioner was Obermann, fictive writer of the letters that the quasi-autobiographical *Obermann* comprises, written in 1804 by Étienne Pivert de Senancour (1770–1846).[1] The eponymous Obermann has left France for Switzerland, from where he sends often-lengthy missives that combine observations of nature with reflective musings. By the time Liszt became familiar with *Obermann*, in the 1830s, the fictive letter writer represented a Romantic type, a melancholy, world-weary figure, and especially one who seeks answers or solace in nature. Senancour's "Observations" that preface *Obermann* introduce him as a man of feeling rather than a man of action: "On verra dans ces lettres l'expression d'un homme qui sent, et non d'un homme qui travaille."[2] Despite commentators' frequent references to the book as a novel, Senancour insists explicitly that it is not a novel. There is no plot. George Sand went even further in her preface to the second edition of *Obermann*, published in 1833: "If one requires of a book progressive coordination of the thoughts and symmetry in the external

197

lines, *Obermann* is not a book."[3] The reason to read the letters is simply to know their fictive writer. In that sense, Obermann comes to represent not a protagonist but a voice.

In 1835 Liszt and his mistress, the Countess Marie d'Agoult, fled Paris to Switzerland to escape the scandal arising from their affair, which had lasted already two years. She was three months pregnant with their first child, Blandine, born in December. They were joined the following year by, among others, their friend George Sand.[4] Apparently, they took with them Senancour's *Obermann*, with the preface by Sand. In a way typical for Romantic travelers, they experienced Switzerland through their reading of Obermann's letters.

In turn, in 1837 and 1838 Liszt composed the pieces that he assembled to make up a three-volume collection called *Album d'un voyageur* with the added descriptor "1re année, Suisse." The books were published out of order. Book 2, titled *Fleurs mélodiques des Alpes*, came out from the publisher Latte in Paris in 1840. Book 1, *Impressions et poésies*, followed the next year, from the Paris press Richault. The complete *Album*, including book 3, *Paraphrases* [of Swiss melodies], was released by Schott in Mainz in 1842. More than a decade later, in 1855, Liszt incorporated substantially revised versions of several of the pieces from the *Impressions et poésies* into a new collection, *Années de pèlerinage, 1re année, Suisse*. One of these pieces is "Vallée d'Obermann." In this chapter I am interested especially in its later manifestation, but some explanation of the differences between the earlier and later versions will help to bring out interesting issues.

The *Album d'un voyageur* constitutes a musical contribution to the literature of travel writing. It followed closely in the footsteps of two literary exemplars by writers in Liszt's Paris circle. Alexandre Dumas *père* published his *Impressions de voyage* beginning in 1833 with an account of his travel to Switzerland, which had begun the previous year. He recounts his route, the scenes that he observed, historical events, local legends and colorful anecdotes, and gastronomical experiences. George Sand wrote a series of *Lettres d'un voyageur*, actually long, often rambling essays on various topics in the form of letters from different places and addressed to different contemporaries, dating from 1834 to 1836, published in 1837. Letter 7, a discourse based on the Swiss Enlightenment writer and physiognomist Johann Kaspar Lavater and on a deserted house, is addressed to Liszt. The composer approached the project of creating a musical traveler's album with these models of travel writing, together with Senancour. As Michele Calella has discussed, Switzerland was for Liszt, as for the Romanticists generally, not merely an actual geographical location but a construction, a fictive landscape that enabled imagination.[5] It was a place of unspoiled nature, the awe-inspiring sublime, and political independence. Wolfgang Fuhrmann likewise points out factors that play into the conception of Switzerland for Liszt and his generation: its representation of a political tradition of self-sufficiency and self-determination, its literary significance for poetry and natural morality, and its embodiment of the sublime and the consequent inspiration toward melancholy self-reflection.[6]

"Vallée d'Obermann" and Its Literary Source

By titling his piece after Obermann, Liszt associates the music with this more spiritual and reflective Romantic experience of Switzerland rather than the country's scenery. The titles of other pieces from the *Album d'un voyageur* (and the *Années de pèlerinage*) refer to places either by simple description, as in the case of "Au bord d'une source," or by actual geographical locations, as in "Le lac [in the later version Au lac] de Wallenstadt," "Les cloches de Genève," and "La chapelle de Guillaume Tell." The valley in question in *Obermann*, as we shall see, was a specific valley, but Liszt's title does not identify it. Liszt encourages the listener to experience not the valley itself but the responses and reflections that it inspires.

In both the *Album* and the *Années*, two brief excerpts from *Obermann* stand as epigrams before the score:

> What do I want? what am I? what may I ask from nature? . . . Every cause is invisible, every end deceiving; every form changes, every period of time exhausts itself: . . . I feel, I exist in order to consume myself in uncontrollable desires, to steep myself in the seduction of a fantastical world, to remain overwhelmed by its voluptuous wandering.[7]

> Unutterable sensitivity, charm and torment of our vain years; vast consciousness of a nature that is everywhere crushing and everywhere impenetrable, universal passion, advanced wisdom, voluptuous abandon; all that a mortal heart can contain of needs and profound ennuis, I have felt it all, tested it all in this memorable night. I have taken a step to the left toward the age of enfeeblement; I have eaten up ten years of my life.[8]

These come from widely separated parts of Senancour's book and in the reverse of their order there. The first is from letter 63 in the eighth year of Obermann's correspondence—yes, Senancour's book was divided into *années*, serving as the model for Liszt's pilgrimage books. In this passage Obermann looks back over his own life experiences and human life generally. The second quotation had appeared much earlier, in letter 4 from the first year, when he looks forward rather than back at his life. Obermann has gone out on a July night to walk along the river Thièle, to sit on the sand at the edge of Lake Neuchâtel until morning. Nature seems to him in one night to have given him so much experience that a decade has drained away. The title of "Vallée d'Obermann" does not identify the specific location in Neuchâtel and the Thièle valley, because the essential experience takes place not along the river and by the lakeside but in Obermann's reflections. To enter Obermann's valley does not mean to follow Obermann to a spot in Switzerland but to find one's way into Obermann's spiritual province.

The Traveler's Tale:
The First Version of "Vallée d'Obermann"

The version of "Vallée d'Obermann" in the *Album d'un voyageur* follows the outer conventions of sonata form (of Type 3, the default approach for the 1830s) in a recognizable fashion.[9] After an introductory passage (mm. 1–22) comes a section in E minor (mm. 23–42), followed by a contrasting idea in G major (beginning at m. 43). The close of the second section moves back toward E minor, leading into a developmental passage (mm. 76–141). The E-minor area is recapitulated, and then a version of the G-major idea returns, now in E major (mm. 142–79). An apotheosis-like close ends the piece (mm. 180–209).

One distinctive aspect of the form is the presence through most of the piece of a recurring motive, introduced in the first measure, three notes descending stepwise in amphibrachic rhythm. This figure marks the beginning of each theme and section, so that the form might be described as monothematic sonata, although "monomotivic" might suit the case even better (example 10.1, a–c). This motive does indeed lend unity to the form. It also allows the introduction, in itself a rather aimless string of gestures, each launched by the motive and broken up by pauses, to appear as a sort of generative improvisational musing that turns into an actual piece of music only at the beginning of the first section of the sonata form at measure 23.[10]

Example 10.1a. Liszt, *Album d'un voyageur*, "Vallée d'Obermann," mm. 1–5.

Example 10.1b. Liszt, *Album d'un voyageur*, "Vallée d'Obermann," mm. 23–26.

Example 10.1c. Liszt, *Album d'un voyageur*, "Vallée d'Obermann," mm. 43–46, lyrical theme (S).

Another important aspect of this "Vallée" is that the major-key sections—section 2 and its reprise—replay their theme in a series of character variations. The first of these adopts an amorous character, indicated by Liszt as "dolcissimo con amore" (m. 43). It comprises a pair of two-measure phrases, with the melody in octaves above the treble staff, accompanied by left-hand arpeggios, answered by a variant with the melody in a baritone register. After a brief extension, the tune shifts to B♭, but it quickly returns to G for a reinterpretation "con forza e passione" in the baritone range with a right-hand accompaniment in intense repeated sixteenth notes.

In the developmental third section, which Liszt marked "Recitativo," the descending three-note motive undergoes modifications in its rhythm, including diminution, and in its pitch configurations. This section takes on the character of a battle or storm. The section is to be performed "sempre a capriccio," and the expressive instructions include "appassionato," "agitato," "precipitato," "furioso," "energico." A continuous increase of energy and excitement comes from the increasing compression of the main motivic ideas here, the descending third alternating with downward-rushing octaves in one hand or the other, so that at the start of the section this alternation takes two measures, then one, then half-measures, until it devolves into virtuosic octaves and tremolos. Over the course of all this the register expands from a low rumble until the right-hand tremolos at the end lie entirely above the treble staff, while left-hand octaves leap between the mid and low ranges. The rhythmic energy comes to a sudden halt in half-note chords, and the entire section collapses into isolated iterations of the motive, chords in the bass range, and pauses. A rhythmically free descending scale to B3 sets up the return of E minor.

After the reprise of the first theme, the second, now in E major, begins with the theme once again in the baritone and accompanied by wide-spanning arpeggios in the right hand, marked "dolcissimo armonioso"; this is then reversed to put the melody in the soprano and harp accompaniment in the left hand. The overall effect is a sort of celestial consolation. The motive is then inverted to create yet another character, this time of hopeful aspiration. A grand crescendo brings the apotheosis-like coda (mm. 180–209), at first employing the upward form of the motive but restoring the original, descending form just before the end. The piece concludes on a plagal cadence from the minor subdominant to the major tonic. Table 10.1 summarizes the form.

Table 10.1. Form and character in "Vallée d'Obermann," 1842

Section O (mm. 1–22)	**Motivic content:** motive (m)—basic form and diminution **Harmony:** E minor—ends on 5 **Expression markings:** pesante (m. 1); lugubre (m. 3); recitando marcato (m. 9); agitato ed acceler (m. 16)
Section 1. P (mm. 23–42)	**Motivic content:** m—used as head of descending P theme **Harmony:** E minor—ends on V7 with A changing to A♯ to lead to B in melody at start of next section **Expression markings:** *avec un profond sentiment de tristesse* (m. 23); dolce plintivo (m. 33); molto agitato (m. 40)

Section 2. S (mm. 43–75)	**Motivic content:** m—used as head of lyrical melody **Harmony:** G—extension at end without clear cadence to lead to section 3 **Expression markings:** dolcissimo con amore (m. 43); dolce molto espressivo (m. 55); più cresc. con agitazione (m. 59); stringendo (m. 61); con forza e passione (m. 62); raddolente (m. 68)
Section 3. (mm. 76–141)	**Motivic content:** m—altered in rhythm, diminution, interval changes **Harmony:** unstable **Expression markings:** recitativo (mm. 76–141); sotto voce (m. 77); appassionato (m. 80); un poco agitato (m. 86); recitativo (m. 89); molto rinforz. ed appassionato (m. 96); marcato espressivo (m. 98); dolce marcato (m. 101); precipitato (mm. 103, 105), agitato assai (m. 105); prestissimo furioso (m. 108), energico (m. 117); marcatissimo (m. 135); recitativo (mm. 131, 136); appassionato (m. 141)
Section 4. P (mm.142–58)	**Motivic content:** m—as in section 1 **Harmony:** E minor **Expression markings:** "Come prima"
Section 4 (continued). S (mm. 159–79)	**Motivic content:** m—as in section 2; later inverted as head of new melodic idea **Harmony:** E major **Expression markings:** dolcissimo armonioso, dolce espressivo il canto (m. 159); marcato ed espressivo il canto (mm. 170–71)
Section 4 (concluded). Coda (mm. 180–209)	**Motivic content:** m **Harmony:** E major—ends with plagal cadence **Expression markings:** energico sempre marcato il Tema (m. 182); ffff con strepito (m. 197); martellato (m. 201)

The Pilgrim's Tale:
The Revised Version of "Vallée d'Obermann"

When Liszt returned to the "Vallée d'Obermann" to create the new piece to be published in the *Années de pèlerinage*, he did not simply revise the work but reconceived it in fundamental ways. Indeed, he framed the entire set differently from the *Album.* The title of the new collection already alters our viewpoint. No longer are these souvenirs gathered into an album by a traveler; now we encounter a pilgrim. More than in the 1842 collection, its 1855 successor represents an explicitly spiritual journey. The addition of a new epigram from Byron's *Childe Harold's Pilgrimage* also reinforces Liszt's new collection's title. One of these joins the earlier quotations from Senancour as preface to "Vallée d'Obermann":

> Could I embody and unbosom now
> That which is most within me,—could I wreak
> My thoughts upon expression, and thus throw
> Soul, heart, mind, passions, feelings, strong or weak,
> All that I would have sought, and all I seek,
> Bear, know, feel, and yet breathe—into *one* word
> And that one word were Lightning, I would speak;
> But as it is, I live and die unheard,
> With a most voiceless thought, sheathing it as a sword. (canto
> 3, stanza 97)

We should expect the revised "Vallée d'Obermann" to reflect the new representation of the protagonist—no longer merely traveler but now pilgrim. The music is recognizable as a successor of the former version, but it has changed in remarkable ways. As pianists and critics have always noted, although the second version still challenges the player, it does not present the transcendent challenges of the first. At the same time, the variety of expressive references has become clearer. Further, it eschews sonata form (or any of the types recognized in Sonata Theory) to emphasize a different principle.[11]

The new piece begins with an introduction derived not from the earlier version's opening but from its sonata form's principal theme. Here it has become longer and much more harmonically unstable. It has a form of its own. The opening descending melody turns unexpectedly from E minor to G minor in the first four measures. These measures repeat in sequence, leading to B♭ minor (example 10.2). A four-measure transitional cantilena leads back to the main descending line, reiterated in a sequence of two-measure units starting successively on A♭5, B♭5, C6, D6, and G6. The scale then decelerates as it descends in parallel octaves to the bass staff and pauses after the interval C4–D♯3, implying the vii°7 in E minor at measure 25.

Example 10.2. Liszt, *Années de pèlerinage,* "Vallée d'Obermann," mm. 1–8.

Abruptly the texture and tonality change to a slowly unfolding chromatic progression supporting a melodic line whose upward inflection seems interrogative. This repeats in sequence at the tritone, ending on iv6 in E, and there follows a dominant seventh and another pause. At this point the first measures of the piece return (mm. 34–41), but the continuation in the transitional cantilena takes place a major third higher than before. The descending scales follow in a new harmonic context, first over an E♭-major $^6_4$ and then a B-major $^6_4$. The questioning phrase also returns, leading to an F-minor sixth chord. A few more iterations of the descending theme wander back to three short E-minor chords in a low register. There is a long rest (m. 74) marking the end of the introduction.

What is now the main body of the work derives from the secondary area of the sonata form in the predecessor version. Here the key is C major, and the lyrical theme first appears in a high register over gently pulsing eighth notes, first in an *una corda*, pianissimo, dolcissimo statement and then rescored more fully *a tre corde*. A duet-like interlude culminating più appassionato (m. 107) brings the section to a transitional close on a descending arpeggio and then scale ("quasi cadenza," m. 118) implying the V7 of E♭ major.

The developmental Recitativo section in the revised "Vallée" largely follows the course of the first version. Here again the character of storm or battle is clarified by some of the same interpretive instructions and some new ones: "appassionato" (mm. 127, 129), "agitato molto" (m. 128), "precipitato" (mm. 134, 136), "stringendo" (m. 137), "presto tempestuoso" (m. 139, replacing "prestissimo furioso"). The whole section, though rewritten somewhat on the surface, follows the development section of the *Album d'un voyageur* version nearly measure for measure. At the end, rather than a simple descending scale, there is a new "quasi cadenza" settling on B3.

This arrival leads to E major for another transformation of the lyrical melody. Here it is played lento and dolce, with a gently rocking, slightly syncopated inner-voice accompaniment. The texture evokes calm Nature, placid and yet vibrant. The four-measure period is extended by one measure, a feature that gives asymmetry and a feeling of relaxed expansion and anticipation to this version. This repeats, still dolce, with the melody in upper octaves and denser texture. This time the fifth-measure extension is marked "smorzando" and concludes on a G♯-major chord and then a fermata over a breath mark. There follow the inverted form of the motive and the rising line that extends it. Here, for the first time in this piece, the left-hand accompaniment employs arpeggios, while the right hand rolls chords under the very high-range melody. The effect is of celestial peace, and the religious reference becomes explicit if the listener recognizes the citation of the "Dresden Amen," a liturgical formula well known in the nineteenth century.[12] A few measures developing the rising gesture initiate a transition to the next segment.

The apotheosis passage begins with the original lyric melody played in three parallel octaves, starting mezzo forte and with a continuous crescendo, accompanied by chords in driving repeated triplet sixteenth notes. After eight measures the rising version returns, still with the driving repeated notes but also in contraposition to rushing octaves in the bass. The original motive reemerges, fortississimo, reiterated every half measure and descending to the lowest range, finally simply cut off by an E-major rising arpeggio, played in four parallel octaves, a sort of triumphal shout.

Following this apparent ending, after a rest marked by a fermata, come two appended measures that finally seem to revert to the very beginning of the piece. Here the motive begins in the first measure, but it loses track of its amphibrachic rhythm and staggers down stepwise in a failed recollection of the left-hand melody from the start of the piece, descending from E4 through D♯, C♮, B, and A, to G♯3, all over the dyad F–A. The final measure is an E-major triad with an appoggiatura moving from C4 to B3. This is all doubled in the two hands, producing a dark, brooding effect. The bass motion from F♮ to E gives the impression of a sort of Phrygian half cadence in A minor, so that the listener might hear the ending as somewhat open-ended. The pitch vocabulary in these two measures, featuring the two augmented whole tones F–G♯ and C–D♯, comprises a form of the so-called Gypsy scale, occurring here for the only time in the work. Table 10.2 summarizes the design of this final version.

Table 10.2. Form and character in "Vallée d'Obermann," 1855

Opening (mm. 1–74)	**Character:** speaking, questioning (mm. 26ff, 60ff) • **Motivic content:** m • **Harmony:** briefly E minor, then modulatory • **Expressive markings:** espressivo (m. 1); sotto voce (m. 9); espressivo (m. 42); dolcissimo (m. 51); sempre dolciss. (m. 55); dolente (m. 67); pesante (m. 71)	Grabócz's description • **Structural unit:** first thematic complex; theme and its rhetorical development • **Character:** lamenting, solo and mournful; MACABRE QUEST
Theme and variations (mm. 75–118)	**Character:** pastoral, amorous • **Motivic content:** m in lyrical melody • **Harmony:** C major • **Expressive markings:** dolcissimo (mm. 75, 85); smorzando (m. 93); espr. (m. 94); più appassionato (m. 107)	Grabócz's description • **Structural unit:** second thematic complex; theme and its formal variations • **Character:** pastoral-amoroso, bel canto fragments; PASTORAL-AMOROSO
Recitative (mm. 119–69)	**Character:** stormy • **Motivic content:** m modified • **Harmony:** unstable • **Expressive markings:** recitativo (m. 119); appassionato (m. 127); agitato molto (m. 128); appassionato (m. 129); precipitato (mm. 134, 136); stringendo (m. 137); presto tempestuoso (m. 139)	Grabócz's description • **Structural unit:** third thematic complex; motto and its "development" • **Character:** storm semes, macabre semes, fanfare semes; MACABRE FIGHT
Further variations of the theme (mm. 170–214)	**Character:** pantheistic, religious, joy • **Motivic content:** m in lyrical melody • **Harmony:** E major • **Expressive markings:** lento dolce (m. 170); dolce (m. 175); dolce armonioso (m. 180); sempre animando sin' al fine (m. 188)	Grabócz's description • **Structural unit:** fourth thematic complex; theme and its formal variations • **Character:** bel canto, pathetic, pastoral-pantheistic semes; RELIGIOUS-PANTHEIST
Coda (mm. 215–16)	**Character:** reflective, brooding • **Motivic content:** m in staggering rhythm • **Harmony:** E ("Gypsy scale"; quasi-Phrygian half-cadence)	

The design of this "Vallée d'Obermann" does not correspond well to the conventions of sonata form, as we have observed, but its structural conception is clear enough.[13] Leaving aside for the moment the introduction and the two-measure closing envoi, it adopts a principle of variation, of the free type that operates by thematic transformation. First comes the lyrical theme that opens with the main motive (mm. 75–84) in a setting evoking innocent nature, in C major, a conventional key for pastoral scenes. This repeats in a thicker texture (mm. 85–94). Measures 95–117 form a duet passage that grows more impassioned as it progresses. These two transformations are followed by the much freer, developmental Recitativo section (mm. 119–69). The arrival at E major brings a revision of the theme that again suggests nature, this time in a more spiritually animated experience (mm. 170–74), a richer reiteration (mm. 175–79), and then the celestial or religious transformation using the inverted, rising line (mm. 180–84). The "apotheosis" (mm. 188–214) joins the descending (mm. 188–95) and ascending (mm. 196–99) melodic extensions of the motive in a continuous style, before it carries itself away in multiple statements of the three-note original motive (mm. 200–213).

The opening seventy-four measures and the final two relate to the variation/transformation process somewhat differently. The first part of the piece does not sound like a sonata form principal theme, but it does sound like an introduction, which should immediately lead us away from analyzing the piece as in any sense a parallel design to the Type 3 sonata form of its predecessor. The motive in this case does not form into the relatively cantabile melodic style that underlies the bulk of the work. The approach is more parlando, and the unfolding less clearly stanzaic. Its harmonic structure, especially the modulation by rising minor thirds in the first eight measures, makes it evidently too unstable to act as a unit suitable for conventional variation (or sonata) procedures.[14] Nevertheless, the first passage immediately introduces the main motive and makes evident its importance. While this opening and the ending remain remote from the sense of variation form that prevails, they obviously participate in their own way in the conceptual scope of thematic transformation.

Unlike, for example, sonata form, thematic transformation does not carry a tradition of conventional functions. On the other hand, we can discover a certain degree of convention within Liszt's own approach to forms based on thematic transformation. As table 10.2 indicates, Márta Grabócz chooses to regard the piece as an example of character variations, and she outlines a "canonical" strategy for such works in four stages (starting point and three variations affecting character and form):

Stage 1 expresses the macabre interrogation related to spleen, painful soul-searching or *lamento*. . . .

Stage 2 finds an immediate answer to Stage 1 in the pastoral character, in the possible solace of the *amoroso* affect. . . .

Stage 3 often marked as *recitativo* by Liszt. Dramatically expressive, it often comes with the musical depiction of storms, battles or macabre fights. . . .

Stage 4 refers to meditation, to the topics of religion, and imitates the ringing of church bells.[15]

Clearly, as she points out, "Vallée d'Obermann" exemplifies this plan—in fact, it might even serve as a template for other works, as Grabócz suggests by placing it at the top of her tables of Liszt works that employ these expressive genres.[16] It is worth noticing here that she does not describe the first stage in the schema as the "theme" but only as a starting point. Thus, in the case of "Vallée d'Obermann," its melodic and harmonic content and its formal unfolding place the first passage outside the variations that follow.

Eero Tarasti has tracked the course of the piece in five isotopies.[17] The first passage he calls "boredom" (97), although he also describes it as iconically representing the Alpine peaks and valleys in its use of high and low registers. He observes that it does not seem to represent past action being narrated but something in the present. The C-major section seems then to come from the past. He calls it "wandering." The isotopy of the middle of the piece is, not unusually, "fight or storm" (98). For Tarasti this pursues latent aspects of the first ("boredom") isotopy, and it therefore seems to return to the present. The fourth isotopy is "pastoral," the characterization most commentators apply to the C-major section. He says that it is like "the sun casting its last rays upon a field full of corpses after the struggle," and he places it in the past tense (which begs the question how the fallen combatants in the past can follow the fight in the present). Tarasti does not recognize the character of religion or meditation that Grabócz and I, like other listeners, hear. The final passage he describes as "Pantheist Apotheosis of a sense of Nature" and "an epico-dramatic culmination of the preceding lyrical isotopy, a movement from 'then' to 'now'" (99). To some extent, then, Tarasti attempts an explanation of the same sort as Grabócz's, but by working too hard at separating both the expressive scene types and the past and present, this interpretation ties itself into impossible knots. Nevertheless, both treatments aim at a kind of narrative explication independent of sonata form, which the work certainly calls for.

Narrative Voice in "Vallée d'Obermann"

Based on its difference in style from the body of the piece, the listener will very likely hear the passage that occupies the first seventy-four measures as communicating on a different level of discourse from what follows. In some sense it might be said to preface or frame the remainder of the music, but that would not describe it adequately. Among the features that differentiate this passage from the rest of the work are its parlando—speaking or prosaic—diction, its isolation of questioning phrases, and its unsettled harmony. Yet the shared dependence on the descending (initially) three-note amphibrachic motive enforces the perception of the entire piece as belonging together. The body of the piece acts in the way that we expect in music that performs action or lived experience. In relation to activity—even if retrospectively—we justifiably understand the introduction as inactive, melancholy, reflective. The body of the piece thus seems to be the recounting of events that the introduction has mentioned by its statement of the motive. The action is then set up as if by a colon at the *lunga pausa* in measure 74. As explicitly as possible (even blatantly), Liszt constructed this piece to represent a narrator and the narration of the narrator's own experiences. Liszt quotes aptly from *Obermann*, "J'ai tout senti, tout éprouvé dans cette nuit mémorable."

We might, however, still probe the identity of the narrative voice. The immediate and natural answer, which Andrew Fowler represents, is that "the composer/pianist becomes Obermann, and through the piano, which acts as conduit, the hero experiences the overwhelming, unpenetrable forces of Nature."[18] For Michele Calella, who considers the entire cycle of pieces, the case is more complicated:

> Whose voice do we perceive in the *Album d'un voyageur* and in
> the Swiss volume of the *Années de pèlerinage*? Perhaps the question
> would better be asked: How many voices? Those of Liszt, Byron,

Senancour, or George Sand? Or of an imaginary musical traveler, of Childe Harold, Obermann—in which Rousseau's hero Saint-Preuve also resonates? And which Liszt does one hear here, the traveler, the reader of poetry, the sensitive-melancholy subject, the Hungarian subject, or the representative of a new Weimar Classicism? A multiplicity of subject voices emerges consciously in this interpretation, which through their overlapping create from Liszt's piano collections a dynamic process of polyphonic narration, which sketches out a diversely culturally loaded geography of Switzerland, a musical landscape whose places can be construed beyond their empirical locations in an intertextual and at the same time discursive process.[19]

As little as we can justify simply naming the voice of this piece as Obermann, we can no more merely label it Liszt. Katharine Ellis notes the obvious problem of knowing how to understand the composer himself. As she points out, Liszt, the Romantic artist, was a "divided self."[20] One might argue that all Romantic artists (if not all of us) have divided selves. Nevertheless, no self-respecting narrator of a single work can be content to remain unidentifiable except by assuming some vague admixture of the composer's selves, so that we give up as hopeless the effort to identify that voice.

"Vallée d'Obermann" makes a sort of textbook example of the application of paratext to direct the performer, hearer, or critic to the identity of the speaker. We read the peritextual excerpts from Senancour and Byron as quotations selected by the same "I" whose voice we hear in the music, and we understand them as asserting a personal empathy with the figures of Obermann and Harold. Liszt left as epitext a statement about *Obermann* that helps to clarify the basis of this empathy in a letter to Schott, the publisher of the *Années de pèlerinage*, expressing his gratitude for the beautiful edition but also objecting to the engraving that accompanied "Vallée d'Obermann," which showed a party of hunters at their ease among the mountains (see Figure 10.1). He wrote,

Geography has nothing to do with this piece, for it refers specifically and only to the French novel *Obermann* by Senancour, whose action purely deals with the development of a particular state of the soul.—This book has had a profound influence on a not inconsiderable part of French literature—especially on Mme George Sand, who has written a long essay about it. One could

Figure 10.1. Title-page engraving for Liszt's "Vallée d'Obermann" in the first edition of *Années de pèlerinage* (Mainz: B. Schott's Söhne, 1855). *Source:* Public domain.

call Obermann the *monochord* of the unremitting loneliness of human suffering. It is a wild, confused, and sublime book. The melancholy, hyperelegiacal fragment "La Vallée d'Obermann" that is entered into the Swiss year of *Années de pèlerinage* (for the book's setting is likewise Switzerland) brings out several main impulses of Senancour's work, as the selected epigraphs also indicate. Shotguns and hunters have nothing to do with it! And as prettily as the title page may have been executed, it stands in the most glaringly laughable *contresens* to the piece.[21]

There are two important points to emphasize in this letter. First, "Vallée d'Obermann" does not depict any actual place, but rather the piece encompasses multiple experiences from Senancour's work. The listener must understand therefore that the music does not depict Switzerland's rugged Alps and placid lakes—and certainly not a hunting party—nor does it record the sounds of waterfalls or cowherds' horns and their charges' clunking bells. Second, in terms of the voice, the book portrays simply the development of the state of a particular soul, and, like a monochord, it sounds the fundamental pitch for the unrelenting loneliness of human suffering. The speaker of this piece (unlike some others in the collection) need not be associated with Switzerland but certainly knows the sublime but desolate, confused malaise suffered by all Romantics—as Norbert Miller has put it, the "state of emptiness in which every genius who is inclined toward inactivity after his heroic beginnings and the flight into interiority must end."[22] The narrative voice of "Vallée d'Obermann" is not Senancour or Byron (or Dumas or Sand), Obermann or Harold—nor, we should emphasize once again, the composer Liszt. We know much about the speaker in the music, however, who shares as much with all of them as they do with each other: the profound calm and the terrifying awe of nature, the excitement and tensions of love, the struggle of conflict, the consolations of religious faith. We know as we experience the music how those experiences feel or have felt to the musical narrator. The music does not offer a specific name, but it makes the listener intimately familiar with the speaker's personality. We cannot help but know this narrative persona.

As we observed about the fictive Obermann at the beginning of this excursion, we do not read the letters in order to follow the story of the exploits of a dramatic character, although we do empathically experience various impressions from a life. Even if in Liszt's music we imagine the narrator formerly to have been the protagonist in the episodes that the music evokes (i.e., that the piece is a first-person narrative), which we might—even then we should not intend to listen to the music to trace the protagonist's life in a sort of *Bildungsdrama*. Most importantly, we come to know their fictive writer. In the music we become acquainted not so much with a protagonist as with a voice.

A Postscript—Or a Signature?

There is still another aspect of the voice in "Vallée d'Obermann" in the *Années de pèlerinage*, one that was not a feature of the personality in the piece of the same title in the *Album d'un voyageur*. The distinction goes beyond the obvious difference between traveler and pilgrim in the two collections. Like the excerpts from *Obermann* that stand as the epigrams for both pieces, the stanza from *Childe Harold's Pilgrimage* that Liszt added for the later version of the piece has nothing to do with a definite place (although Harold is at that moment by Lake Leman), nor does it even suggest any location at all. It expresses a feeling of frustration with the inability to capture the intensity of the speaker's own thoughts and feelings. Even if one had the capacity to express oneself verbally in a way as charged and powerful as lightning, it would not serve. Thus the speaker is reduced to silence.

Harold's stanza is not the only addition in the later version of the "Vallée" that conveys this confession from the speaker. Also new was the little musical envoi in the last two measures. Unlike the early version of the piece, this one does not conclude in a blaze of glory. After the flash of the main coda, it ends modestly with no brilliance at all. The listener surely recognizes that the narration of escapades and episodes has ended, and we are back alone with the narrator from the introduction. The inadequacy of even the most transcendental technique—an inadequacy equally in Lisztian pianism and in Lisztian facility with the harmony of the tonal vocabulary—to express what is most important leaves a stammering, ungrammatical phrase, sounding like a half cadence in a new key, or like nothing much at all. Unmistakably in the music, the narrator discovers that his expression of his experience (or her expression of her experience, because nothing explicitly determines the narrator's gender, and a woman—Marie d'Agoult or George Sand, for example—might also express these Romantic experiences) possesses no voice: ". . . as it is, I live and die unheard, / With a most voiceless thought . . ." There is just one more curious feature of the identification of the voice here. As we noted earlier, these two measures employ the pitch configuration of a "Gypsy scale." As much as the narrator might share with the western European Romantics, the narrative voice at the last moment also reveals Otherness in its own identity. And leaves us there.

Chapter 11

"The Real Author of the Drama"

Deconstruction in Verdi's *Otello*

Thoughts on Music in Opera

On an obvious level, the primary task of the music in an opera is to support and reflect the words and actions of the characters. Much of this work follows well-established conventions. Tempo and harmony express the feelings of characters; scoring represents anything from shepherds' pipes to hunters' horns to the slashes and thrusts of swords in a duel. Vocal lines can distinguish the patter of major generals from the virtuosic rages of nocturnal queens and the lyric raptures of lovers. Music also sets the scene and frames the story. It places the action in an exotic locale or in a storm on the ocean. Overtures raise the curtain, and interludes underlie scene changes. Leitmotifs make references to characters, objects, and ideas that reinforce or play in counterpoint to the statements that singers make. The music in these cases adopts what we might regard as a sort of enriching function in a generalized sense. We would not necessarily encounter any of these instances as manifestations of a narrative voice with any distinct personality.

Sometimes in an opera, as in any story, characters engage in internal narration within the action. Marco Beghelli has discussed instances in opera of analepsis, the recounting of past events, and of teichoscopy, the description of offstage actions as they take place. His points might equally apply to prolepsis, the foretelling of future occurrences. Most importantly, he observes that in such cases the representation of conditions or actions in musical terms has the effect of making them actually present to the audience's experience in a way more immediate than would be the case in a stage play.[1] In a way, we might hypothesize that the music itself would have a narrative function in such cases. On the other hand, we might better think of the music as performing separate dramatic events, embedded within the plot, so that it becomes a kind of parenthetical, musical action, not narration.

We certainly recognize the *authorial* voice in an opera, since different periods and composers have distinct styles. Some composers have their own different creative periods—the creator of Verdi's *Otello* is not the same artist as the creator of Verdi's *Macbeth* almost forty years earlier. In addition to details of musical style, an opera composer's approach to musical dramaturgy can change over the course of a career. Nevertheless, while changes in a composer's style might lead us to understand different works by the same biographical composer in contrasting ways, in themselves the differences remain the attributes of the author. And, as is always the case, the author is not the same as the narrative persona in any work.

A narrative stance would have to manifest itself in some controlling relationship to the characters and action that goes beyond the conventional or even the distinctively authorial. We can uncover an instance of this in Jago's "Credo" from the beginning of act 2 of Verdi's *Otello*. In this case, the music engages the story in a narratorial way, bringing to the fore a specific aspect of the plot, which it presents by means of critical deconstruction.

The Composition of *Otello*

First, however, it will be helpful to remind ourselves of the place of *Otello* in Verdi's oeuvre. Verdi had been the undisputed master of Italian opera in his generation. His first great masterpieces included *Il Trovatore*, *Rigoletto*, and *La Traviata*, all dating from around 1850, when he was approaching forty years old. There followed a series of successful works during the 1850s and 1860s, culminating and terminating with *Aida* in 1871. Then, at the age of fifty-eight, Verdi retired from composing operas. After a hiatus of seventeen years, he was lured back to work by the prospect of composing an opera based on Shakespeare's *Othello*, collaborating with the younger composer and librettist Arrigo Boito (1842–1918). The plans for the project began around 1880, but the opera was not completed until 1886, a very long period of creative effort as compared to Verdi's earlier output. In the course of this extended compositional period, fortunately for us, Verdi, Boito, and several of their collaborators wrote quite a lot about the opera.[2]

It is easy to understand the reasons for Boito's and Verdi's interest in Shakespeare's *Othello* as a source. For one thing, in comparison to most of Shakespeare's plays, the action holds to a single strong, controlling plot. Julian Budden writes, "Of all Shakespeare's dramas it is the best constructed and the most vividly theatrical; it is also the one which most nearly conforms to the canon of Aristotle's *Poetics* in everything apart from its time-scale. There are no sub-plots, no episodes that fail to bear on the central action. . . . Even the most ardently lyrical passages are all harnessed to the dramatic purpose."[3] And he quotes George Bernard Shaw's insight that "instead of Otello being an Italian opera written in the style of Shakespear, Othello is a play written by Shakespear in the style of Italian opera. . . . With such a libretto, Verdi was quite at home: his success with it proves, not that he could occupy Shakespear's plane, but that Shakespear could on occasion occupy his, which is a very different matter."[4] The tale is full of passion, of good and evil, of innocence and violent death. The audience understands the characters easily. Othello is impressive as a powerful military hero; as a Black man, exotic; and as the husband of Desdemona, erotically fascinating. Verdi once described his Otello as "now the warrior, now the passionate lover, . . . now ferocious like a savage."[5] Desdemona, on the other hand, is white and pure, the very image of innocence. As Victor Maurel, who created the role of Jago, put it, she is an "earthly angel."[6] Iago, jealous and bitter, is the perfect villain, tricking his general, Othello, into believing that Desdemona is unfaithful and finally driving him into such jealous rage that he murders her. In his character description in the opera's production book, Boito wrote, "He is an artist in deception."[7] More about these characters later.

With Boito, as with his earlier librettists and with others involved in the production, Verdi engaged in extensive correspondence about the opera—the plot, the characters, details of the poetry, and nuances of staging and performance. Despite the play's appeal as an opera topic, constructing the libretto was not a simple matter. The essence of the plot and most of the main characters were retained, but everything had to be concentrated. Boito omitted act 1 of Shakespeare's play, the Venetian prologue to the Cyprus action, relocating a few necessary details into later parts of the story. Minor characters had to be dropped, such as Bianca (Cassio's girlfriend) and the Clown, or their roles reduced, as with Roderigo. The end of the story was abbreviated so that, unlike in Shakespeare's play, Jago does not kill his own wife, Emilia, and his punishment is not mentioned. Some of Shakespeare's sexual references are toned down, and philosophical material is eliminated. Besides the need to compact the story, musical considerations also played a part in the plan. The play gave little opportunity for exploitation of a chorus, so the collaborators created occasions for that. And an extensive passage featuring the orchestral double basses replaced Othello's last-act soliloquy ("It is the cause . . .").

Iago's "Credo"

Importantly, the opera is mostly about Jago. In a letter of August 24, 1881, Boito wrote to Verdi, "On the lyric side, the principal character is Desdemona; on the dramatic side, the principal character is Jago."[8] The correspondence between composer and librettist a year later shows that at one time Boito and Verdi thought of naming the opera *Jago*. For this reason it is especially useful to study Jago's "Credo," beginning with the scene that opens act 2, a bit of dialogue between Jago and Cassio, whom Jago is setting up to be the object of Otello's unjust jealousy, and continuing through Jago's solo.

The first part of this scene derives from *Othello*, act 2, scene 3, where Iago advises gullible Cassio to appeal to tender-hearted Desdemona to regain the favor of Othello, his underlying motive being to set up a situation in which Othello will believe that Desdemona is involved in an affair with Cassio. Here is the original from Shakespeare:

> I'll tell you what you shall do. Our general's wife is now the general—I may say so in this respect, for that he hath devoted and given up himself to the contemplation, mark, and denotement of her parts and graces. Confess yourself freely to her; importune her help to put you in your place again. She is of so free, so kind, so apt, so blessed a disposition she holds it a vice in her goodness not to do more than she is requested. This broken joint between you and her husband entreat her to splinter; and, my fortunes against any lay worth naming, this crack of your love shall grow stronger than it was before.

In the opera the orchestra begins with two measures of unison, consisting of nothing but a repeated turn motive in the low register. As the curtain rises, Jago and Cassio are revealed on the stage, already in mid-conversation (example 11.1). At this moment the orchestra introduces a one-measure melodic phrase (mm. 3–4), which leads to a sort of spinning out in increasing chromaticism that debouches in a diatonic lyrical, two-measure cadential

Example 11.1. Verdi, *Otello*, act 2, mm. 1–11.

refrain phrase in F major (mm. 9–11). Succeeding this comes a bit of short-breathed, repeating material that moves from F minor momentarily to A♭ and then to a descending sequence through C minor, B♭, A♭, G♭, back to F for a return of the brief refrain (mm. 15–17). Cassio and Jago continue their exchange through this passage, although we do not hear what they say.

At this point the dialogue becomes audible as recitative, accompanied by the repeated turn motive.

JAGO.
Non ti crucciar.
Se credi a me, tra poco, farai ritorno
ai follegianti amori di Monna Bianca,
altiero capitano, coll'elsa d'oro
e col balteo fregiato.
CASSIO.
Non lusingarmi . . .

(JAGO. Do not worry. If you trust me, in a little while you will
return to the playful caresses of Monna Bianca, proud captain,
with your gold hilt and embroidered baldric. CASSIO. Do not
flatter me . . .)

The quick turn figure shifts to a slower, legato ostinato, over which Jago
continues,

Attendi a ciò ch'io dico.
Tu dèi saper che Desdemona è il Duce
del nostro Duce, sol per essa ei vive.
Pregala tu, quell'anima cortese
per te interceda e il tuo perdono è certo.

(JAGO: Listen to what I am telling you. You must know that
Desdemona is the general of our general; he lives only for her.
If you beseech this kind soul to intercede for you, your pardon
is assured.)

His last half-line, "e il tuo perdono è certo," is set to the lyrical refrain, which
we now understand to have been throughout his false assurance to Cassio
that Desdemona's intervention will soften Otello's attitude. The recitative
continues, supported by the figure from measures 12 to 13:

CASSIO.
Ma come favellarle?
JAGO.
È suo costume girsene a meriggiar
fra quelle fronde colla consorte mia.

Quivi l'aspetta.
Or t'è aperta la via di salvazione.
Vanne.

(CASSIO. But how to speak with her? JAGO. It is her custom
to stroll as a noontime rest among these branches with my
wife. Wait for her here. Now the way of salvation opens for
you. Go on.)

Once again Jago's assurance of Cassio's success with Desdemona's help, "la
via di salvazione," merges into the brief refrain melody (mm. 35–36).

The succeeding soliloquy for Jago has no true model in the play. It
begins in blasphemy and ends in nihilism. As soon as Cassio leaves, the
orchestral turn motive returns in four detached iterations, rising through
four octaves of Fs. Then it suddenly comes four times on octave G♭s in the
bass register, fortississimo and accented, as a snarl. Dismissing Cassio, Jago
says,

Vanne; la tua meta già vedo.
Ti spinge il tuo dimone,
e il tuo dimon son io.
E me trascina il mio, nel quale io credo,
inesorate Iddio.

"Go on; I already see your end. Your daemon drives you forward, and I am your daemon. And mine draws me, in which I
believe, inexorable god."

This ends on a half cadence on D♭, as V of G♭.

There follows the "Credo" itself, conjured by Boito from the barest
fragments in Shakespeare. The librettist had originally provided a rather
straightforward, poetic aria text in *versi lirici*, consisting of four regular
quatrains of *doppio quinario*.⁹ That version did not satisfy Verdi, who
wanted something less songlike. The replacement that Boito created and
Verdi ultimately composed employs the more prose-like rhythms of *versi
sciolti*, free verse of the sort commonly used in Italian opera for recitative
but not for arias; Boito called it "broken and nonsymmetrical meter."¹⁰ In
turn, Verdi's declamatory rather than lyrical treatment reflects that Iago is

(to quote from entirely elsewhere in Shakespeare) the perfect example of a man who has "no music in himself" and is "fit for treasons, stratagems, and spoils."

> Credo in un Dio crudel che m'ha creato
> simile a sè e che nell'ira io nomo.
> Dalle viltà d'un germe o d'un atòmo
> vile son nato.
> Son scellerato
> perchè son uomo;
> e sento il fango originario in me.
> Si! questa è la mia fè!
> Credo con fermo cuor, siccome crede
> la vedovella al tempio,
> che il mal ch'io penso e che da me procede,
> per il mio destino adempio.
> Credo che il giusto è un istrion beffardo,
> e nel viso e nel cuor,
> che tutto è in lui bugiardo:
> lagrima, bacio, sguardo,
> sacrificio ed onor.
> E credo l'uom gioco d'iniqua sorte
> dal germe della culla
> al verme dell'avel.
> Vien dopo tanta irrision la Morte.
> E poi? La Morte è il Nulla.
> È vecchia fola il Ciel.

"I believe in a cruel god, who created me like himself and whom I name in anger. From the baseness of a germ or an atom I was born abject. I am a villain because I am a man; and I feel the primeval slime in myself. Yes! this is my belief! I believe with a firm heart, as the young widow in the church believes, that the evil that I conceive and that comes from me arises from my destiny. I believe that the honest man is a mocking actor in his face and in his heart, that everything in him is a lie: tear, kiss, glance, sacrifice, and honor. And I believe man to be the jest of wicked fate from the germ of the cradle to the worm of the grave. After such mockery comes Death. And then? Death is Nothingness. Heaven is an old wives' tale."

The Credo opens with the full orchestra fortissimo in a bold, angular unison line that establishes the key of F minor (example 11.2). Jago begins on a sort of mock-liturgical reciting tone C4 over a "horror" trill[11] and continues over diminished seventh chords that lead to a cadence on E♭ major at the end of the second line of the text (mm. 55–56). An infernal dance figure, which Julian Budden aptly describes as belonging to the Lisztian Mephistophelian type,[12] abruptly enters in E major (example 11.3), and the following lines move to a new close on C minor at "e sento il fango originario in me" (mm. 65–67). Over the return of the opening unison, again in F minor, Jago proclaims, "Si! Quest'è la mia fè!" (mm. 67–71) to close the first part of the "Credo."

The middle of the number digresses through a disorienting series of keys. This section begins in C minor and passes via F minor on the way through D♭—actually avoided by the addition of a C♭ in the bass at the cadence—ultimately to a second-inversion dominant seventh of B at the end of the line "al verme dell'avel" (mm. 100–101). Several accompaniment figurations occur here, notably the hellish dance motive, as well as prominent agitated tremolos.

The brief concluding segment of the "Credo" starts by returning to the opening angular melody, now not in the bold unison but harmonized in a chorale-like texture and legato, fading from forte to pianissimo (mm. 102–6). After "Vien dopo tanta irrision la Morte" ends on a diminished seventh chord, the melody returns, again reharmonized and fragmented

Example 11.2. Verdi, *Otello*, act 2, mm. 46–49.

Example 11.3. Verdi, *Otello*, act 2, mm. 57–59.

by rests for Jago's "E poi? E poi? La Morte è il Nulla." The final line, "È vecchia fola il Ciel," is set to a plagal cadence to D♭, which disappears immediately into a return to the Mephistophelian dance, now in F major. In some stagings Jago bursts into an evil, mocking laugh at this point, but the original stage directions from Boito and Verdi say that he merely shrugs his shoulders and turns away.[13]

Deception

Certainly the musical setting suits the bitter sentiments of the "Credo" text convincingly throughout. Beyond that, it also mirrors Jago's deceptiveness with musical illustrations of deception. If we did not know it already, the text of the scene, moving from Jago's assurances to Cassio to his derisive comment after Cassio's exit and the "Credo" itself, would make it clear that Jago is a deceiver entirely untroubled by conscience. His whole action is based on deception—primarily of Otello but also, as a means of accomplishing that, of Cassio, as well. What might interest us first of all, then, is to find the ways in which Verdi placed instances of musical deception in this scene. Musicians are familiar with a particular image of deception, the deceptive cadence,[14] in which the expected resolution of the dominant chord is thwarted and the harmonic progression led off to some other place, usually the submediant. Such a passage occurs toward the end of the Credo, in the orchestra just preceding the line "dopo tanta irrision" (example 11.4), where the phrase begins on V $\frac{4}{2}$ of G♭ and closes on vi in F major. The musical image of deception is unmistakable.

Another, less conventional instance of deception occurs at the very beginning of the scene, and it has to do with rhythm rather than harmony. At the opening of the act, one hears the rhythm in four-beat measures,

Example 11.4. Verdi, *Otello*, act 2, mm. 103–7.

starting with a static line of beats consisting of four iterations of a sixteenth-note-triplet turn embellishing a quarter-note F2 (see example 11.1). In this motive the triplet constitutes an anacrusis and the quarter note comes on the beat, but the effect also tends to deceive the listener, because the position of the measure is obscured. The beginning with the triplet anacrusis leads the listener to hear the first quarter-note F2 as the start of a measure, whereas in fact it is the second beat and thus itself merely part of an extended three-quarter-measure anacrusis that resolves only on the downbeat of measure 2. We think that the first four beats are 1—2—3—4, but they are really 2—3—4 | 1. We learn only gradually, as the music proceeds, that the very first sound is really the second beat of a measure, so that we have been hearing upbeats as downbeats and vice versa. What is more, conductors typically do not help to clarify the issue. In many cases they play the four successive occurrences of the motive without any shaping of the measure, and not uncommonly they actually give a slight diminuendo, so that the fourth one does not come across as a downbeat at all. The music establishes deception at the start of the scene, even before we hear Jago speak.

Jago as Author of the Action

Otello offers another, much more sophisticated view of the figure of Jago, however, which will occupy the remainder of this chapter. In order to get at this point, we need to amplify the understanding of Jago. Describing Jago in the production book for the opera, Boito wrote, intriguingly,

> Jago is Envy. Jago is a scoundrel. Jago is a critic. In his cast of characters, Shakespeare characterizes him like this: "Jago, a Villain," and he does not add a word more. In the square of Cyprus, Jago defines himself like this: "I am nothing if not critical. Io non sono che un critico." He is a spiteful and malicious critic. . . . He is an artist in deception. . . . Jago is the real author of the drama. He creates the threads, he gathers them up, he arranges them, he intertwines them.[15]

The first two statements here, the statements that describe Jago's character, require little justification beyond the text of the play and the opera. Anyone who knows the plot at all is aware that Jago is the villain of the drama. The assertion that he is Envy (with a capital *E*) suggests not merely that he is envious but that he personifies the vice itself. The paragraph also describes Jago's way of engaging in the plot, an artist in deception.

Jago does not merely participate in the same way that the other characters do in the dramatic action, however. He is more than the villain of the piece. Jago controls the other characters and the direction of the plot, and in this sense he guides the action. His function has been described in various ways. Although insisting that the title of the work finally had to be *Otello*, Verdi wrote, "[Jago] is (it's true) the Demon who sets everything in motion."[16] James Hepokoski calls him a "puppeteer and trickster," not merely deceiving the other characters but pulling the strings to control them.[17] Scott Balthazar calls him "an instigator."[18] Jane Hawes uses various terms: "mover and shaker," "master manipulator," "the Master Manipulator, the Evil Genius, the Demon who drives the action."[19] In this sense Boito's representation of Jago as the "real author" must intend to capture the distinction between Jago and all the other characters, who become the actors in his theater and end as his victims.

Theodore Albritton Conner proposes another way to understand the position of Jago.[20] He refers to Jago's role as that of a narrator: "the narrator whose authority controls the action" (214–15). Simply controlling the action might, however, make Jago no more than the strongest character in the drama—or, in the sense in which Boito uses the term, its author. On the other hand, Conner offers some reasons to view Jago's function as narrative. Describing the moment at which Jago says that he plans to place the handkerchief in Cassio's residence, Conner says that he "explicitly establishes his authority as narrator. . . . Jago quite literally 'speaks' to the audience, informing them of his ability to control the events which will shape the outcome of the opera" (218). Later he writes, "Beyond his increased power over the other characters, Jago has also established his position as narrator. He controls the unfolding events within the opera and flaunts his authority by reveling in his victory through utterances directed specifically towards the audience" (222). Assuming that we accept the idea that for a character to speak explicitly to the audience about his motives and their effects is a device that reveals a narrative position, Jago's role goes beyond that of a character or even a puppet master. Conner also draws attention to the use of both textual and musical framing devices associated with Jago. One of these is the return of the line "Il mio velen lavora" (My poison is working), and the other is the recurrence in Jago's part of the descending melodic line starting from a high $F\flat4$, earlier noted by Frits Noske, that "marks the inception and successful completion of his plot to destroy Otello." Conner suggests that such a framing device "reaffirms [Jago's] position as the narrator."[21]

One way of approaching Jago's function emerges from discussions of the music that place the character in charge not only of the dramatic action but also of the musical course of the work. An example is Hepokoski's introduction to his discussion of Jago's "Credo." Hepokoski writes that "Iago cunningly conceals his actual tonal goals. One is never quite certain where he is headed. At times the listener (with Cassio—and, later in the opera, with Otello) can only hang on dizzily to see how it all turns out."[22] This again places Jago in the position of dictating the course of the drama, now the drama of the music as well as of the action. In that sense we might regard him as more than an actor—either author or narrator.

Nevertheless, all these assertions depend on some degree of argument based on preconceptions about specific situations, and we might or might not find any of them convincing. Dramatic protagonists might influence the action of a plot without taking narrative control. Actors in plays and operas can express their thoughts aloud, even in asides to the audience, without seeming to be authors or narrators. Recurring melodic units might serve as reminiscence motives or leitmotifs without rising to the level of narrative-framing devices. The consistency between the harmonic direction or errancy in a passage and our understanding of a character need not be attributed to manipulations by the character. (We would hardly say, to apply this idea in reverse, that every aria that employs conventional, predictable tonal goals is being guided by the singing character's lack of imagination.) Jago does stand out as a remarkable figure. We surely should accept the original production book's description of him as "the real author of the drama," since this way of describing his management of his plot comes directly from his creators Boito and Verdi in the production book. Hepokoski asserts that

> the truth [of this authorship] exceeds its superficial meaning. *Otello* is the only non-comic opera of Verdi in which the perspective is predominantly ironic, and, as several commentators on the [Shakespeare] play have remarked, Iago forces us to see things through his eyes. . . . the audience, powerless to intervene, must watch these machinations 'from above,' alone with Iago knowing what nobody else on stage knows. . . . We sink into Iago's world with him, a soulless world of artifice, high polish, cool objectivity, and intellectual manipulation.[23]

Jago as Critic

Another aspect of Jago, equally rooted in the understanding of the character as he is described in the production book, has remained remarkably unexplored. This is the curious observation "Jago is a critic." A bit of history helps to shed light on this statement, which itself appears to derive from a line in Shakespeare's play, act 2, scene 1 (line 119). Here Iago banters with Desdemona and his wife, Emilia, mocking women as a sex. Desdemona challenges him, saying, "What wouldst thou write of me, if thou shouldst praise me?" and he replies, "O gentle lady, do not put me to't, / For I am nothing if not critical." Which is not at all the same thing as claiming to be "a critic."

To see how the line in Shakespeare's play became transformed into the characterization in the production book, we need to note that Boito derived much of his understanding of *Othello* from the French translation by François-Victor Hugo, first published in 1860. Hugo's version of this exchange reads,

DESDEMONA.
Qu'écrirais-tu de moi si tu avais à me louer?

IAGO.
Ah! noble dame, ne m'en chargez pas.—Je ne suis qu'un critique.[24]

In other words, "I am nothing but a critic." Moreover, in his prefatory character study, which, as Hepokoski has demonstrated, obviously influenced Boito's libretto,[25] Hugo quotes this very line, actually including the English: "Iago lui-même en convient; il n'est qu'un critique, *I am nothing if not critical*; mais c'est un critique qui ne voit jamais que les mauvais côtés" (Iago himself admits it: he is nothing but a critic, but he is a critic who never sees anything but the worst).[26] It would have been possible to translate Iago's line as "Je ne suis que critique," allowing the understanding of "critique" as an adjective—as in, "I am only critical" or "I am nothing but critical"—but Hugo's version, "un critique," forces a reading of the word as a noun and alters the meaning considerably.

The direct Italian translation of the English line would likely have been "Io sono nulla, se non critico"—"I am nothing, if not critical." Very clearly, however, Boito's version derives from Hugo's, translating the French rather than the English. What is more, Boito then placed the line in quite a different context, where the adjective *critical* would make no sense. In act 1 of the opera, Cassio urges Jago to sing in praise of Desdemona, and Jago demurs, according to the production book "jokingly, with an affected humility,"[27] on the grounds that he is not a singer—we have noted already from the style of his "Credo" that he has no music in himself—but rather only a critic:

CASSIO.
Tu, Jago, canterai le sue lodi!

JAGO.
(piano a Roderigo) (Lo ascolta.)
Io non sono che un critico.

(CASSIO. You, Jago, shall sing her praises! JAGO. *[softly to Roderigo]* [Listen to him.] I am nothing but a critic.)

Thus, when Boito approached the writing of the libretto, he had in mind this notion of Jago as a critic, and this characterization continued into the production book. Furthermore, coming from a composer and writer, we can be sure that this was not meant as a favorable comment about Jago; in fact, just as Hugo wrote "mais c'est un critique qui ne voit jamais que les mauvais côtés," Boito went on to say, "He is a spiteful and malicious critic." Whether simply as villain or as author or as narrator, therefore, Jago also works by the methods of a critic.

Although it is not a term that Verdi and Boito would have known, one of the things that we now expect from criticism is *deconstruction*, an approach that, although the opera's creators did not know the term, they must have had in mind, as we shall see. Because deconstruction can be a rather complicated matter and has been framed in a variety of ways in the literature of critical theory, let me explain as concisely as I can how I engage it and apply it here. Deconstruction has been defined as "a particular method of textual analysis and philosophical argument . . . to reveal logical or rhetorical incompatibilities between the explicit and implicit planes of discourse in a text and to demonstrate . . . how these incompatibilities are disguised and assimilated by the text."[28] The term *text* here can mean any object of discourse, not necessarily stated in words but including institutions or any other means of articulating ideas. Essential to the concept of deconstruction is the observation that any truth claim carries with it an unarticulated *supplement*—the undercutting idea that lies hidden behind the statement. In particular, in the analysis of assertions of political or cultural principles, deconstruction exposes how an expression of values incorporates but also suppresses some implicit but complicating truths.

Certainly, Jago as the "real author of the drama" and as "critic" engages in a kind of deconstruction. Just as "Jago is Envy" in an allegorical sense, the characters Otello and Desdemona stand for particular positive values in Western culture. Otello represents strength and valor, a soldier who sees the world in terms of absolutes and for whom the idea of defeat is inconceivable; Otello is a winner. Jago plays on Otello's strength and turns it into weakness, because Otello's way of seeing things in black and white allows Jago to create a situation in which Otello must interpret Desdemona's actions as representing either faithfulness or betrayal, overlooking the possibility that the situation might have nothing to do with her love for him. Sandra Corse writes, "Because Otello cannot abide uncertainty, he rushes too quickly into certainty, the certainty that Desdemona has deceived him."[29] Since it is inconceivable to Otello not to be the winner, he destroys his own happiness in his refusal to cope with what he can only see as losing. By the same token, Desdemona represents innocence; as we have seen, she was described by Maurel as an angel. Verdi wrote that "Desdemona is not a woman, she's a type! She is the type of goodness, of resignation, of sacrifice!"[30] What Jago shows us is that innocence can mean not only the virtue of purity but also the weakness that comes from a lack of understanding. Desdemona is such an innocent that in her ingenuousness she cannot perceive that her kindness to Cassio could be misrepresented as unfaithfulness to Otello. Thus Otello is vulnerable because he is determined to be invincible, and Desdemona is punished because she is an innocent. In this way Jago the critic approaches Otello and Desdemona as texts and deconstructs the values that they allegorically represent. Further, Jago not only has to succeed as a villain in making his victims betray themselves but also, as a critic, has to make sure that they understand he has deconstructed them. As Corse observes, "he is obsessed not only with destroying Otello but in showing Otello that the values the Moor believes in—honor, faith, and love—are debased and worthless."[31]

Although she never notes the reference to Jago as a critic, Corse arrives at something like the idea of deconstruction in her view of Jago's exploitation of the instability that arises from the unreliability of meaning, pointing out the contrast between Otello and Jago and the latter's way of dealing with the world. She writes, "What is contrasted, then, in Boito's opposition of Otello and Jago is, on the one hand, a will to believe in stability and meaning in human actions and words and, on the other, a compulsion to share a belief in chaos and lack of meaning."[32] Similarly, "Desdemona retains to the end her unquestioning faith in the eternity of love and efficacy of prayer. . . . She never sees Otello as anything but her idealized image of him."[33] Corse notes that at the end of the opera "Jago's manipulation of meaning is rejected, by both the audience and the final outcome of the play, but the near success of his plot indicates that his manipulation of meaning is powerful."[34] Similarly without mention of Jago as critic or his work as deconstruction, Hepokoski also approaches this way of conceiving Jago, observing that "Hugo's exegetical point [that Iago is motivated by envy] is obviously also a main source of the 1884 Credo, which relies so heavily on the reversal of values—the ridiculing of positives into negatives."[35]

Deconstruction in Music

Just as with deception, we can hear the music actually engaged in deconstruction. In fact, this takes place in close connection with the same deceptive features of the scene and the "Credo" that we focused on earlier. Let us listen to them again.

The opening music quite notably illustrates the use of a melodic ornament. The triplet turn decorates those first repeated beats and then embellishes the melody that follows. As an ornament, decoration, or embellishment, it represents the addition of beauty to the melodic line. But then the music deconstructs the idea of ornament. As soon as Cassio is out of earshot and Jago is alone on the stage, we abruptly hear that same turn as an ugly snarl (example 11.5). As Budden puts it, "by a masterstroke the triplet figure is transformed into a brutal gesture in preparation for Iago's Credo of evil."[36] This change of tone reveals that there is nothing inherently beautiful about the melodic gesture employed as embellishment. It might draw our attention to the fact that decoration is often a means either of obscuring nakedness or of distracting attention from an ugly flaw. Here beautification is deconstructed as deception.

Example 11.5. Verdi, *Otello*, act 2, mm. 38–39.

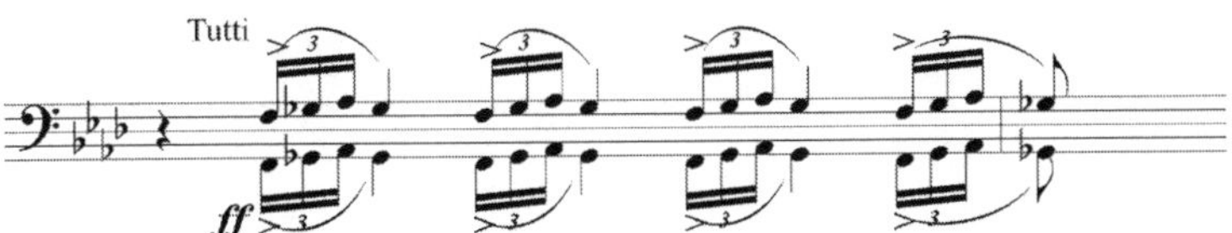

Even more striking is what happens to the first theme in the "Credo" itself in its recurrences. Hepokoski calls these "the celebrated unison-pillars of *negative affirmation*" (my emphasis), hinting at a critical attitude but without exploring or even raising the concept of deconstruction.[37] Stated in a bold unison by the orchestra, the phrase serves in purely musical terms to set the key of F minor, in which the entire passage is framed. Such unison passages used as forceful means to establish or confirm the key of a piece had constituted part of composers' stock in trade since the early eighteenth century. The archetypal model for the sort of thing that I have in mind here is an extremely familiar example (example 11.6), but we can easily find many instances at least from the beginning of the eighteenth century well into the nineteenth. Exactly this is what takes place at the beginning of Jago's "Credo." The boldness of the *tutta forza* unison stands as an assertion of stability and security in the key of F minor. Now let us follow what happens to this as the music continues. After its first statement, this melody reappears in the same form to accompany Jago's affirmation "Si! quest'è la mia fè!" (Yes! This is my belief!). Later, however, the music deconstructs the convention that it has represented. We discover, just before the end of the solo, that the very definiteness of the unaccompanied melody makes it vulnerable to reharmonization—in fact, in the first instance, just that deceptive harmonization that we noted earlier. There, as we will recall, it no longer confirmed but slipped away from F minor to the submediant in F major. But there is more to this moment than simply that we were deceived in our assumption about the harmonic underpinning of that melodic statement. Almost immediately it reappears in yet another harmonization, this time starting on the vii°7 of E♭ minor and twisting its way through D♭ major to an evasion on a first-inversion B♭ minor chord and then to a low D♭2 (example 11.7). In the end, this is not merely a case of deception but one of deconstruction. Precisely the device that we

Example 11.6. Mozart, *Eine kleine Nachtmusik*, K. 525, mvt. 1, mm. 1–4.

Example 11.7. Verdi, *Otello*, act 2, mm. 109–14.

suppose to have the function of clarifying tonality is revealed to represent no particular tonality. It is not that we were misled by the harmonic progression but that a convention employed to secure harmony is in reality a texture and scoring that in its essence, the "Credo" reminds us, provides no harmony at all. The seemingly positive assertion carries with it this supplement—that in the "Credo" it inherently opens up doubt.[38]

Narration as an Act of Critical Theory, Critical Theory as an Act of Narration

To summarize, we can now understand how, rather more strongly than most operas, Verdi's *Otello* allows for a narrative interpretation. Jago is, as the production book points out, the "author of the drama," in the sense that as the villain he manipulates the other characters and controls the action. Conner regards his function as that of a narrator, although his argument conflates narrator and author. Perhaps Jago behaves like a narrator in those moments when he speaks to the audience, although not every aside makes an actor a narrator, or when he offers framing devices, but these might merely be the kinds of recurring phrases in text or music common in many operas. In any case, at most, Jago could be author or narrator of the action, but not of the opera.

Nevertheless, two cues unmask for us the narrative identity behind *Otello*. The first is the identification of Jago as a critic, an insight that came to mind for François-Victor Hugo and Boito by an accident of translation combined with the nature of Jago's actions in the drama. Second, with this in mind, we find ourselves listening to the music of the opera—here specifically the "Credo," as the passage in which Jago is directly revealed—attuned to the critical process of deconstruction that unfolds in the music itself. To put this the other way around, when we hear how the music actually works, the French and Italian translators' assertion about Jago steers us toward identifying the scene's persona as likewise a critic. The music confronts us with a brilliant performance of critical deconstruction.

Chapter 12

The Painter Sings

Historicity in Wolf's "Auf ein altes Bild"

A Poem About a Painting

When Edward Cone undertook his explication of the nature of musical expression in *The Composer's Voice*, he began with Schubert's "Erlkönig." The song foregrounds the question of persona—first, because the text itself draws attention to the dialogic relationship between the narrator of and the characters within Goethe's ballad; and second, because the music so obviously enters into the telling of the story.[1]

Hugo Wolf's song "Auf ein altes Bild" similarly presents an unusual opportunity to investigate and to clarify some issues in the aesthetics of art song. In a different way from "Erlkönig," but equally strikingly, the text of the song opens issues of artistic expression. The music relates not only to Eduard Mörike's 1838 poem but by implication also to the picture that the poem describes (a picture never explicitly identified by the poet). Moreover, the song's musical style, quite unusual for its post-Romantic composer, offers a particular opening for consideration of alternative hypotheses regarding the interpretation of this interestingly multilayered song itself, as well as of the relationships of text and music in song generally (example 12.1).

Mörike's brief poem, consisting of only six lines of iambic tetrameter, describes a picture of the Madonna in an outdoor setting, with the Christ child playing on her lap:[2]

In grüner Landschaft Sommerflor,
Bei kühlem Wasser, Schilf und Rohr,

237

Example 12.1. Wolf, "Auf ein altes Bild."

spie - let auf der Jung - frau Schoss!
Und dort im Wal - de won - ne - sam,
ach, grü - net schon des Kreu - zes Stamm!

> Schau, wie das Kindlein Sündelos
> Frei spielet auf der Jungfrau Schoß!
> Und dort im Walde wonnesam,
> Ach, grünet schon des Kreuzes Stamm!

"In a green, summer-luxuriant landscape, by cool water, rush and reed, see how the child, sinless, plays freely on the Virgin's lap! And there in the wood joyfully, ah, already the cross's trunk grows green."

The season is summer, and there is water nearby. In the wood in the background of this peaceful scene, the viewer sees the tree from which will come the cross of the Crucifixion.

The textual detail certainly suggests that Mörike referred to a specific picture. Indeed, Mörike wrote a number of poems based on actual visual works, including drawings he made himself as well as works by others. "Auf ein altes Bild" appears to be the earliest such poem.[3] In her very helpful study "Eduard Mörikes Gedichte zu Bildern und Zeichnungen," however, Renate von Heydebrand, who tracked down many of the visual sources and parallels to Mörike's poetry, confessed that she was unable to locate a specific picture to correspond to this poem.[4] Disappointing as this might be, let me admit, too, that I have not discovered such a picture.

Heydebrand makes two points in this regard. First, she suggests that "It might certainly be conceivable that Mörike, like August Wilhelm Schlegel in the painting poems of his 'Gespräche,' only had in his imagination the genre of painting," but she is not fully convinced that this is the case, for, as she points out, in that case "he would perhaps more likely have headed the poem instead 'Madonna and child' or something of the sort."[5] Second, she notes that this very situation opens interpretive possibilities: "Whether the artist himself already suggested the symbol of the cross in the wood is doubtful but not out of the question. For Mörike the least optical stimulus sufficed. . . . More important than the question of the model seems to me the observation that Mörike does not co-opt the meditation to which he invites the spectator through a 'view' but rather opens up the space for its play around the pictorial symbol."[6]

Susan Youens takes a similar position, suggesting that Mörike's poem is an instance of "notional ekphrasis," in which the work of art exists purely in the poet's imagination. As she points out, in such a case the imaginatively envisioned picture offers the advantage that it certainly incorporates the images and expresses the meanings that the text ascribes to it, whereas a poem about an actual picture would be only a hypothetical interpretation, even if it were a compelling one.[7]

Before proceeding to the song, it will be useful to note what this composition of one work based on another—whether actual or imaginary—suggests. We might read the poem convincingly in either of two ways. In the first, probably the obvious one, we understand the poem as conveying the observations of a speaker or lyric persona whom we imagine to be the fictive spectator, viewing a picture. The eye traverses the scene in the painting from middle ground to foreground to background, ending at the wood in the distance and there discovering or imagining the cross. The emotional response to this foreshadowing of the Crucifixion comes as the "Ach!" of lament or sympathetic anguish with which the last line opens.

In a second reading, however, we might imagine the speaker in the poem as representing the fictive artist at the moment of inspiration, at the moment when the artist discovers the potential for the juxtaposition of images of the Christ child and the cross. The "Ach!" of the last line of the text represents the "Aha!" of artistic inspiration. This means that we would think of the relationship of text and picture as reversed, for in this latter case we understand the poem as representing the thoughts of the artist, preceding the creation of the fictive picture itself. Moreover, this is not farfetched, for after all it is one way to apply the idea of ekphrasis, regarding the text as representing no actual painting but rather Mörike's own envisioning of a possibility in the genre of Madonna paintings.

Song and Voice

Hugo Wolf set Mörike's poem almost exactly a half century after it had been written, on April 14, 1888. Now, it is possible to suggest that, whether or not Mörike wrote about a particular work of art, when Wolf composed the song, he did have a specific picture in mind. This is worth noting because in song music assimilates its text,[8] and therefore the song would necessarily refer to the composer's image of the picture, whether or not it is the same picture that the poet had in mind.

What might that image be? The music itself is suggestive here, for it seems to specify how old this "old picture" actually is. In several ways the song unmistakably evokes the style of Renaissance music. This is not to claim that the music accurately reproduces Renaissance musical style but merely that within Wolf's late-nineteenth-century context there are plenty of signifiers of the Renaissance. Most immediately evident is the modal harmony.[9] The song is in F♯ minor, but it opens with the prominent use of the subtonic E♮, so that at least initially the listener recognizes the harmony as governed by what would be Glarean's Aeolian mode. Another feature of the harmony that would strike the nineteenth-century ear as archaizing is the treatment of the cadences—notably, plagal cadences resolving to chords with the so-called Picard third.[10] Added to this must be the texture, on the surface *stile famigliare* in four parts, with vocal-style lines.[11] When the singer enters—and, at least tentatively, I think we may presume that the song is for a male voice—it becomes evident that the principal melody is not that of the cantus in the keyboard part but rather the lowest part; the vocal line of measures 5 to 6 takes up the bassus of measures 1 to 2. Even within the familiar-style texture of the instrumental opening, there is a further embedded archaism. One reason the texture sounds as old-fashioned as it does, I think, is that one hears within it a simple fauxbourdon, which is not obscured by the addition of the fourth tone in each harmony (example 12.2).[12]

This musical style suggests that Wolf had in mind a Renaissance picture rather than one, say, contemporary with Mörike. To understand the song, we do not need to know that Wolf envisioned a specific picture; it remains possible that the image suggested in the song existed only in Wolf's imagination. Nevertheless, to help us establish a sense of the piece, one familiar and plausible candidate surely would be Raphael's *Madonna del Prato* (now in the Vienna Kunsthistorisches Museum), which had been in Vienna since 1773 and which the composer must have known (see figure 12.1). This painting, dating from 1505 or 1506, would certainly suggest the music's generalized style references to the Renaissance.

An examination of Raphael's painting confirms that Wolf might have found in it the scene described in Mörike's poem. The *Jungfrau* sits in a green summer landscape, not far from a lake. The infant Jesus, leaning into his mother's lap, plays with his cousin John (later the Baptist). The figure of John is not mentioned by Mörike, but here we are considering not Mörike's picture but a candidate for a painting that might have been suggested to

Example 12.2. Wolf, "Auf ein altes Bild," analytical reduction of mm. 1–2.

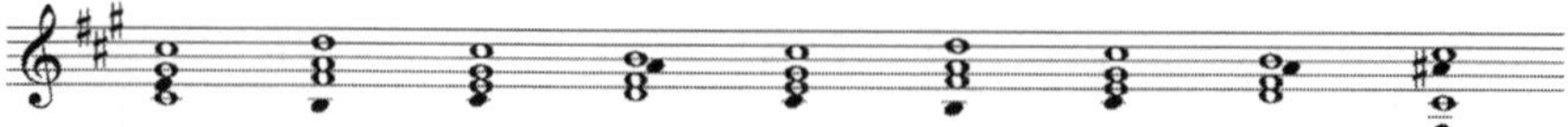

Figure 12.1. Raphael, *Madonna del Prato*. *Source:* Kunsthistorisches Museum Wien / KHM Museumsverband. Used with permission.

Wolf by Mörike's words. In the trees in the background we can see where Wolf might have found the cross of Mörike's poem.

The relation of music to text in a song may be conceived in various ways. We are accustomed—especially as music historians—to regarding this from the perspective of the song's compositional history. When the music and the words of a song are closely related, we are in the habit of saying (as Cone does) that the music comments on the words. We say that the composer has supplied music that illustrates the meanings or serves to evoke the mood of the preexisting text. From this point of view, we might say of

"Auf ein altes Bild" that in it the archaizing music responds to the poem's suggestion of a sixteenth-century painting. We might likewise hypothesize, as I have just done, that in the song Wolf's music looks back to Mörike's poem and simultaneously further back to Raphael's *Madonna del Prato*.

Romantic Song—Some General Principles

But I would like to argue that this is not really how the song itself works (or most other nineteenth-century songs, for that matter), either in terms of the strongest aesthetic premises for the genre or in terms of the actual hearing of the piece or singing of the text. For certainly in our listening to this song—not in its compositional history now, but in the hearing of the work itself—as in many others, the music precedes the text. In such songs the music can have either (or perhaps both?) of two types of expressive effect, which I should like to pursue in what follows. In either case, this can be stated by saying that the music expresses the experience of the lyric persona of the text as it comes to us in the song.[13]

First, the music can represent an actual physical experience of hearing that sets the speaker of the poem into context. In this sort of song, while the singer takes the role of a quasi-theatrical character, the keyboard part suggests a sensory environment, aurally setting the scene, either by way of a visual (or even tactile) metaphor or in the sense that the environment contains actual sound. Schubert's songs abound in this sort of thing. Remember that the idea here is that the vocal persona hears the music as an actual sound, and this sound inspires the speech that he sings (still assuming a male singer, based on the register of the voice and the voicing in the piano part). In the second song of Schubert's *Die schöne Müllerin*, "Wohin?," to take an obvious example, anyone listening to the first two measures of the piano's introduction inevitably "hört ein Bächlein rauschen." My point here, however, is that even when the vocal persona does not identify the sound in a statement so explicit—even comical when it is taken out of context—this is how songs actually should be understood to work. Historically speaking, the poem inspired the music, but in the song itself, exactly to the contrary, the music inspires the words.

The music need not represent anything so actual in the singer-persona's experience as a brook (or spinning wheel or galloping horse), however. Alternatively, it can represent the quality of emotional experience, making explicit to the listener the speaker's feeling, out of which the text emerges.

The role of music in this case, as Mendelssohn would certainly assert (see chapter 6), is to express that feeling to the listener in the direct and precise way that words cannot. This is what Wolf implied when he once wrote to a friend, upon completing his song "Nun wandre, Maria," "If you wish to experience this event, then you must hear my music."[14] Clearly, he did not mean that the music reproduced the physical or sensory events along the route of the holy family's flight into Egypt. The statement makes the claim that the emotional experience is immanent in the music, and that the music thus allows the listener to experience the feeling of the persona in the song. The words then serve, essentially, as an instance of speech that arises from that musically embodied feeling. In such songs we are accustomed, misleadingly, to describe the music as more "abstract" than in cases of metaphorical word-painting or actual auditory onomatopoeia. In the sense that it is not scenic, the music certainly seems less easy to translate into verbal language. On the other hand, in that it expresses its emotional content without recourse to visual imagery, it is more immediate than either words or scenic music. To take another familiar example from Schubert, we might choose "Du bist die Ruh," D. 776. There is no visual image here. If we were to claim that the music paints the physical sensory world of the speaker, if we tried to describe a setting here, without adequate textual or other evidence, we would rightly be accused of a self-indulgent and arbitrary approach to the song. The music is peaceful, but the singer-persona is not seeing a peaceful scene—unruffled water, motionless trees—but rather feeling the peace that the character being addressed brings to the speaker.

But that is not to say that the relation of keyboard part to vocal persona is fundamentally different in these two situations. The text still must arise from the music, whether from a particular scenic environment or from feeling.

Several comments ought to be made here. Whereas in the former type of song the scene setting generally operates through the rhythms and figurations of the keyboard part, the latter type is more likely to derive its more directly emotive content through harmony. Naturally, most successful songs employ the entire palette of musical style elements. Indeed, what makes a scene-setting song most effective—as in the hands of Schubert—is that the visual or aural image also resonates with the internal feeling of the vocal persona.

Moreover, there is a crucial lesson in this for singers. The singer should never forget that whether the music represents the lyric persona's sensory environment or internal, emotional condition, it is prior to the text. The music is emphatically not accompaniment or even really commentary. The vocal persona must hear the music and be motivated by it. My wife teaches an acting class in which one of the essential principles is that student actors should not say a line unless they genuinely feel that it is what they need to say. A parallel principle applies for the Lieder-singer. Unless singers hear the keyboard part and recognize it as the cause for the vocal line, they have no business singing at all. It does not matter whether the score provides an introduction. The music must resonate in the singer's ear and feeling.

So the most productive aesthetic theory for the understanding of the Romantic song takes the music as representing the sensory and/or emotional experience of the speaker of the poem. In this manner, the understanding of a song stems from the sense that both the lyric persona and the persona's perspective are made determinate via the music.

Looking at and Listening to the Old Picture Once More

Let us turn again to "Auf ein altes Bild" to see how this aesthetic affects the hearing and understanding of the song. Imagine first what happens if we understand the archaizing keyboard part of "Auf ein altes Bild" as representing the actual auditory experience of the lyric persona. The music first of all locates the fictive speaker at some time around the year 1500, hearing the music before and during the course of what he says. The music forms a backdrop, like the painted scene on a stage. In such a case, as we have just noted, we should understand the music to inspire the words. Further, when the fictive lyric persona speaks, he describes the painting. This understanding of the music, in other words, corresponds to our earlier reading of the poem as an enactment of the painter conceiving the painting—the "Aha" moment. The vocal persona then represents the painter thinking out loud, hearing the music—perhaps even creatively inspired by the music—in the background.

The other reading requires that we understand the speaker of the lyric as having looked at the painting and as speaking his observations of the picture in the text. In contradistinction to the hypothesis just advanced, the fictive painting now stands temporally earlier than the music and the words. The music, in this case, might possibly be regarded as actually part of the fictive physical experience of the viewer, assuming that we imagine the viewer to be roughly contemporary with the sixteenth-century painting.[15] More likely, though, if we regard the singer as a viewer of the painting, the music would be understood either as an evocation of historical music in the mind's ear of a more modern viewer or as the expression of the feeling corresponding to that archaic music.

Naturally, from our position, it is easy to take this song as representing an actual event in the composer's life. Wolf certainly viewed a picture, or at least read a vivid description of one, and heard this music in his mind's ear. The song seems fictively to enact that experience. On the other hand, we might also imagine that, from Wolf's point of view, this fictive viewer might be a representation of Mörike. As is well known, the title of Wolf's published collection is *Gedichte von Mörike*, and it is Mörike's portrait that stands as the frontispiece of the volume of music.[16] Commentators on Wolf have generally drawn attention to this as a way of emphasizing his respect for his literary texts or even as evidence of humility in his personality. Equally plausible is the implication that in music the composer could bring to life a fictive reincarnation of the poet and his emotional experience, suggesting that we are to approach the songs as spoken by this "Mörike," a fictive character in a songbook of which Wolf is the author.

Ultimately, the music does not finally force on us a single reading of the poem. It does, however, restrict the possible stylistic range of the picture we imagine, placing it in the Renaissance. The interplay of the musical style Wolf chose and the likelihood that the composer was familiar with Raphael's *Madonna del Prato* combine to suggest that, whatever the poem's remaining vagueness about the specific image, the "altes Bild" of the song could be understood to be this particular painting. The fact that the poem might be read as if it came before rather than after the picture raises our consciousness in regard to the relationship between genres in composite works. In this context the song reminds us that the relationship of music and text in the work is the reverse of their historical chronology. In turn, this observation opens us up to some interesting hearings of the song itself.

Aesthetical Postscript

There is one further aesthetic principle to be adduced from Wolf's song. To this point, I have tried to press to the limits of specificity in proposing possible personalities and situations to be understood from the song, but, as I hope you have noticed, I have also left open the choices among these proposals. The nature of the work is to validate these interpretations as complementary. A work of art stands in a pivotal position between its creator and its receiver, and it acts as a shared experience between them. With regard to Mörike's poem, whatever the fictive painter envisions and describes in our one reading, the fictive viewer sees and describes in the other. The music of Wolf's song extends this principle further still. To the extent that the keyboard part represents the actual musical environment of our fictive painter, it represents as identical to that music the fictive viewer's imagined music, in which his emotional response is manifested as immanent.

The aesthetic fact that this song, its poem, and its picture together demonstrate is that, at some level, the work of art—especially a work of music—brings about a meeting of experiences. For all our usual hesitation about saying so, in a real and profound sense any work of art constitutes a truly shared experience—shared by the actual creator, the fictive persona, the performer, and the audience.

Chapter 13

Representing the Narrator's Voice

MacDowell's "Keltic" Sonata

Edward MacDowell's Piano Sonata in E Minor, op. 59, called "Keltic," dates from 1901, at the peak of interest in exoticism and nationalism in late Romantic or post-Romantic music. Despite the strongly favorable critical judgment the Sonata received from its contemporaries, histories of American music have generally given it only the most superficial treatment. Both the work itself and its neglect can serve to open up critical and aesthetic questions. Here I steer away from looking at MacDowell from the viewpoint of American (or at least Americanist) music history. I then consider various aspects of his relationship to the Celtic. In the end, however, I argue that we can hear MacDowell's "Keltic" Sonata as representing not an example of an American composer who could not break away from his European education but an instructive paradigm for Romanticism.

MacDowell and Americanism

That the music does not bear obvious traces of American nationalism probably accounts for the Sonata's neglect by historians of music in the United States. The Sonata might even seem an embarrassment to American music history, since it could exemplify the failure of American composers to find a distinctive style.

MacDowell certainly did concern himself with the problem of finding a style of music that would belong distinctively to his own country, and his contemporaries hoped ardently that he would do so. As John Erskine points out in his article on MacDowell for the *Dictionary of American Biography*, "His interest in America was genuine and deep, reaching far beyond the field of music, but it is doubtful whether he knew how close he was to his country, how ready it was to welcome him, how instinctively it looked to him to be its spokesman in his art."[1] Quoting MacDowell from a conversation in Chicago in the fall of 1894, Hamlin Garland recalled the composer's saying, "I am working toward a music which shall be American in the creative sense. Our music thus far is mainly a scholarly re-statement of Old World themes. In other words, it is derived from Germany, as all my earlier pieces were."[2]

MacDowell's manner of dealing with this issue, however, was complex and ambivalent. We know how he disagreed with Dvořák's idea that American composers should base their national music on melodies taken from Native American song and African American spirituals. Garland quotes him as arguing that "I do not believe in 'lifting' a Navajo theme and furbishing it into some kind of a musical composition. That is not American music. Our problem is not so simple as all that."[3] Garland also reports MacDowell as having said that "[national style in music] is a question of personality. If a composer is sincerely American at heart, his music will be American. Almost any hack composer can imitate the Persian, Chinese, or any other racial music, but the spirit of it is not caught. The weakness of our music is in its borrowing . . . A national music can not be founded on the songs of reds and blacks."[4] MacDowell's unfortunate, dated form of reference to Native Americans and African Americans here should not distract from his essential point that he could not accept as American for himself and his fellow late-nineteenth-century white composers a style that would absorb what in more modern terms would likely be condemned as exploitative appropriation, some sort of imitation of the music of the country's oppressed populations.

MacDowell argued,

> before a people can find a musical writer to echo its genius it must first possess men who truly represent it—that is to say, men who, being part of the people, love the country for itself: men who put into their music what the nation has put into its life; and in the case of America it needs above all, both on the part of the public and on the part of the writer, absolute freedom from the restraint that an almost unlimited deference to European thought and prejudice has imposed upon us. Masquerading in

the so-called nationalism of Negro clothes cut in Bohemia will not help us. What we must arrive at is the youthful vitality and the undaunted tenacity of spirit that characterizes the American man. This is what I hope to see echoed in American music.[5]

MacDowell and Celtic Musical Style Traits

MacDowell's belief that his own American music should derive from his Celtic roots also did not lead him to use folk-music-based melodies or rhythms, scorings, or harmony. Indeed, MacDowell remained deeply suspicious of exoticist adaptations of style traits of folk musics. MacDowell's important early biographer Lawrence Gilman quotes MacDowell's lecture on "Folk-Music":

> So-called Russian, Bohemian, or any other purely national music has no place in art, for its characteristics may be duplicated by anyone who takes the fancy to do so. . . . We have seen the Strauss family adopting the cross rhythms of the Spanish—or, to be more accurate, the Moorish or Arab—school of art. Moszkowski the Pole writes Spanish dances. Cowen in England writes a Scandinavian Symphony. Grieg the Norwegian writes Arabian music; and, to cap the climax, we have here in America been offered a pattern for an "American" national musical costume by the Bohemian Dvořák—though what the Negro melodies have to do with Americanism in art still remains a mystery. Music that can be made by "recipe" is not music, but "tailoring." To be sure, this tailoring may serve to cover a beautiful thought; but—why cover it? and, worst of all, why cover it (if covered it must be: if the trademark of nationality is indispensable, which I deny)—why cover it with the badge of whilom slavery rather than with the stern but at least manly and free rudeness of the North American Indian? . . . But the means of "creating" a national music to which I have alluded are childish.[6]

Again here, as noted earlier, MacDowell's reference to the appropriation of the musics of victimized minorities, while it might strike us today as insensitive, should instead be read as respectful. It reveals his sensitivity to the fact that the melodies of spirituals are not neutral material to be adopted to create an artificial Americanism but carry the bitter history of enslaved people. He regards Native American peoples as characterized by strength and freedom; his use of the word "rudeness" means not "unmannerly" but "rugged" or "vigorous." Centrally, he argues that he cannot create American music in any authentic sense by extracting and exploiting features of others' musics with which he could not pretend empathy.

The "Keltic" Sonata, then, does not incorporate thematic material or any colorings that might be regarded as derived from any repertoire of Irish music. Thus the Sonata fails not only as an instance of American nationalism but equally as an example of exoticist Irishism. These two obvious keys by which we might presume to interpret it, therefore, are unavailable.

The Identification of MacDowell as Celtic

Although the music of the Sonata does not, as MacDowell might have put it, masquerade in specially tailored Irish costume, we must not be too hasty in casting aside the significance of its drawing upon Celtic connections in some way. Plenty of evidence exists of the composer's own identification with his Scottish and Irish heritage, both from the composer himself and from his contemporaries. MacDowell stated explicitly that "I am now on the way to being myself and as I am myself I will be Celtic-American rather than German-American or Afro-American."[7] At the outset of his 1908 biography, Gilman hastened to establish MacDowell's Celtic ancestry, for the composer was, after all, only a second-generation American. He actually makes MacDowell Celtic rather than American, opening his biography with the statement that "Edward MacDowell, the first Celtic voice that has spoken commandingly out of musical art, achieved that priority through natural if not inevitable processes."[8]

The identification of MacDowell as Celtic extended to other attributes and other writers, as well. Gilman attributes the composer's personality to his family roots, suggesting that he had inherited from his father a "Celtic sensitiveness of temperament";[9] later he also makes a similar claim for MacDowell's sense of humor, "which was of true Celtic richness, . . . fluent and inexhaustible."[10] The writer Hamlin Garland, reporting on a concert by MacDowell one Friday afternoon in the fall of 1888 in Boston Music Hall, says, "With what Celtic fire he played!"[11] Whatever this idea that MacDowell was Celtic may have meant to the various critics—sensitivity, richness, or fire—it appears to have formed a central part of MacDowell's understanding of himself and others' understanding of him.

The "Keltic" Sonata and Programmatic Content

When MacDowell dealt with the Celtic aspect of the Sonata, he did not claim that it incorporated an Irish musical style. Rather, he identified the work with the Irish epic tale, as it was popularized in his time, and this will occupy the remainder of the following discussion.

Despite its title and a brief motto referring to Irish legends of Deirdre and Cuchullin,[12] however, the "Keltic" Sonata is not explicitly programmatic. In fact, it adopts conventional forms for three movements of a nonprogrammatic sonata, with bold outer movements in E minor and the more lyrical central movement in G major.

The first of the sonata's three movements, clearly in conventional (Type 3) sonata form, sets up the tonic E minor by a majestic, chordal theme punctuated by a stern two-note falling-third motive (example 13.1). The

Example 13.1. MacDowell, Sonata No. 4 in E Minor, op. 59, "Keltic," mvt. 1, mm. 1–14.

contrast key, G major, is expressed through a more rhapsodic idea, and the two-note motive now appears in the high register, evoking perhaps nature and distance (example 13.2).[13] The development brings impressive (Lisztian) virtuosity, with a free succession of figurations. A very compact recapitulation quickly leads to a coda organically developed from earlier ideas.

The second movement opens with a melody so reminiscent of the theme associated with the principal key in the first movement as perhaps to appear an organically evolved variant of it. A second melody does suggest nationalism—but only of the generic sort—by the use of a pentatonic melody (example 13.3). (We might, however, hear less of the folk musician

Example 13.2. MacDowell, Sonata No. 4 in E Minor, op. 59, "Keltic," mvt. 1, mm. 51–58.

Example 13.3. MacDowell, Sonata No. 4 in E Minor, op. 59, "Keltic," mvt. 2, mm. 17–24.

here than the nineteenth-century American parlor song.) Again a middle section full of post-Romantic virtuoso figurations leads to a reprise that grows ever gentler.

The third and final movement, a scherzo in style, unfolds in a free form. Highly energetic, it adopts intense, galloping compound-meter rhythms (example 13.4). The two-note motive provides cyclic connections to the previous movements. At the finale's end, as coda to the entire sonata, comes a briefly major-brightened reminiscence of the first movement (hence also of the second), fading to near silence before a bold rush to the final E-minor chords.

So far, the Sonata constitutes a typical nineteenth-century example of the genre. It need not be understood as programmatic, any more than as nationalistic. It belongs to the Romantic tradition that included the not-explicitly-programmatic sonatas of Chopin, Liszt, Brahms, and MacDowell's own teacher Joachim Raff (1822–82).

Our understanding of the Sonata can take into account both peritextual and epitextual evidence stemming from the composer. MacDowell prefaced the score with an epigrammatic quatrain:

> Who minds now Keltic tales of yore,
> Dark Druid rhymes that thrall;
> Deirdré's song, and wizard lore
> Of great Cuchullin's fall.[14]

Writing to Lawrence Gilman about the sonata, MacDowell supplied some lines of poetry of his own, which, although he disclaimed them as program-

Example 13.4. MacDowell, Sonata No. 4 in E Minor, op. 59, "Keltic," mvt. 3, mm. 13–20.

matic in the sense of outlining a plot for the music, he suggested "may serve, however, to aid the understanding of the *stimmung* of the sonata." He places "Cuchullin's story . . . in touch with the Deirdré-Naesi tale." He emphasized, though—in a phrasing reminiscent of Beethoven's about the Pastoral Symphony—"the music is more a commentary on the subject than an actual depiction of it."[15] MacDowell's poetic evocation of the Sonata's mood, sent privately to Gilman, reads as follows:

> Cuchullin fought and fought in vain,
> 'Gainst faery folk and Druid thrall:
> And as the queenly sun swept down,
> In royal robes, red gold besown,
> With one last lingering glance
> He sate himself in lonely state
> Against a giant monolith,
> To wait Death's wooing call.
> None dared approach the silent shape
> That froze to iron majesty,
> Save the wan, mad daughters of old Night,
> Blind, wandering maidens of the mist,
> Whose creeping fingers, cold and white,
> Oft by the sluggard dead are kissed;
> And yet the monstrous Thing held sway,
> No living soul dared say it nay;
> When lo! upon its shoulder still,
> Unconscious of its potent will,
> There perched a preening birdling gray,
> A'weary of the dying day;
> And all the watchers knew the lore:
> Cuchullin was no more.[16]

Despite MacDowell's disclaimer of a programmatic outline in the sonata, commentators have—seemingly inevitably—risen to the bait. Descriptions range from the uselessly general to the embarrassing.

Gilman, resisting excessively specific programmaticism, restricts himself mostly to vague characterizations that might be applied to any large sonata of the late nineteenth century:

> It is cast in a mould essentially heroic; it has its moods of
> tenderness, of insistent sweetness, but these are incidental: the

governing mood is signified in the tremendous exordium with which the work opens, and which is sustained, with few deviations, throughout the work. Deirdré he has realised exquisitely in his middle movement: that is her image, in all its fragrant loveliness. MacDowell has limned her musically in a manner worthy of comparison with the sumptuous pen-portrait of her in Standish O'Grady's "Cuculain": "a woman of wondrous beauty, bright with gold her hair, eyes piercing and splendid, tongue full of sweet sounds, her countenance like the colour of snow blended with crimson."

In the close of the last movement we are justified in seeing a translation of the sublime tradition of Cuchullin's death. This it is which furnished MacDowell with the theme that he celebrates in the lines of verse which I have quoted above.[17]

Alan H. Levy, self-admittedly a historian and not a musician, hazards a more detailed speculation:

The music opens in E minor, "with great power and dignity." There is a grand chordal declamation, depicting both the king [Conchobar] and the craggy, misty landscape of the tale. The motif here involves descending intervals, sometimes thirds, sometimes second or fourths. But they are always descending, symbolizing, simultaneously, the tragedy in the offing and the shift of power from gods to humans. This percussive motif precedes a contrasting, more whimsical melodic theme, which hints at major modality, implying a bit of hopefulness, in Dierdre's [*sic* throughout] heart. The two themes are then developed and recapitulated, as love and foreboding tragedy, hope and failure, mingle. The descending interval dominates.

The second movement, "with naive tenderness," ascends to G major. The opening chords link to the powerful opening of the first movement. But here, instead of stern block chords, MacDowell casts harp-like arpeggios in high registers with hints of Wagnerian chromaticism. This gentle, almost casual aura evokes Dierdre. The descending chords, seconds and fourths in this case, never completely disappear, symbolizing Dierdre's never being free of the power from which she has fled. "As heard from afar," MacDowell writes of the movement. A Celtic melody then enters, illustrating Dierdre's true romantic yearnings and where they seek fruition. The original intervals reappear, but now intermittently they descend and ascend. Immortal power has been challenged and jarred. Human aspiration has a flicker of hope. The melody then develops, with triplet accompaniment. For a time then the original, powerful intervals appear gone, eclipsed. The sweet melody dominates, and the movement ends serenely, as on a note of love.

The third movement, "very swift and fierce," returns to E minor. Here MacDowell depicts Cuchullin's exploits and battles. The movement begins rushing into an arpeggiated, pointed melody. In 6/8 time the melody grows in range and dynamics. The theme ends at its tonal zenith, then it shifts to a falling second interval, symbolizing the greater powers with which Cuchullin must contend. A second melody appears, with brilliant runs, full of surging dynamics. the tonal center is at mid-register, indicative of the essential human features of Cuchullin, versus his god-like features or the low evil with which he must do battle. In Celtic legend Cuchullin died in battle but stood upright against a rock. No one dared attack, fearing he was still alive, until a bird landed on his shoulder and sang. "With tragic pathos," as MacDowell marks it, Cuchullin's fall then comes from this middle "human" register. Dierdre's theme and descending fourth intervals interweave. The section begins pianissimo (pp) and becomes più più pianissimo (pppp), where all that remains is the spirit of Dierdre's love, the sonata ending with four measures of peroration. One need know nothing of the mythic text to feel the tragedy at hand.[18]

The error in this kind of program invention stems neither from its naive (sometimes inaccurate) descriptions of the music nor from its simplistic interpretations. Such efforts themselves are misplaced, for the "Keltic" Sonata does not consist of programmatic depiction, and not even of symbolic associations, such as descending lines with tragedy or the shift of power from gods to mortals. The title and motto have significance, but it must reside entirely elsewhere.

The "Keltic" Sonata and Narrative Voice

Rather than attempt to understand the "Keltic" Sonata by way of looking for traces of the American or the Irish in its musical style, or by attempting to tease out of it some sort of programmatic story, it is more fruitful to approach the music through genre study and musical narratology to ground our appreciation. MacDowell's own statements about the work justify this methodology. What MacDowell was really after, though it seems to have been underestimated by critics from his own time to ours, was not so much a musical nationalism—neither American nor Irish—or a detailed programmatic plot, but a voice.

MacDowell makes this quite clear in a letter to Mr. N. J. Corey, quoted by Gilman, writing, "This fourth sonata is more of a 'bardic' rhapsody on the subject than an attempt at actual presentation of it."[19] The harp-like rolled harmonies of the opening themes in the first two movements of the "Keltic" Sonata immediately call to mind the bardic harp in an onomatopoeic manner. Beyond merely mimicking the instrument, however, the whole idiom of the music should bring to mind the diction of a bard.[20] The implication is that it is the narrative persona of the storyteller rather than the dramatic characters who inhabit the stories of Irish legend on which criticism might best concentrate. Narratology thus provides a better methodology for approaching this work than nationalism or simple program writing. The narrative aspect of the "Keltic" Sonata enters into the process of interpretation through the evocation of the bardic voice. The composer again gives the clue, directing attention not to the exploits of the characters of legend but to the manner of the voice of the bard. In the letter just quoted, MacDowell continued, "I have made use of all the suggestion of tone-painting in my power,—just as the bard would have reinforced *his* speech with gesture and facial expression."[21] The rhapsodic gestures of the music, therefore, do not represent the characters or actions of legendary heroines and heroes but rather enact the bard who evokes the feeling of the music's action. It is thus not story (the plottedness of epic or dramatic action) but the act of storytelling (narrative or diegetic) that constitutes the crux of this sonata.

This bardic quality is quite a different matter from sounding like Irish folk music (or like historical Irish music, whatever MacDowell might have imagined that to be). Instead it is a heightened—"reinforced," as MacDowell put it—style of diction. The models for this were the versions of the ancient bardic tales of Celtic legend familiar to MacDowell, those of Standish O'Grady and Fiona MacLeod. To demonstrate these we can consider the following examples, which represent two quite different genres within the literature.

Gilman refers to the literary historian and historical novelist Standish O'Grady (1846–1928) as the model, as we have already noted. The following will serve as an example:

Within as from far distance there arose reverberations and horrid echoes as from deep caverns, and voice calling to voice, as of troop encouraging troop, and a noise of a crash, as of giants falling, a clangour of brass, and the thunder-pealing cry of the son of Sualtam amid the deafening uproar. Through rolling clouds there gleamed lurid lightnings, revealing things nameless, not to be described. From their tombs brake forth the ancient dead at the noise of that strife like the shock of worlds, for the earth stirred herself, and the dead arose out of their sleep of ages. Then time gave up her secrets and births to be, and her veiled nations and generations arose rank behind rank. Like a torrent's fall their voices sounded from afar, summoning him to their deliverance, their thin voices unheard in the crash and roar of that awful strife.

Then were the hosts of Erin disordered, and the battalions clashed together; then sprang champions forth out of their chariots, and the steeds were panic-stricken, and flew through the plain with the war-cars.[22]

On the other hand, MacDowell originally intended to dedicate the Sonata to the pseudonymous poet Fiona MacLeod (William Sharp, 1855–1905), who, like O'Grady, transmitted Celtic—though more characteristically Gaelic—tales, and who also wrote several collections of poetry derived from an imagined Hibernian or Caledonian past. MacDowell wrote to the poet, "Your work has so grown into my life that I venture to ask you to permit my placing your name on some music of mine. Your poems have been an inspiration to me and I trust you will accept a dedication of music that is yours already by right of suggestion. By this I do not mean that my music in any way echoes your words but that your words have been a most powerful incentive to me in my music and I crave your sympathy for it."[23] Fiona MacLeod's poems do not adopt the grandiloquent intonations of O'Grady's. Instead, they are lyrical and mystical.

Deirdrê Is Dead . . .

"Deirdrê the beautiful is dead . . . is dead!"
                      (The House of Usna)

The grey wind weeps, the grey wind weeps,
    the grey wind weeps:

Dust on her breast, dust on her eyes, the grey
    wind weeps!

Cold, cold it is under the brown sod, and cold
    under the grey grass:
Here only the wet wind and the flittermice and
    the plovers pass:

I wonder if the wailing birds, and the soft
    hair-covered things
Of the air, and the grey wind hear what sighing
    song she sings

Down in the quiet hollow where the coiled
    twilights of hair
Are gathered into the darkness that broods on
    her bosom bare?

It is said that the dead sing, though we have
    no ears to hear,
And that whoso lists is lickt up of the Shadow,
    too, because of fear—

But this would give me no fear, that I heard
    a sighing song from her lips:
No, but as the green heart of an upthrust
    towering billow slips

Down into the green hollow of the ingathering
    wave,
So would I slip, and sink, and drown, in her
    grassy grave.

For is not my desire there, hidden away under
    the cloudy night
Of her long hair that was my valley of whispers
    and delight—

And in her two white hands, like still swans
    on a frozen lake,

Hath she not my heart that I have hidden
    there for dear love's sake?

Alas, there is no sighing song, no breath in
    the silence there:
Not even the white moth that loves death flits
    through her hair

As the bird of Brigid, made of foam and the
    pale moonwhite wine
Of dreams, flits under the sombre windless
    plumes of the pine.

I hear a voice crying, crying, crying: is it the
    wind
I hear, crying its old weary cry time out of
    mind?

The grey wind weeps, the grey wind weeps,
    the grey wind weeps:
Dust on her breast, dust on her eyes, the grey
    wind weeps![24]

These approaches to a literary style gave MacDowell the bardic narrative voice as the means to identify the heightened manner of diction in the music. The lines the composer sent to Gilman attempt to resonate sympathetically with the writing of O'Grady and MacLeod. The music manifests this in a declamatory rhythmic/melodic style, highly gestural figures, post-Romantic richness of harmony and density of texture, and registral extremes. Its virtuosity foregrounds the act of performance, as MacDowell suggested in likening its expression to that of his idea of "reinforced" bardic intonation. For the "Keltic" Sonata, a better literary parallel than any episode from Irish legend would be the description of a bard's performance in O'Grady's *History of Ireland*:

> the sacred bard drew from its sheath, made of the grey fell of badgers, lined with soft white doeskin, the gold-adorned harp, which had delighted the minds of warriors at many a great feast. . . . Anon, beneath his swift and eager hands, there arose

a storm of sweet sounds, taking captive the souls of those who listened; but as a thunder shower dies away in heavy single drops, so subsided that great prelude, note by sweet dissolving note, and the bard's voice arose singing.[25]

To the extent, then, that the "Keltic" Sonata derives from ancient Irish legend, it does so via its bardic voice. It is the narrative quality of the music, and not action, that we should hear in the work. This gives the piece a special place among those Romantic works that explicitly identify their narrative persona. It commends itself not as a nationalistic work but as a Romantic one, an instructive example, therefore, as we come to understand how essential to Romanticism the identity of voice was.

In summary, neither the events of Irish legend as topic nor American or Irish musical traits make the "Keltic" Sonata especially interesting. The work may not appear particularly useful to the historian as an example of Irish or American exoticism or nationalism at the turn of the century. Attempts to discover the characters, events, or themes of Irish legend programmatically in the "Keltic" Sonata founder in futility. On the other hand, MacDowell's reference to Irish legend was not without purpose, for it offered him a means to make explicit the central aesthetic premise of Romanticism, foregrounding the fictive speaker's persona. Coming at the end of the century of artistic Romanticism, this work centrally manifests the voiced-ness that is Romanticism's essential characteristic.

Chapter 14

Recognizing Romantic Voices

The recognition of narrative or lyric voices in Romanticism is such a natural part of hearing a Romantic piece (as it is of viewing a painting or reading a poem) that we generally experience the music this way, without stopping to analyze it. The experience of hearing a Romantic work as the utterance of a recognizable individual voice responds to the essential aesthetic foundation of the music: Art expresses a speaking subject's personality. Identifying the particular voices in a way that understands them as fictive, created voices requires close reading combined with broad context. The scholarly application of this principle is the business of narratology, the study of narrativity.

A common usage of the term *narrative* in music analysis treats it as a matter of recounting musical structures in words. Description that follows the development of motives through their tracks of tensions to resolution over the form of a piece is sometimes called narrative analysis. It claims validity on the basis of its approaching a work not as a design best represented spatially by a visual outline or diagram but as a plot that unfolds in action.

But a plot alone does not make a narrative; it only makes a plot. To be sure, in this book we have followed plots in a number of different pieces, but, just as not every plotted work reveals a Romantic voice, voice is not limited to plotted works. We have also identified voices in nonplotted, lyric works.

What makes the concept of narrativity (or lyrical voice) in this book different from other studies that claim to approach music as narrative is that here we have treated the work not as a dramatic object to explicate as plot but as the utterance of a personality. We have dealt with the music not primarily as an object of detailed analysis but as the expressive act of a mind or personality, whose acquaintance we make and to whom we listen in a personal way. Romantic music asks of us not that we analyze it, or even interpret it, but that we attend to it and become acquainted with the mind from which it comes.

Listeners listen in this way instinctively. They probably think of it, in a sort of shorthand, as getting to know the composer through the music. In most cases listeners probably imagine the voice of the work as the composer's voice or at least refer to it in those terms. They perceive the lyric ego or narrative persona, but they name it with the name of the composer. This might lead to the so-called biographical—or (auto)biographical—fallacy, the assumption that the mind of the work is congruent with that of the composer. From the narratologist's point of view, we would say that they impose the composer's name on the fictive Romantic voice that the music creates. A more thoughtful approach enables us to recognize the distinction between the biographical composer and the fictive voice to which the work belongs.

Analysis

From the vantage point of narratology, we have various means to pursue closely the identities of Romantic voices in the music we listen to and study. First, naturally, is the music itself. Analysis is not the end goal, but it is certainly one component of the project. Just as we learn about people in life—or learn about the speakers in poems or the narrators in novels—from what they say, the content of a musical work represents its voice. In every case in the preceding chapters, close listening has held a central place. We have been especially intrigued by the least easily explained features of the music. In fact, we learn most where, for example, harmony surprises us or form departs from our expectations.

The first movement of Beethoven's "Tempest" Sonata stands as the archetypal instance of this, as critics have repeatedly struggled with the question of how to locate a principal theme in that form, a question stubbornly left unanswered by the recitative interruption. Some forms give more help, as in the case of Liszt's "Vallée d'Obermann," which represents the class of pieces in which a passage outside the main action of the form—often, as in this instance, an introduction—can suggest the persona who directs the listener to the body of the music. In that piece we encounter also a closing, past the conclusion of the form, that serves as an envoi or even a signature. Idiosyncrasies in the treatment of form, especially sonata forms, commonly open questions that challenge us to pursue a narratological hearing. We found that to be the case in Hensel's Piano Trio and Chopin's B-Minor Piano Sonata, where our asking what kinds of narrators would recount those particular plots led to two different feminist voices.

Listening to the works might draw our attention to features of musical style other than form that offer insight into their narrative voices—scoring, rhythm, melody, harmony. In Berlioz's *Harold en Italie*, the simple observation of instrumentation opens the way to finding the narrator. The scoring and placement of the viola apart from the orchestra sets up the distinct planes in the discourse. To track the narrative function, we pay attention to the ways in which the viola inserts or recalls ideas, comments, or focalizes the scene. In the case of the opening scene of act 2 of Verdi's *Otello*, it was first the misleading rhythm in the placement of the measures at the opening of the curtain, then the reconception of the embellishing motive as an ugly snarl, and later the double instance of deceptive cadences that revealed the underlying Iago-like, deconstructive nature of the narrative persona.

Musical References

The inclusion of musical references in a work also leads to the discovery of persona. Most transparently, the adoption of a familiar opera tune as the basis for a series of variations comes into play by leading us to consider how that treatment manifests an identifiable voice. The use of musical references appears most strikingly in Schumann's C-Major Symphony, because that work is replete with quotations and allusions—to Bach (both musical allusions and the spelling of his name), Haydn, Mozart, Beethoven (in quotations from *An die ferne Geliebte* and the Ninth Symphony, as well as in the adoption of an archetypally heroic overall plot), possibly Mendelssohn, and finally Schumann himself. We also heard Chopin recalling his own music in the nocturnal secondary theme in the first movement of his B-Minor Sonata.

Musical references need not be to specific works. Hensel's Piano Trio references devotional and domestic music in its inner movements as well as the csárdás in its finale. Wolf's "Auf ein altes Bild" evokes music of a bygone era. The music does not exactly adopt the technique or texture of fauxbourdon, but we cannot fail to recognize the historicizing effect. The reference or allusion unmistakably locates in the fictive past the image that the text describes. The voice becomes either that of the fictive painter in the imagined Renaissance or the contemporary viewer in a historical museum of art.

Gender

A special type of reference in nineteenth-century music is to gender. Gender differences intersect inextricably with genre. The references to devotional and domestic genres in Hensel's Trio must direct our attention toward the milieu of women in nineteenth-century European culture, and this has to affect our understanding of the work's voice. Gender implications likewise locate virtuosic variations on aria tunes in the realm of the prima donna. Other features of the music or external factors can work either to reinforce or to counter such default implications.

In addition to genre, thematic styles in music can imply gender. This applies particularly to the themes in sonata forms. We can easily understand why the decisive establishment of tonic keys and metrical frameworks to open Classic sonata forms tended to demand characteristically triadic and clearly metrical themes. To achieve contrast, the themes associated with secondary keys naturally and increasingly tended toward lyricism. By the middle of the nineteenth century, theoretical explanations of sonata design characterized this contrast as one of masculine and feminine. The form itself, in which the secondary theme resolves into the tonal territory of the principal theme, can reasonably be criticized as reinforcing gender stereotypes and power dynamics. This is the default plot for sonata-form movements, at least those classified in Sonata Theory as Type 3. For that reason, awareness of the normatively masculine plan and alertness to forms that contravene the norm offer insights into particular works. In the examples here, they have guided us to understanding contrasting feminist perspectives: the representation of the heroic feminine in Hensel's Piano Trio, the strategy of nonaggression in the first movement of Chopin's B-Minor Sonata.

Style

In many works we become acquainted with the personality of a poetic speaker or narrator partly by our recognition of style or idiom. In the case of Schubert's Heine songs, we cannot help noticing the turn away from the folklike style of strophic song with simple, figurational accompaniment toward a declamatory vocal style and quasi-orchestral piano part. The style marks the lyric speaker as urbane and sophisticated. The same principle applies to our understanding of the narrative voice in MacDowell's "Keltic" Sonata, which intentionally adopts a high-flown, bardic rhetoric.

Paratext

Different sorts of paratexts, both peritexts and epitexts, inevitably come into play as elements of Romantic voiced-ness. We might consider the texts of songs or opera either as part of the text of the work or as peritext. The interplay of words and tones has not only exemplified text-setting in the sense that tones illustrate images or express emotion in a lyric poem but also led us to an acquaintance with the specific Romantic voices in all the songs we have studied: Schubert's Heine songs, Schumann's Eichendorff songs, and Wolf's setting of Mörike's poem. In the case of Verdi's *Otello*, the text of Jago's "Credo" reveals the character, but other passages in the libretto of the opera, together with the ideas taken over from Shakespeare's play (which adoptively becomes epitext), suggest the deconstructive machinations of Iago and turn our attention to the devices that represent deconstruction in the rhythm, melody, and harmony.

Although they are not literally the musical tones themselves, performance indications in a score cannot be held strictly separate from the musical text. In this sense they might seem to belong to a gray area between text and peritext. Performance instructions have played a part most notably in our understanding of the narrative position of the viola in *Harold en Italie*. The statement at the beginning of the score that the solo viola stands apart from the orchestra with the harp beside it might be the most obvious example of an explicitly staged distinction in planes of discourse in a narrative work.

More in the usual meaning of peritext as we encounter it in literature are titles and epigrams attached to instrumental works. The title of *Harold en Italie* serves as a cue not only to the content of the work but also to the planes of discourse and action in Byron's poem—the scenes, the figure of Harold as the pilgrim, and the narrative voice that sets up and comments on Harold's experiences. The titles of the individual movements specify scenes, of which only "Harold in the Mountains" directly references Byron's poem; the other titles as peritext save listeners from scouring *Childe Harold's Pilgrimage* for episodes that cannot be found there.

Likewise, the title and epigram in MacDowell's "Keltic" Sonata let us know that the music comes from an Irish and legendary world. If we know the literary references to the writing of Standish O'Grady and Fiona MacLeod, we will bring more to the identification of the sort of voice we recognize in the music. The title of Liszt's "Vallée d'Obermann" locates the voice in Switzerland and specifically in the landscape encountered by Senancour's protagonist. The epigram from "Obermann" identifies the speaker's experience of loneliness and world-weariness, and the one from *Childe Harold's Pilgrimage* more directly reveals the frustration with his inability to find adequate expression for profound, intense feelings. Such references also tend to make the original works by Senancour and Byron part of our access to the personality of the voice in Liszt's character piece.

An unexpected perspective on paratext comes from Mendelssohn, who adamantly rejected the application of peritextual verbiage to his songs without words, and indeed to music in general. The effect of this, as we realized, is to turn the inclination to provide titles back onto the listener, with the result that whatever words one might find to characterize the pieces derive their meaning from the fact that they account for the unmistakable musical feeling as the listener's own expressions. In that sense the listener becomes also the Romantic voice and welcome to add whatever sort of personal epitext she or he finds meaningful.

Epitexts can come to a work even quite late. A good example is the way in which Berlioz's *Mémoires* interface with *Harold en Italie*. Although the *Mémoires* date from considerably later than the symphony, the episodes of pilgrims' processions and the Abruzzi mountaineer's serenade color the listener's image of the narrative persona's experiences.

Composer Biography

The biographies of composers can suggest aspects of voice, but we have to approach them cautiously to avoid the (auto)biographical fallacy. As I have emphasized, the voice of a work is not the writer of the work in a simple sense. Berlioz traveled to Italy, and Liszt spent considerable time in Switzerland, but the voices of *Harold en Italie* and "Vallée d'Obermann" owe far more to their reading than to their actual experiences. On the other hand, what we know of the way in which Paganini presented himself reveals that he had in mind to create and nurture a persona, even though he worried that listeners who regarded his virtuosity as enabled by supernatural forces consequently failed to credit his own talent and application.

Biography can also come into play in purely fortuitous ways. The title "Tempest" attached to Beethoven's Piano Sonata in D Minor, op. 31, no. 2, does not stem from the composer, and we might dismiss it as irrelevant to understanding the music. The story that Schindler tells of his exchange with Beethoven about his piano sonatas does not reveal that Beethoven offered him the key to the music. Nevertheless, it happened to enact the same sort of resistance against supplying answers to questions that the D-Minor Sonata teases us to ask and then refuses to answer. Then it leads us to an understanding of Beethoven's retort to Schindler that he should go read Shakespeare's play, which in turn suggests the insight that the narrative voice of the first movement of the Sonata has a Prospero-like personality.

External Agency

At times the observations or interpretations of people other than composers can guide our understanding of a particular voice. We have had a strong example of this in the reception history of Chopin's B-Minor Sonata, for which later critics—whether favorable or not—both confirm that the themes conform to conventions of gender and identify the secondary theme as embodying the figure of Chopin.

Equally in the case of Chopin's variations on "Là ci darem la mano" we saw the influence of an individual critic. Schumann's review advanced the position that the voice does not emerge as that of a virtuoso performer (which Chopin certainly was) but of an opera composer. As such, the voice would be gendered male rather than female.

Not surprisingly, another critic helps to identify a lyric voice in Schumann's own work. The problem of understanding the nature of cyclicity in his op. 39 *Liederkreis* can be resolved by attending to Brendel's contemporary observation that the work represents not a linear story but the voice of the Romantic poets by absorbing within its orbit the poets' "fantastic opulence."[1]

The Problem of a Methodology

In the end, musical narratology distinctively possesses no systematic methodology. The discussions in this book should, however, at least point to some of the means by which listeners can—and indeed do—discover and recognize voices, whether narrative or lyric, in Romantic music.

We must place at the center of our thinking the sound of the music, including its representation in scores as well, perhaps, as whatever we can discover about performance practice, historical instruments, and acoustic spaces. Music analysis has an important place. Rigorous method in Schenkerian analysis or Sonata Theory helps to uncover the internal content of a lyric or dramatic work. Most suggestive should always be the aspects of the music that resist analysis most stubbornly, because those moments likely hold the most individual meaning.

What composers or other creators of musical works, such as librettists, say should carry some weight. They sometimes reveal their points of departure or their intentions in a work, but we're lucky if they do so explicitly in the terms that we would use. Rarely, however, we do find situations such as Verdi's *Otello*, in which we have documents making direct statements that Jago is a critic and the true author of the drama. Composers are not critical theorists. Even though they do not intend to answer the questions that we bring, what they have written or said can provide insights into how they think the voice of the music will emerge. In the case of Berlioz's *Mémoires* or MacDowell's talks and interviews, they might offer a fairly direct invitation to meet the narrative persona. Beethoven's impatient dismissal of Schindler gives a clue entirely fortuitously to the character of the voice in the first movement of the "Tempest" Sonata. It is important to exercise caution, however, because in some cases an autobiographical observation might mislead us, as in the instance of Schumann's report that he was ill during the composition of the C-Major Symphony, which distracts us from giving adequate attention to the much more significant allusions in the work.

In looking to know the personas of music as listeners actually encounter them, we should not overlook observations by others. Schumann's review of Chopin's Mozart variations identifies the persona directly as a composer. The later critics of Chopin's B-Minor Sonata heard the themes as gendered and the secondary theme as embodying the composer's personal style, and this was true both for the Sonata's admirers and for d'Indy, who despised the work.

Identifying the personalities of voices in Romantic music remains, in the end, a matter of learning everything we can and thinking synthetically. As Lawrence Kramer wrote about method in *Music as Cultural Practice, 1800–1900*, "throw away this map before you use it."[2] Because each work has its own narrative or lyric voice, and each speaks in its own idiom from its particular place, the fictive personas of musical works, like the real persons in our lives, reveal themselves more intimately as we discover more about them and listen to them more carefully and sympathetically.

Notes

Chapter 1

1. I choose the term *Classic* rather than *Classical* for this period and its music because it avoids confusion with the common usage of *classical music*, of which the Romantic repertoire forms a very large part.

2. Peter Brooks, "Reading for the Plot," in *Essentials of the Theory of Fiction*, 3rd ed., ed. Michael J. Hoffman and Patrick D. Murphy (Durham, NC: Duke University Press, 2005), 329; reprinted from Peter Brooks, *Reading for the Plot* (New York: Alfred A. Knopf, 1984).

3. Charles Rosen, *The Classical Style: Haydn, Mozart, Beethoven* (New York: Norton, 1971), 43.

4. Friedrich Schiller, "On the Tragic Art," in *Works of Friedrich Schiller*, vol. 8, *Aesthetical and Philosophical Essays* (Boston, MA: S. E. Cassino, 1884), 360–64.

5. The terminology "modes of representation" goes back to Aristotle; see the *Poetics* 1448a19–b3. Following Gérard Genette, I distinguish here between two modes, drama and narrative (leaving aside lyric poetry for the moment). Gérard Genette, *Fiction and Diction*, trans. Catherine Porter (Ithaca, NY: Cornell University Press, 1993), 8.

6. Arthur Schopenhauer, *The World as Will and Idea*, 7th ed., trans. R. B. Haldane and J. Kemp (London: Kegan Paul, Trench, Trübner, 1909), 211.

7. Tzvetan Todorov, *Introduction to Poetics*, trans. Richard Howard (Brighton, UK: Harvester, 1981), 51.

8. Stanley Cavell, *Must We Mean What We Say?* (New York: Scribner, 1969; updated ed., Cambridge: Cambridge University Press, 2002), 320–21.

9. James Hepokoski and Warren Darcy, *Elements of Sonata Theory: Norms, Types, and Deformations in the Late-Eighteenth-Century Sonata* (New York: Oxford University Press, 2006). While I find that Hepokoski and Darcy locate and label with impressive thoroughness the vast variety of options that composers devised within the form, it has not been necessary to adopt their elaborate approach to sonata forms in this book. Instead, I employ a somewhat more straightforward

framework and nomenclature deliberately based on the discussions of the form by late-eighteenth- and nineteenth-century writers, together with abbreviations adapted from Jan LaRue's *Guidelines for Style Analysis* (2nd ed., Warren, MI: Harmonie Park Press, 1992). Thus, the basic abbreviations for thematic material in a sonata movement are, as in Sonata Theory, P for themes associated with the principal key and S for those associated with the secondary key, but O is used rather than I to represent introductory material, in order to avoid confusion with the roman numeral I for numbering a section or for a harmonic function. Transition themes appear as T instead of Sonata Theory's clumsier TR. A closing-function theme is indicated by K rather than C, which might also represent a pitch class or key. Likewise, different P themes in a movement are 1P, 2P, etc. (read as "first theme associated with the principal key" and "second theme associated with the principal key") rather than P^1, P^2, etc., which might suggest variations of a single P theme.

10. Hepokoski and Darcy, *Elements of Sonata Theory*, 15–16.

11. Hepokoski and Darcy, 251–52.

12. The principal allusion to the idea of *loci topici* in music by a period writer appears in Johann David Heinichen's *Der General-Bass in der Composition* (Dresden, 1728). Heinichen is mainly interested in the resources for the expression of affect in operatic compositions. To explain how music can evoke affects, he turns to the techniques of rhetoric as it was taught in contemporary manuals. See George J. Buelow, "The *Loci Topici* and Affect in Late Baroque Music: Heinichen's Practical Demonstration," *The Music Review* 27 (1966): 161–76.

13. Leonard Ratner, *Classic Music: Expression, Form, and Style* (New York: Schirmer, 1980), followed by *Romantic Music: Sound and Syntax* (New York: Schirmer, 1992). A notable essay in creating a glossary of "topics" in nineteenth-century music is Janice Dickensheets, "The Topical Vocabulary of the Nineteenth Century," *Journal of Musicological Research* 31, nos. 2–3 (2012): 97–137.

14. Wye J. Allanbrook, *Rhythmic Gesture in Mozart: "Le nozze di Figaro" and "Don Giovanni"* (Chicago: University of Chicago Press, 1983); V. Kofi Agawu, *Playing with Signs: A Semiotic Interpretation of Classic Music* (Princeton, NJ: Princeton University Press, 1991).

15. Raymond Monelle, *The Musical Topic: Hunt, Military and Pastoral* (Bloomington: Indiana University Press, 2006). The book is largely a demonstration of numerous examples of hunt, march, and pastoral styles rather than analysis or interpretation. See also his discussion of topics in chapter 2, "The Search for Topics," in his earlier book *The Sense of Music: Semiotic Essays* (Princeton, NJ: Princeton University Press, 2000), 14–40.

16. Monelle, *The Musical Topic*, 7; my emphasis.

17. Kofi Agawu, *Music as Discourse: Semiotic Adventures in Romantic Music* (Oxford: Oxford University Press, 2009), 41–50.

18. The diversity of applications of the term is obvious in the collection of essays edited by Danuta Mirka, *The Oxford Handbook of Topic Theory* (New York:

Oxford University Press, 2014). John A. Rice notes the difficulties of topic theory in his review of the *Oxford Handbook* in the *Journal of the American Musicological Society* 68 (2015): 447.

19. For another discussion of the problems inherent in applying a methodology of topic theory to nineteenth-century music, see Julian Horton, "Listening to Topics in the Nineteenth Century," in Mirka, *Oxford Handbook*, 642–64. Although Horton does not set aside the concept for nineteenth-century music, arguing instead for interpreting it in ways different from the previous century, the foreignness of the term to nineteenth-century writing always leads me to prefer the term *character* for the music explored here.

20. My translation from Daniel Gottlob Türk, *Klavierschule, oder Anweisung zum Klavierspielen für Lehrer und Lernende, mit kritischen Anmerkungen* (Leipzig: Schwickert / Halle: Hemmerde und Schwetschke, 1789), 114–16: "Ein jedes gute Tonstück hat irgend einen bestimmten (herrschenden) Charakter, das heisst, der Komponist hat einen gewissen Grad der Freude oder Traurigkeit, des Scherzes oder Ernstes, der Muth oder Gelassenheit, u.s.w. darin ausgedruckt."

21. Johann Georg Sulzer, *Allgemeine Theorie der schönen Künste* (Leipzig: Weidmann, 1792; repr. Hildesheim: George Olms, 1970), 1:273; my translation. The passage comes from the article "Ausdruck," in the section "Ausdruck in der Musik":

> Jedes Tonstück, es sey ein würklicher von Worten begleiteter Gesang, oder nur für die Instrumente gesetzt, muss einen bestimmten Charakter haben, und in dem Gemüthe des Zuhörers Empfindungen von bestimmter Art erweken. Es wäre thöricht, wenn der Tonsetzer seine Arbeit anfangen wollte, ehe er den Charakter seines Stücks festgesetzt hat. Er muss wissen, ob die Sprache, die er führen will, die Sprache eines Stolzen oder eines Demüthigen, eines Beherzten oder Furchtsamen, eines Bittenden oder Gebietenden, eines Zärtlichen oder eines Zornigen sey. Wenn er auch durch einen Zufall sein Thema erfunden, oder wenn es ihm von ohngefehr eingefallen ist, so untersuche er den Charakter desselben, damit er ihn auch bey der Ausführing beybehalten könne.
>
> Hat er den Charakter des Stücks festgesetzt, so musst er sich selbst in die Empfindung setzen, die er in andern hervorbringen will. Das beste ist, dass er sich eine Handlung, eine Begebenheit, einen Zustand vorstelle, in welchem sich dieselbe natürlicher Weise in dem Lichte zeiget.

22. My translation from Anton Reicha, *Traité de mélodie* (Paris: Chez l'auteur, impr. de J. L. Scherff, 1814), 62: "La Mélodie exprime differens caractères. . . . Deux airs composés dans le même ton et avec la même mesure, modulés de la même manière, et ayant le même rhythme et la même coupe, peuvent être néanmoins entièrement opposés de caractère." For recent treatments of the idea of character

as applied to entire works, see Robert Riggs, "'On the Representation of Character in Music': Christian Gottfried Körner's Aesthetics of Instrumental Music," *The Musical Quarterly* 81, no. 4 (Winter 1997): 599–631; Matthew Pritchard, "'The Moral Background of the Work of Art': 'Character' in German Musical Aesthetics," *Eighteenth-Century Music* 9, no. 1 (March 2012): 63–80.

23. In a 1988 article, Fred Maus interrogates the relationship between "structural" and "dramatic" analysis of a piece, with a discussion of the first eighteen measures of Beethoven's String Quartet in F Minor, op. 95; Fred Maus, "Music as Drama," *Music Theory Spectrum* 10 (1988): 56–73. He concludes that "for at least some music, a satisfactory account of structure must already be an aesthetically oriented narration of dramatic action" (73), but he remains noncommittal about the identity of agents for the action. Eero Tarasti, who approaches this issue from the perspective of theoretical musical semiotics, also arrives at this idea of theme as agent, specifically in the context of sonata form, which he implies represents a "'rule' built into the aesthetics of Western art music": "When a dominant musical element is chosen for a certain section, then one is in the narrative process of the achronic, hierarchic relation of opposition, which lies so close to the surface of the discourse and to the latter's more or less anthropomorphic configurations, so that a new actorial isotopy enters: a theme identifiable as a musical actant." Eero Tarasti, *A Theory of Musical Semiotics* (Bloomington: Indiana University Press, 1994), 32. Like numerous other authors, as I shall consistently observe, Tarasti uses the term "narrative" to mean what I designate as "plotted" or "dramatic" process.

24. Hepokoski and Darcy, *Elements of Sonata Theory*, 252.

25. Seth Monahan, "'Inescapable' Coherence and the Failure of the Novel-Symphony in the Finale of Mahler's Sixth," *19th-Century Music* 31, no. 1 (Summer 2007): 61, 74.

26. Carl Czerny, *School of Practical Composition*, trans. John Bishop (London: R. Cocks, 1848; repr. New York: Da Capo, 1979), 1:34. The treatise was published in German as *Die Schule der praktischen Composition* (Bonn: Simrock, 1848).

27. Lawrence Kramer, in "Musical Narratology: A Theoretical Outline," *Indiana Theory Review* 12 (1991): 141–62, rejects structuralist approaches to narrativity in music and instead offers some examples of the hermeneutic work performed by narratological study of music. While I clearly find more to justify the discovery of narrative in analysis than Kramer does, we would certainly agree that narratological approaches are more likely to help us deal with music that lacks structural coherence than to demonstrate coherence, as well as that narrative thinking offers social and cultural or epistemic and self-reflective insights (or insights that combine any or all of these).

28. My translation from Jean-Jacques Rousseau, *Confessions* (Paris, 1819), 81: "Je ne suis fait comme aucun de ceux que j'ai vus; j'ose croire n'être fait comme aucun de ceux qui existent. Si je ne vaux pas mieux, au moins je suis autre. Si la nature a bien ou mal fait de briser le moule dans lequel elle m'a jeté, c'est ce dont on ne peut juger qu'après m'avoir lu."

29. Russell Millard, "Telling Tales: A Survey of Narratological Approaches to Music," *Current Musicology* 103 (Fall 2018): 5–44, undertakes a roughly chronological overview of much of the major scholarship that purports to apply the idea of narrativity in music analysis or criticism. Most of this literature has to do with plot rather than narrative per se in the more rigorous sense that will be developed here.

30. Robert Scholes and Robert Kellogg, *The Nature of Narrative* (New York: Oxford University Press, 1966), 4.

31. Seymour Chatman, "Discourse: Nonnarrated Stories," in Hoffman and Murphy, *Essentials of the Theory of Fiction*, 247; reprinted from Seymour Chatman, *Story and Discourse: Narrative Structure in Fiction and Film* (Ithaca, NY: Cornell University Press, 1978). The reference is to Plato, *Republic*, bk. 3, 392c–398b.

32. The usage here is regrettably somewhat complicated by the backward use of the terms *diegetic* and *nondiegetic* or *extradiegetic* in the field of film theory, where the term *mimetic* is largely if not entirely disregarded. In this literature those sounds (such as musical performances) that are made or heard by the characters in the plot/action of the film are referred to as "diegetic," while those that come from outside the characters' experience (such as voice-over commentary or background underscoring) are "extradiegetic." In fact, the material that is called diegetic would belong to mimesis in the sense that Plato and Aristotle had in mind, and the so-called extradiegetic sounds would be precisely the ones that reflect the controlling narrative position—in other words, diegetic. In order to avoid contamination by this confusing usage, I shall avoid the use of these terms as much as possible.

33. Schiller, "On the Tragic Art," 362–63.

34. Genette, *Fiction and Diction*, 8.

35. Michael J. Toolan, *Narrative: A Critical Linguistic Introduction* (New York: Routledge, 1988), 7.

36. Tzvetan Todorov, *The Poetics of Prose*, trans. Richard Howard (Ithaca, NY: Cornell University Press, 1977), 111; originally published as *Poétique de la prose* (Paris: Seuil, 1971).

37. To be fair, Toolan does not by any means neglect the narrative voice in his book. He had already said, "Narratives have to have a teller, and that teller, no matter how backgrounded or remote or 'invisible,' is always important." Toolan, *Narrative*, 5.

38. See the quotation at the end of the section "Plot and Musical Form," cited in note 11.

39. Byron Almén, *A Theory of Musical Narrative* (Bloomington: Indiana University Press, 2008). See my review in the *Journal of Musicological Research* 30, no. 1 (2011): 72–76.

40. Northrop Frye, *Anatomy of Criticism: Four Essays* (Princeton, NJ: Princeton University Press, 1957).

41. Seth Monahan, "Action and Agency Revisited," *Journal of Music Theory* 57, no. 2 (Fall 2013): 321–71. This article expands on the earlier discussion in Monahan's dissertation of ways in which analyses employ the concept of agency;

see Seth Monahan, "Mahler's Sonata Narratives" (PhD diss., Yale University, 2008), esp. chap. 1 and the summarizing matrix in figure 1.1 on p. 305.

42. Robert S. Hatten, *A Theory of Virtual Agency for Western Music* (Bloomington: Indiana University Press, 2018), especially the introduction (pp. 1–13) and the prelude (pp. 15–29). I am grateful to Professor Hatten for sharing an unpublished version of his paper of the same title, which became the prelude of the book.

43. Karol Berger, "Narrative and Lyric: Fundamental Poetic Forms of Composition," in *Musical Humanism and Its Legacy: Essays in Honor of Claude V. Palisca*, ed. Nancy Kovaleff Baker and Barbara Russano Hanning, Festschrift series no. 11 (Stuyvesant, NY: Pendragon, 1992), 454–56. See also Paul Ricoeur, *Time and Narrative* (Chicago: University of Chicago Press, 1984), 1:32–37.

44. Michael Klein, *Intertextuality in Western Art Music* (Bloomington: Indiana University Press, 2005), 116–17.

45. Klein, *Intertextuality in Western Art Music*, 135.

46. Jean-Jacques Nattiez, "Can One Speak of Narrativity in Music?," *Journal of the Royal Musical Association* 115 (1990): 240–57.

47. It is worth noting that Northrop Frye described his project in *The Anatomy of Criticism* as that of finding for literature the equivalents of such musical concepts as rhythm and key, sonata form and fugue, not the reverse; see Frye, *Anatomy of Criticism*, 133–34.

48. Nattiez, "Can One Speak of Narrativity in Music?," 244.

49. Monelle, *The Sense of Music*, 115–46. The most concise statement of the idea appears on page 117.

50. Michael Klein, "Chopin's Fourth Ballade as a Musical Narrative," *Music Theory Spectrum* 26 (2004): 38–39.

51. Andrew Davis, *Sonata Fragments: Romantic Narratives in Chopin, Schumann, and Brahms* (Bloomington: Indiana University Press, 2017), 14.

52. Hatten, *A Theory of Virtual Agency*, 170.

53. This point and the usage of the terms are neatly outlined in Brooks, "Reading for the Plot," 335.

54. Gérard Genette, "Time and Narrative in *A la recherche du temps perdu*," in *Essentials of the Theory of Fiction*, 3rd ed., ed. Michael J. Hoffman and Patrick D. Murphy (Durham, NC: Duke University Press, 2005), 189.

55. Paul Ricoeur, "Narrative Time," *Critical Inquiry* 7, no. 1 (1980): 175.

56. Carolyn Abbate, "What the Sorcerer Said," *19th-Century Music* 12, no. 3 (1989): 221–30.

57. Seymour Chatman, "What Novels Can Do That Films Can't (and Vice Versa)," *Critical Inquiry* 7, no. 1 (1980): 122.

58. Thomas Christensen, "Narrative Theory and Music Analysis," in *Musik-konzepte—Konzepte der Musikwissenschaft: Bericht über den Internationalen Kongreß der Gesellschaft für Musikforschung, Halle (Saale) 1998*, ed. Kathrin Eberl and Wolfgang Ruf (Kassel: Bärenreiter, 2000), 1:51–52.

59. Robert S. Hatten, "Interpreting Beethoven's *Tempest* Sonata Through Topics, Gestures, and Agency," in *Beethoven's "Tempest" Sonata: Perspectives of Analysis and Performance*, ed. Pieter Bergé et al. (Leuven: Peeters, 2009), 164. For a later discussion of virtual narrative agency in music, with demonstrative examples, see Hatten, *A Theory of Virtual Agency*, 202–18.

60. David Loberg Code, "Narrative Strategies in Tonal Compositions" (PhD diss., University of Maryland, College Park, 1990), 234.

61. Code, "Narrative Strategies," 300–301.

62. Code, 301–2.

63. Carolyn Abbate, *Unsung Voices: Opera and Musical Narrative in the Nineteenth Century* (Princeton, NJ: Princeton University Press, 1991), 19.

64. See the reviews by Lawrence Kramer, "Song and Story," *19th-Century Music* 15, no. 3 (Spring 1992): 235–39; and Robert P. Morgan, review of *Unsung Voices: Opera and Musical Narrative in the Nineteenth Century*, by Carolyn Abbate, *The Journal of Modern History* 64, no. 3 (September 1992): 576–81.

65. Edward T. Cone, *The Composer's Voice* (Berkeley: University of California Press, 1974); Wayne C. Booth, *The Rhetoric of Fiction* (Chicago: University of Chicago Press, 1961). Another stimulus to my initial thinking about the signs of voice in musical works was Lawrence Kramer's discussion of the "Malinconia" movement of Beethoven's String Quartet op. 18, no. 6, in a chapter titled "As If a Voice Were in Them," in Lawrence Kramer, *Music as Cultural Practice 1800–1900* (Berkeley: University of California Press, 1990).

66. Abbate, "What the Sorcerer Said," 222; Michael Klein, *Music and Narrative Since 1900* (Bloomington: Indiana University Press, 2013), 22.

67. A related, somewhat complicating issue is that of a work's implied author, as distinct from the speaker or narrator. Booth gave significant consideration to this figure, who is also constructed by the actual writer of a novel and whose position is that of neither the writer nor the narrator but who stands between those two. See Booth, *The Rhetoric of Fiction*, 70–77. This raises interesting issues for music, where the identification of implied composers manifests in different ways than in literature.

It is possible, of course, to find instances in which implied composers emerge very clearly. Sometimes the choice of a musical genre or style easily lends an identity to an implied composer. To give a simple example, we might think, for instance, of the works of Bach and notice that we hear a different implied composer in a concerto grosso, such as the Concerto in D Minor for two violins, from those whom we hear in the chorale prelude in "Nun komm der Heiden Heiland" that opens the *Orgelbüchlein* or in *The Musical Offering*. The implied composer in a Mendelssohn song without words is not the same as in *Elijah*.

In nineteenth-century music we could of course pursue many questions about implied composers, thinking about matters ranging from milieux and audiences to compositional and performance techniques. What will concern us here, however, are the personalities of lyric speakers and narrators, who speak more intimately from each work. It is in this part of our experience of a piece that we hear the Romantic voice.

68. See in particular Peter Kivy, "Contra the Hypothetical Persona in Music," in *Emotion and the Arts*, ed. Mette Hjort and Sue Laver, 95–109 (Oxford: Oxford University Press, 1997).

69. Mark Evan Bonds has explored this issue in *The Beethoven Syndrome: Hearing Music and Autobiography* (New York: Oxford University Press, 2020); see esp. pp. 82–93, 120–42.

70. Bonds, *The Beethoven Syndrome*, 15. Bonds gives a revealing account of how "hearing music as autobiography" (his subtitle) developed in the nineteenth century. He does not clearly keep in the reader's mind the fact that this approach leads to both misinterpretation of individual works and a failure to recognize the aesthetic significance of the narrative or lyrical voice in Romantic music. See my review, Douglass Seaton, review of *The Beethoven Syndrome*, by Mark Evan Bonds, *Music & Letters* 102, no. 1 (February 2021): 155–58.

71. Throughout this book, *idiom* will mean a manner of expression that we recognize as characteristic of a person, group, or the like, as in *folk idiom* or *pianistic idiom*. (In just one case, where the meaning will be obvious, it refers to a particular figurative use of a word.)

72. Robert Hatten, "On Narrativity in Music: Expressive Genres and Levels of Discourse in Beethoven," *Indiana Theory Review* 12 (1991): 75–98. The issue of levels of discourse formed an important part of the narrative theory of Mikhail Bakhtin, represented in his essays published as *The Dialogic Imagination*, ed. Michael Holquist, trans. Caryl Emerson and Michael Holquist (Austin: University of Texas Press, 1981). For a more extensive development of Hatten's ideas, see also his *Musical Meaning in Beethoven: Markedness, Correlation, and Interpretation* (Bloomington: Indiana University Press, 1994). Hatten returns to the topic in his *A Theory of Virtual Agency*; see esp. pp. 203–5. On the whole, I would distinguish Hatten's approach from mine in the sense that he proposes to develop an aesthetic theory, with the intention to arrive at something like general applicability, in contrast to my turn to critical and Romantic approaches to the idiosyncrasies of individual works.

73. For the Ossianic in Mendelssohn, see R. Larry Todd, "Mendelssohn's Ossianic Manner, with a New *Source*: 'On Lena's Gloomy Heath,'" in *Mendelssohn and Schumann: Essays on Their Music and Its Context*, ed. Jon W. Finson and R. Larry Todd, 136–60 (Durham, NC: Duke University Press, 1984), reprinted in R. Larry Todd, *Mendelssohn Essays*, 51–79 (New York: Routledge, 2008); R. Larry Todd, *Mendelssohn: "The Hebrides" and Other Overtures* (Cambridge: Cambridge University Press, 1993). On the suggestion of the German Männerchor in the symphony's coda, see Peter Mercer-Taylor, "Mendelssohn's 'Scottish' Symphony and the Music of German Memory," *19th-Century Music* 19, no. 1 (Summer 1995): 68–82. Narrative persona in Mendelssohn's orchestral music is also discussed in Douglass

Seaton, "Symphony and Overture," in *The Cambridge Companion to Mendelssohn*, ed. Peter Mercer-Taylor (Cambridge: Cambridge University Press, 2004), 91–111.

74. Gérard Genette, *Paratexts: Thresholds of Interpretation*, trans. Jane E. Lewin (Cambridge: Cambridge University Press, 1997), originally published as *Seuils*.

75. Among the commentaries on these six songs, the usual issue is the significance in biographical terms of the misattribution. That is, they represent something of Fanny's relation to the social and family contexts in which she worked. But the critical and narratological issues, which have not been pursued, merit consideration in their own right, as well.

76. For discussion related to the usage of the terms *thematic* and *rhematic* in this context, see Genette, *Fiction and Diction*, viii, and *Paratexts*, ch. 4.

77. Tia DeNora, *Beethoven and the Construction of Genius: Musical Politics in Vienna, 1792–1803* (Berkeley: University of California Press, 1995); Scott Burnham, *Beethoven Hero* (Princeton, NJ: Princeton University Press, 1995).

78. In recent years a number of musicological and music-theoretical scholars have made important contributions to the analysis of musical plot, often referring to this as "narrative," but obviously not using the term in the focused sense in which I employ it here. Already mentioned is Almén's *A Theory of Musical Narrative* (see note 39). Edward Klorman, *Mozart's Music of Friends: Social Interplay in the Chamber Works* (Cambridge: Cambridge University Press, 2016) develops what I would classify as a plot-based rather than narrative approach to analysis, generating accounts of what goes on in Mozart chamber works by treating the instrumental parts as agents and the interplay between them as exchanges of bits of conversation, responsive gestures, and strategies.

Chapter 2

1. Anton Felix Schindler, *Beethoven as I Knew Him* (originally published in 1840; rev. 3rd ed. 1860), ed. Donald W. MacArdle, trans. Constance S. Jolly (Chapel Hill: University of North Carolina Press, 1966), 404–6.

2. See Carl Czerny, *On the Proper Performance of All Beethoven's Works for the Piano: Czerny's "Reminiscences of Beethoven" and Chapters II and III from Volume IV of the "Complete Theoretical and Practical Piano Forte School Op. 500,"* ed. and with a commentary by Paul Badura-Skoda (Vienna: Universal, 1970), 60:

Perhaps Beethoven (who was ever fond of representing natural scenes) imagined to himself the waves of the sea in a stormy night, whilst cries of distress are heard from afar:—such an image may always furnish the player with a suitable idea for the proper performance of this great musical picture. It is certain that, in many of his finest works, Beethoven was inspired by similar visions and images, drawn either from reading or created by his own excited imagination, and that we should obtain the real key to his compositions and to their performance only through the thorough knowledge of these circumstances, if this were always practicable.

3. Schindler, *Beethoven as I Knew Him*, 406. The original text of this final paragraph reads as follows: "Eines Tages, als ich dem Meister den tiefen Eindruck geschildert, den die Sonaten in **D moll** und **F moll** (Op. 31 und 57) in der Versammlung bei C. Czerny hervorgebracht und er in guter Stimmung war, bat ich ihn, mir den Schlüssel zu diesen Sonaten zu geben. Er erwiderte: 'Lesen Sie nur Shakespeare's Sturm.' Dort also soll er zu finden seyn; aber an welcher Stelle? Frager, lese, rathe und errathe!" Anton Felix Schindler, *Biographie von Ludwig van Beethoven* (4th ed., Münster: Aschendorff, 1871; reprinted in Hildesheim: Olms, 1970; originally published in 1840; rev. 3rd ed. 1860), pt. 2, 221. The English edition translates "in der Versammlung bei C. Czerny" as "Carl Czerny's playing," although the German only suggests a gathering at Czerny's home or organized by him. Czerny need not have been the performer of the two sonatas on this occasion. (Schindler titled his book *Biographie von Ludwig van Beethoven*, but MacArdle's title seems to represent the nature of the book more appropriately.)

4. See, for example, Dagmar Beck and Grita Herre, "Einige Zweifel an der Überlieferung der Konversationshefte," in *Bericht über den Internationalen Beethoven-Kongress: 20.–23. März 1977 in Berlin*, ed. Harry Goldschmidt et al., 257–74 (Leipzig: Deutscher Verlag für Musik, VEB, 1978); Peter Stadlen, "Zu Schindlers Fälschungen in Beethovens Konversationsheften," *Österreichische Musikzeitschrift* 32, nos. 5–6 (1977): 246–52; Peter Stadlen, "Schindler's Beethoven Forgeries," *The Musical Times* 118 (1977): 549–52; Peter Stadlen, "Schindler und die Konversationshefte," *Österreichische Musikzeitschrift* 34, no. 1 (1979): 2–18; Dagmar Beck and Grita Herre, "Anton Schindlers fingierte Eintragungen in den Konversationsheften," in *Zu Beethoven 1: Aufsätze und Annotationen*, ed. Harry Goldschmidt, 11–89 (Berlin: Neue Musik, 1979).

5. K. M. Knittel, for example, says, "The supposed 'poetic' relationship between op. 31 no. 2 and Shakespeare's *The Tempest* [is] also unlikely to be true." K. M. Knittel, "Schindler, Anton Felix," in *The New Grove Dictionary of Music and Musicians*, 2nd ed., ed. Stanley Sadie (London: Macmillan, 2001), 22:510.

6. Donald Francis Tovey, *A Companion to Beethoven's Pianoforte Sonatas* (London: Associated Board of the Royal Schools of Music, 1948), 128. Tovey did not by any means intend to promote such an idea. Immediately preceding this, he writes, "With all the tragic power of its first movement the D minor Sonata is, like Prospero, almost as far beyond tragedy as it is beyond mere foul weather," and he continues, "but people who want to identify Ariel and Caliban and the castaways, good and villainous, may as well confine their attention to the exploits of the Scarlet

Pimpernel when the *Eroica* or the C minor Symphony is being played." Tovey's own discussion simply describes the musical events.

7. Arnold Schering, *Beethoven in neuer Deutung* (Leipzig: C. F. Kahnt, 1934), 80. "1. Satz. Largo, Allegro usw. 1. Akt, 2. Szene. Fernando hört den Lockruf des unsichtbaren Ariel und lauscht in Ergriffenheit dessen Ballade vom ertrunkenen Vater. / 2. Satz. Adagio. 3. Akt, 1. Szene. Liebesduett zwischen Fernando und Miranda. / 3. Satz. Allegretto. Charakterbild des Luftgeistes Ariel nach dessen Lied im 5. Akt, 1. Szene."

8. Schering, *Beethoven in neuer Deutung*, 84. "Hätte Beethoven die Sonate viersätzig gestalten wollen, so würde er wahrscheinlich nicht gezögert haben, in einem grotesken Scherzo dem ungestalten Kaliban ein musikalisches Denkmal zu setzen."

9. Josef Pembaur, *Ludwig van Beethovens Sonaten op. 31 Nr. 2 u. op. 57* (Munich: Wunderhorn, 1915), 3–4.

10. Czerny, *Proper Performance*, 13.

11. Charles Rosen, *The Classical Style*, 43. Rosen does not speak of "plot" but of "drama," but the point is the same. As we noted in the preceding chapter, Rosen formulates the difference between the musical presuppositions of the Baroque and the Enlightenment very succinctly here.

12. See the discussion in chapter 1, referring to James Hepokoski and Warren Darcy, *Elements of Sonata Theory*, 251–52. This quotation appears on page 252.

13. On the distinction of gender in nineteenth-century views of musical character, see James Hepokoski, "Masculine—Feminine," *The Musical Times* 135 (August 1994): 494–99. This distinction does not apply to the contrasting themes in Beethoven's "Tempest" Sonata, but we shall return to it in a very important way in chapter 8.

14. Among recent treatises on the analysis of sonata forms, it is worth pointing here to Charles Rosen, *Sonata Forms* (New York: Norton, 1988), and Hepokoski and Darcy, *Elements of Sonata Theory*. My approach does not differ from Hepokoski and Darcy's Sonata Theory in its essentials, but I rely more self-consciously on the formulations in the historical sources from the period of the music that I discuss. Some of my preferences for terminology and abbreviations have been explained in chapter 1.

15. John Neubauer, "Tales of Hoffmann and Others: On Narrativizations of Instrumental Music," in *Interart Poetics: Essays on the Interrelations of the Arts and Media*, ed. Ulla-Britta Lagerroth et al., 117–36 (Amsterdam: Rodopi, 1996), discusses the "emplotment" of musical works by various writers, representing various degrees of such metaphorical storytelling. See my discussion of Mendelssohn's views on music and words in chapter 6.

16. For a helpful discussion of the "Tempest" Sonata, see Timothy Jones, *Beethoven: The "Moonlight" and Other Sonatas, op. 27 and op. 31* (Cambridge: Cambridge University Press, 1999), 103–8. The continuing variety of views about

the form of the first movement is represented by the essays included in Pieter Bergé et al., eds., *Beethoven's "Tempest" Sonata: Perspectives of Analysis and Performance* (Leuven: Peeters, 2009) and by the detailed analytical graphs provided by five of the contributors to that volume and to Pieter Bergé, ed., *Beethoven's Tempest Sonata (First Movement): Five Annotated Analyses for Performers and Scholars* (Leuven: Peeters, 2012)—demonstrating motivic (Pieter Bergé and Jeroen D'hoe), Schenkerian (Poundie Burstein), form-functional (William E. Caplin), Sonata Theory (James Hepokoski), and metrical (William Rothstein) approaches.

A detailed description of the compositional process of op. 31, no. 2, is included in Barry Cooper, *Beethoven and the Creative Process* (Oxford: Clarendon Press, 1990), 177–96.

17. Hatten, "Interpreting Beethoven's *Tempest* Sonata," 166. An early identification of the "recitative chord" in Beethoven's music appears in the discussion of recitative as an expressive genre (he also refers to it as a topic) that can affect the level of discourse in Hatten, "On Narrativity in Music," 90–93. See also Hatten, *Musical Meaning in Beethoven*, esp. 174–84. In both instances the concept is demonstrated particularly by Beethoven's String Quartet in B♭, op. 130.

18. Schmitz, *Beethovens "zwei Prinzipe,"* 50: "nur ein Versuch zu einem Thema, eine Improvisation."

19. Kenneth Hamilton, "Beethoven's Tempest Sonata in Performance," in Bergé et al., *Beethoven's "Tempest" Sonata*, 140–44.

20. See Hepokoski and Darcy, *Elements of Sonata Theory*, 101, for a description of how this usually works.

21. A summary of representative attempts to locate the sonata's principal area may be found in Steven Vande Moortele, "The First Movement of Beethoven's *Tempest* Sonata and the Tradition of Twentieth-Century 'Formenlehre,'" in Bergé et al., *Beethoven's "Tempest" Sonata*, 293–314. A recent article by Edgardo Salinas describes this failure of the sonata to recapitulate as a "production of absence" and connects the movement to Schlegel's concept of Romantic irony. For Salinas the principal thematic character would have to be "an inchoate theme we never quite hear in the tonic." Edgardo Salinas, "The Form of Paradox as the Paradox of Form: Beethoven's 'Tempest,' Schlegel's Critique, and the Production of Absence," *Journal of Musicology* 33, no. 4 (Fall 2016): 519.

22. Adolf Bernhard Marx, *Anleitung zum Vortrag Beethovenscher Klavierwerke* (Berlin: Otto Janke, 1863), 124–25:

Alles bisher Betrachtete bis an den Takt 21 ist Einleitung, Anlauf zu dem mit Takt 21 beginninden Satze; es ist in sich unbefriedigend, den es ist unfertig, liegt noch und bleibt im Werden, stellt zwei gänzlich verschiedne Motive gegen einander. Dieses Ringen, dieses Unentschiedenheit muss zum Ausdruck kommen, und daher ist kein festes Zeimaass möglich, aber auch kein schroffer Einsatz des Allegro. Denn noch ist nichts, durchaus nichts bestimmt und entschieden, alles unsicher, schwankend, fraglich. Daher aber, im rechten Sinne gefasst, ist alles anregend, spannend auf das Kommende, aufregend.

Mit Takt 21 tritt der Hauptsatz ein, und sogleich in voller Entschiedenheit, also gleich in festem und lebhaften Zeitmaass und mit voller Kraft. Hiermit beginnt also der erste Satz des Allegro.

23. Hugo Leichtentritt, *Musical Form* (Cambridge, MA: Harvard University Press, 1951), 154; translated from *Musikalische Formenlehre*, 4th ed. (Leipzig: Breitkopf & Härtel, 1948), 162; Vande Moortele, "First Movement," 294.

24. Hugo Riemann, *L. van Beethovens sämtliche Klavier-Solosonaten* (Berlin: Max Hesse, 1919), 2:379–80.

25. Ludwig Misch, "The 'Problem' of the D Minor Sonata," chapter 5 of his *Beethoven Studies* (Norman: University of Oklahoma Press, 1953), 41; originally published as "Das 'Problem' der D-moll-Sonate von Beethoven," in *Beethoven-Studien* (Berlin: Walter de Gruyter, 1950). This argument does not hold up, however, when we consider that movements in what Sonata Theory classifies as Type 2 sonata form do not return to the material originally presented in the tonic—such as the first movements of Mozart's Symphony No. 1 in E-flat, K. 16, or Chopin's Piano Sonata No. 3 in B Minor (discussed elsewhere in this book)—and, by this reasoning, they would seem to have no principal themes at all, which clearly is not a tenable position.

26. Misch, "The 'Problem,'" 42; "Das 'Problem,'" 43: "Sie verleugnet überdies aber auch in einem entscheidenden Wesenszuge den Charakter eines Hauptthemas: Das Hauptthema eines Beethovenschen Sonatensatzes repräsentiert und umschreibt . . . regelmässig die Hauptonart."

27. Janet Schmalfeldt, "Form as the Process of Becoming: The Beethoven-Hegelian Tradition and the 'Tempest' Sonata," *Beethoven Forum* 4 (1995): 37–71. The analysis is laid out in the diagram on pp. 58–59; the description of the consequent as "fantasialike" appears on p. 62.

28. James Hepokoski, "Approaching the First Movement of Beethoven's *Tempest* Sonata Through Sonata Theory," in Bergé, *Beethoven's "Tempest" Sonata*, 181–212. The quoted statements are on pages 184 and 193, respectively. This point of view seems to differ slightly from an earlier treatment that acknowledged more explicitly the introductory function of mm. 1–21, when Hepokoski and Warren Darcy wrote that the opening "may also be understood simultaneously as both *an introduction—clearly its principal role—*and the onset of a deformational P." Hepokoski and Darcy, *Elements of Sonata Theory*, 299 (emphasis added).

29. Dahlhaus refers to the treatment of the movement by August Halm, who pointed to m. 21 as the arrival of the music at "the Now" (das Jetzt). See August Halm, *Von zwei Kulturen der Musik* (Munich: G. Müller, 1913), 49, 58.

30. Carl Dahlhaus, *Ludwig van Beethoven: Approaches to His Music*, trans. Mary Whittall (Oxford: Clarendon, 1991), 89, 170; see also pp. 117–18.

31. See note 27.

32. Erwin Ratz, *Einführung in die musikalische Formenlehre: Über Formprinzipien in den Inventionen und Fugen J. S. Bachs und ihre Bedeutung für die Kompositionstechnik Beethovens,* 3rd ed. (Vienna: Universal Edition, 1973), 155.

33. My translation from Carl Dahlhaus, *Ludwig van Beethoven und seine Zeit* (Laaber: Laaber-Verlag, 1988), 154. The German text says, "Ein Hörer, der sich adäquat verhält, dringt nicht etwa allmählich und über Hindernisse hinweg zu der Erkenntnis vor, dass die unscheinbare Dreiklangsbrechung, die er zunächst als Introduktion verkannte, in Wahrheit bereits das Thema war, sondern durchläuft einen Transformationsprozess, in dem die Bestimmung 'Praeludium,' 'Anticipation,' und 'Exposition' sich gleichsam übereinanderschichten, ohne dass die eine durch die andere verdrängt würde."

34. Dahlhaus, *Beethoven: Approaches to His Music,* 170.

35. Schmalfeldt, "Form as the Process of Becoming," 70.

36. Schmalfeldt, 70. Schmalfeldt's wording is echoed in Jones, *Beethoven,* 107: "In short, this section refuses to behave in a conformational recapitulatory manner. It marks a return to the opening idea, but in an altered state that obfuscates rather than clarifies."

37. Walter Riezler, *Beethoven* (New York: E. P. Dutton, 1938), 130.

38. Salinas, "Form of Paradox," 516.

39. Eduardo Marx, *Heidegger und der Ort der Musik* (Würzburg: Königshausen & Neumann, 1998).

40. Scott Burnham, "Singularities and Extremes: Dramatic Impulses in the First Movement of Beethoven's *Tempest* Sonata," in Bergé et al., *Beethoven's "Tempest" Sonata,* 47.

41. Riezler, *Beethoven,* 129–30.

42. Paul Bekker, *Beethoven* (Berlin: Schuster & Loeffler, [1912]), 151–52:

Ein einfacher Dominantdreiklang erklingt, dessen gespannt fragender Ausdruck noch durch die Basston verwendete Terz unheimlich verschärft wird. Und dieser mystischen Tiefe entsteigt eine gespenstige Erscheinung, mit leisen Schritten nach oben tappend. Heftig abwehrende energische Achtelrhythmen, festgeschlagene Bassviertel drängen fort von dem drohenden Spuk, beruhigen sich erst langsam auf einem breit ausklingenden Adagiotakt. Doch das Phantom kehrt wieder, ernster noch mahnend durch die überraschende C-dur-Wendung. Heftiger als zuvor antworten die abwehrende Figuren, in furchtbarer Erregung auffahrend bis zum F3 und dann in die Tiefe stürzend, wo eine chromatische Skala den Sturm entfesselt. Unter rollenden Achteltriolen erscheint das Thema: es ist die Largovision. Mit dämonischer Gewalt dring es empor. Eine schmerzlich flehende, chromatisch um einen Ton sich windende Phrase antwortet zweimal. Dann wird sie vom Thema verdrängt, das, von Stufe zu Stufe in lapidaren Akkordschritten aufsteigend, sich mit vernichtender

Gewalt durchsetzt. Die wogenden Achtelrhythmen stürmen weiter, bis ihnen ein scheinbar neues Motiv Halt gebietet. Scheinbar neu. Es ist die chromatische Antwortphrase, von rückwärts gelesen, die in dieser Form Rhythmen von drohend trotziger Kraft annimmt: die Klage formt sich durch Umkehrung zur entschlossenen Abwehr. Langsam lässt die Erregung nach. Die düstere Ruhe des Anfangs kehrt wieder, doch mit ihr auch die Largovision. Aus den tiefsten Registern emporwallende Arpeggien steigern noch den Ausdruck des Grausig-Phantastischen. Eine Durchführung schliesst sich an, die, unter Fortfall des Zweiten Themas, dem Vordersatz durchaus ähnelt. Der Hauptgedanke allein dominiert. Da—bei der zweiten Wiederkehr des Anfanges scheint der Bann gebrochen zu sein. Das Thema beginnt zu sprechen. Aus dem Akkordmotiv ringt sich ein Rezitativ von schmerzlich bittendem Ausdruck hervor. Umsonst. In dumpf pochenden Akkorden und sich aufbäumenden Akkordgängen verkündet sich eine nur unterdrückte, nicht beruhigte Erregung. Gewaltsam strebt sie nach Befreiung, das zweite Thema ringt sich nochmals heraus, um ebenso, wie beim erstenmal, in dunklen Bassgängen zu verschwinden. Eine grosszügig einfache Kadenz beschliesst das in finsteren Mollharmonien verhallende Stück.

43. Halm, *Von zwei Kulturen der Musik*, 39ff.

44. Hepokoski, "Approaching the First Movement," 199, 190.

45. Hepokoski, 204.

46. Hatten, "Interpreting Beethoven's *Tempest* Sonata," 171.

47. William S. Newman, *Beethoven on Beethoven: Playing the Piano Sonatas His Way* (New York: Norton, 1988), 246. Newman points out that this report comes very indirectly—Beethoven told Czerny, who told Theodor Kullak, who told his son Franz, who told Carl Krebs, and Newman's source was Paul Mies.

48. Czerny, *Proper Performance*, 43.

49. Karol Berger, "Beethoven and the Aesthetic State," *Beethoven Forum* 7 (1999): 22 (see also p. 32).

50. For a breakdown of these possibilities, see Michael Heinemann, "Lesen Sie nur Shakespeares Sturm," *Musica* 45, no. 5 (1991): 301–2.

51. The composer's familiarity with *The Tempest* and his identification with Prospero is discussed in Theodore Albrecht, "Beethoven and Shakespeare's *Tempest*: New Light on an Old Allusion," *Beethoven Forum* 1 (1992): 81–92.

52. Lawrence Kramer also regards the recitative as external to the action—*parergon*—a position that corresponds to some extent with mine in the present discussion. He finds in this movement, and in the sonata taken as a whole, the legitimation of "the human subject in its own interiority." He does not pursue very closely the significance of the specific position of the vocal intrusion in the plot of the sonata's first movement. See Lawrence Kramer, "Beethoven's Tempest Sonata: Musical Meaning and Enlightenment Anthropology," *Beethoven Forum* 6 (1998): 31–65.

53. Halm, *Von zwei Kulturen der Musik*, 67: "als ob der Autor auf einmal dozierte, als ob der Künstler redete, anstatt zu bilden."

54. Riezler, *Beethoven*, 130.

55. Ratz, *Einführung in die Musikalische Formenlehre*, 155: "Das Rezitativ tritt an die Stelle des noch in der Durchführung mit elementarer Gewalt auftretenden Überleitungsmotivs, das in der Reprise nicht mehr erscheint, womit wohl von Beethoven auf etwas sehr Wesentliches hingewiesen werden soll." He goes on with a hypothetical suggestion of what that significant idea might be: "Vielleicht können wir es den Sieg des Zarten über das Gewaltsame nennen" ("Perhaps we could call it the victory of the gentle over the powerful").

56. Martin Geck, "Das wilde Denken: Ein Strukturalistischen Blick auf Beethovens op. 31, 2," *Archiv für Musikwissenschaft* 57 (2000): 64–77. "Es ist die Geschichte, die sie ist" (73); "Das Rezitativ, so scheint es, hat dieses stabile, fast konventionell zu nennende Element beiseitegeschoben, um dem Satz neue Räume zu öffnen—keine thematischen, jedoch Freiräume" (69); "entringt sich die binären Opposition des Anfangs diesmal ein ausdrucksvoller Ruf, der kaum anders denn als prononcierte Äusserung oder gar als Einspruch eines Subjekts gedeutet werden kann" (71).

Chapter 3

1. Instances of multiple singers raise the issue of whether we might seek to identify a persona guiding the interlocutors, although in enacted drama we typically focus more on the speaking or acting characters than on the dramatist's voice or personality. The Heine cycle under discussion in this chapter does not require that additional level of interpretation.

2. Cone, *The Composer's Voice*, 1–19.

3. Michael Hall, for example, insists that Schubert's Heine songs constitute a set rather than a cycle, because they are not plot-like in the sense of following events in chronological order and because they manifest a sort of balance he finds typical of other Schubert song sets; Michael Hall, *Schubert's Song Sets* (Aldershot: Ashgate, 2003), 246. Hall even suggests that the songs make up a symphonic movement structure (253), linking the final three songs into one composite fourth movement.

4. This is suggested in passing, without any music-analytical grounds, in Maurice J. E. Brown, *Schubert Songs* (London: British Broadcasting Corporation, 1967), 59. The idea is developed with analytical support by Harry Goldschmidt, "Welches war die ursprüngliche Reihenfolge in Schuberts Heine-Lieder?" *Deutsches Jahrbuch der Musikwissenschaft für 1972* (1974): 52–62, reprinted in *Um die Sache der Musik* (Leipzig: Reclam, 1976), 141–54; and by Richard Kramer, "Schubert's Heine," *19th-Century Music* 8 (1985): 213–25, reprinted as ch. 5 of *Distant Cycles: Schubert and the Conceiving of Song* (University of Chicago Press, 1994), 125–47. The case of *Winterreise* is somewhat complicated by the fact that the Müller poems

appeared in two sets, of which Schubert knew only the first when he composed an initial group of songs, which forced some divergence from Müller's order in the complete cycle.

5. My translation from "Liederkreis, Liedercyclus," in Heinrich Christoph Koch, *Musikalisches Lexicon: Auf Grundlage des Lexicon's von H. Ch. Koch*, 2nd ed. (Heidelberg: J. C. B. Mohr, 1865), 513–14:

> Ein zusammenhängender Complex verschiedener lyrischer Gedichte. Jedes derselben ist in sich abgeschlossen, kann hinsichts des Versmaasses und Strophenbaues von den anderen auch äusserlich verschieden sein; alle aber stehen in innerer Beziehung zu einander, den durch alle zieht sich ein- und derselbe Grundgedanke, die einzelnen Dichtungen geben immer nur verschiedener Wendung desselben, stellen ihn in mannigfachen und oft auch contrastirenden Bildern und von verschiedenen Seiten dar, so dass das Grundgefühl in ziemlich umfassender Vollständigkeit ausgetragen wird. . . . Zur dramatisirenden Solocantate fehlt dem Liederkreis eigentlich nichts mehr als das Recitativ, und die arienartige Form der Gesänge anstatt der liedartigen; im übrigen wird man ihn der Cantate ziemlich nahestehend finden, oder als eine Mittelgattung zwischen durchcomponirtem Liede und Cantate ansehen.

6. As will become clear, I find the arguments of the scholars I cite in this chapter generally unconvincing. It should also be obvious that I both credit them with their identification of crucial details and take inspiration from their pathbreaking attempts to demonstrate the cyclicity in these works.

7. Goldschmidt, "Welches war die ursprüngliche Reihenfolge," 14: "der unüberhörbare einheitliche 'Ton' der Heine-Lieder, seine tragische Akzentuierung und nicht zuletzt die hohe stylistische Einheit, gebunden an den neuen deklamatorisch-melodischen Sprachgestus."

8. Edward T. Cone, "Schubert's Heine Songs," in *Hearing and Knowing Music: The Unpublished Essays of Edward T. Cone*, ed. Robert P. Morgan, 106–15 (Princeton, NJ: Princeton University Press, 2009).

9. Hall, *Schubert's Song Sets*, 254–59.

10. Numerous analyses point out details in individual songs. Helpful for the tracking of harmonic features across the six songs is Louise Litterick, "Recycling Schubert: On Reading Richard Kramer's *Distant Cycles: Schubert and the Conceiving of Song*," *19th-Century Music* 20, no. 1 (Summer 1996): 77–95. Litterick's purpose is to defend Schubert's ordering of the songs against Kramer's (and other) arguments that they should properly follow Heine's sequence.

11. Goldschmidt, "Welches war die ursprüngliche Reihenfolge," 55–58.

12. Richard Kramer, "Schubert's Heine," 218 (*Distant Cycles*, 137).

13. Douglass Seaton, "Interpreting Schubert's Heine Songs," *The Music Review* 53, no. 2 (May 1992): 85–99.

14. The composer had used this mode-based symbolism from as early as "Erlkönig." Gernot Gruber notes this in his article "Romantische Ironie in den Heine-Liedern?" in *Schubert-Kongress Wien 1978*, ed. Otto Busatti (Graz: Akademische Druck- und Verlagsgesellschaft, 1979), 325, but he merely notes that four of the six Heine songs are in minor keys, not mentioning the internal move to the major in "Der Atlas." Gruber cites Hans Heinrich Eggebrecht, "Prinzipien des Schubert-Liedes," *Archiv für Musikwissenschaft* 27, no. 2 (1970): 96: "Dur und Moll stehen in Schuberts Liedern häufig sich gegenüber wie die Illusionswelt des schönen, hellen Traumes und die Realitätswelt der banalen, elenden, barfüssigen Wirklichkeit, wobei Dur musikalisch die Traumsphäre (die Ausschaltung den wachen Willens und Wollens, die Entrücktheit) als die Eigentliche, helle, schöne Wirklichkeit bezeichnet."

15. Susan Youens, *Heinrich Heine and the Lied* (Cambridge University Press, 2007), 19, 20.

16. Hall, *Schubert's Song Sets*, 254.

17. Litterick, "Recycling Schubert," 86.

18. Although Hall argues that the songs form a set rather than a cycle, he finds that they share a single lyric ego, but he falls into the biographical fallacy: "[Schubert's] ordering of the poems makes sense only if it is seen as a character study of Heine himself. . . . The interest lies in the person's capacity to suffer, and ultimately to find a measure of inner peace" (*Schubert's Song Sets*, 247). The second sentence here can certainly be true, whether one regards the lyric persona as Heine, which is not especially convincing, or more aptly as a speaker created in the songs themselves.

19. The distinctively unmusical style of this text was noted immediately after the publication of *Schwanengesang*. G. W. Fink, in his review of *Winterreise* and *Schwanengesang* in *Allgemeine musikalische Zeitung* 31, no. 40 (October 1829): col. 661, wrote, "Nr. 8. 'Der Atlas.' Mit diesem für musikalische Behandlung nicht ausgezeichneten, kurzen Gesange, aus dem der Tonsetzer alles was möglich war, zu machen wusste, beginnen H. Heine's Gedichte, von denen die übrigen sämmtlich wohl gewählt sind." Walburga Litschauer, "The Origin and Early Reception of *Schwanengesang*," in *A Companion to Schubert's "Schwanengesang": History, Poets, Analysis, Performance*, ed. Martin Chusid (New Haven: Yale University Press, 2000), 9, translates this rather loosely as "With this short poem, not especially suitable for musical setting, the composer contrived to do everything possible to imitate H. Heine's poems."

20. Litterick, on the other hand, does not regard the third song as necessarily a reference to an actual past event. For her, "the scenario of *Das Fischermädchen* makes sense only as an escape fantasy" (Litterick, "Recycling Schubert," 85). Likewise, Xavier Hascher seems to place the moment (and that in "Am Meer") not in the past but in the speaker's imagination: "'Das Fischermädchen' (no. 3) and 'Am Meer' (no. 5) can be parenthesized as fantastical digressions or interpolations, brought in by

association." Xavier Hascher, "'In dunkeln Träumen': Schubert's Heine-Lieder Through the Psychoanalytical Prism," *Nineteenth-Century Music Review* 5, no. 2 (2008): 53.

21. Litterick writes, "The use of C♭ major here can best be explained through its emotional and narrative association with the [B-major] passage in *Der Atlas*" ("Recycling Schubert," 86).

22. As Youens sees it, the key of B/C♭ corresponds to the possibility of happiness, which resembles my interpretation here, but I hear it as creating a more specific association with the heart itself, which, as we shall see, extends farther across the cycle.

23. Youens anticipates the Doppelgänger of the final song, but she does not make this explicit: "Schubert, I suspect, understood that *the sailor who steers the boat to a sad beat is actually the persona himself*, split off into one who narrates and one who plies the oars on this same journey *over and over again*. There is truth of a most uncomforting sort in this recognition of an inner being who 'steers,' dictating what we do, but who is also an incomprehensible Other" (*Heinrich Heine and the Lied*, 60; italics added). Here Youens also leaves unstated the reinforcing observation that if the boat is headed toward the city, then the rower cannot see it, so that in this interpretation one member of the split persona—the oarsman, weary with effort—struggles along but remains unable even to perceive the place that the speaker identifies with loss.

24. Youens likens this music to a dead march and mentions that it shares its regular two-bar-phrase structure with Handel's famous Sinfonia from *Saul*; see Youens, *Heinrich Heine and the Lied*, 55, 58. Although the key of that piece is the same as that of "Die Stadt," Handel's music actually is a march (in duple meter), unlike Schubert's, and it does not feature the shuddering rhythm of Schubert's song. We might accept the suggestion that the loss would feel like a death to the speaker here, but the song really suggests something more bitter than death—deliberate betrayal and abandonment.

25. As Youens points out, in literary convention the drinking of tears can serve as a metaphor for the sexual act. That interpretation offers the opportunity to associate the song with Schubert's own experience with venereal disease, but I hesitate to fall into the trap of the (auto)biographical fallacy; Schubert might well have identified with this poem personally, but if we treat the Heine songs as the personal outpouring of a still minor and mainly pitiable Viennese composer, they become sordidly specific and the listener little more than a voyeur. While I would not rule out the reading that links drinking tears to a sex act (an image found elsewhere in *Die Heimkehr*), this poem only speaks of dying of longing, not of any sort of fulfillment or consummation.

26. Dietrich Fischer-Dieskau points out the ironic potential here in his *Schubert's Songs: A Biographical Study*, trans. Kenneth S. Whitton (New York: Alfred A. Knopf, 1981), 281, but to my ear his performances instead treat this turn with

simple, gentle tenderness: legato, diminuendo, and poco ritardando. Most singers adopt the same approach, but this is not the only option. Max van Egmond, for example, takes the turn as an opportunity for a heavily articulated, sobbing effect; hear his recording with pianist Kenneth Slowik. Max van Egmond, baritone, and Kenneth Slowik, fortepiano, *Franz Schubert: "Schwanengesang" / Robert Schumann: "Dichterliebe," The Romantics*, vol. 3, Musica Omnia MO0102, 2005.

27. Freud later wrote about "repetition compulsion" (*Wiederholungszwang*) as a manifestation of neurosis related to oedipal childhood experience; see Sigmund Freud, *Beyond the Pleasure Principle*, trans. C. J. M. Hubback (London: International Psycho-Analytical Press, 1922), 17–25. Lawrence Kramer approaches this issue in psychoanalytic terms when he writes, "If Maurice J. E. Brown was right to suggest that the appropriate sequence for the Heine songs is not the posthumously published one, but the order in which the poems appear in Heine's *Die Heimkehr*, then the second half of *Schwanengesang* forms a coherent little song cycle that portrays the tragic lapse of the self into obsessive repetition as the result of sexual grief. . . . The speakers [plural *sic*] in the Heine poems that Schubert set in 1828 are victims of compulsive repetition who return endlessly to the scene of their worst loss," and in "Der Doppelgänger" "the musical persona surrenders his allegiance to the moment of erotic failure in which his inner life was formed." Lawrence Kramer, "The Schubert Lied: Romantic Form and Romantic Consciousness," in *Schubert: Critical and Analytical Studies*, ed. Walter Frisch (Lincoln: University of Nebraska Press, 1986), 219, 223–24. These observations would obtain, of course, regardless of whether the songs were reordered according to the chronology of their events. We should be cautious, further, about attributing a Freudian psychoanalytic understanding to the works of Heine or Schubert. Neither the Atlas nor his heart appears to have repressed past events and experiences the memory of which might be brought to consciousness in the lyric persona. (Unless the woman of "Am Meer" is his mother—and I'm not willing to go there!)

28. Lawrence Kramer observed that the speaker in "Der Doppelgänger" finds "the extremity of despair in a confrontation between the halves of a divided self: the subject who desires, and a double who represents that subject's worst aspects—anxiety, self-torment, self-contempt" ("The Schubert Lied," 218). Kramer sees a similarity to the protagonist of *Winterreise* but inexplicably neglects to mention the even more obvious opportunity to point out the connection to "Der Atlas."

29. David Ferris, "Dissociation and Declamation in Schubert's Heine Songs," in *Rethinking Schubert*, ed. Lorraine Byrne Bodley and Julian Horton (New York: Oxford University Press, 2016), 383–403, draws attention to concepts and features that "Der Atlas" and "Der Doppelgänger" have in common as well as the differences in the ways that they do somewhat the same things. As he puts it, "In poems Nos. 20 and 24 from Heine's *Heimkehr*, the narrator suddenly experiences a psychological rupture within his own consciousness, which results in the splitting of his narrative voice. In the final stanzas of these poems, the narrator becomes both the *ich* who is

speaking and the *du* who is being addressed" (401). This does not fully capture the sophistication of the relationship between the speakers of the two songs, nor does it incorporate the relevant aspects of the intervening songs in Schubert's composition, but it is on the right track.

30. As Andrew Weaver writes of *Dichterliebe*, "not a coherent plot but a coherent *narrative discourse*." Andrew Weaver, "Memories Spoken and Unspoken: Hearing the Narrative Voice in *Dichterliebe*," *Journal of the Royal Musical Association* 142, no. 1 (2017): 33.

31. Siegbert Salomon Prawer, *Heine: Buch der Lieder* (Great Neck, NY: Barron's Educational Series, 1960), 37.

32. Letter dated June 7, 1826; see Heines Briefe, *Säkularausgabe*, 20, 250n6: "In meinem Gedichten hingegen ist nur die Form einigermassen volkstümlich, der Inhalt gehört der konventionelle Gesellschaft." Quoted in Cristina Urchueguía and Roger Lüdeke, "Der Doppelgänger: Für eine funktionsgeschichtliche Beschreibung von Schuberts Heine-Vertonung," *Deutsche Vierteljahrschift für Literaturwissenschaft und Geistesgeschichte* 74, no. 2 (2000): 283.

33. Gruber, "Romantische Ironie," 322: "Auch ist es denkbar, dass Schuberts Vertonungen seiner Gedichte Heines Vorstellungen von musikalischer Volkstümlichkeit nicht entsprechen."

Chapter 4

1. Friedrich Blume, "Romantik," in *Die Musik in Geschichte und Gegenwart*, ed. Friedrich Blume (Kassel: Bärenreiter, 1963), 11, col. 801; published in English translation in Friedrich Blume, *Classic and Romantic Music*, trans. M. D. Herter Norton (New York: W. W. Norton, 1970), 121. Although obviously a reflection of Blume's German-biased musical values, it was this assertion that prompted my thinking many years ago about the issue of Romantic virtuosity. (It should be noted that Blume's reputation has suffered from his professional positions during the Nazi era and from his study of the musics of different races, although he has been exonerated from complicity in the racial violence perpetrated by the Nazis.)

2. Carl Dahlhaus, *Nineteenth-Century Music*, trans. J. Bradford Robinson (Berkeley: University of California Press, 1989), 137–38.

3. Cone, *The Composer's Voice*.

4. Francis Toye, *Rossini: A Study in Tragi-Comedy* (New York: W. W. Norton, 1963), 25–26: "at an ordinary performance, alike in large or small theatres, people only listened to certain numbers, filling in the rest of the evening by paying visits and playing cards and having refreshments."

5. Rossini reported to Ferdinand Hiller his encounter with the young singer Teresa Adelaide Carpano: "One day, the cadenza that she sang after an aria was of unsurpassably adventurous harmony. I tried to explain to her that she must give some

consideration to the harmony held in the orchestra. And, really, she saw the validity of my point to a certain extent. But at the next performance she again succumbed to her inspiration and made such a cadenza that I couldn't help laughing." Herbert Weinstock, *Rossini: A Biography* (New York: Knopf, 1968), 12.

6. Of course, I have in mind here two specific recordings by Bartoli. The first, recorded in 1988 and released in 1989, is Cecilia Bartoli, *Rossini Arias*, with the Vienna Volksoper Orchestra and Giuseppe Patanè (conductor), London 425 430-2, 1989, compact disc. The second, recorded in 1992 and released in 1993, is Cecilia Bartoli et al., *La Cenerentola*, with the Teatro Comunale of Bologna and Riccardo Chailly (conductor), London 436 902-2, 1993, compact disc.

7. Toye, *Rossini*, 27.

8. One might be inclined to consider the introduction of the minor in the "Non più mesta" variations an imposition of the "composerly" in the music. I don't think that this is the case, however—specifically because, as clearly "più mesta," it absolutely disregards the text, which the listener certainly knows, and therefore can only be heard as a kind of cosmetic shading.

9. Review by G. W. Fink, "Recensionen [on works of Henri Herz]," *Allgemeine musikalische Zeitung* 33 (January 1831): cols. 7–12. I have translated the German as follows: "reiz[end]" (charming), "zierlich" (dainty), "graziöse" (gracious), "glänzend" (glittering), "anziehend" (alluring), "Nettigkeit" (prettiness), "modisch" (fashionable), "Coquetterie" (flirtatiousness), and "die Kunst nicht um der Kunst, sondern um des Gefallens willen getrieben" (not art for art's sake, but rather motivated by the desire to please).

10. François-Joseph Fétis, *Biographical Notice of Nicolo Paganini, Followed by an Analysis of His Compositions, and Preceded by a Sketch of the History of the Violin*, 2nd ed. (London: Schott, 1876), 45.

11. Fétis, *Biographical Notice*, 43. In this case the variations in question were the set titled "Le Streghe" ("The Witches").

12. For a detailed discussion of Paganini's demonic persona, including its relationship to gender, see Maiko Kawabata, "Virtuosity, the Violin, the Devil . . . What *Really* Made Paganini 'Demonic'?," *Current Musicology* 83 (Spring 2007): 85–108. Kawabata cites a number of identifiers used for Paganini—sorcerer, charlatan, carbonaro, wizard, magician, Hexensohn (witch's son), Hexenmeister (witch master), Mephistopheles, Faust, demonic, Zamiel, Satan, devil's spawn—all masculine figures. In addition, she points to examples in which Paganini's treatment of the violin (with its female shape and crying response) was likened to an abusive attack by a man on a woman. See also Maiko Kawabata, *Paganini: The "Demonic" Virtuoso* (Rochester, NY: Boydell, 2013), ch. 2, "'Demonic' Violinist, Magical Virtuosity." Kristen Strandberg cites Kawabata's work in her dissertation, classifying this response to Paganini's virtuosity as an example of the "wizard" image; see Kristen Strandberg, "Art or Artifice? Violin Virtuosity and Aesthetics in Parisian Criticism, 1831–1848" (PhD diss., Indiana University, 2014), 102–4.

13. Robert Schumann, "Ein Opus II," *Allgemeine musikalische Zeitung* 33 (1831): cols. 805–8. Among the most easily accessible English translations is that in Oliver Strunk, ed., *Source Readings in Music History*, rev. ed., Leo Treitler, general editor (New York: W. W. Norton, 1998), 1144–45.

14. Strunk, *Source Readings*, 1144–45.

15. Liszt's treatment of "Là ci darem la mano," which actually occupies much of the central portion of his reminiscence, makes the duet aspect much clearer than Chopin's, so that the voices within the action seem more evident. Such an approach might help to imply the behind-the-scenes presence of the dramatist as narrative persona—as does all the surrounding material. This also already made a difference in Chopin's work, where there is a large amount of introductory and framing material. There is an interesting moment just before the duet theme in the Liszt treatment of *Don Giovanni* where Liszt seems to be reminiscing Chopin.

For an extensive discussion of the Liszt *Réminiscences*, see Charles Rosen's treatment, which points out that Liszt approaches the opera "not as a series of isolated memories but as a synoptic view of the opera, in which the different moments of the drama exist simultaneously: what Liszt reveals is the way they are interrelated" (530). Rosen frames the work as an exploitation of Liszt's own "international reputation for erotic conquest"—a self-portrait of the composer as notorious lover (539). Charles Rosen, *The Romantic Generation* (Cambridge, MA: Harvard University Press, 1995), 528–41.

16. For brief descriptions of some of the forms, see Kenneth Hamilton, "Liszt's Early and Weimar Piano Works," in *The Cambridge Companion to Liszt*, ed. Kenneth Hamilton (Cambridge: Cambridge University Press, 2005), 84.

17. An interesting study of a female virtuoso is Sean M. Parr, "Caroline Carvalho and Nineteenth-Century Coloratura," *Cambridge Opera Journal* 23, nos. 1–2 (2012): 83–117. Parr points out that Carvalho made significant contributions to the levels of vocal virtuosity in nineteenth-century performance, even establishing for vocalists (and thus for her gender) the transcendental capabilities that Paganini and the pianists represented. Parr emphasizes that Carvalho merits recognition as a creative force, but he also recognizes the gender stereotyping and disdain for virtuoso performance that led critics "to actively seek to write her out of history" (117, referring to quotations on p. 84).

Chapter 5

1. George Gordon Byron [Lord Byron], *Childe Harold's Pilgrimage*, in *The Complete Poetical Works*, vol. 2, ed. Jerome J. McGann (Oxford: Clarendon, 1980), 8–9.

2. The dedication of *Childe Harold's Pilgrimage*, added to the seventh edition of the first two cantos, is addressed to Ianthe, about whom we learn that she is

beautiful, animated, warm-hearted, and half the poet's age. In actuality the reference is to Lady Charlotte Harley (daughter of Jane Scott, the Countess of Oxford, with whom Byron had an affair), whom Byron apparently sexually molested when she was eleven, at about the same time he first published cantos 1 and 2. Ianthe may also represent the reader/listener as the fictive narratee of the forthcoming poem. The dedication, if taken in light of the biographical context, might then place us in a position to receive the description of Harold as a personal confession.

3. For Berlioz's account, see *Mémoires de Hector Berlioz, comprenant ses voyages en Italie, en Allemagne, en Russie et en Angleterre 1803–1865* (Paris: Calmann-Lévy, [1896–97]), 1:301–2. For the leading English translation, see *The Memoirs of Hector Berlioz*, trans. and ed. David Cairns (New York: Knopf, 2002), 215–16.

4. Berlioz, *Mémoires*, 2:81–82: "dans cette scène de brigands, l'orchestre était devenu un veritable pandœmonium; il y avait quelque chose de surnaturel et d'effrayant dans la frénésie de sa verve. . . . Vous ne connaissez rein de pareille, vous autres, poëtes, vous n'êtes jamais emportés par de tels ouragans de vie."

5. I have newly translated Berlioz's description of the piece here from the French original found in the *Mémoires*, 1:302–3: "J'imaginais d'écrire pour l'orchestra une suite de scènes, auxquelles l'alto solo se trouverait mêlé comme un personnage plus ou moins actif conservant toujours son caractère propre; je voulus faire de l'alto, en le plaçant au milieu des poétiques souvenirs que m'avaient laissés mes pérégrinations dans les Abruzzes, une sorte de rêveur mélancolique dans le genre du Childe Harold de Byron."

6. Berlioz, *Mémoires*, 1:303: "un thème principal (le premier chant de l'alto) se reproduit dans l'oeuvre entière; . . . le chant d'Harold se superpose aux autres chants de l'orchestre, avec lesquels il contraste par son mouvement et son caractère, sans en interrompre le développement."

7. La Mara, *Franz Liszts Briefe*, vol. 4 (Leipzig: Breitkopf & Härtel, 1899), 87: "Il y a dans cette ouvrage comme dans Lohengrin un chant caractéristique pour Harold. Ce chant se mêle admirable à la mélodie du *Chant des Pèlerins*, à la *Sérénade du Montagnard des Abruzzes*, et même à l'*Orgie des Brigands*—tantôt pour les dominer, tantôt pour leur server de support, de relief ou d'assombrissement."

8. Hugh Macdonald, *Berlioz* (Oxford: Oxford University Press, 1982), 101.

9. D. Kern Holoman, *Berlioz* (Cambridge, MA: Harvard University Press, 1989), 245.

10. Cairns points out that "*Haro!*" was an exclamation formerly used to arrest someone and proceed to summary justice; see Berlioz, *The Memoirs of Hector Berlioz*, 218n.

11. Hepokoski and Darcy do not mention this movement in their formulation of Sonata Theory. Because they reject the idea of a recapitulation with P and S themes in reverse order, they might classify the movement as a Type 2 sonata, regarding the arrival of P in the tonic at measure 290 as the beginning of the coda. See Hepokoski and Darcy, *Elements of Sonata Theory*, 382–86. That seems to fly in

the face of the listener's experience of this movement, however, because the passage beginning with the H theme at measure 323 is so clearly marked as initiating a coda.

The argument against any possibility of a "reversed recapitulation" depends on the insistence that a rotation cannot begin with S. The concept of rotations of thematic modules as the basis of form arises from their observation, derived from analysis of an enormous repertoire mostly from the late eighteenth century, however, whereas the historically contemporary accounts of long-movement forms regard them more flexibly as two-phase tonal plots articulated or enacted by thematic character, without requiring rotations to include P and S modules in a fixed order. Berlioz, of course, felt no compunctions in his treatment of conventions. As the reader will have noticed, my description here simply notes that S and P return in the tonic, and I feel no need to classify the movement's form or explain it away.

12. The introduction and coda occupy 301 of the movement's 493 measures, compared to 192 for the sonata-form body of the movement (repetition of the first part of the sonata form brings that section to 253 and the total to 564). The introduction's adagio tempo actually means that it alone accounts for roughly half the movement's total time in performance.

13. Byron, *Childe Harold's Pilgrimage*, vol. 2, 103, 104–5.

14. It would be a mistake, however, to regard the symphony as actually autobiographical for the composer, as Rainer Schmusch does: "*Harold en Italie*, which would more aptly be called 'Berlioz in Italy'" ("*Harold en Italie*, das treffender 'Berlioz en Italie' hiesse . . ."). Rainer Schmusch, "Programmusik als musikalisch Autobiographie und Katharsis," in *Hector Berlioz: Autopsie des Künstlers*, by Schmusch, Musik-Konzepte 108 (Munich: text+kritik, 2000), 73.

15. Berlioz, *Mémoires*, 1:221: "Lignes de madones couronnant les hautes collines, et que suivent, le soir, en chantant des litanies, les moissonneurs attardés qui reviennent des plaines, au tintement mélancolique de la campanella d'un couvent cache." It is worth noting that Berlioz had earlier experienced a similar episode at home in La Côte Saint-André when he was a teenager, local peasants singing in a springtime rogation procession; see chapter 40 of his *Mémoires*, 1:244–45.

16. This kind of fragmentation also occurs as a way of representing tragedy and lack of fulfillment at the end of the second-movement funeral march in Beethoven's "Eroica" Symphony and in the third-movement "Scène aux champs" in Berlioz's *Symphonie fantastique* 3. Tragedy is presumably not the intention in the procession in *Harold en Italie*, though it might share with the "Scène aux champs" the evocation of isolation and loneliness.

17. Berlioz, *Mémoires*, 1:221:

Une nuit, la plus singulière sérénade que j'eusse encore entendue vint me réveiller. Un *ragazzo* aux vigoureux poumons criait de toute sa force une chanson d'amour sous les fenêtres de sa *ragazza*, avec accompagnement d'une énorme mandoline, d'une musette et d'un petit instrument de fer de la nature du triangle, qu'ils appellent dans le pays *stimbalo*. Son chant, ou plutôt son cri, consistait en quatre ou cinq notes d'une progression descendante, et se terminait, en remontant, par un long gémissement de la note sensible à la tonique, sans prendre haleine.

18. There is no brigands' orgy in Berlioz's memoirs of his visit to Italy. There is one in *Childe Harold's Pilgrimage*, but it takes place in Albania. See canto 2, stanzas 71–72, and the Suliotes' song that follows.

19. Schmusch, "Programmusik," 73: "the Harold theme itself no longer coalesces, and the viola's sound recollects itself as representation of the I as if by forgetting the imago" ("das 'Harold-Thema' selbst nicht mehr gelingt und der Bratschenklang sich als Repräsentant des Ich gleichsam durch Vergessen des Imago an sich selbst erinnert").

20. Wolfgang Dömling emphasizes that "it is a matter of a series of scenes, not of a self-contained drama" ("Es handelt sich um eine 'Folge von Szenen,' nicht um ein geschlossenes Drama"). Wolfgang Dömling, *Hector Berlioz und seine Zeit* (Laaber: Laaber-Verlag, 1986), 101.

21. For a fuller consideration of the relationship of *Harold en Italie* to Beethoven's symphonies and Berlioz's response to them, see Mark Evan Bonds, "*Sinfonia anti-eroica*: Berlioz's *Harold en Italie* and the Anxiety of Beethoven's Influence," *Journal of Musicology* 10, no. 4 (Fall 1992): 417–63; revised and reprinted in his *After Beethoven: Imperatives of Originality in the Symphony* (Cambridge, MA: Harvard University Press, 1996), 28–72. Bonds's interest is principally in Berlioz (as successor to Beethoven) and his Harold (as related to Byron's), while I am concerned with the issues of voice in Byron and Berlioz.

22. The foreword to the edition of *Harold en Italie* edited by Paul Banks and Hugh Macdonald as volume 17 of the *New Edition of the Complete Works*, by Berlioz (Kassel: Bärenreiter, 2001), ix n13, notes that Berlioz "reviewed the performance of the Ninth Symphony in the *Le rénovateur* of 2 February 1834 (Berlioz, *Critique musicale*, 1, Paris 1996, pp. 149–50)."

23. Thomas Austenfeld writes, "in Berlioz the subjective expression of a sentiment caused by, or seen in relation to, an event or a work of art reaches its climax. *Harold en Italie* is thus not a translation of Byron's poem into another artistic medium, but Berlioz's reaction to it, merged with a response to his own Italian experiences and expressed in musical terms." Thomas Austenfeld, "'But, Come, I'll Set Your Story to a Tune': Berlioz's Interpretation of Byron's *Childe Harold*," *Keats-Shelley Journal* 39 (1990): 84. Austenfeld also emphasizes, correctly, that the music is not tone painting.

24. See Ian Wyatt Gerg, "The Virtual Observing Agent in Music: A Theory of Agential Perspective as Implied by Indexical Gesture" (PhD diss., University of Texas at Austin, 2015), 179–85.

25. In the sense that Mieke Bal uses the idea of focalization, this presents an interesting problem of classification. To the extent that we consider Harold an actor or participant in the various scenes, this represents a character-bound focalizer (CF). If,

on the other hand, Harold merely guides our attention to the places and actions, this would exemplify an external focalizer (EF). See Mieke Bal, *Narratology: Introduction to the Theory of Narrative*, 3rd ed. (Toronto: University of Toronto Press, 2009), 145–65.

26. Byron, *Childe Harold's Pilgrimage*, vol. 2, 79, 82, 95.

27. Jeffrey Langford put this exactly right: "the motto theme becomes, in a sense, a mobile musical 'character' just as Berlioz intended." Jeffrey Langford, "The 'Dramatic Symphonies' of Berlioz as an Outgrowth of the French Opera Tradition," *The Musical Quarterly* 69, no. 1 (Winter 1983): 98.

28. The original directions in the score are clear: *"L'exécutant doit être placé sur l'avant-scène, près du public et isolé de l'orchestre"*; *"La harpe doit être placé près de l'Alto solo."*

29. Schmusch refers to levels in the work, but he distinguishes them as action and recollection. He uses the term "Geschehnisebene" (event levels), which fails to capture the different nature of the scene and the narrative voice, because the narrative perspective of the poet does not really constitute separate events but instead an angle of approach to the events observed, reported, and reflected on. See Schmusch, *Der Tod des Orpheus: Entstehungsgeschichte der Programmusik* (Freiburg im Breisgau: Rombach, 1998), 234.

30. Discussions of the symphony have sometimes identified the viola as embodying a narrative voice, but they have not always profited from considering the fictive narrative poet so prominent in Byron's work. Macdonald, for example, writes that "the part the viola plays throughout, so different from Paganini's conception of a concerto part, is as personal as that of the artist in *Lélio*; it speaks with Berlioz's own voice against the background of Italian scenery." Macdonald, *Berlioz*, 103. Like other commentators, this formulation runs into the (auto)biographical fallacy; the composer's experiences of course informed the creation of the scenes, but the voice of the work must be a fictive one, not that of Berlioz himself.

31. Bal, *Narratology*, 18–22, 132–49. Bal argues cogently for the centrality of "focalization" in narratives, but this broadly assumes a fabula conveyed through the story. Unless a musical work is programmatic, the music does not refer to action outside itself, but the concept is particularly applicable in a piece such as *Harold en Italie*.

32. For example, "In the middle section [of the pilgrims' march] basses plod, pilgrims chant and Harold quietly caresses his strings." Macdonald, *Berlioz*, 102. But Harold is represented by a theme, as characters generally are, and it is not he but the poet who plays the arpeggios.

33. Edward T. Cone, "Inside the Saint's Head: The Music of Berlioz (Part II)," *Musical Newsletter* 1, no. 4 (October 1971): 19.

34. Gerg, "Virtual Observing Agent," 183.

35. Hatten, *A Theory of Virtual Agency*, 205–7.

36. Dömling, employing another image, observes that "the representation of an actor's role—the figure of Harold—is *entwined* with the presentation of an internal subject, an epic Ego as in the novel, which in a supplementary fashion also

exhibits the aspect of the autobiographical" (emphasis added; "Die Repräsentierung einer Rollenfigur—die Gestalt des Harold—ist verschränkt mit der Darstellung eines inneren Subjekts, eines epischen Ich wie im Roman, das zusätzlich noch den Aspekt des Autobiographischen aufweist"; Dömling, *Berlioz und seine Zeit*, 101).

Chapter 6

1. For a closely researched and penetrating discussion of the aesthetics of the songs without words, see Thomas Christian Schmidt, *Die ästhetischen Grundlagen der Instrumentalmusik Felix Mendelssohn Bartholdys* (Stuttgart: M & P Verlag für Wissenschaft und Forschung, 1996), 285–300. Frieder Reininghaus, "Studie zur bürgerlichen Musiksprache Mendelssohns 'Lieder ohne Worte' als historisches, ästhetisches und politisches Problem," *Die Musikforschung* 28, no. 1 (January–March 1975): 34–51, situates the songs without words as not only a key to Mendelssohn's oeuvre but as a signpost for nineteenth-century music after the appearance of his first collection of these pieces in 1830.

2. The lineage of the songs without words was outlined briefly by Louise Tischler and Hans Tischler, "Mendelssohn's *Songs Without Words*," *The Musical Quarterly* 33, no. 1 (January 1947): 2. The character piece indeed has a clear history dating back to the Baroque, with the keyboard *ordres* of Couperin representing the most prominent examples. The Baroque character piece might take its topic from any number of places. Couperin's and Rameau's works illustrate music based on actual living people, "types" taken from the theater or other public entertainment, and even animals or mechanical devices.

One might regard Schumann's *Carnaval* as belonging to this tradition, since it includes real or pseudonymous characters (Chopin, Paganini; Estrella, Chiarina; Lettres dansantes), fictional personalities (Eusebius and Florestan), and ball-costumed figures (Pierrot, Arlequin, Papillons). In the tradition of the dance suite, it also features dances (Valse noble, Valse allemande). In fact, its tradition attaches more directly to the sets of dances for actual use composed by Schumann's Classic and early-nineteenth-century predecessors. Schumann's character pieces belong to the Romantic aesthetic because they appear as cycles and are therefore at least loosely plotted. For a discussion of the plotting of Schumann's *Papillons*, see Eric Frederick Jensen, "Explicating Jean Paul: Robert Schumann's Program for *Papillons*, Op. 2," *19th-Century Music* 22, no. 2 (Fall 1998): 127–43.

3. Robert Schumann, "Felix Mendelssohn, sechs Lieder ohne Worte für das Pianoforte. Zweites Heft," *Neue Zeitschrift für Musik* 2 (June 23, 1835): 202:

Wer hätte nicht einmal in der Dämmrungsstunde am Clavier gesessen (ein Flügel scheint schon zu hoftonmässig) und mitten im Phantasiren sich unbewußt eine leise Melodie dazu gesungen? Kann man nun zufällig die Begleitung mit der Melodie in den Händen allein verbinden, und ist

man hauptsächlich ein Mendelssohn, so entstehen daraus die schönsten
Lieder ohne Worte. Leichter hätte man es noch, wenn man geradezu
Texte componirte, die Worte wegstriche und so der Welt übergäbe,
aber dann ist es nicht das rechte, sondern sogar eine Art Betrug,—man
müßte denn damit eine Probe der musikalischen Gefühlsdeutlichkeit
anstellen wollen und den Dichter, dessen Worte man verschwiege,
veranlassen, der Composition seines Liedes einen neuen Text unterzulegen. Träfe er im letzten Falle mit dem alten zusammen, so wäre
dies ein Beweis mehr für die Sicherheit des musikalischen Ausdruckes.
Zu unsern Liedern. Klar wie die Sonne sehen sie einen an. Das erste
kommt an Lauterkeit und Schönheit der Empfindung dem in E-Dur
im ersten Heft beinahe gleich; denn dort quillt es noch näher von
der ersten Quelle weg. Florestan sagte: "wer solches gesungen, hat
noch langes Leben zu erwarten, sowohl bei Lebzeiten als nach dem
Tode; ich glaube, es ist mir das liebste." Die Anfangs doppelstimmige
Begleitung in der Mitte wird später hie und da einstimmig, wodurch
aber gerade die Monotonie vermieden wird; das letzte klingt beinahe
wie Widerspruch. Beim zweiten Lied fällt mir Jägers Abendlied von
Göthe ein: "im Felde schleich' ich still und wild, gespannt mein Feuerrohr u.s.w."; an zartem duftigen Bau erreicht es das des Dichters. Das
dritte scheint mir weniger bedeutend, und fast wie ein Rundgesang in
einer Lafontainischen Familienscene; indeß ist es echter unverfälschter
Wein, der an der Tafel herumgeht, wenn auch nicht der schwerste und
seltenste. Das dritte find' ich äußerst liebenswürdig, ein wenig traurig
und in sich gekehrt, aber in der Ferne spricht Hoffnung und Heimath.
In der französischen Ausgabe finden sich, wie in allen Stücken so vor-
züglich in diesem bedeutende Abweichungen von der deutschen, die
indessen Mendelssohn nicht anzugehören scheinen.—Das nächste trägt
etwas Unentschiedenes im Charakter, selbst in Form und Rhythmus
und wirkt demgemäß. Das letzte, eine venetianische Barcarole, schließt
weich und leise das Ganze zu.—So wollet euch von Neuem an diesem
edlen Geist erfreuen!

4. Marc-André Souchay, letter to Felix Mendelssohn, October 12, 1842,
transcribed by John Michael Cooper in his article "Words Without Songs? Of Texts,
Titles, and Mendelssohn's *Lieder ohne Worte*," in *Musik als Text*, papers from the
International Congress of the Gesellschaft für Musikforschung 1993, Freiburg im
Breisgau, ed. Hermann Danuser (Kassel: Bärenreiter, 1998), 2:344:

Die liebsten Sachen, die ich für das Clavier geschrieben, kannte, waren
mit seit Jahren Ihre "Lieder ohne Worte." Ich fand schon früher, da
ich eigentlich noch Kind war, einen eigenthümlichen Reiz, ein so
allesdurchdringendes Gefühel, in ihnen, daß sie mir stests die liebste

und Teuerste aller Claviercompositionen waren. Dieses dunkle Gefühl, das schon früher in mir entstieg, hat sich aber immer mehr ausgebildet und jetzt, da ich mir bei jedem dieser herrlichen Stücke einen festen Gedanken gebildet, bewähren sie den doppelten Genuß, die bloße Liebe und Hinneigung zu ihnen hat sich zur vollen Begeisterung umgewandelt.

Oft freilich werde ich ausgelacht mit meinen phantasti[s]chen Ideen, selbst von Leuten, die ich als tüchtige Musiker anerkennen und ehren muß, wie z.B. von meinem jetzigen Lehrer dem hiesigen Kammermusicus Deichert, der von gar keinen Gedanken, sondern nur von bloßen Tönen wissen will!—Aber es kann nicht sein, ich kann es nur nicht vorstellen, daß diesen herrlichen Gemälden kein Gedanke zu Grunde liegen sollte.—Ich bitte Eur. Hochwohlgeb. mir es nicht als Anmaßung auszulegen wenn ich wage Ihnen meine Meinung offen mitzusprechen, sondern vielmehr den Grund zu dieser Dreistigkeit in meiner ungemeinen Verehrung für Sie, und meiner Wißbegierde zu suchen. Ich glaube mich nicht zu irren, wenn ich meine, daß die verschiedenen Bedeutungen der Lieder etwa folgende sein könnten: Heft 1 Nro 1, Resignation, Nro 2: Melancholie Nro 3, Tableau einer Parforce-Jagd, Nro 4: Lob der Güte Gottes, Nro 6: Venetianisches Gondellied. Heft 2 Nro 1, Schilderung eines frommen dankbaren Gesuchtes, Nro 2, Jagdtableau, Nro 4: Heftiger Wunsch an die Welt hinaus zuziehen. Nro 5: Schlummerlied. Nro 6: Venetianisches Gondellied. Heft 3 Nro 1: Unbegrenzte aber unglücklicher Liebe, die daher oft in Sehnsucht, Schmerz, Wehmuth u. Verzweiflung beigeht, aber immer wieder ruhig wird. Nro 2: Bange Erwartung (abwechselnd Sehnsucht, Angst und Schmerz) Nro 3: Liebeslied. Nro 4: Zufriedenheit Nro 5: Verzweiflung Nro 6. Duett. Heft 4 Nro 2: Sehnsucht Nro 3: Verzweiflung Nro 5: Kriegerisches Volkslied.

The translation here is by John Michael Cooper, in Strunk, *Source Readings in Music History*, 1200.

5. Letter to Marc-André Souchay, 15 October 1842, in Felix Mendelssohn Bartholdy, *Sämtliche Briefe*, ed. Helmut Loos and Wilhelm Seidel (Kassel: Bärenreiter, 2008–17), 9:74:

[Wörter] scheinen mir so vieldeutig, so unbestimmt, so misverständlich im Vergleich zu einer rechten Musik, die einem die Seele erfüllt mit tausend bessern Dingen, als Worten. Das bringt mich eher zum Gegentheil von der Meinung Ihres jetzigen Lehrers, der blos von hübschen Tönen und von keinen Gedanken wissen will. Das was mir eine Musik ausspricht, die ich liebe, sind mir nicht zu unbestimmte Gedanken, um sie in Worte zu fassen, sondern zu bestimmte.

So finde ich in allen Versuchen, diese Gedanken auszusprechen, etwas richtiges, aber auch in allen etwas Ungenügendes, nicht Allgemeines, und so geht es mir auch mit den Ihrigen. Das ist aber nicht Ihre Schuld, sondern die Schuld der Worte, die es eben nicht besser können. Fragen Sie mich, was ich mir dabei gedacht habe, so sage ich: gerade das Lied, wie es da steht. Und habe ich bei dem einen oder andern auch ein bestimmtes Wort oder bestimmte Worte im Sinne gehabt, so kann ich die doch keinen andern Menschen aussprechen, weil dem einen das Wort nicht heißt was es dem andern heißt, weil nur das Lied dem einen dasselbe sagen, dasselbe Gefühl in ihm erwecken kann, wie im andern—ein Gefühl, das sich aber nicht durch dieselben Worte ausspricht. Resignation, Melancholie, Lob Gottes, Parforcejagd,—der eine denkt dabei nicht das, was der andere; dem einen ist Resignation, was dem andern Melancholie; der dritte kann sich bei beiden Worten gar nichts rechtes, lebhaftes denken,—ja, wenn einer von Natur ein rechter, frischer Jäger wäre, dem könnte gar das Lob Gottes und die Jagd ziemlich auf eins herauskommen und für den wäre auch wirklich und wahrhaftig der Hörnerklang das rechte Lob Gottes. Wir hörten darin nichts als die Parforcejagd, und wenn wir uns mit ihm noch so viel darüber herumstritten, wir kämen nicht weiter, das Wort bleibt vieldeutig und die Musik verständen wir beide doch recht.

6. The editions are Felix Mendelssohn Bartholdy, *Songs Without Words* (Boston: F. M. Gilson, [ca. 1885])—"Gilson (ca. 1885)" in table 6.1; Felix Mendelssohn, *Songs Without Words (Lieder ohne Worte): An Analytic Edition*, ed. Percy Goetschius, introduction by Daniel Gregory Mason (Boston: Oliver Ditson, 1906)—"Ditson/ Goetschius"; and Felix Mendelssohn-Bartholdy, *Songs Without Words for the Piano*, ed. Constantin von Sternberg (New York: G. Schirmer, 1915)—"Schirmer/Sternberg."

7. The following list is assembled from the entries in the Mendelssohn thematic catalog, Ralf Wehner, *Felix Mendelssohn Bartholdy: Thematisch-systematisches Verzeichnis der musikalischen Werke (MWV)*, Leipziger Ausgabe der Werke von Felix Mendelssohn Bartholdy, series 13, vol. 1A (Wiesbaden: Breitkopf & Härtel, 2009).

8. Thomas Schmidt points out that the title was dropped at the time of publication, when the tempo changed from Allegro di molto (already uncharacteristically fast for the barcarolle genre) to Presto agitato (*Die ästhetischen Grundlagen*, 297). The title "Agitation" clearly derives simply from the tempo direction. As indicated earlier, Souchay considered the piece's emotion to be "despair."

9. R. Larry Todd, *Mendelssohn: A Life in Music* (Oxford: Oxford University Press, 2003), 567–68.

10. Letter to Josephine von Miller, 30 January 1833, in Mendelssohn Bartholdy, *Sämtliche Briefe*, 3:114:

> Sie wollen Worte zu dem kleinen Liede aus a dur, welches ich Ihnen hinterließ, von mir wissen; aber wie soll ichs anfangen, um welche dazu zu finden? Denn das ist eben die Hauptsache bei solchem Lied ohne Worte, daß sich jeder seine Worte und seinen Sinn hinzu denkt, und sichs auf seine eigne Weise auslegt; das habe ich allerdings wohl auch gethan, aber nur sehr unzusammenhängend, hier und da mal auf eine Note ein Wort, dann wieder eine Menge Noten ohne alle Worte, dann wieder Worte ohne Sinn—und das darf ich Ihnen doch nicht so schreiben, zumal da es eigentlich nur auf den Sinn ankommt. Also erfinden Sie selbst sich nur die Verse, daß Sie die Bedeutung verstehen, weiß ich doch, wenn Sie es auch abläugnen oder um mit Ihren Worten zu reden 'trotz aller Bescheidenheit' und wenn Sie die nicht wüßten, so wäre das ganze Lied nichts nütz und verfehlt; ich wollte mich denn hiedurch feierlich verpflichten Ihnen ein besseres diesen Herbst zu bringen, das seine Stimmung deutlicher ausspräche, als dies es wohl thut.

11. See John Michael Cooper, "Words Without Songs?," 341.

12. Reininghaus, "Studie zur bürgerlichen Musiksprache," 44: "ganz individualisiert für den einsamen Pianisten, für eine hermetisch sich abriegelnde private Sphäre. Zwar ist das Klavierwerk Mendelssohns sprachlos in begriflichen Sinn; es vermag aber doch zu reden."

13. Felix Mendelssohn, *Songs Without Words (Selection)*, Péter Nagy (piano), Naxos 8.554055, 1997, compact disc.

14. The use of the C5 here, neither prepared nor resolved in conventional fashion, reflects the importance of dissonances on the beat to the expressive content of this piece. There is obviously no available conventional nonchord tone remaining in the linear motion from B♭4 through A♭4 on the way to G4. In order to create a dissonance here, Mendelssohn had to abandon standard practices for nonchord tones in melodic writing and simply skip up to C5 and back.

15. For relevant discussions of these instances, see Christa Jost, *Mendelssohns Lieder ohne Worte* (Tutzing: Hans Schneider, 1988), esp. 19n38, 88–90, 127–33; R. Larry Todd, "'Gerade das Lied wie es dasteht': On Text and Meaning in Mendelssohn's *Lieder ohne Worte*," in *Musical Humanism and Its Legacy: Essays in Honor of Claude V. Palisca*, ed. Nancy Kovaleff Baker and Barbara Russano Hanning (Stuyvesant, NY: Pendragon, 1992), 367–77; Cooper, "Words Without Songs?," 341–45; R. Larry Todd, "Mendelssohn's *Lieder ohne Worte* and the Limits of Musical Expression," in *Mendelssohn Perspectives*, ed. Nicole Grimes and Angela R. Mace, 197–222 (Farnham, UK: Ashgate, 2012). For a discussion of the application of Mendelssohn's aesthetic position to vocal songs, see Douglass Seaton, "The Problem of the Lyric Persona in Mendelssohn's Songs," in *Felix Mendelssohn Bartholdy: Kongreß-Bericht 1994*, ed. Christian Martin Schmidt, 167–86 (Wiesbaden: Breitkopf & Härtel, 1997).

16. Cooper, "Words Without Songs?," 345.

17. My translation, based on the German text as given in *The Letters of Fanny Hensel to Felix Mendelssohn*, ed. Marcia Citron (Pendragon, 1987), 547:

Lieber Felix, wenn Singliedern die Worte weggenommen warden, um sie als Concertstück zu brauchen, so ist das ein richtiges Gegenstück zu den Experiment, Deinen Spielliedern Worte unterzulegen, die andre Hälfte von der verkehrten Welt. . . . Soll man nun aber nicht eine ungeheure Meinung von sich bekommen (nein, man soll nicht) wenn man sieht, daß die Späße, womit wir uns als halbe Kinder die Zeit vertrieben haben, jetzt von den großen Talenten nacherfunden, u. als Futter furs Publikum gebraucht warden?

18. The autograph manuscript is on page 9 in volume 18 of the Mendelssohn-*Nachlass* in the Staatsbibliothek zu Berlin, Preussischer Kulturbesitz. A facsimile of the letter to Fanny, which includes Mendelssohn's fair copy of the piece, may be found in the selection of Mendelssohn's letters edited by Peter Sutermeister, *Felix Mendelssohn Bartholdy: Lebensbild mit Vorgeschichte, Reisebriefe von 1830/31 aus Deutschland, Italien und der Schweiz* (Zurich: Ex Libris-Verlag, 1949), between pages 136 and 137.

19. Jost, *Mendelssohns Lieder ohne Worte*, 31; Cooper, "Words Without Songs?," 342–43.

20. "ich möchte gern bei Dir sein und Dich sehn und Dir was erzählen, es will aber nicht gehn. Da habe ich Dir den ein Lied aufgeschrieben, wie ichs wünsche und meine; dabei habe ich Dein gedacht und es ist mir sehr weich zu Muthe dabei." Letter to Fanny Hensel, 14 June 1830, in Mendelssohn Bartholdy, *Sämtliche Briefe*, 1:547.

21. Jost, *Mendelssohns Lieder ohne Worte*, 127–33; Todd, "'Gerade das Lied wie es dasteht,'" 363–67.

22. Todd, 367–77.

23. "Ich habe bei Deinen Worten das eigne Gefühl, dass ich keine Musik zu machen brauche, es ist als läse ich sie heraus und als stände sie schon vor mir." Mendelssohn Bartholdy, *Sämtliche Briefe*, 2:184. For a fuller discussion of this position, see Seaton, "Problem of the Lyric Persona."

24. Louise H. and Hans Tischler pointed out how much of Mendelssohn's musical style is represented in the songs without words in two articles from 1947, Tischler and Tischler, "Mendelssohn's *Songs Without Words*" (see note 2), and Louise Tischler and Hans Tischler, "Mendelssohn's Style: The *Songs Without Words*," *The Music Review* 8 (1947): 256–73.

25. Johann Peter Lyser, "Felix Mendelssohn-Bartholdy," *Wiener Musik-Zeitung* 2, no. 154 (December 24, 1842): 617–18: "da merkt' ich den bald, daß Mendelssohn's Lieder ohne Worte richtiger so bezeichnet würden: '*Empfindungen wofür es keine Worte gibt.*'"

Chapter 7

1. Joseph Freiherr von Eichendorff, *Gedichte von Joseph Freiherr von Eichendorff* (Berlin: Duncker und Humblot, 1837).

2. Herwig Knaus, *Musiksprache und Werkstruktur in Robert Schumanns "Liederkreis,"* Schriften zur Musik 27 (Munich: Katzbichler, 1974), 13.

3. A convenient comparative table showing all four orderings may be found in Patrick McCreless, "Song Order in the Song Cycle: Schumann's *Liederkreis*, Op. 39," *Music Analysis* 5, no. 1 (1986): 19. A list of the songs as they appear in the manuscript sources, with other songs interspersed as Schumann actually composed them, appears in David Ferris, *Schumann's Eichendorff "Liederkreis" and the Genre of the Romantic Cycle* (Oxford: Oxford University Press, 2000), 187. Both the first and the eighth songs are titled "In der Fremde."

4. This point is well made by Jürgen Thym, "A Cycle in Flux: Schumann's Eichendorff *Liederkreis*," in *Of Poetry and Song: Approaches to the Nineteenth-Century Lied*, ed. Jürgen Thym (Rochester, NY: University of Rochester Press, 2010), 377: "Indeed, in many of Eichendorff's poems, springs or brooks are murmuring, idyllic lakes are located in mysterious forests, treetops and leaves are rustling, horn calls can be heard echoing in the woods, and nightingales sing of love. These images recur in Eichendorff's poetry with an almost mannered frequency in ever-new constellations, and anyone who selects a group of his poems is bound to generate correspondences because of the formulaic nature of the poet's language."

5. John Daverio, *Robert Schumann: Herald of a New Poetic Age* (New York: Oxford University Press, 1997), 212.

6. Ferris, *Schumann's Eichendorff "Liederkreis,"* 19.

7. Benedict Taylor, "Absent Subjects and Empty Centers: Eichendorff's Romantic Phantasmagoria and Schumann's *Liederkreis*, Op. 39," *19th-Century Music* 40, no. 3 (Spring 2017): 221.

8. Thym, "A Cycle in Flux," 377. See note 4.

9. Wilhelm Killmayer, "Schumann und seine Dichter," *Neue Zeitschrift für Musik* 142, no. 3 (1981): 233: "Er schwelgt dann in einer Handwerksburschenseligkeit, wo einer munteren Aug's auf froher Fahrt in frischer Luft in eine antiquarische Adelsaffäre verstrickt wird, wo er im Mondenschimmer im Tale ein altes Schloss liegen sieht, in dessen Garten voll Rosen weiss und rot die Geliebte auf ihn warten scheint, die aber tot ist, und die Nachtigallen wollen ihm was von der schönen, alten Zeit sagen." For a similar but more choppy than run-on presentation illustrating the kaleidoscope of images in Eichendorff/Schumann, see Taylor, "Absent Subjects and Empty Centers," 201.

10. Numerous analysts have pointed this out. Barbara Turchin notes that, in the sense that the songs share mottos rather than whole, more expansive themes, the song cycle resembles Schumann's earlier "variation cycles" for piano. Barbara Turchin, "Robert Schumann's Song Cycles: The Cycle Within the Song," *19th-Century Music* 8, no. 3 (1985): 232–33. McCreless gives lists of motive forms in "Song Order in

the Song Cycle," 15–17. See also Knaus, *Musiksprache und Werkstruktur*, 5–12, where Knaus makes much of the use of descending tetrachords in the vocal line; Jürgen Thym, "The Solo Song Settings of Eichendorff's Poems by Schumann and Wolf" (PhD diss., Case Western Reserve University, 1974), 215–17; and Daverio, *Robert Schumann*, 215–16. I take a somewhat cautious approach to the list that follows in this and the next paragraph, since some gestures are so ubiquitous in songs that they hardly stand out to the listener (as Knaus's examples of the descending tetrachord in songs by many composers demonstrate). As a rule of thumb, to achieve prominence as a recurring motive, a figure should be clearly audible and marked by its position in the musical texture or form in multiple songs.

11. The motive resembles that developed in the finale of Schumann's Symphony No. 4 in D Minor, op. 120, although in that movement, at a much faster tempo, it takes on a very different character.

12. Taylor, "Absent Subjects and Empty Centers," 219, 217.

13. McCreless emphasizes that throughout the composition and publication process (after the initial selection of poems), Schumann's reorderings of the songs took place only within each group of six ("Song Order in the Song Cycle," 21).

14. Taylor's assertion that "the successive episodes are held together merely by an abstract linear thread" exaggerates the linearity of the *Liederkreis* while validating the claim by suggesting that the thread is mere abstraction ("Absent Subjects and Empty Centers," 209). We might even find it difficult to apply to the Eichendorff songs the concept of "coherent *narrative discourse*," which Andrew Weaver raises in discussing *Dichterliebe*, which possesses narrativity at a level that the songs of op. 39 do not approach at all (Weaver, "Memories Spoken and Unspoken").

15. Taylor, "Absent Subjects and Empty Centers," 201–2.

16. Ferris, *Schumann's Eichendorff "Liederkreis,"* 202.

17. Andrew H. Weaver, *Narrative and Robert Schumann's Songs: A New Approach to the Romantic Lied* (Rochester, NY: University of Rochester Press, 2024). The main discussion of the Eichendorff *Liederkreis* is on pages 237–42. Weaver considerably strains the application of the concept of telos, because while the yearning for transcendence provides a shared poetic theme for the different voices that he finds in the songs, that does not meet his definition of telos: "the ultimate goal toward which the subject of a fabula aspires, and the arc toward that goal over the course of the fabula" (259). Weaver, like other recent critics, does not find any fabula or arc at all in the cycle.

18. Weaver's narratological approach to the Lied sets considerable store by the claim that the pianist and singer form a performer-narrator, but he admits that this performer-narrator "cannot, however, be construed as providing cyclic coherence to a collection of songs, for if that were the case, then any song recital—even one consisting of contrasting works composed over a span of centuries—must be considered a song cycle if performed by the same pianist and singer throughout" (*Narrative and Robert Schumann's Songs*, 237). Intriguing as his concept of the performer-narrator is for a theory of narrativity in performances, it falls apart here in the face of the necessity to disallow its narrative function when it becomes inconvenient.

19. The text in the first song does not specify the speaker's gender. The singer in the novel in which the poem first appeared, *Viel Lärmen um Nichts*, is, in fact, a woman. No songs in Schumann's *Liederkreis* require the speaker to be a woman, but several clearly imply a man's voice, most notably the last, "Frühlingsnacht" ("Sie ist deine, sie ist dein!"). For the sake of simplicity, I shall use the masculine pronoun, although my conclusion here would allow for a female voice in the opening song.

Critics tend to regard "Die Stille" as potentially an outlier among songs that might all otherwise be for male speakers, asserting that the speaker is a woman, possibly because the song's title identifies a silent woman. I read "Die Stille" as meaning "Quietude," not a reference to the speaker's gender. The reference in the text to "nur Einer" does suggest someone who wants to be understood by a male person, but that need not require a female speaker. In any case, if all the poems are quoted by the speaker of "In der Fremde (I)," this has no bearing on my argument.

20. Taylor writes, "The identity is created, perhaps just [*sic*] a regulative fiction" ("Absent Subjects and Empty Centers," 221). The identity of voice in all literary work is, of course, created and serves as a regulative fiction. It is the critic's obligation to find that identity without contriving it artificially.

21. Jon Finson observes that the beginning with "Der frohe Wandersmann" leaves the order of the following songs confusing, but he accepts this as a manifestation of irony. Jon W. Finson, "The Intentional Tourist: Romantic Irony in the Eichendorff *Liederkreis* of Robert Schumann," in *Schumann and His World*, ed. R. Larry Todd (Princeton, NJ: Princeton University Press, 1994), 164, 167. The defense of apparent incoherence by assigning it to irony, however, is not convincing.

22. In the autograph these songs and "Intermezzo" bear dates that indicate that they were composed in sequence, which might reinforce the sense of these four optimistic love lyrics as a group. Schumann did not write them in immediate succession, however, but over a period of almost two weeks: May 4, "Die Stille"; May 9, "Mondnacht"; before May 16, "Intermezzo"; May 16–17, "Schöne Fremde" (Knaus, *Musiksprache und Werkstruktur*, 14). During this period Schumann also composed other songs, by other poets; see Thym, "A Cycle in Flux," 378.

23. Taylor conceives the intriguing idea that a work might take the nature of the nineteenth-century phantasmagoria, which "creates the illusion of movement but offers no narrative and is marked by a sense of irreality and the capacity for provoking cognitive uncertainty or fear" ("Absent Subjects and Empty Centers," 205). While I find the reference interesting from the point of view of broad cultural context, I am skeptical about the relevance of the phantasmagoria here. As I hope to show, there is at least an overall lyric persona in Schumann's op. 39; nor do I find a sense of irreality or that the work provokes the disturbing feelings that Taylor suggests.

24. Ferris, *Schumann's Eichendorff "Liederkreis,"* 6.

25. Ferris (67–69) cites August Wilhelm Schlegel's discussion of drawings that illustrate poetry in August Wilhelm Schlegel,"Über Zeichnungen zu Gedichten und Johann Flaxmanns Umrisse," in *Athenaeum: Eine Zeitschrift von August Wilhelm*

Schlegel und Friedrich Schlegel, vol. 2, ed. Curt Grützmacher (Munich: Rowohlt, 1969), 73–104, esp. 78–80.

26. Ferris, 64.

27. Friedrich Schlegel, "Brief über den Roman," in *Kritische Friedrich-Schlegel Ausgabe,* vol. 2, ed. Hans Eichner (Zurich: Thomas, 1967), 336; "Ja ich kann mir einen Roman kaum andre denken, als gemischt aus Erzählung, Gesang und andern Formen."

28. Other instances of such miscellanies with introductory personas readily come to mind. For example, we can think of the speaker of the *Liederkreis* similarly to Blake's Piper and Bard of the introductions to the *Songs of Innocence and Experience.*

29. I owe the argument here to a perceptive observation in Turchin, "Robert Schumann's Song Cycles," 240. Turchin does not mention there the striking appearance of the G-major triad, however, which for me nails down the conclusion.

30. Michael Musgrave, "Fragments of a Secret Life," *Times Literary Supplement,* no. 5141 (October 12, 2001): 18.

31. McCreless finds the person of the poet specifically in the forest traveler of the third song of op. 39: "While the Lorelei's assertion that the poet will come 'nimmermehr aus diesem Wald' most obviously suggests his death, it may also figuratively suggest that he is inextricably entrapped in her world of magic, nature and the past—that is, that he is a poet" ("Song Order in the Song Cycle," 24). It seems difficult to argue, however, that the speaker entrapped by the Lorelei in the third song continues as the lyric voice across the cycle as a whole.

32. Franz Brendel, "Robert Schumann mit Rücksicht auf Mendelssohn-Bartholdy und die Entwicklung der modernen Tonkunst überhaupt," *Neue Zeitschrift für Musik* 22 (1845): 122: "Schumann ist Romantiker—hierin liegt hauptsächlich die Erklärung für die so eben erwähnte altdeutsche naivität—und sein Empfindungskreis ist daher sehr verwandt mit dem, welchen die Dichter unserer romantischer Schule aufgeschlossen haben. Die phantastische Pracht, von welcher diese träumte, hat Sch. in dem *Liederkreis von Eichendorff* musikalisch zur Darstellung gebracht." (No translator would be inclined to understand the root *-kreis* in *Empfindungskreis* as suggesting the arrangement of feelings along a circumference.)

33. Booth, *The Rhetoric of Fiction,* 70–77.

34. Daverio, *Robert Schumann,* 212.

35. Taylor, "Absent Subjects and Empty Centers," 218.

36. Ferris, *Schumann's Eichendorff "Liederkreis,"* 6.

Chapter 8

1. For a brief synopsis, launching an important discussion, see Mark Evan Bonds, *Absolute Music: The History of an Idea* (Oxford: Oxford University Press, 2014), 1–9. Predecessors of Bonds's study on the subject include Carl Dahlhaus,

Die Idee der absoluten Musik (Kassel: Bärenreiter, 1978), published in English as *The Idea of Absolute Music*, trans. Roger Lustig (Chicago: University of Chicago Press, 1989), and Daniel Chua, *Absolute Music and the Construction of Meaning* (Cambridge: Cambridge University Press, 1999), see esp. chap. 28, pp. 224–27, for a discussion of Wagner and Hanslick.

2. Charles Rosen, *Sonata Forms* (New York: Norton, 1988), esp. 96–104.

3. Rosen, *The Classical Style*, 43, 57, and passim, gave a groundbreaking articulation of this point.

4. Adolf Bernhard Marx, *Die Lehre von der musikalischen Komposition, praktish theoretisch*, 3rd ed. (Leipzig: Breitkopf & Härtel, 1856–63), 3:282:

> In diesem Paar von Sätzen ist . . . der Hauptsatz das zuerst, also in erster Frische und Energie Bestimmte, mithin das energischer, markiger, absoluter Gebildete . . . , das Herrschende und Bestimmende. Der Seitensatz dagegen ist das nach der ersten energischen Feststellung Nachgeschaffene, zum Gegensatz Dienende, von jenem Vorangehenden Bedingte und Bestimmte, mithin seinem Wesen nach nothwendig das Mildere, mehr schmiegsam als markig Gebildete, das Weibliche gleichsam zu jenem vorangehenden Männlichen. Eben in solchem Sinn ist jeder der beider Sätze ein Andres und erst beide mit einander ein Höheres, Vollkommneres." For a discussion of Marx's statements, with references to other relevant bibliography, see Scott Burnham, "A. B. Marx and the Gendering of Sonata Form," in *Music Theory in the Age of Romanticism*, ed. Ian Bent, 163–86 (Cambridge: Cambridge University Press, 1996). See also Hepokoski, "Masculine—Feminine.

5. See Susan McClary, *Feminine Endings: Music, Gender, and Sexuality* (Minneapolis: University of Minnesota Press, 1991), esp. 7–17; Marcia Citron, *Gender and the Musical Canon* (Cambridge: Cambridge University Press, 1993), 132–45. Indeed, plot itself has been claimed to be modeled on male sexual experience; see Robert Scholes, *Fabulation and Metafiction* (Urbana: University of Illinois Press, 1979), 26.

6. Françoise Tillard, *Fanny Mendelssohn*, trans. Camille Naish (Portland, OR: Amadeus, 1992), 329.

7. Anonymous, Review of Piano Trio in D Minor, op. 11, by Fanny Hensel, *Neue Berliner Musik Zeitung* 1 (1847): 231–32; "finden wir in diesem Trio breite, schwungvolle Fundamente, die sich in stürmenden Wogen zu einem herrlichen Gebäude hinaufbauen. Der erste Satz ist in dieser Beziehung ein Meisterstück, das Trio höchst eigentümlich."

8. R. Larry Todd, *Fanny Hensel: The Other Mendelssohn* (Oxford: Oxford University Press, 2010), xvi, 148, 341.

9. Waldura refers specifically to Beethoven's "Tempest" Sonata as an example of this kind of procedure. See Markus Waldura, "Vier romantische Klaviertrios in d Moll im Vergleich: Mendelssohn-Schumann-Hensel-Berwald," in *Schumanniana nova:*

Festschrift Gerd Nauhaus zum 60. Geburtstag, ed. Bernhard Appel et al., 785–813 (Sinzig: Studio, 2002), 810–13.

10. Suzanne Cusick, "Feminist Theory, Music Theory, and the Mind/Body Problem," *Perspectives of New Music* 32, no. 1 (Winter 1994): 13.

11. Cusick, "Feminist Theory," 13.

12. Hepokoski, "Masculine—Feminine," 497–98. The quoted passage appears on p. 498.

13. Hensel, *Letters of Fanny Hensel to Felix Mendelssohn Bartholdy*, 349, 612.

14. Todd, *Fanny Hensel*, 341.

15. Todd, 341–42.

16. The place of an implied author in literature, as distinct from the narrator, was discussed notably by Wayne Booth; see Booth, *The Rhetoric of Fiction*, 70–77.

17. Cusick, "Feminist Theory," 13; italics added.

18. "Otto Dresel's Soirees," *Dwight's Journal of Music* 8, no. 22 (March 1, 1856): 174.

19. Two helpful recent discussions of sonata form in Chopin appear in the proceedings of the Second International Musicological Congress, "Chopin and His Works in the Context of Culture," held in Warsaw October 10–17, 1999: Wojciech Nowik, "Chopin's Sonata Counter-Type: Error of Construction or Innovative Ideas" (pp. 334–40), and Tetiana Zolozowa, "La forme sonate de Chopin" (pp. 341–48), in *Chopin and His Work in the Context of Culture*, ed. Irena Poniotwoska (Kraków: Polska Akademia Chopinowska, 2003).

20. "Ein mehr 'kombiniertes' Stück ist die h-moll-Sonate Chopins; die Gedanken strömen in derartiger Fülle, daß die sinfonische Arbeit thematischer Entwicklung zurückstehen muß; gleichwohl wird dieses Klavierstück in Ansehung des zierlichen zweiten, des gesanglichen dritten und des dramatischen Schlußsatzes mit seinem Zug ins Große immer neben den ersten Klavierstücken aus dem vorigen Jahrhundert bestehen können." Paul Egert, *Friedrich Chopin* (Potsdam: Akademische Verlagsgeschellschaft Athenaion, [1936]), 111.

21. "Le *style pianistique*, style dont les effets ont été et sont encore déplorables à bien des point de vue. . . . Tout esprit de construction et de coordination des idées y est malheureusement absent; . . . véritable devoir d'un élève bien décidé à faire ici un développment parce que c'est l'usage; mais toute logique en est jalousement bannie. [And as for a recapitulation, it is] à peu près inexistante, car le meilleur élément, le th. A, par une omission inexplicable, n'y reparaît pas: . . . enfantine esquisse qui nous laisse bien loin des monuments d'ordre et d'harmonie, tant et si justement admirés, des Bach et des Beethoven." Vincent d'Indy, *Cours de composition musicale*, bk. 2, pt. 1 (Paris: Durand, 1909), 407–8.

22. Hugo Leichtentritt, *Analyse von Chopins Klavierwerken* (Berlin: Max Hesse, 1922), 245–57; see also Ursula Dammeier-Kirpal, *Der Sonatensatz bei Frédéric Chopin* (Wiesbaden: Breitkopf & Härtel, 1973), 91–102.

23. Rosen, *Sonata Forms*, 393–94.

24. Hepokoski and Darcy, *Elements of Sonata Theory*, see chap. 17, pp. 353–87. Hepokoski and Darcy list the first movements of Chopin's B-flat minor and

B-minor sonatas among instances of the form, but they do not discuss these pieces. It must be emphasized that the present discussion does not attempt to render a thorough analysis of the movement. It focuses on the gendered contrast between the principal and secondary themes, which—as the form was codified—were regarded as normative, and whose abandonment in this movement thus caused analysts and critics trouble with it. For the present purpose, such matters as the use of transitional and closing themes are set aside. As not conventionally gendered components of the form, they do not engage the listener's assumptions and expectations in the same manner, and therefore they would not affect the line of argument here. For a detailed and insightful analysis of the movement, especially with regard to the process of the transition and closing areas, see Andrew Davis, "Chopin and the Romantic Sonata: The First Movement of Op. 58," *Music Theory Spectrum* 36 (2014): 270–94. A more compact discussion is Andrew Davis, "Mixed Genres and Narrativity in Chopin's B-Minor Sonata," in *Music: Function and Value—Proceedings of the 11th International Congress on Musical Signification: Cracow, 27 September–2 October 2010*, ed. Teresa Malecka and Małgorzata Pawłowska (Kraków: Akademia Muzyczna w Krakowie, 2013), 2:281–91. For more on Sonata Theory applied in interpretations of nineteenth-century sonatas—overwhelmingly dealing with Brahms—see also Davis, *Sonata Fragments*.

25. For further discussion of gender in Chopin, see Eero Tarasti, "Chopin and the Transcendental Subject: Body and Transcendence in Chopinian Aesthetics," in *Chopin and His Work in the Context of Culture*, ed. Irena Poniotwoska (Kraków: Polska Akademia Chopinowska, 2003), 195–214, esp. 195–203.

26. D'Indy, *Cours de composition musicale*, 407–8.

27. "Energie," "Zielstrebigkeit"; "Die Melodie wiegt sich in der Höhe." Leichtentritt, *Analyse von Chopins Klavierwerken*, 245.

28. "Bestimmtheit und Klarheit" (Dammeier-Kirpal, *Der Sonatensatz bei Fré-déric Chopin*, 91), "ruhigen, kantablen" (95), "immer häufigere Verzierungen" (94).

29. Hepokoski, "Masculine—Feminine," 499.

30. Scholes and Kellogg, *The Nature of Narrative*, 4.

31. Davis, "Chopin and the Romantic Sonata," 292.

32. For a discussion of metanarrativity, see Gerald Prince, *Narratology: The Form and Functioning of Narrative* (Berlin: Mouton, 1974), 115–28.

33. Klein, "Chopin's Fourth Ballade as Musical Narrative."

34. See Davis, "Mixed Genres and Narrativity"; "Chopin and the Romantic Sonata"; *Sonata Fragments*, esp. chap. 2 (pp. 34–47).

35. Davis, *Sonata Fragments*, 40.

36. Scholes and Kellogg, *The Nature of Narrative*, 207.

37. My adoption of Scholes and Kellogg's term "dynamic" here applies the word to the main thematic elements, referring to both their characters and the types of activity in which they engage within the plot.

38. Hayden White, "The Value of Narrativity in the Representation of Reality," *Critical Inquiry* 7, no. 1 (1980): 5–27.

39. See Booth, *The Rhetoric of Fiction*, 211–40; Bal, *Narratology*, 12–23. Note that this makes the situation essentially unlike that of the persona in Cone's well-known application of the concept of persona in *The Composer's Voice*, where the persona is behind the music but not actually heard in it. Unlike the present essay, Cone's work belongs to aesthetics, not hermeneutics.

40. "Einem ächt Chopin'schen liedmässigen, von Triolen unterstützten Cantabile." Review of Chopin's Sonata No. 3 in B Minor, op. 58, *Allgemeine musikalische Zeitung* 48, no. 5 (February 4, 1846): 74–75; the quotation is in column 75.

41. "Er hat in der Aeußerung . . . einige Besonderheiten, die, weil sie vom Herkömmlichen sehr auffallend abweichen, beim ersten Blick bemerkbar sind . . . . [Diese Sonate] *ist von Chopin*." "1716," *Neue Zeitschrift für Musik* 23 (September 16, 1845): 89–90; the phrases quoted appear on p. 89.

42. "Ce défaut est assez fréquent chez Chopin. . . . Il a recours alors à des tournures italiennes, empruntées à la mode des théâtres et des salons de son temps." D'Indy, *Cours de composition musicale*, 408.

43. "Lauschen wir nun nicht wieder entzückt dem Kantilenensänger Chopin?" Adolf Weissmann, *Chopin* (Berlin: Schuster & Loeffler, 1922), 156.

44. "Eine echt Chopinsche Melodie"; Dammeier-Kirpal, *Der Sonatensatz bei Frédéric Chopin*, 93.

45. The salon itself was a feminine-gendered environment; see Jeffrey Kallberg, "The Harmony of the Tea Table: Gender and Ideology in the Piano Nocturne," *Representations* 39 (1992): 102–33; reprinted in *Chopin at the Boundaries: Sex, History, and Musical Genre* (Cambridge, MA: Harvard University Press, 1996), 30–61.

46. See note 24.

47. Kallberg, "The Harmony of the Tea Table," 104–6.

48. Wayne C. Petty, "Chopin and the Ghost of Beethoven," *19th-Century Music* 22, no. 3 (Spring 1999): 294; Klein, "Chopin's Fourth Ballade as Musical Narrative," 32.

49. This is self-evident in the theory of narrativity. For further discussion of the "Chopinian transcendental subject," see Tarasti, "Chopin and the Transcendental Subject," 203–6.

50. To reiterate a point central to this study, the voice of this Sonata is not "the" voice of the merely biographical Chopin. Such a voice does not and cannot exist. Equally important is the voice identified by Cheng Wei Lim in his article "Heroic Narratives and Chopin's Polonaise in A♭ Major, Op. 53," *19th-Century Music* 46, no. 2 (2022): 163–93. Lim locates the meaning of the Polonaise in the context of the Polish aspiration for national integrity. As part of that discussion, Lim identifies the voice of that piece as that of the wieszcz, a prophetic bard. But, again, not every work by Chopin speaks with that voice, either, as the reception history of the B-Minor Sonata shows.

Chapter 9

1. An important critique of the Symphony from the point of view of its structure may be found in Carl Dahlhaus, "Studien zu romantischen Symphonien—Das 'Finalproblem' in Schumanns Zweiter Symphonie," in *Jahrbuch des Staatlichen Instituts für Musikforschung Preussischer Kulturbesitz*, ed. Dagmar Droysen (Berlin: Staatliches Institut für Musikforschung Preussischer Kulturbesitz, 1973), 104–19.

2. Robert Schumann, letter to Mendelssohn, September 20, 1845, in *Briefe: Neue Folge*, 2nd ed., ed. F. Gustav Jansen (Leipzig: Breitkopf & Härtel, 1904), 249: "In mir paukt und trompetet es seit einigen Tagen sehr (Trombe in C); ich weiss nicht, was daraus werden wird."

3. Clara Schumann reported to Felix Mendelssohn in a letter of December 27, 1845, that Robert Schumann had surprised her at Christmas with his symphony sketches; see Nancy B. Reich, "The Correspondence Between Clara Wieck Schumann and Felix and Paul Mendelssohn," in Todd, *Schumann and His World*, 222. Schumann noted some of the important stages of the symphony's drafting in his journal; see Robert Schumann, *Tagebücher*, vol. 3, *Haushaltbücher: Teil I, 1837–47*, ed. Gerd Nauhaus (Leipzig: VEB Deutscher Verlag für Musik, 1982), 408ff.:

12 December 1845 – "Symphonistiche Gedanken"
13 December 1845 – "Symphonistiche Gedanken"
14 December 1845 – "Symphoniaca"
15 December 1845 – "Symphoniaca"
16 December 1845 – "Symphonie"
17 December 1845 – "1ster Satz fast fertig"
18 December 1845 – "Scherzo angefangen"
19 December 1845 – "Musik – am Scherzo –"
20 December 1845 – "Am Scherzo – fleißig –"
21 December 1845 – "Am Adagio Einiges"
25 December 1845 – "Mus.[ikalisches] Aufregung im letzten Satz d. Symphonie"
26 December 1845 – "Musik.[alisches] Glück – beinahe fertig mit d. letzten Satz"
27 December 1845 – "Musik.[alische] Aufregung"
28 December 1845 – "Fast ganz fertig m.[it] d. Symphonie"

The orchestration is not mentioned often, but it does appear in a couple of entries (there is no *Haushaltbuch* for the period between March 28, 1846, and May 11, 1847, which would include most of the period in question):

12 February 1846 – "d. Symphonie zu instr.[umentieren] angefangen"
22 February 1846 – "Nur kleine Fortschritte in d. Symphonie"

4. Preparations for the concert are discussed in Clara Schumann's letters to Mendelssohn; see Reich, "Correspondence," 223–25.

5. Most notable among them is Anthony Newcomb, "Once More 'Between Absolute and Program Music': Schumann's Second Symphony," *19th-Century Music* 7, no. 3 (April 3, 1984): 233–50, a detailed study that lays out much of the central evidence both analytical and documentary. Newcomb's bibliography is also especially useful.

6. For an extensive analysis of the harmonic progress of the Symphony, see Linda Correll Roesner, "Tonal Strategy and Poetic Content in Schumann's C-Major Symphony, Op. 61," in *Probleme der symphonischen Tradition im 19. Jahrhundert: Internationales Musikwissenschaftliches Colloquium, Bonn, 1989, Kongreßbericht*, ed. Siegfried Kross and Marie Luise Maintz, 295–306 (Tutzing: Hans Schneider, 1990), esp. pp. 296–301. Roesner's conclusion that the key of C major is connected to the initial of Clara's name seems unconvincing, despite the material that she finds in the Symphony's allusions (in the presumed allusion to Schumann's "Widmung," a pretty thin one) to song tunes that can be connected to Robert's feelings for her.

7. Newcomb, "Once More," 247. The finale of Schumann's op. 61 is sufficiently idiosyncratic that it has generated several studies. Among the most useful articles specifically devoted to the movement are Jon R. Finson, "The Sketches for the Fourth Movement of Schumann's Second Symphony," *Journal of the American Musicological Society* 39 (1986): 143–68; Gerd Nauhaus, "Final-Lösungen in der Symphonik Schumanns," in Kross and Maintz, *Probleme der symphonischen Tradition im 19. Jahrhundert*, 307–20, translated by Susan Gillespie as "Schumann's Symphonic Finales," in Todd, *Schumann and His World*, 113–28; and Ingeborg Maass, "Zwischen absoluter und Progammusik? Zum Finale von Schumanns C-Dur Symphonie op. 61," in *Aspekte historischer und systemmatischer Musikforschung: Zur Symphonie im 19. Jahrhundert, zu Fragen der Musiktheorie, der Wahrnehmung von Musik und Anderes*, Schriften zur Musikwissenschaft 5, ed. Christoph-Hellmut Mahling and Kristina Pfarr, 133–40 (Mainz: Are, 2002).

8. Newcomb emphasizes this point in a footnote, 242n21. Roesner (see note 6) also demonstrates thematic evolution from the third-movement theme (which becomes the secondary-area theme in the finale) to the section 4 theme of the finale.

9. Ernst Gottschald, "Robert Schumann's zweite Symphonie: Zugleich mit Rücksicht auf andere, insbesondere Beethoven's Symphonien. Vertraute Briefe a A. Dörffel," *Neue Zeitschrift für Musik* 32 (1850): 137–38: "das *sieggekrönte* Ringen der besonderen Individualität nach ihrer innigsten Verschmelzung mit der geistigen Allgemeinheit in der alle egoistischen Schranken, welche die einzelnen Geister von einander trennten, die sich non als Gleiche lieben, denn sie wohnen im Reiche der Freiheit, Gleichheit und Brüderlichkeit."

10. Gottschald, "Robert Schumann's zweite Symphonie," 138: "des Tondichters Gemüth, noch mitten in befremdeter Einsamkeit befangen."

11. Michael P. Steinberg, "Schumann's Homelessness," in Todd, *Schumann and His World*, 75. He also denies the plot framework that others find in the work.

12. Schumann, letter to Otten, April 2, 1849, *Briefe: Neue Folge*, 300: "Die Symphonie schrieb ich im December 1845 noch halb krank; mir ist's als müsste man ihr dies anhören. Erst im letzten Satz fing ich an mich wieder zu fühlen; wirklich wurde ich auch nach Beendigung des ganzen Werkes wieder wohler. Sonst aber, wie gesagt, erinnert sie mich an eine dunkle Zeit."

13. Newcomb, "Once More," 237.

14. In this regard, Mark Evan Bonds, in his brief discussion in *The Beethoven Syndrome* (151–52), reports the critical reception of the C-Major Symphony, quoting some of the relevant documentary evidence, but misses the opportunity to rule out the misunderstanding of the work as a representation of Schumann's health.

15. Schumann, letter to Taubert, March 3, 1847, *Briefe: Neue Folge*, 273: "im ganzen ein finsteres Stück,—erst im letzten Teil tun ein Paar freundlichen Strahlen hervorbrechen." Quoted in Newcomb, "Once More," 237n12.

16. Robert Hatten's memorably alliterative descriptor for this expressive generic schema, "tragic to triumphant," has gained some currency; see Hatten, *Musical Meaning in Beethoven*, 80. I find it problematic because whether a work is a tragedy depends not on a mood that it sets but on its outcome. By definition, a plot with a triumphant ending is not a tragedy, no matter how dismal, funereal, or even catastrophic it might have seemed earlier in the course of its plot.

17. A useful exploration of intertextuality in music is Klein, *Intertextuality in Western Art Music*. Klein's first chapter provides a tidy survey of the most important literary, and some musical, contributions to today's thinking about intertextuality, with convincing examples.

18. R. Larry Todd, "On Quotation in Schumann's Music," in Todd, *Schumann and His World*, 80 and 109n3.

19. See Berthold Litzmann, ed., *Clara Schumann, Johannes Brahms: Brief aus den Jahren 1853–1896* (Leipzig: Breitkopf & Hartel, 1927), 1:158.

20. Ingeborg Maass, "Zur Bach-Rezeption in Schumanns C-Dur Symphonie op. 61," in *Robert Schumann: Philologische, analytische, sozial- und rezeptionsgeschichtliche Aspekte*, Saarbrücker Studien zur Musikwissenschaft No. 8, ed. Wolf Frobenius et al. (Saarbrücken: Saarbrücker Drückerei, 1998), 101. Maass understands this "organismus-fremdes Strukturelement" on an abstract compositional level rather than as a process of recollection (105).

21. Roesner, "Tonal Strategy," 299n9. See also Christopher Alan Reynolds, *Motives for Allusion: Context and Content in Nineteenth-Century Music* (Cambridge, MA: Harvard University Press, 2003), 41 and 195n31.

22. Daverio, *Robert Schumann*, 319.

23. Newcomb, "Once More," 247. As critics have long noticed, this recalls Schumann's earlier use of the same phrase in the final Adagio passage of the first movement of his *Phantasie*, op. 17, possibly with a similar effect. It is important to

exercise some caution about this allusion to Beethoven, because the same melodic contour appears elsewhere in nineteenth-century music, without a similar semiotic or affective purpose and possibly without conscious borrowing. A notable instance is in the Allegretto un poco agitato of the orchestral first number of Mendelssohn's *Lobgesang* (mm. 398–400, etc.)

24. Daverio, *Robert Schumann*, 318–19, regards this as an allusion by both Mozart and Schumann to Baroque music, but unlike my reading his takes it to suggest a move from the secular to the spiritual.

25. Finson, "Sketches," 155n29.

26. Arnfried Edler, "Ton und Zyklus in der Symphonik Schumanns," in Kross and Maintz, *Probleme der symphonischen Tradition*, 194. The letter to Verhulst is cited from F. Gustav Jansen, ed., *Robert Schumanns Briefe, Neue Folge*, 2nd ed. (Leipzig, 1904), 517n314.

27. Edler, 202: "die symphonische Tradition selber, repräsentiert durch das Haydn-Zitat."

28. "Der Begriff der musikalischen Arbeit thematisiert wird—es gibt vor Brahms kaum eine andere Symphonie, in der substantielle und strukturelle Verein-heitlichung so rigoros und so angestrengt erzwungen sind wie hier, und kaum eine, in der der Begriff der musikalischen Arbeit zugleich so geschichtstief gefaßt wird." Ludwig Finscher, "'Zwischen absoluter und Programmusik': Zur Interpretation der deutschen romantischen Symphonie," in *Über Symphonien: Beiträge zu einer musikalischen Gattung*, Festschrift Walter Wiora zum 70. Geburtstag, ed. Christoph-Hellmut Mahling (Tutzing: Hans Schneider, 1979), 112.

29. Mark Evan Bonds, *After Beethoven: Imperatives of Originality in the Symphony* (Cambridge, MA: Harvard University Press, 1996).

30. I take the expression from its appearance in Akio Mayeda, *Robert Schumanns Weg zur Symphonie* (Zurich: Atlantis / Mainz: Schott, 1992), 523. Mayeda refers to "Das Beethovensche Grundkonzept: 'Durch Leiden zur Freude'" and cites Beethoven's letter to Countess Maria von Erdödy of October 19, 1815.

31. Schumann, *Briefe: Neue Folge*, 262.

32. Klaus W. Niemöller discusses fugato in the nineteenth century, pointing out that it represented a "harkening-back" to earlier music. He identifies a class of pieces that use fugato as a representation of ritual and sacrament, and he traces the origins of this usage to Mozart's duet for the two Armed Men in *The Magic Flute*. He notes the resemblance between Mozart's passage and the fugato in the slow movement of Schumann's C-Major Symphony as an example, but he does not pursue any further hermeneutic significance in this observation. See Klaus W. Niemöller, "Das Fugato als Ausdrucksmittel im 19. Jahrhundert," in *Festschrift Walter Wiora zum 30. Dezember 1966*, ed. Ludwig Finscher and Christoph-Helmut Mahling (Kassel: Bärenreiter, 1967), 415.

33. The duet's text and the music together represent an example of a usage of walking bass that, as Christopher Reynolds has noted, can serve to reference

"faith, resolve, and strength, whether in the sacred context of the Credo . . . or in operatic scenes that portray the same traits" (*Motives for Allusion*, 10).

34. "Die Musik ist keine solche, die ein glücklicher Geist gefunden: sie ist eine errungene und hat eine große Weltanschauung, ein großes Leben hinter sich." Alfred Dörffel, "Für Orchester: Robert Schumann, Op. 61. Zweite Symphonie für großes Orchester," *Neue Zeitschrift für Musik* 28 (1848): 99.

35. Gottschald, "Robert Schumann's zweite Symphonie," 138: "innerste Seele, welche fest und unerschütterlich die Feuerprobe der 'Gestalten' besteht."

36. See note 9.

37. "Wenn in den Werken der ersten Epoche bei R. Schumann das Phantastische überwog, so ist es hier, vermittelt durch seine contrapunktischen Studien, die plastische, objective Ausprägung der Gedanken, eine Richtung, welche überhaupt die Werke seiner zweiten Epoche charakterisirt." Franz Brendel, report on Leipzig Abonnementskonzerte, *Neue Zeitschrift für Musik* 25 (1846): 181.

38. Reynolds, *Motives for Allusion*, 138.

39. Newcomb, "Once More," 240. Newcomb does not relate the citations of the earlier masters to the plot archetype of the Symphony, which he reads as representing the illness-to-recovery or struggle-to-victory contour.

40. Nauhaus, "Final-Lösungen in der Symphonik Schumanns," 128n51.

Chapter 10

1. The author's name often appears erroneously with an acute accent as Sénancour. The title of the work on its first publication was spelled *Oberman*, but the second *n* became standard in later editions, beginning in 1833.

2. Étienne Pivert de Senancour, *Obermann* (Paris: Charpentier, 1847), 17.

3. "Si l'on exige dans un livre la coordination progressive des pensées et la symétrie des lignes extérieures, Obermann n'est pas un livre." George Sand, preface to Obermann, by Étienne Pivert de Senancour (Paris: Charpentier, 1847), 6.

4. For a summary of this period and these events, see Alan Walker, *Franz Liszt*, vol. 1: *The Virtuoso Years* (New York: Knopf, 1990), 190–231.

5. Michele Calella, "Musik und imaginative Geographie: Franz Liszts *Années de pèlerinage* und die kulturelle Konstruktion der Schweiz," *Die Musikforschung* 65 (2012): 211–30.

6. Wolfgang Fuhrmann, "Das Land der Schweiz mit der Seele suchend: Franz Liszt's Schweiz-Erfahrung zwischen dem *Album d'un voyageur* (1840–42) und den *Années de pèlerinage 1: Suisse* (1855)," *Jahrbuch der Staatlichen Instituts für Musikforschung Preußischer Kulturbesitz* (2012): 221–22.

7. Senancour, *Obermann*, 280: "Que veux-je? Que suis-je? Que demander à la nature? . . . Toute cause est invisible, toute fin trompeuse; toute forme change, toute durée s'épuise: . . . Je sens, j'existe pour me consumer en désirs indomptables,

pour m'abreuver de la séduction d'un monde fantastique, pour rester atterré de sa voluptueuse erreur."

8. Senancour, 43: "Indicible sensibilité, charme et tourment de nos vaines années; vaste conscience d'une nature partout accablante et partout impénétrable, passion universelle, sagesse avancée, voluptueux abandon; tout ce qu'un cœur mortel peut contenir de besoins et d'ennuis profonds, j'ai tout senti, tout éprouvée dans cette nuit mémorable. J'ai fait un pas sinistre vers l'âge d'affaiblissement; j'ai dévoré dix années de ma vie." This is one of the passages from Senancour that Sand quoted at length (preface to *Obermann*, 7–8).

9. Scholars who discuss the forms of both versions of "Vallée d'Obermann" generally take a somewhat tentative approach to especially the form of the early one, despite its relatively straightforward design. A detailed general discussion is in William H. Hughes Jr., "Liszt's *Première année de pèlerinage: Suisse*: A Comparative Study of Early and Revised Versions" (DMA diss., Eastman School of Music, University of Rochester, 1985), 154–94. Hughes gives basic diagrams aligning the two forms of the two versions, as do other writers, but does not explicitly distinguish the use of sonata form in the first or the abandonment of that form in the second.

10. John Rink hears other recurring features in the piece, specifically references to the "reaching-over" motive of a rising third and descending second and the progression of an augmented-sixth chord resolving to a G♯-major chord, both of which he connects to Schubert's song "Der Wanderer," which Liszt had transcribed in 1838. Both features might be found in other works, as well. Some of the instances of the "reaching-over" motive that Rink cites might seem rather buried in "Vallée d'Obermann." If one accepts this as a convincing intertextual reference, then, as Rink points out, there is another reference to consider in a programmatic interpretation of Liszt's music, but Rink does not explore its implications. John Rink, "Translating Musical Meaning: The Nineteenth-Century Performer as Narrator," in *Rethinking Music*, ed. Nicholas Cook and Mark Everist (Oxford: Oxford University Press, 1999), 226–28. By his use of the metaphor of "narration," Rink aims to suggest how the player shapes the intensity of the music in performance, an issue that should not fail to take into consideration the central aspects of narrativity discussed here. Rink does not, in fact, arrive at a conclusion about the nineteenth-century performer at all but has in mind to provide guidance to twenty-first-century players.

11. In his discussion of the piece in *The Cambridge Companion to Liszt*, Kenneth Hamilton compared the first version unfavorably to the second on structural grounds: "Liszt's recasting of this piece turned it into one of his most sublime achievements. Many of the problems with the earlier version can be traced to its almost pedantic sonata structure. . . . In the later version resemblances to a sonata layout are far more distant . . . the result is striking and directly moving in a way that far surpasses the earlier version. The vast expansion of Liszt's compositional range and technique is rarely so evident as here." Hamilton, "Liszt's Early and Weimar Piano Works," 69.

In the relatively brief discussion that his chapter allowed, Hamilton did not discuss the influence of paratexts or the relationship of form to voice.

12. The brief Dresden Amen formula was composed by Johann Gottlieb Naumann (1741–1801) for the Dresden court chapel. Other notable references occur in Mendelssohn's "Reformation" Symphony and Wagner's *Parsifal*.

13. Some commentators have, nevertheless, read the piece as a sonata form. See, for example, the generalized diagram offered by Dolores Pesce, "Expressive Resonance in Liszt's Piano Music," in *Nineteenth-Century Piano Music*, ed. R. Larry Todd (New York: Schirmer Books, 1990), 361. Andrew Fowler considers both versions of "Vallée d'Obermann" as having a ternary design, although he gives more detailed diagrams than Pesce, neither of which seems convincingly regarded as ternary. Andrew Fowler, "Motive and Program in Liszt's 'Vallée d'Obermann,'" *Journal of the American Liszt Society* 29 (January–June 1991): 5.

14. See the observation in Konstantin Zenkin, "Fluidity of Structures in the Music of Franz Liszt: From Romantic 'Form as Process' to 'Open Form,'" *Quaderni dell'Instituto Liszt* 12 (2012): 49, that "the harmonic structure of the theme dramatically contradicts its expositional function: the theme immediately obtains transitional features." In fact, the opening does not attempt to constitute the theme in this piece at all, and it is the lyrical melody introduced at measure 75 that serves as the actual theme for the variation-like continuation of the form. Comparison with the early version is also helpful here, since the harmonic treatment of the material there, which did serve as principal theme for a sonata form, was much more stable.

15. Márta Grabócz, "The Two Faces of the 'mal du siècle' in Literature and in Liszt's Piano Works," *Studia musicologica* 55, nos. 1–2 (June 2014): 58. See also her two earlier monographs, *Morphologie des œuvres pour piano de Liszt* (Budapest: MTA Zenetudományi Intezét, 1987; 2nd ed., Paris: Kimé, 1996) and *Musique, narrativité, signification* (Paris: L'Harmattan, 2009).

16. Grabócz, "Two Faces," 61 (table 5), and an earlier version in Márta Grabócz, "The Role of Semiotical Terminology in Musical Analysis," in *Musical Semiotics in Growth*, ed. Eero Tarasti et al. (Bloomington: Indiana University Press / Imatra: International Semiotics Institute, 1996), 217 (example 6).

17. Eero Tarasti, "The Case of *Obermann*: Franz Liszt and Marie d'Agoult in Switzerland," in *Interdisciplinary Studies in Musicology: Report from the First Interdisciplinary Conference, Poznań, November 23–24, 1991*, ed. Maciej Jabłoński and Jan Stęszewski, 90–105 (Poznań: Ars nova, 1993). This article attempts a sophisticated critical consideration of the piece, but it takes a rather unsophisticated approach to analysis. In some important places it is simply inaccurate; for example, the end of the introduction in measure 74 is not on a "six-four chord of the E minor tonic," as Tarasti claims, and there is no F♯ in the penultimate measure, as his music example shows.

18. Fowler, "Motive and Program," 11.

19. Calella, "Musik und imaginative Geographie," 229:

Wessen Stimme nehmen wir im *Album d'un voyageur* und im Schweizer Heft der Années de pèlerinage wahr? Vielleicht sollte die Frage besser lauten: Wie viele Stimmen? Jene von Liszt, Byron, Senancour oder George Sand? Oder von einem imaginären musikalischen Reisenden, von Childe Harold, Obermann, in dem noch Rousseaus Held Saint-Preuve mitschwingt? Und welchen Liszt hört man hier, den Reisenden, den Leser von Dichtungen, das empfindsam-melancholische Subjekt, das "ungarische" Subjekt, oder der Vertreter einer neuen Weimarer Klassik? In dieser Interpretation wurde bewusst von einer Vielfalt von Subjektstimmen ausgegangen, die durch ihre Überschneidung aus Liszts Klaviersammlungen einen dynamischen Prozess der polyphonen Erzählung machen, die eine unterschiedlich kulturell aufgeladene imaginative Geographie der Schweiz entwerfen, eine musikalische Landschaft, deren Orte jenseits ihrer empirischen Lokalisierung in einem intertextuellen, zugleich diskursiven Prozess konstruiert werden.

20. Katharine Ellis, "Liszt: The Romantic Artist," in Hamilton, *The Cambridge Companion to Liszt*, 4–6.

21. Franz Liszt, letter to Schott, May 18, 1855, in Edgar Istel,

Elf ungedrückte Briefe Liszts an Schott," *Die Musik* 5, no. 19 (1906): 46. "Die Geographie hat aber bei diesem Stück durchaus nichts zu thun, den es bezieht sich einzig und allein auf den französischen Roman Obermann von Sénancourt [*sic*] dessen Handlung blos die Entwickelung eines besonderen Seelen Zustandes bildet.—Dies Buch hat eine tiefe Einwirkung auf einen nicht unbedeutsamen Theil der französischen Litteratur ausgeübt—insbesondere auf Mme. George Sand welche einen längeren Aufsatz darüber geschreiben. Obermann könnte man das *Monochord* der unerbittlichen Einsamkeit der menschlichen Schmerzen nennen. Es ist ein wüstes, verworrenes und sublimes Buch. Das düstere, hyper-elegische Fragment "la Vallée d'Obermann" welches in den Schweizer Jahrgang der *Années de pèlerinage* aufgenommen (da die Szene des Buches ebenfalls die Schweiz ist) bringt mehrere Hauptmomente des Werkes von Sénancourt worauf auch die gewählten Epigraphen hinweisen. Flinten und Jäger passen da keineswegs hinzu! und so hübsch auch das Title Blatt ausgeführt sein mag, so steht es im grellst lächerlichen *contresens* zu dem Stück.

22. Norbert Miller, "In Obermans Tal: Franz Liszt und die Alpenbegeisterung der Jahre nach 1830," in *Die Schweiz und ihre Landschaft in slavischer Lyrik*, ed. Peter Brang (Mainz: Akademie der Wissenschaften und der Literatur, 2000), 82.

Chapter 11

1. Marco Beghelli, "Analessi, ticoscopio, ipotiposi," in *La vera storia ci narra: Verdi narrateur / Verdi narrator*, ed. Camillo Faverzani, 17–32 (Lucca: Libreria Musicale Italiana, 2014).

2. The correspondence between Verdi and Boito is available in Italian in Marcello Conati and Maria Medici, eds., *Carteggio Verdi-Boito* (Parma: Istituto di Studi Verdiani, 1978), translated as *The Verdi-Boito Correspondence*, English-language edition by William Weaver (University of Chicago Press, 1994) and also in English in Hans Busch, ed. and trans., *Verdi's "Otello" and "Simon Boccanegra" in Letters and Documents*, rev. ed. (Oxford: Clarendon, 1988), vol. 1.

3. Julian Budden, *The Operas of Verdi*, rev. ed. (Oxford: Clarendon, 1992), 3:302.

4. George Bernard Shaw, *Shaw's Music: The Complete Musical Criticism in Three Volumes*, 2nd rev. ed., ed. Dan H. Laurence (London: Bodley Head, 1989), 3:579.

5. Letter to Giulio Ricordi, May 11, 1887, in Busch, *Verdi's "Otello" and "Simon Boccanegra,"* 1:311.

6. Victor Maurel, "À propos de la mise en scène du drame lyrique *Otello*," in Victor Maurel, *Dix ans de carrière: 1887–1897* (Paris: Paul Dupont, 1897; reprinted in New York: Arno, 1977), 49.

7. Busch, *Verdi's "Otello" and "Simon Boccanegra,"* 2:485.

8. Busch, 1:112. See Conati and Medici, *Carteggio Verdi-Boito*, 1:58: "La figura principale del lato Lirico è Desdemona, la figura principale del lato dramatico è Jago."

9. For the Italian text and a translation, see Daniel Taddie, "The Devil, You Say: Reflections on Verdi's and Boito's Iago," *The Opera Quarterly* 7, no. 1 (Spring 1990): 68–69.

10. Boito, letter to Verdi, April 26, 1884, in *The Verdi-Boito Correspondence*, 74. The text appears on the following page in this edition, and a facsimile is given in the "Plates" section as figure 13.

11. For Jane Hawes the trill represents Jago's contempt. Jane Hawes, *An Examination of Verdi's "Otello" and Its Faithfulness to Shakespeare* (Lewiston, NY: Edwin Mellen, 1994), 66.

12. Budden, *The Operas of Verdi*, 3:297.

13. Busch, *Verdi's "Otello" and "Simon Boccanegra,"* 2:529.

14. Verdi would have used the equivalent term *cadenza d'inganno*.

15. Busch, *Verdi's "Otello" and "Simon Boccanegra,"* 2:485. Also see Mariangela Tempera, "Otello: Da Verdi a Shakespeare," in *Tre secoli di Otello*, ed. Elena Sala Di Felice and Laura Sanna (Rome: Bulzoni, 1999), 78–79.

16. Busch, 1:200. See Conati and Medici, *Carteggio Verdi-Boito*, 1:58: "Egli è (è vero) il Demonio, che muove tutto."

17. James A. Hepokoski, *Giuseppe Verdi: Otello* (Cambridge: Cambridge University Press, 1987), 146.

18. Scott L. Balthazar, "Desdemona's Alienation and Otello's Fall," in *The Cambridge Companion to Verdi*, ed. Scott L. Balthazar (Cambridge: Cambridge University Press, 2004), 254.

19. Hawes, *Examination*, 38, 39, 123.

20. Theodore Albritton Conner, "Towards an Interpretive Model of Text-Music Relations: An Analysis of Selected Scenes from Verdi's *Otello*" (PhD diss., University of Connecticut, 1997).

21. Conner, "Towards an Interpretive Model," 227. See Frits Noske, *The Signifier and the Signified: Studies in the Operas of Mozart and Verdi* (The Hague: Martinus Nijhoff, 1977), 148. Noske does not, however, claim that this makes Jago a narrator.

22. Hepokoski, *Giuseppe Verdi: Otello*, 146.

23. Hepokoski, 183. As an example of a study of the play that points this out, Hepokoski cites Jane Adamson, *"Othello" as Tragedy: Some Problems of Judgment and Feeling* (Cambridge: Cambridge University Press, 1980), 66–67.

24. William Shakespeare, *Œuvres complètes de W. Shakespeare: Les Jaloux: Cymbeline – Othello*, vol. 5, pt. 2, trans. François-Victor Hugo (Paris: Pagnerre, 1860), 266.

25. James A. Hepokoski, "Boito and F.-V. Hugo's 'Magnificent Translation': A Study in the Genesis of the *Otello* Libretto," in *Reading Opera*, ed. Arthur Groos and Roger Parker (Princeton, NJ: Princeton University Press, 1988), 34–50. Hepokoski does not mention the translation of Iago's self-characterization or compare the character studies in Hugo's translation and the production book.

26. François-Victor Hugo, preface to his translation of *Othello*, in Shakespeare, *Œuvres complètes*, 67.

27. Busch, *Verdi's "Otello" and "Simon Boccanegra,"* 2:508.

28. J. Douglas Kneale, "Deconstruction," in *The Johns Hopkins Guide to Literary Theory and Criticism*, ed. Michael Groden and Martin Kreiswirth (Baltimore: Johns Hopkins University Press, 1994), 185.

29. Sandra Corse, *Opera and the Uses of Language: Mozart, Verdi, and Britten* (Rutherford, NJ: Fairleigh Dickinson University Press, 1987), 83.

30. Busch, *Verdi's "Otello" and "Simon Boccanegra,"* 1:301.

31. Corse, *Opera and the Uses of Language*, 81.

32. Corse, 87–88.

33. Corse, 85–86.

34. Corse, 87.

35. Hepokoski, "Boito and F.-V. Hugo's 'Magnificent Translation,'" 57.

36. Julian Budden, *Verdi*, 3rd ed. (Oxford: Oxford University Press, 2008), 297.

37. Hepokoski, *Giuseppe Verdi: Otello*, 146. Hepokoski gives a reference to Budden, *The Operas of Verdi*, 3:358. Budden, however, only calls this a "unison of negative emotion," and so treats the phrase only as expressive, with no implication of a critical stance. See also Budden, *Verdi*, 297, where the "Credo" as a

whole is described as "one of the most powerful expressions of negative emotion in all music."

38. In something like this sense, Katherine Bergeron questions whether Jago's "Credo" should be understood as a creed at all—given its continuously self-denying content, poetic design, musical structure, and the shrug called for in the stage directions of the production book. Katherine Bergeron, "How to Avoid Believing (While Reading Iago's 'Credo')," in *Reading Opera*, ed. Arthur Groos and Roger Parker, 184–99 (Princeton, NJ: Princeton University Press, 1988).

Chapter 12

1. See Cone, *The Composer's Voice*, 5–17.

2. Much of Mörike's poetry is religious in subject, not surprising for works by a pastor. Mörike (1804–75) was trained in theology at Tübingen and, after several years in minor posts, settled in 1834 as pastor in the village of Cleversulzbach near Württemberg. He retired on a small pension in 1843 and moved to Mergentheim. In 1851, after his marriage, he earned extra money by lecturing on German literature at the Katharinenstift, a school for girls in Stuttgart. He resigned from this position in 1866. Susan Youens, "Doubters and Believers: Case Studies in the *Geistliche Lieder* of Eduard Mörike and Hugo Wolf," *The American Journal of Semiotics* 13, nos. 1–4 (Fall 1996 [1998]): 103–46, includes a helpful discussion of the poet's somewhat vexed experience of his vocation.

3. For a detailed discussion of these poems and the corresponding pictures, see Renate von Heydebrand, "Eduard Mörikes Gedichte zu Bildern und Zeichnungen," in *Bildende Kunst und Literatur: Beiträge zum Problem ihrer Wechselbeziehungen im neunzehnten Jahrhundert*, ed. Wolfdietrich Rasch, Studien zur Philosophie und Literatur des neunzehnten Jahrhunderts 6, 121–56 (Frankfurt am Main: Vittorio Klostermann, 1970), and plates on pp. lvii–lxxxv.

4. Heydebrand, "Eduard Mörikes Gedichte," 147.

5. Heydebrand, 147: "Denkbar wäre wohl, daß Mörike, wie August Wilhelm Schlegel in den Gemäldegedichten seiner 'Gespräche,' nur den Bildtypus in seiner Vorstellung gehabt hat; aber dann hätte er das Gedicht vielleicht doch eher 'Madonna mit dem Kind' oder ähnlich überschrieben."

6. Heydebrand, 147–48: "Ob der Künstler das Symbol des Kreuzes im Wald schon selbst angedeutet hat, ist fraglich, aber nicht ausgeschlossen. Für Mörike hätte die geringste optische Anregung genügt: . . . Wichtiger als die Frage nach der Vorlage erscheint mir die Beobachtung, daß Mörike die Meditation, zu der er den Betrachter durch ein 'Schau' auffordert, nicht schon vorwegnimmt, sondern auf das Bildsymbol des künftigen Schicksals nur den Spielraum für sie eröffnet."

7. Susan Youens, "Doubters and Believers," 131–32. Her interpretation concerns theological issues rather than the narratological ones I explore here, and there is therefore no reason that our readings cannot apply simultaneously.

8. For a discussion of the assimilation of text by music, see Susanne K. Langer, *Feeling and Form: A Theory of Art* (New York: Scribner's, 1953), chap. 10, 149–68.

9. Frank Walker, in his biography of the composer, identifies the melody as "modal, chorale-like," and Helmut Thürmer notes the song's "partly ecclesiastically colored harmony" ("zum Teil kirchlich gefärbte Harmonik"), but neither connects this style explicitly with a historical period, nor with the painting viewed in the poem. See Frank Walker, *Hugo Wolf: A Biography* (New York: Alfred A. Knopf, 1968); Helmut Thürmer, *Die Melodik in den Liedern von Hugo Wolf*, Schriften zur Music 2, ed. Walter Kolneder (Giebing über Prien am Chiemsee: Emil Katzbichler, 1970), 109.

10. Youens understands the major thirds in these cadences as inevitably, for anyone in the late nineteenth century, a reference to Bach's music. She regards this device as a symbol for redemption ("Doubters and Believers," 136).

11. For Youens, the use of inversional counterpoint between the lowest and highest voices in the texture constitutes a sort of symbolic reference to Renaissance polyphony, as well as suggesting the model of Schubert's expressive use of such contrary motion in "Der Wegweiser" in *Winterreise* (135).

12. Jean Haywood provides a description of the devices and expressive effects in this song, but she rather misleadingly refers to the texture as resembling organum, and she erroneously states that the melody moves parallel with rather than in contrary motion to the bass line. Jean I. Haywood, *The Musical Language of Hugo Wolf* (Ilfracombe, UK: Arthur H. Stockwell, 1986), 31.

13. It should be noted that I am discussing a slightly different problem from Cone's. Cone's purpose was to construct a theory that explained the *function* of the music. He proposes that the song accompaniment corresponds to a narrator in a literary work. The accompaniment, as "composer's voice," "seems to evoke and to comment on the words and implied actions of the persona portrayed by the singer" (Cone, *The Composer's Voice*, 12–13). As a way of explaining the accompaniment's function, this strikes me as a very credible model, and I do not believe my position here contradicts it. My concern, however, is not the function but the *expressiveness* of the music itself.

14. Letter to Friedrich Eckstein, a composer himself and a friend of Wolf, dated November 5, 1889, one day after the completion of "Nun wandre, Maria." Ernst Decsey, *Hugo Wolf* (Berlin: Schuster and Loeffler, 1903–6), 2:31; cited in Susan Youens, *Hugo Wolf: The Vocal Music* (Princeton, NJ: Princeton University Press, 1992), 256.

15. One could also imagine the spectator viewing the painting centuries later and actually hearing Renaissance music. This requires that we ourselves fictionalize a considerable degree of coincidence—especially for Raphael's painting, which had long been not in a church but in the Austrian imperial private collection. It would be a case of special pleading for no particular purpose.

16. Ernest Newman, *Hugo Wolf* (London: Methuen, 1907), 183. The statement about the frontispiece is Newman's; the idea about the Mörike persona is mine.

Chapter 13

1. John Erskine, "MacDowell, Edward Alexander," in *Dictionary of American Biography*, ed. Dumas Malone (New York: Scribner's, 1933), 12:26.

2. Hamlin Garland, *Roadside Meetings* (New York: Macmillan, 1931), 320.

3. From a conversation in New York in the winter of 1896. Garland, *Roadside Meetings*, 322.

4. Garland, 322–23. Erskine's recounting of MacDowell's comments to the next generation of American composers, represented by his Columbia University students in the period 1896–98, is interesting in this regard:

> In the composition class one day he spoke his mind about the material that we used. Our work, when of good enough quality, he said might pass for that of Europeans. Neither our themes nor our rhythms suggest that we lived in New York. He hastened to add that he set no value on conscious or deliberate nationalism, but an artist must accept himself for better or for worse. What we whistled, sang or played in moments of relaxation, more often than not was ragtime. Well, if syncopated rhythms were natural to us, why not try to make of them something important? "I would do it myself," he went on, "if I had not lived so long in Europe. Ragtime is not instinctive with me as it is with you—though I did make an attempt at it in the scherzo of my *Second Concerto*."

Erskine continues, "That was the first good word for jazz I ever heard." John Erskine, *The Memory of Certain Persons* (Philadelphia: J. B. Lippincott, 1947), 76–77.

5. From MacDowell's lecture on "Folk-Music." Lawrence Gilman, *Edward MacDowell: A Study* (New York: John Lane, 1908; reprinted in New York: Da Capo, 1969), 84–85.

6. Gilman, *Edward MacDowell*, 83–84.

7. Garland, *Roadside Meetings*, 323.

8. Gilman, *Edward MacDowell*, 1.

9. Gilman, 2.

10. Gilman, 64.

11. Garland, *Roadside Meetings*, 319.

12. The name of the hero is spelled variously but most authoritatively in Irish as Cú Chulainn. In the present discussion, I shall use MacDowell's spelling, which is not unusual in English.

13. This motive has been variously interpreted. Hyunjung Cho suggests that it resembles the sound of bells, but there are no bells in the legend of Cuchullin and Deirdre; see Hyunjung Cho, "The Four Piano Sonatas of Edward MacDowell" (DMA diss., Boston University, 2001). Yuchi Sophie Wang refers to it as a "fate"

motive but also refers to the idea that it imitates a bird call; see Yuchi Sophie Wang, "Edward MacDowell: A Poetic Voice as Seen in the 'Eroica' and 'Keltic' Sonatas" (DMA diss., University of Cincinnati College-Conservatory of Music, 2014), 70. Wang cites an article by Dolores Pesce, but the reference is incorrect. The bird in question should in any case be a raven, and anyone who has ever heard a raven could hardly connect its croak to the cuckoo-like two-note motive in the "Keltic" Sonata.

14. Most commentators have suggested that this quatrain is of MacDowell's own devising, but Levy attributes it to Fiona MacLeod, and Mumper says it came from the *Cycle of the Red Branch*. Alan H. Levy, *Edward MacDowell: An American Master* (Lanham, MD: Scarecrow, 1998), 167; Dwight Robert Mumper, "The Four Piano Sonatas of Edward MacDowell" (DMA diss., Indiana University, 1971).

15. Gilman, *Edward MacDowell*, 156.

16. Gilman, 157.

17. Gilman, 159–60.

18. Levy, *Edward MacDowell*, 169–70.

19. Levy, 158.

20. Dickensheets discusses the bardic "dialect" (her word) and points out the common incorporation of the harp or harp-like gestures ("Topical Vocabulary," 126–28).

21. Gilman, *Edward MacDowell*, 158.

22. Standish O'Grady, *History of Ireland: Cuculain and His Contemporaries*, vol. 2 (London: Sampson, Low, Searle, Marston, & Rivington, 1880), 280–81.

23. Elizabeth Sharp, *William Sharp (Fiona MacLeod): A Memoir* (New York: Duffield, 1910), 389–90. In the end, however, the Sonata, like MacDowell's Sonata No. 3, "Norse," was dedicated to Edvard Grieg.

24. From the cycle *Foam of the Past*, in Fiona MacLeod [William Sharp], *Poems and Dramas* (London: William Heinemann, 1912), 108–10.

25. O'Grady, *History of Ireland*, 126–27.

Chapter 14

1. Brendel, "Robert Schumann mit Rücksicht auf Mendelssohn-Bartholdy," 122.

2. Lawrence Kramer, *Music as Cultural Practice, 1800–1900*, 14.

Bibliography

Abbate, Carolyn. *Unsung Voices: Opera and Musical Narrative in the Nineteenth Century.* Princeton, NJ: Princeton University Press, 1991.

Abbate, Carolyn. "What the Sorcerer Said." *19th-Century Music* 12, no. 3 (1989): 221–30.

Abbiati, Franco. *Giuseppe Verdi.* Milan: Ricordi, 1959. 4 vols.

Adamson, Jane. *"Othello" as Tragedy: Some Problems of Judgment and Feeling.* Cambridge: Cambridge University Press, 1980.

Agawu, Kofi. *Music as Discourse: Semiotic Adventures in Romantic Music.* Oxford: Oxford University Press, 2009.

Agawu, V. Kofi. *Playing with Signs: A Semiotic Interpretation of Classic Music.* Princeton, NJ: Princeton University Press, 1991.

Albrecht, Theodore. "Beethoven and Shakespeare's *Tempest*: New Light on an Old Allusion." *Beethoven Forum* 1 (1992): 81–92.

Allanbrook, Wye J. *Rhythmic Gesture in Mozart: "Le nozze di Figaro" and "Don Giovanni."* Chicago: University of Chicago Press, 1983.

Almén, Byron. *A Theory of Musical Narrative.* Bloomington: Indiana University Press, 2008.

Austenfeld, Thomas. "'But, Come, I'll Set Your Story to a Tune': Berlioz's Interpretation of Byron's *Childe Harold.*" *Keats-Shelley Journal* 39 (1990): 83–94.

Baker, Nancy Kovaleff, and Barbara Russano Hanning. *Musical Humanism and Its Legacy: Essays in Honor of Claude V. Palisca.* Festschrift series no. 11. Stuyvesant, NY: Pendragon, 1992.

Bakhtin, Mikhail. *The Dialogic Imagination: Four Essays.* Edited by Michael Holquist, translated by Caryl Emerson and Michael Holquist. Austin: University of Texas Press, 1981.

Bal, Mieke. *Narratology: Introduction to the Theory of Narrative.* 4th ed. Toronto: University of Toronto Press, 2017.

Balthazar, Scott L. "Desdemona's Alienation and Otello's Fall." In *The Cambridge Companion to Verdi*, edited by Scott L. Balthazar, 237–54. Cambridge: Cambridge University Press, 2004.

Banks, Paul, and Hugh Macdonald. Foreword to Berlioz, *Harold en Italie*, viii–xi.

Beck, Dagmar, and Grita Herre. "Anton Schindlers fingierte Eintragungen in den Konversationsheften." In *Zu Beethoven* 1: *Aufsätze und Annotationen*, edited by Harry Goldschmidt, 11–89. Berlin: Neue Musik, 1979.

Beck, Dagmar, and Grita Herre. "Einige Zweifel an der Überlieferung der Konversationshefte." In *Bericht über den Internationalen Beethoven-Kongress: 20.–23. März 1977 in Berlin*, edited by Harry Goldschmidt et al., 257–74. Leipzig: Deutscher Verlag für Musik, VEB, 1978.

Beghelli, Marco. "Analessi, ticoscopio, ipotiposi." In *La vera storia ci narra: Verdi narrateur / Verdi narrator*, edited by Camillo Faverzani, 17–32. Lucca: Libreria Musicale Italiana, 2014.

Bekker, Paul. *Beethoven*. Berlin: Schuster & Loeffler, [1912].

Bergé, Pieter, editor. *Beethoven's Tempest Sonata (First Movement): Five Annotated Analyses for Performers and Scholars*. Leuven: Peeters, 2012.

Bergé, Pieter, Jeroen D'hoe, and William E. Caplin, editors. *Beethoven's "Tempest" Sonata: Perspectives of Analysis and Performance*. Leuven: Peeters, 2009.

Berger, Karol. "Beethoven and the Aesthetic State." *Beethoven Forum* 7 (1999): 17–44.

Berger, Karol. "Narrative and Lyric: Fundamental Poetic Forms of Composition." In Baker and Hanning, *Musical Humanism*, 451–70.

Bergeron, Katherine. "How to Avoid Believing (While Reading Iago's 'Credo')." In Groos and Parker, *Reading Opera*, 184–99.

Berlioz, Hector. *Harold en Italie*. Vol. 17 of *New Edition of the Complete Works*, by Hector Berlioz, edited by Paul Banks and Hugh Macdonald. Kassel: Bärenreiter, 2001.

Berlioz, Hector. *Mémoires de Hector Berlioz, comprenant ses voyages en Italie, en Allemagne, en Russie et en Angleterre 1803–1865*. Paris: Calmann-Lévy, [1896–97].

Berlioz, Hector. *The Memoirs of Hector Berlioz*. Translated and edited by David Cairns. New York: Knopf, 2002.

Blume, Friedrich. *Classic and Romantic Music: A Comprehensive Survey*. Translated by M. D. Herter Norton. New York: W. W. Norton, 1970.

Blume, Friedrich. "Romantik." In *Die Musik in Geschichte und Gegenwart*, edited by Friedrich Blume. Kassel: Bärenreiter, 1963.

Bonds, Mark Evan. *Absolute Music: The History of an Idea*. Oxford: Oxford University Press, 2014.

Bonds, Mark Evan. *After Beethoven: Imperatives of Originality in the Symphony*. Cambridge, MA: Harvard University Press, 1996.

Bonds, Mark Evan. *The Beethoven Syndrome: Hearing Music and Autobiography*. New York: Oxford University Press, 2020.

Bonds, Mark Evan. "*Sinfonia anti-eroica*: Berlioz's *Harold en Italie* and the Anxiety of Beethoven's Influence." *Journal of Musicology* 10, no. 4 (Fall 1992): 417–63. Revised and reprinted in Bonds, *After Beethoven*.

Booth, Wayne. *The Rhetoric of Fiction*. Chicago: University of Chicago Press, 1961.

Brauner, Charles S. "Irony in the Lieder of Schubert and Schumann." *The Musical Quarterly* 67 (1981): 261–81.

Brendel, Franz. Report on Leipzig *Abonnementskonzerte. Neue Zeitschrift für Musik* 25 (1846): 180–82.

Brendel, Franz. "Robert Schumann mit Rücksicht auf Mendelssohn-Bartholdy und die Entwicklung der modernen Tonkunst überhaupt." *Neue Zeitschrift für Musik* 22 (1845): 63–67, 81–83, 89–92, 113–15, 121–23, 145–47, 149–50. Translated by Jürgen Thym as "Robert Schumann with Reference to Mendelssohn-Bartholdy and the Development of Modern Music in General," in Todd, *Schumann and His World,* 317–37.

Brinkmann, Reinhold. "Schumann und Eichendorff: Studien zum Liederkreis, Opus 39." *Musik-Konzepte* 95 (1997): 1–89.

Brooks, Peter. "Reading for the Plot." In Hoffman and Murphy, *Essentials of the Theory of Fiction,* 201–20.

Brown, Maurice J. E. *Schubert Songs.* London: British Broadcasting Corporation, 1967.

Budden, Julian. *The Operas of Verdi.* Rev. ed. Oxford: Clarendon, 1992.

Budden, Julian. *Verdi.* 3rd ed. Oxford: Oxford University Press, 2008.

Buelow, George J. "The *Loci Topici* and Affect in Late Baroque Music: Heinichen's Practical Demonstration." *The Music Review* 27 (1966): 161–76.

Burnham, Scott. "A. B. Marx and the Gendering of Sonata Form." In *Music Theory in the Age of Romanticism,* edited by Ian Bent, 163–86. Cambridge: Cambridge University Press, 1996.

Burnham, Scott. *Beethoven Hero.* Princeton, NJ: Princeton University Press, 1995.

Burnham, Scott. "Singularities and Extremes: Dramatic Impulses in the First Movement of Beethoven's *Tempest* Sonata." In Bergé et al., *Beethoven's "Tempest" Sonata,* 39–59.

Busch, Hans, editor and translator. *Verdi's "Otello" and "Simon Boccanegra" in Letters and Documents.* Rev. ed. Oxford: Clarendon, 1988.

Byron, George Gordon [Lord Byron]. *Childe Harold's Pilgrimage.* In *The Complete Poetical Works,* edited by Jerome J. McGann. Oxford: Clarendon, 1980.

Calella, Michele. "Musik und imaginative Geographie: Franz Liszts *Années de pèlerinage* und die kulturelle Konstruktion der Schweiz." *Die Musikforschung* 65 (2012): 211–30.

Cavell, Stanley. *Must We Mean What We Say?* Updated ed. Cambridge: Cambridge University Press, 2002. Originally published in 1969 by Scribner.

Chatman, Seymour. "Discourse: Nonnarrated Stories." In Hoffman and Murphy, *Essentials of the Theory of Fiction,* 139–49.

Chatman, Seymour. *Story and Discourse: Narrative Structure in Fiction and Film.* Ithaca, NY: Cornell University Press, 1978.

Chatman, Seymour. "What Novels Can Do That Films Can't (and Vice Versa)." *Critical Inquiry* 7, no. 1 (1980): 122–40.

Cho, Hyunjung. "The Four Piano Sonatas of Edward MacDowell." DMA diss., Boston University, 2001.

Christensen, Thomas. "Narrative Theory and Music Analysis." In *Musikkonzepte—Konzepte der Musikwissenschaft: Bericht über den Internationalen Kongreß der Gesellschaft für Musikforschung, Halle (Saale) 1998*, edited by Kathrin Eberl and Wolfgang Ruf, 1:48–56. Kassel: Bärenreiter, 2000.

Chua, Daniel. *Absolute Music and the Construction of Meaning*. Cambridge: Cambridge University Press, 1999.

Chusid, Martin, editor. *A Companion to Schubert's Schwanengesang: History, Poets, Analysis, Performance*. New Haven, CT: Yale University Press, 2000.

Chusid, Martin. "Verdi's Own Words: His Thoughts on Performance, with Special Reference to *Don Carlos, Otello*, and *Falstaff*." In *The Verdi Companion*, edited by William Weaver and Martin Chusid. New York: W. W. Norton, 1979.

Citron, Marcia. *Gender and the Musical Canon*. Cambridge: Cambridge University Press, 1993.

Code, David Loberg. "Narrative Strategies in Tonal Compositions." PhD diss., University of Maryland, College Park, 1990.

Cone, Edward T. *The Composer's Voice*. Berkeley: University of California Press, 1974.

Cone, Edward T. "Inside the Saint's Head: The Music of Berlioz (Part II)." *Musical Newsletter* 1, no. 4 (October 1971): 16–21.

Cone, Edward T. "Schubert's Heine Songs." In *Hearing and Knowing Music: The Unpublished Essays of Edward T. Cone*, edited by Robert P. Morgan, 106–15. Princeton, NJ: Princeton University Press, 2009.

Conner, Theodore Albritton. "Towards an Interpretive Model of Text-Music Relations: An Analysis of Selected Scenes from Verdi's *Otello*." PhD diss., University of Connecticut, 1997.

Cooper, Barry. *Beethoven and the Creative Process*. Oxford: Clarendon, 1990.

Cooper, John Michael. "Words Without Songs? Of Texts, Titles, and Mendelssohn's *Lieder ohne Worte*." In *Musik als Text: Bericht über den 19. Kongress der Gesellschaft für Musikforschung, Freiburg im Breisgau 1993*, edited by Hermann Danuser, 2:341–45. Kassel: Bärenreiter, 1998.

Corse, Sandra. *Opera and the Uses of Language: Mozart, Verdi, and Britten*. Rutherford, NJ: Fairleigh Dickinson University Press, 1987.

Cusick, Suzanne. "Feminist Theory, Music Theory, and the Mind/Body Problem." *Perspectives of New Music* 32, no. 1 (Winter 1994): 8–27.

Czerny, Carl. *On the Proper Performance of All Beethoven's Works for the Piano: Czerny's "Reminiscences of Beethoven" and Chapters II and III from Volume IV of the "Complete Theoretical and Practical Piano Forte School op. 500."* Edited and with a commentary by Paul Badura-Skoda. Vienna: Universal, 1970.

Czerny, Carl. *School of Practical Composition*. Translated by John Bishop. London: R. Cocks, 1848. Reprinted in 1979 by Da Capo. Published in German as *Die Schule der praktischen Composition* (Bonn: Simrock, 1848).

Dadelsen, Georg von. "Robert Schumann und die Musik Bachs." *Archiv für Musik-wissenschaft* 14 (1957): 46–59.

Dahlhaus, Carl. *Die Idee der absoluten Musik.* Kassel: Bärenreiter, 1978. Published in English as *The Idea of Absolute Music,* translated by Roger Lustig. Chicago: University of Chicago Press, 1989.

Dahlhaus, Carl. *Ludwig van Beethoven: Approaches to His Music.* Translated by Mary Whittall. Oxford: Clarendon, 1991.

Dahlhaus, Carl. *Ludwig van Beethoven und seine Zeit.* Laaber: Laaber-Verlag, 1988.

Dahlhaus, Carl. *Nineteenth-Century Music.* Translated by J. Bradford Robinson. Berkeley: University of California Press, 1989.

Dahlhaus, Carl. "Studien zu romantischen Symphonien—Das 'Finalproblem' in Schumanns Zweiter Symphonie." In *Jahrbuch des Staatlichen Instituts für Musikforschung Preussischer Kulturbesitz,* edited by Dagmar Droysen, 104–19. Berlin: Staatliches Institut für Musikforschung Preussischer Kulturbesitz, 1973.

Dammeier-Kirpal, Ursula. *Der Sonatensatz bei Frédéric Chopin.* Wiesbaden: Breitkopf & Härtel, 1973.

Daverio, John. *Nineteenth-Century Music and the German Romantic Ideology.* New York: Schirmer Books, 1993.

Daverio, John. *Robert Schumann: Herald of a "New Poetic Age."* New York: Oxford University Press, 1997.

Davis, Andrew. "Chopin and the Romantic Sonata: The First Movement of Op. 58." *Music Theory Spectrum* 36 (2014): 270–94.

Davis, Andrew. "Mixed Genres and Narrativity in Chopin's B-Minor Sonata." In *Music: Function and Value—Proceedings of the 11th International Congress on Musical Signification: Cracow, 27 September–2 October 2010,* edited by Teresa Malecka and Małgorzata Pawłowska, 2:281–91. Kraków: Akademia Muzyczna w Krakowie, 2013.

Davis, Andrew. *Sonata Fragments: Romantic Narratives in Chopin, Schumann, and Brahms.* Bloomington: Indiana University Press, 2017.

Decsey, Ernst. *Hugo Wolf.* Berlin: Schuster and Loeffler, 1903–6. 4 vols.

DeNora, Tia. *Beethoven and the Construction of Genius: Musical Politics in Vienna, 1792–1803.* Berkeley: University of California Press, 1995.

Deutsch, Otto Erich. *Schubert: Die Dokumente seines Lebens.* Kassel: Bärenreiter, 1964.

Dewey, John. *Art as Experience.* New York: Capricorn, 1958.

Dickensheets, Janice. "The Topical Vocabulary of the Nineteenth Century." *Journal of Musicological Research* 31, nos. 2–3 (2012): 97–137.

D'Indy, Vincent. *Cours de composition musicale.* Bk. 2, pt. 1. Paris: Durand, 1909.

Dömling, Wolfgang. *Hector Berlioz und seine Zeit.* Laaber: Laaber-Verlag, 1986.

Dörffel, Alfred. "Für Orchester: Robert Schumann, Op. 61. Zweite Symphonie für großes Orchester." *Neue Zeitschrift für Musik* 28 (1848): 97–101.

Edler, Arnfried. "Ton und Zyklus in der Symphonik Schumanns." In Kross and Maintz, *Probleme der symphonischen Tradition,* 187–202.

Egert, Paul. *Friedrich Chopin.* Potsdam: Akademische Verlagsgeschellschaft Athenaion, [1936].

Eggebrecht, Hans Heinrich. "Prinzipien des Schubert-Liedes." *Archiv für Musikwissenschaft* 27, no. 2 (1970): 89–109.

Eichendorff, Joseph Freiherr von. *Gedichte von Joseph Freiherr von Eichendorff.* Collected by Adolf Schöll. Berlin: Duncker und Humblot, 1837.

Ellis, Katherine. "Liszt: The Romantic Artist." In *The Cambridge Companion to Liszt,* edited by Kenneth Hamilton, 1–13.

Erskine, John. "MacDowell, Eduard Alexander." In *Dictionary of American Biography,* edited by Dumas Malone. New York: Scribner's, 1933.

Erskine, John. *The Memory of Certain Persons.* Philadelphia: J. B. Lippincott, 1947.

Ferris, David. "Dissociation and Declamation in Schubert's Heine Songs." In *Rethinking Schubert,* edited by Lorraine Byrne Bodley and Julian Horton, 383–403. New York: Oxford University Press, 2016.

Ferris, David. *Schumann's Eichendorff "Liederkreis" and the Genre of the Romantic Cycle.* New York: Oxford University Press, 2000.

Fétis, François-Joseph. *Biographical Notice of Nicolo Paganini, Followed by an Analysis of His Compositions, and Preceded by a Sketch of the History of the Violin.* 2nd ed. London: Schott, 1876.

Fink, G. W. "Recensionen [on works of Henry Herz]." *Allgemeine musicalische Zeitung* 33 (January 1831): cols. 7–12.

Fink, G. W. Review of *Winterreise* and *Schwanengesang. Allgemeine musikalische Zeitung* 31, no. 40 (October 1829): cols. 653–62.

Finscher, Ludwig. "'Zwischen absoluter und Programmusik': Zur Interpretation der deutschen romantischen Symphonie." In *Über Symphonien: Beiträge zu einer musikalischen Gattung. Festschrift Walter Wiora zum 70. Geburtstag,* edited by Christoph-Hellmut Mahling, 316–27. Tutzing: Hans Schneider, 1979.

Finson, Jon W. "The Intentional Tourist: Romantic Irony in the Eichendorff *Liederkreis* of Robert Schumann." In Todd, *Schumann and His World,* 156–70.

Finson, Jon W. "The Sketches for the Fourth Movement of Schumann's Second Symphony." *Journal of the American Musicological Society* 39 (1986): 143–68.

Fischer-Dieskau, Dietrich. *Schubert's Songs: A Biographical Study.* Translated by Kenneth S. Whitton. New York: Alfred A. Knopf, 1981.

Fowler, Andrew. "Motive and Program in Liszt's 'Vallée d'Obermann.'" *Journal of the American Liszt Society* 29 (January–June 1991): 3–11.

Freud, Sigmund. *Beyond the Pleasure Principle.* Translated by C. J. M. Hubback. London: International Psycho-Analytical Press, 1922.

Frye, Northrop. *Anatomy of Criticism: Four Essays.* Princeton, NJ: Princeton University Press, 1957.

Fuhrmann, Wolfgang. "Das Land der Schweiz mit der Seele suchend: Franz Liszt's Schweiz-Erfahrung zwischen dem *Album d'un voyageur* (1840–42) und den *Années de pèlerinage 1: Suisse* (1855)." *Jahrbuch der Staatlichen Instituts für Musikforschung Preußischer Kulturbesitz* (2012): 213–46.

Garland, Hamlin. *Roadside Meetings*. New York: Macmillan, 1931.

Geck, Martin. "Das wilde Denken: Ein strukturalistischen Blick auf Beethovens op. 31,2." *Archiv für Musikwissenschaft* 57 (2000): 64–77.

Genette, Gérard. *Fiction and Diction*. Translated by Catherine Porter. Ithaca, NY: Cornell University Press, 1993.

Genette, Gérard. *Narrative Discourse: An Essay in Method*. Translated by Jane Lewin. Ithaca, NY: Cornell University Press, 1980.

Genette, Gérard. *Paratexts: Thresholds of Interpretation*. Translated by Jane E. Lewin. Cambridge: Cambridge University Press, 1997. Originally published as *Seuils*.

Genette, Gérard. "Time and Narrative in *A la recherche du temps perdu*." In Hoffman and Murphy, *Essentials of the Theory of Fiction*, 121–38.

Gerg, Ian Wyatt. "The Virtual Observing Agent in Music: A Theory of Agential Perspective as Implied by Indexical Gesture." PhD diss., University of Texas at Austin, 2015.

Gilman, Lawrence. *Edward MacDowell: A Study*. New York: John Lane, 1908. Reprinted in New York: Da Capo, 1969.

Goldschmidt, Harry. "Welches war die ursprüngliche Reihenfolge in Schuberts Heine-Lieder?" *Deutsches Jahrbuch der Musikwissenschaft für 1972* (1974): 52–62. Reprinted in Harry Goldschmidt, *Um die Sache der Musik: Reden und Aufsätze* (Leipzig: Reclam, 1976), 141–54.

Gottschald, Ernst. "Robert Schumann's zweite Symphonie: Zugleich mit Rücksicht auf andere, insbesondere Beethoven's Symphonien. Vertraute Briefe a A. Dörffel." *Neue Zeitschrift für Musik* 32 (1850): 137–39, 141–42, 145–48, 157–59.

Grabócz, Márta. *Morphologie des œuvres pour piano de Liszt*. Budapest: MTA Zenetudományi Intezét, 1987 / 2nd ed., Paris: Kimé, 1996.

Grabócz, Márta. *Musique, narrativité, signification*. Paris: L'Harmattan, 2009.

Grabócz, Márta. "The Role of Semiotical Terminology in Musical Analysis." In *Musical Semiotics in Growth*, edited by Eero Tarasti, Paul Forsell, and Richard Littlefield, 195–218. Bloomington: Indiana University Press / Imatra: International Semiotics Institute, 1996.

Grabócz, Márta. "The Two Faces of the 'mal du siècle' in Literature and in Liszt's Piano Works." *Studia musicologica: An International Journal of Musicology of the Hungarian Academy of Sciences* 55, nos. 1–2 (2014): 43–64.

Groos, Arthur, and Roger Parker, editors. *Reading Opera*. Princeton, NJ: Princeton University Press, 1988.

Gruber, Gernot. "Romantische Ironie in den Heine-Liedern?" In *Schubert-Kongress Wien 1978*, edited by Otto Busatti, 321–34. Graz: Akademische Druck- und Verlagsgesellschaft, 1979.

Hall, Michael. *Schubert's Song Sets*. Aldershot: Ashgate, 2003.

Halm, August. *Von zwei Kulturen der Musik*. Munich: G. Müller, 1913.

Hamilton, Kenneth. "Beethoven's Tempest Sonata in Performance." In Bergé et al., *Beethoven's "Tempest" Sonata*, 127–61.

Hamilton, Kenneth, editor. *The Cambridge Companion to Liszt*. Cambridge: Cambridge University Press, 2005.

Hamilton, Kenneth. "Liszt's Early and Weimar Piano Works." In Hamilton, *The Cambridge Companion to Liszt*, 57–85.

Hascher, Xavier. "'In dunkeln Träumen': Schubert's Heine-Lieder Through the Psychoanalytical Prism." *Nineteenth-Century Music Review* 5, no. 2 (2008): 43–70.

Hatten, Robert S. "Interpreting Beethoven's *Tempest* Sonata Through Topics, Gestures, and Agency." In Bergé et al., *Beethoven's "Tempest" Sonata*, 163–80.

Hatten, Robert S. *Musical Meaning in Beethoven: Markedness, Correlation, and Interpretation*. Bloomington: Indiana University Press, 1994.

Hatten, Robert S. "On Narrativity in Music: Expressive Genres and Levels of Discourse in Beethoven." *Indiana Theory Review* 12 (1991): 75–98.

Hatten, Robert S. *A Theory of Virtual Agency for Western Music*. Bloomington: Indiana University Press, 2018.

Hawes, Jane. *An Examination of Verdi's "Otello" and Its Faithfulness to Shakespeare*. Lewiston, NY: Edwin Mellen, 1994.

Haywood, Jean I. *The Musical Language of Hugo Wolf*. Ilfracombe, UK: Arthur H. Stockwell, 1986.

Heinemann, Michael. "Lesen Sie nur Shakespeares Sturm." *Musica* 45, no. 5 (1991): 301–2.

Heinichen, Johann David. *Der General-Bass in der Composition*. Dresden, 1728.

Hensel, Fanny. *The Letters of Fanny Hensel to Felix Mendelssohn*. Edited by Marcia Citron. Pendragon, 1987.

Hepokoski, James. "Approaching the First Movement of Beethoven's *Tempest* Sonata Through Sonata Theory." In Bergé et al., *Beethoven's "Tempest" Sonata*, 181–212.

Hepokoski, James. "Boito and F.-V. Hugo's 'Magnificent Translation': A Study in the Genesis of the *Otello* Libretto." In Groos and Parker, *Reading Opera*, 34–50.

Hepokoski, James. *Giuseppe Verdi: Otello*. Cambridge: Cambridge University Press, 1987.

Hepokoski, James. "Masculine—Feminine." *The Musical Times* 135 (August 1994): 494–99.

Hepokoski, James, and Warren Darcy. *Elements of Sonata Theory: Norms, Types, and Deformations in the Late-Eighteenth-Century Sonata*. New York: Oxford University Press, 2006.

Heydebrand, Renate von. "Eduard Mörikes Gedichte zu Bildern und Zeichnungen." In *Bildende Kunst und Literatur: Beiträge zum Problem ihrer Wechselbeziehungen im neunzehnten Jahrhundert*, edited by Wolfdietrich Rasch, Studien zur Philosophie und Literatur des neunzehnten Jahrhunderts 6, 121–56. Frankfurt am Main: Vittorio Klostermann, 1970.

Hoffman, Michael, and Patrick D. Murphy, editors. *Essentials of the Theory of Fiction*. 3rd ed., Durham, NC: Duke University Press, 2005.

Holoman, D. Kern. *Berlioz*. Cambridge, MA: Harvard University Press, 1989.

Horton, Julian. "Listening to Topics in the Nineteenth Century." In Mirka, *Oxford Handbook of Topic Theory*, 642–64.

Huber, Annegret. "Das 'Lied ohne Worte' Mendelssohns: Zu seiner Zeit und zur 'Biedermeierdiskussionszeit.'" *Zeit in der Musik—Musik in der Zeit*, edited by Diether de La Motte, 105–21. Frankfurt am Main: Peter Lang, 1997.

Hughes, William H., Jr. "Liszt's *Première année de pèlerinage: Suisse*: A Comparative Study of Early and Revised Versions." DMA diss., Eastman School of Music, University of Rochester, 1985.

Istel, Edgar. "Elf ungedrückte Briefe Liszts an Schott." *Die Musik* 5, no. 19 (1906): 43–52.

Jensen, Eric Frederick. "Explicating Jean Paul: Robert Schumann's Program for *Papillons*, Op. 2." *19th-Century Music* 22, no. 2 (Fall 1998): 127–43.

Jones, Timothy. *Beethoven: The "Moonlight" and Other Sonatas, Op. 27 and Op. 31.* Cambridge: Cambridge University Press, 1999.

Jost, Christa. *Mendelssohns Lieder ohne Worte.* Frankfurter Beiträge zur Musikwissenschaft 14. Tutzing: Schneider, 1988.

Jung-Kaiser, Ute. "'O wer sehen könnte . . .': Eduard Mörikes Bildgedichte und ihre klangliche Visualisierung bei Hugo Wolf." In *Wie Bilder klingen: Neue Innsbrucker Beiträge zur Musikwissenschaft*, no. 1, edited by Lukas Christensen and Monika Fink, 3–53. Vienna: Lit, 2011.

Kallberg, Jeffrey. "The Harmony of the Tea Table: Gender and Ideology in the Piano Nocturne." *Representations* 39 (1992): 102–33. Reprinted in Jeffrey Kallberg, *Chopin at the Boundaries: Sex, History, and Musical Genre* (Cambridge, MA: Harvard University Press, 1996), 30–61.

Kawabata, Maiko. *Paganini: The "Demonic" Virtuoso.* Rochester: Boydell, 2013.

Kawabata, Maiko. "Virtuosity, the Violin, the Devil . . . What *Really* Made Paganini 'Demonic'?" *Current Musicology* 83 (Spring 2007): 85–108.

Killmayer, Wilhelm. "Schumann und seine Dichter." *Neue Zeitschrift für Musik* 142, no. 3 (1981): 231–36.

Kirby, F. E. "Liszt's Pilgrimage." *Piano Quarterly* 89 (Spring 1975): 17–21.

Kivy, Peter. "Contra the Hypothetical Persona in Music." In *Emotion and the Arts*, edited by Mette Hjort and Sue Laver, 95–109. Oxford: Oxford University Press, 1997.

Klein, Michael. "Chopin's Fourth Ballade as a Musical Narrative." *Music Theory Spectrum* 26 (2001): 23–55.

Klein, Michael. *Intertextuality in Western Art Music.* Bloomington: Indiana University Press, 2005.

Klein, Michael. *Music and Narrative Since 1900.* Bloomington: Indiana University Press, 2018.

Klorman, Edward. *Mozart's Music of Friends: Social Interplay in the Chamber Works.* Cambridge: Cambridge University Press, 2016.

Knaus, Herwig. *Musiksprache und Werkstruktur in Robert Schumanns "Liederkreis."* Schriften zur Musik 27. Munich: Katzbichler, 1974.

Kneale, J. Douglas. "Deconstruction." In *The Johns Hopkins Guide to Literary Theory and Criticism*, edited by Michael Groden and Martin Kreiswirth. Baltimore: Johns Hopkins University Press, 1994.

Knittel, K. M. "Schindler, Anton Felix." In *The New Grove Dictionary of Music and Musicians*, 2nd ed., edited by Stanley Sadie, 22:51. London: Macmillan, 2001.

Koch, Heinrich Christoph. *Musikalisches Lexicon: Auf Grundlage des Lexicon's von H. Ch. Koch.* 2nd ed. Heidelberg: J. C. B. Mohr, 1865.

Kolb, Jocelyne. "'Die Puppenspiele meines Humors': Heine and Romantic Irony." *Studies in Romanticism* 26 (1987): 399–419.

Konold, Wulf. "'Credo in un Dio crudel . . .': Die Figur des Jago bei Shakespeare und Boito/Verdi." *Musik und Bildung* 20, no. 2 (1988): 121–27.

Kramer, Lawrence. "Beethoven's Tempest Sonata: Musical Meaning and Enlightenment Anthropology." *Beethoven Forum* 6 (1998): 31–65.

Kramer, Lawrence. "Musical Narratology: A Theoretical Outline." *Indiana Theory Review* 12 (1991): 141–62.

Kramer, Lawrence. *Music as Cultural Practice 1800–1900.* Berkeley: University of California Press, 1990.

Kramer, Lawrence. Review of *Unsung Voices: Opera and Musical Narrative in the Nineteenth Century*, by Carolyn Abbate. *19th-Century Music* 15, no. 3 (Spring 1992): 235–39.

Kramer, Lawrence. "The Schubert Lied: Romantic Form and Romantic Consciousness." In *Schubert: Critical and Analytical Studies*, edited by Walter Frisch, 200–237. Lincoln: University of Nebraska Press, 1986.

Kramer, Richard. "Schubert's Heine." *19th-Century Music* 8 (1985): 213–25. Reprinted in Richard Kramer, *Distant Cycles: Schubert and the Conceiving of Song* (Chicago: University of Chicago Press, 1994), 125–47.

Kross, Siegfried, and Marie Luise Maintz. *Probleme der symphonischen Tradition im 19. Jahrhundert: Internationales Musikwissenschaftliches Colloquium, Bonn 1989.* Tutzing: Hans Schneider, 1990.

Kurtzmann, Jeffrey. "The Iagoization of *Otello*: A Study in Verdi's Musical Translation of Shakespeare's Linguistic Dramaturgy." In *Sonic Transformations of Literary Texts: From Program Music to Musical Ekphrasis*, edited by Siglind Bruhn, 69–101. Hillsdale, NY: Pendragon, 2008.

La Mara. *Franz Liszts Briefe.* Vol. 4. Leipzig: Breitkopf & Härtel, 1899.

Langer, Susanne K. *Feeling and Form: A Theory of Art.* New York: Scribner's, 1953.

Langford, Jeffrey. "The 'Dramatic Symphonies' of Berlioz as an Outgrowth of the French Opera Tradition." *The Musical Quarterly* 69, no. 1 (Winter 1983): 85–103.

LaRue, Jan. *Guidelines for Style Analysis.* 2nd ed. Warren, MI: Harmonie Park Press, 1992.

Leichtentritt, Hugo. *Analyse von Chopins Klavierwerken.* Berlin: Max Hesse, 1922.

Leichtentritt, Hugo. *Musical Form*. Cambridge, MA: Harvard University Press, 1951. Originally published as *Musikalische Formenlehre*, 4th ed. (Leipzig: Breitkopf & Härtel, 1948).

Levy, Alan H. *Edward MacDowell: An American Master*. Lanham, MD: Scarecrow, 1998.

Lim, Cheng Wei. "Heroic Narratives and Chopin's Polonaise in A♭ Major, Op. 53." *19th-Century Music* 46, no. 2 (2022): 163–93.

Litschauer, Walburga. "The Origin and Early Reception of *Schwanengesang*." In *A Companion to Schubert's "Schwanengesang": History, Poets, Analysis, Performance*, edited by Martin Chusid, 5–13. New Haven, CT: Yale University Press, 2000.

Litterick, Louise. "Recycling Schubert: On Reading Richard Kramer's *Distant Cycles: Schubert and the Conceiving of Song*." *19th-Century Music* 20, no. 1 (Summer 1996): 77–95.

Litzmann, Berthold, editor. *Clara Schumann, Johannes Brahms: Brief aus den Jahren 1853–1896*. Leipzig: Breitkopf & Hartel, 1927.

Lyser, Johann Peter. "Felix Mendelssohn-Bartholdy." *Wiener Musik-Zeitung* 2, no. 154 (December 24, 1842): 617–18.

Maass, Ingeborg. "Zur Bach-Rezeption in Schumanns C-Dur Symphonie op. 61." In *Robert Schumann: Philologische, analytische, sozial- und rezeptionsgeschichtliche Aspekte*, Saarbrücker Studien zur Musikwissenschaft No. 8, edited by Wolf Frobenius, Ingeborg Maass, Markus Waldura, and Tobias Widmaier, 97–105. Saarbrücken: Saarbrücker Drückerei, 1998.

Maass, Ingeborg. "Zwischen absoluter und Progammusik? Zum Finale von Schumanns C-Dur Symphonie op. 61." In *Aspekte historischer und systematischer Musikforschung: Zur Symphonie im 19. Jahrhundert, zu Fragen der Musiktheorie, der Wahrnehmung von Musik und Anderes*, Schriften zur Musikwissenschaft 5, edited by Christoph-Hellmut Mahling and Kristina Pfarr, 133–40. Mainz: Are, 2002.

Macdonald, Hugh. *Berlioz*. Oxford: Oxford University Press, 1982.

MacLeod, Fiona [William Sharp]. *Poems and Dramas*. London: William Heinemann, 1912.

Marx, Adolf Bernhard. *Anleitung zum Vortrag Beethovenscher Klavierwerke*. Berlin: Otto Janke, 1863.

Marx, Adolf Bernhard. *Die Lehre von der musikalischen Komposition, praktisch theoretisch*. 3rd ed. Leipzig: Breitkopf & Härtel, 1856–63.

Marx, Eduardo. *Heidegger und der Ort der Musik*. Würzburg: Königshausen & Neumann, 1998.

Maurel, Victor. *Dix ans de carrière: 1887–1897*. Paris: Paul Dupont, 1897. Reprinted in New York: Arno, 1977.

Maus, Fred. "Music as Drama." *Music Theory Spectrum* 10 (1988): 56–73.

Mayeda, Akio. *Robert Schumanns Weg zur Symphonie*. Zurich: Atlantis / Mainz: Schott, 1992.

McClary, Susan. *Feminine Endings: Music, Gender, and Sexuality.* Minneapolis: University of Minnesota Press, 1991.

McCreless, Patrick. "Song Order in the Song Cycle: Schumann's *Liederkreis*, Op. 39." *Music Analysis* 5, no. 1 (1986): 5–28.

Mendelssohn Bartholdy, Felix. *Sämtliche Briefe Felix Mendelsson Bartholdy.* Edited by Helmut Loos and Wilhelm Seidel. Kassel: Bärenreiter, 2008–17.

Medici, Mario, and Marcello Conati, editors. *Carteggio Verdi-Boito.* Parma: Istituto di Studi Verdiani, 1978. English-language edition by William Weaver, *The Verdi Correspondence.* Chicago: University of Chicago Press, 1994.

Mercer-Taylor, Peter. "Mendelssohn's 'Scottish' Symphony and the Music of German Memory." *19th-Century Music* 19, no. 1 (Summer 1995): 68–82.

Millard, Russell. "Telling Tales: A Survey of Narratological Approaches to Music." *Current Musicology* 103 (Fall 2018): 5–44.

Miller, Norbert. "In Obermans Tal: Franz Liszt und die Alpenbegeisterung der Jahre nach 1830." In *Die Schweiz und ihre Landschaft in slavischer Lyrik,* edited by Peter Brang, 65–87. Mainz: Akademie der Wissenschaften und der Literatur, 2000.

Mirka, Danuta, editor. *The Oxford Handbook of Topic Theory.* New York: Oxford University Press, 2014.

Misch, Ludwig. *Beethoven Studies.* Norman: University of Oklahoma Press, 1953.

Monahan, Seth. "Action and Agency Revisited." *Journal of Music Theory* 57, no. 2 (Fall 2013): 321–71.

Monahan, Seth. "'Inescapable' Coherence and the Failure of the Novel-Symphony in the Finale of Mahler's Sixth." *19th-Century Music* 31, no. 1 (Summer 2007): 53–95.

Monahan, Seth. "Mahler's Sonata Narratives." PhD diss., Yale University, 2008.

Monelle, Raymond. *The Musical Topic: Hunt, Military and Pastoral.* Bloomington: Indiana University Press, 2006.

Monelle, Raymond. *The Sense of Music: Semiotic Essays.* Princeton, NJ: Princeton University Press, 2000.

Morgan, Robert P. Review of *Unsung Voices: Opera and Musical Narrative in the Nineteenth Century,* by Carolyn Abbate. *The Journal of Modern History* 64, no. 3 (September 1992): 576–81.

Mumper, Dwight Robert. "The Four Piano Sonatas of Edward MacDowell." DMA diss., Indiana University, 1971.

Musgrave, Michael. "Fragments of a Secret Life." *Times Literary Supplement,* no. 5141 (October 12, 2001): 18.

Nattiez, Jean-Jacques. "Can One Speak of Narrativity in Music?" *Journal of the Royal Musical Association* 115 (1990): 240–57.

Nauhaus, Gerd. "Final-Lösungen in der Symphonik Schumanns." In Kross and Maintz, *Probleme der symphonischen Tradition,* 307–20. Translated by Susan

Gillespie as "Schumann's Symphonic Finales," in Todd, *Schumann and His World*, 113–28.

Neubauer, John. "Tales of Hoffmann and Others: On Narrativizations of Instrumental Music." In *Interart Poetics: Essays on the Interrelations of the Arts and Media*, ed. Ulla-Britta Lagerroth, Hans Lund, and Erik Hedling, 117–36. Amsterdam: Rodopi, 1996.

Newcomb, Anthony. "Once More 'Between Absolute and Program Music': Schumann's Second Symphony." *19th-Century Music* 7, no. 3 (April 3, 1984): 233–50.

Newman, Ernest. *Hugo Wolf.* London: Methuen, 1907.

Newman, William S. *Beethoven on Beethoven: Playing the Piano Sonatas His Way.* New York: Norton, 1988.

Niemöller, Klaus W. "Das Fugato als Ausdrucksmittel im 19. Jahrhundert." In *Festschrift Walter Wiora zum 30. Dezember 1966*, edited by Ludwig Finscher and Christoph-Helmut Mahling, 413–18. Kassel: Bärenreiter, 1967.

Noske, Frits. *The Signifier and the Signified: Studies in the Operas of Mozart and Verdi.* The Hague: Martinus Nijhoff, 1977.

Nowik, Wojciech. "Chopin's Sonata Counter-Type: Error of Construction or Innovative Ideas." In Poniotowska, *Chopin and His Work*, 334–40.

O'Grady, Standish. *History of Ireland: Cuculain and His Contemporaries.* Vol. 2. London: Sampson, Low, Searle, Marston, & Rivington, 1880.

"Otto Dresel's Soirees." *Dwight's Journal of Music* 8, no. 22 (March 1, 1856): 174.

Parr, Sean M. "Caroline Carvalho and Nineteenth-Century Coloratura." *Cambridge Opera Journal* 23, nos. 1–2 (2012): 83–117.

Pembaur, Josef. *Ludwig van Beethovens Sonaten op. 31 Nr. 2 u. op. 57.* Munich: Wunderhorn, 1915.

Pesce, Dolores. "Expressive Resonance in Liszt's Piano Music." In *Nineteenth-Century Piano Music*, edited by R. Larry Todd, 395–452. New York: Schirmer Books, 1990.

Petty, Wayne C. "Chopin and the Ghost of Beethoven." *19th-Century Music* 22, no. 3 (Spring 1999): 281–99.

Poniotowska, Irena. *Chopin and His Work in the Context of Culture.* Kraków: Polska Akademia Chopinowska, 2003.

Prawer, Siegbert Salomon. *Heine: Buch der Lieder.* Great Neck, NY: Barron's Educational Series / London: Arnold, 1960.

Prince, Gerald. *Narratology: The Form and Functioning of Narrative.* Berlin: Mouton, 1974.

Pritchard, Matthew. "'The Moral Background of the Work of Art': 'Character' in German Musical Aesthetics." *Eighteenth-Century Music* 9, no. 1 (March 2012): 63–80.

Ratner, Leonard. *Classic Music: Expression, Form, and Style.* New York: Schirmer, 1980.

Ratner, Leonard. *Romantic Music: Sound and Syntax.* New York: Schirmer, 1992.

Ratz, Erwin. *Einführung in die Musikalische Formenlehre: Über Formprinzipien in den Inventionen und Fugen J. S. Bachs und ihre Bedeutung für die Kompositionstechnik Beethovens.* 3rd ed. Vienna: Universal, 1973.

Reich, Nancy B. "The Correspondence Between Clara Wieck Schumann and Felix and Paul Mendelssohn." In Todd, *Schumann and His World*, 205–32.

Reicha, Anton. *Traité de mélodie.* Paris: Chez l'auteur, impr. de J. L. Scherff, 1814.

Reininghaus, Frieder. "Studie zur bürgerlichen Musiksprache Mendelssohns 'Lieder ohne Worte' als historisches, ästhetisches und politisches Problem." *Die Musikforschung* 28, no. 1 (1975): 34–51.

Review of Piano Sonata in B Minor, by Frédéric Chopin. *Neue Zeitschrift für Musik* 23 (September 16, 1845): 89–90.

Review of Piano Trio in D Minor, op. 11, by Fanny Hensel. *Neue Berliner Musik Zeitung* 1 (1847): 231–32.

Review of Sonata No. 3 in B Minor, op. 58, by Frédéric Chopin. *Allgemeine musikalische Zeitung* 48, no. 5 (February 4, 1846): 74–75.

Reynolds, Christopher Alan. *Motives for Allusion: Context and Content in Nineteenth-Century Music.* Cambridge, MA: Harvard University Press, 2003.

Rice, John A. Review of *The Oxford Handbook of Topic Theory*, edited by Danuta Mirka. *Journal of the American Musicological Society* 68 (2015): 447–53.

Ricoeur, Paul. "Narrative Time." *Critical Inquiry* 7, no. 1 (1980): 169–90.

Ricoeur, Paul. *Time and Narrative.* Chicago: University of Chicago Press, 1984–88. 3 vols.

Riemann, Hugo. *L. van Beethovens sämtliche Klavier-Solosonaten.* Vol. 2. Berlin: Max Hesse, 1919.

Riezler, Walter. *Beethoven.* New York: E. P. Dutton, 1938.

Riggs, Robert. "'On the Representation of Character in Music': Christian Gottfried Körner's Aesthetics of Instrumental Music." *The Musical Quarterly* 81, no. 4 (Winter 1997): 599–631.

Rink, John S. "Translating Musical Meaning: The Nineteenth-Century Performer as Narrator." In *Rethinking Music*, edited by Nicholas Cook and Mark Everist, 217–38. Oxford: Oxford University Press, 1999.

Roesner, Linda Correll. "Tonal Strategy and Poetic Content in Schumann's C-Major Symphony, Op. 61." In Kross and Maintz, *Probleme der symphonischen Tradition*, 295–306.

Rosen, Charles. *The Classical Style: Haydn, Mozart, Beethoven.* New York: Norton, 1971.

Rosen, Charles. *The Romantic Generation.* Cambridge, MA: Harvard University Press, 1995.

Rosen, Charles. *Sonata Forms.* New York: Norton, 1988.

Rousseau, Jean-Jacques. *Confessions.* Paris, 1819.

Salinas, Edgardo. "The Form of Paradox as the Paradox of Form: Beethoven's 'Tempest,' Schlegel's Critique, and the Production of Absence." *Journal of Musicology* 33, no. 4 (Fall 2016): 483–521.

Sand, George. Preface to Senancour, *Obermann*, 1–16.

Senancour, Étienne Pivert de. *Obermann*. Rev. ed. Paris: Charpentier, 1847.

Schering, Arnold. *Beethoven in neuer Deutung*. Leipzig: C. F. Kahnt, 1934.

Schiller, Friedrich. "On the Tragic Art." In *Works of Friedrich Schiller*, vol. 8, *Aesthetical and Philosophical Essays*. Boston: S. E. Cassino, 1884.

Schindler, Anton Felix. *Beethoven as I Knew Him*. Edited by Donald W. MacArdle, translated by Constance S. Jolly. Chapel Hill: University of North Carolina Press, 1966.

Schindler, Anton Felix. *Biographie von Ludwig van Beethoven*. 4th ed. Münster: Aschendorff, 1871. Reprinted in Hildesheim: Olms, 1970; originally published in 1840; rev. 3rd ed. 1860.

Schlegel, August Wilhelm. "Über Zeichnungen zu Gedichten und Johann Flaxmanns Umrisse." In *Athenaeum: Eine Zeitschrift von August Wilhelm Schlegel und Friedrich Schlegel*, vol. 2, edited by Curt Grützmacher, 73–104. Munich: Rowohlt, 1969.

Schlegel, Friedrich. "Brief über den Roman." In *Kritische Friedrich-Schlegel Ausgabe*, vol. 2, edited by Hans Eichner. Zurich: Thomas, 1967.

Schmalfeldt, Janet. "Form as the Process of Becoming: The Beethoven-Hegelian Tradition and the 'Tempest' Sonata." *Beethoven Forum* 4 (1995): 37–71.

Schmidt, Thomas Christian. *Die ästhetischen Grundlagen der Instrumentalmusik Felix Mendelssohn Bartholdys*. Stuttgart: M & P Verlag für Wissenschaft und Forschung, 1996.

Schmitz, Arnold. *Beethovens "zwei Prinzipe": Ihre Bedeutung für Themen- und Satzbau*. Berlin: F. Dümmler, 1923.

Schmusch, Rainer. *Der Tod des Orpheus: Entstehungsgeschichte der Programmusik*. Freiburg im Breisgau: Rombach, 1998.

Schmusch, Rainer. "Programmusik als musikalisch Autobiographie und Katharsis." In *Hector Berlioz: Autopsie des Künstlers*, by Rainer Schmusch, Musik-Konzepte 108, 69–86. Munich: text+kritik, 2000.

Scholes, Robert. *Fabulation and Metafiction*. Urbana: University of Illinois Press, 1979.

Scholes, Robert, and Robert Kellogg. *The Nature of Narrative*. New York: Oxford University Press, 1966.

Schopenhauer, Arthur. *Die Welt als Wille und Vorstellung*. Vols. 1–2 of *Sämtliche Werke*, edited by Wolfgang Frhr. von Löheneysen. Stuttgart: Cotta, 1960.

Schopenhauer, Arthur. *The World as Will and Idea*. 7th ed. Translated by R. B. Haldane and J. Kemp. London: Kegan Paul, Trench, Trübner, 1909.

Schumann, Robert. *Briefe: Neue Folge*. 2nd ed., edited by F. Gustav Jansen. Leipzig: Breitkopf & Härtel, 1904.

Schumann, Robert. "Ein Opus II." *Allgemeine musikalische Zeitung* 33 (1831): cols. 805–8. Translated as "An Opus 2" in Strunk, *Source Readings in Music History*, 1144–45.

Schumann, Robert. "Felix Mendelssohn, sechs Lieder ohne Worte für das Pianoforte. Zweites Heft." *Neue Zeitschrift für Musik* 2 (June 23, 1835): 202.

Schumann, Robert. *Gesammelte Schriften über Musik und Musiker.* 5th ed., edited by Martin Kreisig. Leipzig: Breitkopf & Härtel, 1914.

Schumann, Robert. *Tagebücher.* Vol. 3, *Haushaltbücher: Teil I, 1837–47,* edited by Gerd Nauhaus. Leipzig: VEB Deutscher Verlag für Musik, 1982.

Seaton, Douglass. "Interpreting Schubert's Heine Songs." *The Music Review* 53, no. 2 (May 1992): 85–99.

Seaton, Douglass. "The Problem of the Lyric Persona in Mendelssohn's Songs." In *Felix Mendelssohn Bartholdy: Kongreß-Bericht 1994,* edited by Christian Martin Schmidt, 167–86. Wiesbaden: Breitkopf & Härtel, 1997.

Seaton, Douglass. Review of *The Beethoven Syndrome,* by Mark Evan Bonds. *Music & Letters* 102, no. 1 (February 2021): 155–58.

Seaton, Douglass. Review of *A Theory of Musical Narrative,* by Byron Almén. *Journal of Musicological Research* 30, no. 1 (2011): 72–76.

Seaton, Douglass. "Symphony and Overture." In *The Cambridge Companion to Mendelssohn,* edited by Peter Mercer-Taylor, 91–111. Cambridge: Cambridge University Press, 2004.

Shakespeare, William. *Œuvres complètes de W. Shakespeare: Les Jaloux: Cymbeline—Othello.* Vol. 5, translated by François-Victor Hugo. Paris: Pagnerre, 1860.

Sharp, Elizabeth. *William Sharp (Fiona MacLeod): A Memoir.* New York: Duffield, 1910.

Shaw, George Bernard. *Shaw's Music: The Complete Musical Criticism in Three Volumes.* 2nd rev. ed., edited by Dan H. Laurence. London: Bodley Head, 1989.

Souchay, Marc-André, and Felix Mendelssohn. "An Exchange of Letters." In Strunk, *Source Readings in Music History,* 1198–201.

Stadlen, Peter. "Schindler's Beethoven Forgeries." *The Musical Times* 118 (1977): 549–52.

Stadlen, Peter. "Schindler und die Konversationshefte." *Österreichische Musikzeitschrift* 34, no. 1 (1979): 2–18.

Stadlen, Peter. "Zu Schindlers Fälschungen in Beethovens Konversationsheften." *Österreichische Musikzeitschrift* 32, nos. 5–6 (1977): 246–52.

Stein, Jack, "Schubert's Heine Songs." *Journal of Aesthetics and Art Criticism* 24 (1966): 559–66.

Steinberg, Michael P. "Schumann's Homelessness." In Todd, *Schumann and His World,* 47–79.

Strandberg, Kristen. "Art or Artifice? Violin Virtuosity and Aesthetics in Parisian Criticism, 1831–1848." PhD diss., Indiana University, 2014.

Strunk, Oliver, editor. *Source Readings in Music History.* Rev. ed., Leo Treitler, general editor. New York: W. W. Norton, 1998.

Sulzer, Johann Georg. *Allgemeine Theorie der schönen Künste.* Leipzig: Weidmann, 1792. Reprinted in 1970 by George Olms. 5 vols.

Sutermeister, Peter, editor. *Felix Mendelssohn Bartholdy: Lebensbild mit Vorgeschichte, Reisebriefe von 1830/31 aus Deutschland, Italien und der Schweiz.* Zurich: Ex Libris-Verlag, 1949.

Taddie, Daniel. "The Devil, You Say: Reflections on Verdi's and Boito's Iago." *The Opera Quarterly* 7, no. 1 (1990): 52–71.

Tarasti, Eero. "The Case of *Obermann*: Franz Liszt and Marie d'Agoult in Switzerland." In *Interdisciplinary Studies in Musicology: Report from the First Interdisciplinary Conference, Poznań, November 23–24 1991*, edited by Maciej Jabłoński and Jan Stęszewski, 90–105. Poznań: Ars nova, 1993.

Tarasti, Eero. "Chopin and the Transcendental Subject: Body and Transcendence in Chopinian Aesthetics." In Poniotowska, *Chopin and His Work*, 195–214.

Tarasti, Eero. *A Theory of Musical Semiotics*. Bloomington: Indiana University Press, 1994.

Taylor, Benedict. "Absent Subjects and Empty Centers: Eichendorff's Romantic Phantasmagoria and Schumann's *Liederkreis*, Op. 39." *19th-Century Music* 40, no. 3 (Spring 2017): 201–22.

Tempera, Mariangela. "Otello: Da Verdi a Shakespeare." In *Tre secoli di Otello*, edited by Elena Sala Di Felice and Laura Sanna, 71–93. Rome: Bulzoni, 1999.

Thürmer, Helmut. *Die Melodik in den Liedern von Hugo Wolf.* Schriften zur Music 2, edited by Walter Kolneder. Giebing über Prien am Chiemsee: Emil Katzbichler, 1970.

Thym, Jürgen. "A Cycle in Flux: Schumann's Eichendorff *Liederkreis*." In *Of Poetry and Song: Approaches to the Nineteenth-Century Lied*, edited by Jürgen Thym, 375–89. Rochester, NY: University of Rochester Press, 2010.

Thym, Jürgen. "The Solo Song Settings of Eichendorff's Poems by Schumann and Wolf." PhD diss., Case Western Reserve University, 1974.

Tillard, Françoise. *Fanny Mendelssohn*. Translated by Camille Naish. Portland, OR: Amadeus, 1992.

Tischler, Louise, and Hans Tischler. "Mendelssohn's *Songs Without Words*." *The Musical Quarterly* 33, no. 1 (January 1947): 1–16.

Tischler, Louise, and Hans Tischler. "Mendelssohn's Style: The *Songs Without Words*." *The Music Review* 8 (1947): 256–73.

Todd, R. Larry. *Fanny Hensel: The Other Mendelssohn*. Oxford: Oxford University Press, 2010.

Todd, R. Larry. "'Gerade das Lied wie es dasteht': On Text and Meaning in Mendelssohn's *Lieder ohne Worte*." In Baker and Hanning, *Musical Humanism*, 355–79.

Todd, R. Larry. *Mendelssohn: A Life in Music*. Oxford: Oxford University Press, 2003.

Todd, R. Larry. *Mendelssohn Essays*. New York: Routledge, 2008.

Todd, R. Larry. *Mendelssohn: "The Hebrides" and Other Overtures*. Cambridge: Cambridge University Press, 1993.

Todd, R. Larry. "Mendelssohn's *Lieder ohne Worte* and the Limits of Musical Expression." In *Mendelssohn Perspectives*, edited by Nicole Grimes and Angela R. Mace, 197–222. Farnham, UK: Ashgate, 2012.

Todd, R. Larry. "Mendelssohn's Ossianic Manner, with a New *Source:* 'On Lena's Gloomy Heath.'" In *Mendelssohn and Schumann: Essays on Their Music and Its

Context, edited by Jon W. Finson and R. Larry Todd, 136–60. Durham, NC: Duke University Press, 1984. Reprinted in Todd, *Mendelssohn Essays*, 57–79.

Todd, R. Larry. "On Quotation in Schumann's Music." In Todd, *Schumann and His World*, 80–112.

Todd, R. Larry, editor. *Schumann and His World*. Princeton, NJ: Princeton University Press, 1994.

Todorov, Tzvetan. *Introduction to Poetics*. Translated by Richard Howard. Brighton: Harvester, 1981.

Todorov, Tzvetan. *The Poetics of Prose*. Translated by Richard Howard. Ithaca, NY: Cornell University Press, 1977. Originally published as *Poétique de la prose* (Paris: Seuil, 1971).

Toolan, Michael J. *Narrative: A Critical Linguistic Introduction*. New York: Routledge, 1988.

Tovey, Donald Francis. *A Companion to Beethoven's Pianoforte Sonatas*. London: Associated Board of the Royal Schools of Music, 1948.

Toye, Francis. *Rossini: A Study in Tragi-Comedy*. New York: Norton, 1963.

Turchin, Barbara. "Schumann's Song Cycles: The Cycle Within the Song." *19th-Century Music* 8, no. 3 (1985): 231–44.

Türk, Daniel Gottlob. *Klavierschule, oder Anweisung zum Klavierspielen für Lehrer und Lernende, mit kritischen Anmerkungen*. Leipzig: Schwickert / Halle: Hemmerde un Schwetschke, 1789.

Urchueguía, Cristina, and Roger Lüdeke. "Der Doppelgänger: Für eine funktionsgeschichtliche Beschreibung von Schuberts Heine-Vertonung." *Deutsche Vierteljahrschift für Literaturwissenschaft und Geistesgeschichte* 74, no. 2 (2000): 279–304.

Vande Moortele, Steven. "The First Movement of Beethoven's *Tempest* Sonata and the Tradition of Twentieth-Century 'Formenlehre.'" In Bergé et al., *Beethoven's "Tempest" Sonata*, 293–314.

Waldura, Markus. "Vier romantische Klaviertrios in d Moll im Vergleich: Mendelssohn-Schumann-Hensel-Berwald." In *Schumanniana nova: Festschrift Gerd Nauhaus zum 60. Geburtstag*, edited by Bernhard Appel, Ute Bar, and Matthias Wendt, 785–813. Sinzig, Germany: Studio, 2002.

Walker, Alan. *Franz Liszt: The Virtuoso Years, 1811–1847*. Vol. 1. New York: Knopf, 1990.

Walker, Frank. *Hugo Wolf: A Biography*. New York: Alfred A. Knopf, 1968.

Wang, Yuchi Sophie. "Edward MacDowell: A Poetic Voice as Seen in the 'Eroica' and 'Keltic' Sonatas." DMA diss., University of Cincinnati College-Conservatory of Music, 2014.

Weaver, Andrew. "Memories Spoken and Unspoken: Hearing the Narrative Voice in *Dichterliebe*." *Journal of the Royal Musical Association* 142, no. 1 (2017): 31–67.

Weaver, Andrew. *Narrative and Robert Schumann's Songs: A New Approach to the Romantic Lied*. Rochester, NY: University of Rochester Press, 2024.

Wehner, Ralf. *Felix Mendelssohn Bartholdy: Thematisch-systematisches Verzeichnis der musikalischen Werke (MWV)*, Leipziger Ausgabe der Werke von Felix Mendelssohn Bartholdy, series 13, vol. 1A. Wiesbaden: Breitkopf & Härtel, 2009.

Weinstock, Herbert. *Rossini: A Biography*. New York: Knopf, 1968.

Weissmann, Adolf. *Chopin*. Berlin: Schuster & Loeffler, 1922.

Westrup, Jack. "Some Settings of Heine." In *Festival Essays for Pauline Alderman*, edited by Burton L. Karson. Provo, UT: Brigham Young University Press, 1976.

White, Hayden. "The Value of Narrativity in the Representation of Reality." *Critical Inquiry* 7, no. 1 (1980): 5–27.

Youens, Susan. "Brief Reflections on the Two Müller Cycles of Franz Schubert: *Die schöne Müllerin*, D. 795, and *Winterreise*, D. 911." *NATS Journal* 43, no. 4 (January/February 1987): 16–18.

Youens, Susan. "Doubters and Believers: Case Studies in the *Geistliche Lieder* of Eduard Mörike and Hugo Wolf." *The American Journal of Semiotics* 13, nos. 1–4 (Fall 1996 [1998]): 103–46.

Youens, Susan. *Heinrich Heine and the Lied*. Cambridge: Cambridge University Press, 2007.

Youens, Susan. *Hugo Wolf: The Vocal Music*. Princeton, NJ: Princeton University Press, 1992.

Youens, Susan. "Retracing a Winter's Journey: Reflections on Schubert's *Winterreise*." *19th-Century Music* 9 (1985): 128–35.

Zenkin, Konstantin. "Fluidity of Structures in the Music of Franz Liszt: From Romantic 'Form as Process' to 'Open Form.'" *Quaderni dell'Instituto Liszt* 12 (2012): 45–61.

Zolozowa, Tetiana. "La forme sonate de Chopin." In Poniotowska, *Chopin and His Work*, 341–68.

Discography

Bartoli, Cecilia. *Rossini Arias*. With Vienna Volksoper Orchestra, conducted by Giuseppe Patanè. London 425 430-2, 1989. Compact disc.

Bartoli, Cecilia, Enzo Dara, William Matteuzzi, Alessandro Corbelli, and Michele Pertusi. *La Cenerentola*. With Teatro Comunale of Bologna, conducted by Riccardo Chailly. London 436 902-2, 1993. Compact disc.

Egmond, Max von, baritone, and Kenneth Slowik, fortepiano. *Franz Schubert: "Schwanengesang" / Robert Schumann: "Dichterliebe."* The Romantics, vol. 3. Musica Omnia MO0102, 2005. Compact disc.

Mendelssohn, Felix. *Songs Without Words (Selection)*. Péter Nagy (piano). Naxos 8.554055, 1997. Compact disc.

Index

NOTE: For chapters 2–13 the index generally does not list occurrences of the titles of the major works discussed, nor of their composers and poets, for pages within their respective chapters. The pages containing the analytical discussions of the works are, however, listed. Significant mentions of those works and names elsewhere in the book are indexed as usual.